Reports of the Research Committee
of the
Society of Antiquaries of London

No. XXI

Published in conjunction with the Corporation of the Borough of Colchester

The Roman Potters' Kilns of Colchester

By

M. R. Hull, M.A., F.S.A.

Oxford

Printed at the University Press by Vivian Ridler for

The Society of Antiquaries

Burlington House, London

and

The Corporation of the Borough of Colchester

1963

PRINTED IN GREAT BRITAIN
AT THE UNIVERSITY PRESS, OXFORD
BY VIVIAN RIDLER
PRINTER TO THE UNIVERSITY

CONTENTS

CONTENTS

CONTENTS

LIST OF PLATES

LIST OF PLATES

LIST OF FIGURES IN THE TEXT

LIST OF FIGURES IN THE TEXT

LIST OF ABBREVIATIONS USED IN REFERENCES

Antiq. Journ. The Antiquaries Journal.

Aquincum, see Kuzsinszky.

Arch. Archaeologia (Society of Antiquaries).

Arch. Ael. Archaeologia Aeliana (Newcastle).

Arch. Cant. Archaeologia Cantiana (Maidstone).

Arch. Journ. The Archaeological Journal (Royal Archaeological Institute).

Arch. Scot. Archaeologia Scotica (Society of Antiquaries of Scotland, 1782–1890).

Arentsburg. J. H. Holwerda, *Arentsburg, een Romeinsch militair Vlootstation* (Leiden, 1923).

Argonne, see Chenet.

Artis, *Durobrivae.* E. T. Artis, *The Durobrivae of Antoninus . . .* (London, 1828).

Atkinson, *Wroxeter.* D. Atkinson, *Report on Excavations at Wroxeter, 1923–27* (Oxford, 1942).

Balmuildy. S. N. Miller, *The Roman Fort at Balmuildy* (Glasgow, 1922).

Bingen Mus. Cat. G. Behrens, *Katalog, Städtische Altertumssammlung* (Bingen, 1920).

Birdoswald Turret (49*b*). *Transactions of the Cumberland and Westmorland Antiquarian and Archaeological Society*, xiii. 347.

Blickweiler. R. Knorr and F. Sprater, *Die westpfälzischen Sigillata-Töpfereien von Blickweiler und Eschweiler Hof* (1927).

B.J. Bonner Jahrbücher, published by the Verein von Altertumsfreunden im Rheinlande.

Brecon Gaer. R. E. M. Wheeler, *The Roman Fort near Brecon* (Cymmrodorion Society Publications, 1926).

B.M. British Museum.

Cam. ⎱ C. F. C. Hawkes and M. R. Hull,
Camulodunum ⎰ *Camulodunum, First Report on the Excavations at Colchester, 1930–39.* (Society of Antiquaries, 1947).

Cat. Devizes Mus. Catalogue of Antiquities in the Museum . . . at Devizes, part ii (Devizes, 1934).

Chenet, M. G. *La Céramique gallo-romaine d'Argonne du IVe siècle.*

C.I.L. Corpus Inscriptionum Latinarum.

Cohen, H. *Monnaies frappées sous l'Empire romain* (1880).

C.M. Report ⎱ The Colchester and Essex
Colch. Mus. Rep. ⎰ Museum: *Annual Report.*

Coll. Ant. C. Roach Smith, *Collectanea Antiqua*, i–vii (London, 1848–80).

Cumb. and Westm. Trans. Transactions of the Cumberland and Westmorland Antiquarian and Archaeological Society.

Curle, *see* Newstead.

Déch. J. Déchelette, *Les Vases céramiques ornés de la Gaule romaine* (1904).

Forrer, R. *Die römischen Terrasigillata-Töpfereien von Heiligenberg-Dinsheim und Ittenweiler im Elsaß* (1911).

Gellygaer. J. Ward, *The Roman Fort of Gellygaer* (1902).

Gillam. J. P. Gillam, 'Types of Roman Coarse Pottery Vessels in Northern Britain', *Arch. Ael.*[4] xxxv (1957).

Germ. Rom. Germania Romana (Römisch-Germanische Kommission).

Haltwhistle Burn. Archaeologia Aeliana[3], v. 263.

Heiligenberg, see Forrer.

Hermet, F. *La Graufesenque* (Paris, 1934).

J.B.A.A. Journal of the British Archaeological Association (London).

Joslin. See *Transactions of the Essex Archaeological Society*, N.S. i (1878), 192 ff.

J.R.S. Journal of Roman Studies (Society for the Promotion of Roman Studies, London).

Kuzsinszky, B., *Das große römische Töpferviertel in Aquincum* (Budapest, Régiségei XI, 1932).

Knorr and Sprater, *see Blickweiler.*

L.M. London Museum.

Loeschcke, S., Keramische Funde in Haltern, *Mitt d. Altertums-Kommission f. Westfalen*, V (1909), 103 ff.

Ludowici, W. I. Stempelnamen röm. Töpfer . . . in Rheinzabern (1901–1904).
II. Stempelbilder röm. Töpfer . . . in Rheinzabern (1901–1905).
III. Urnengräber . . . in Rheinzabern (1905–1908).

LIST OF ABBREVIATIONS USED IN REFERENCES

IV. Röm. Ziegelgräber, 1908–1912.
V. Stempelnamen und Bilder röm. Töpfer (1927).
VI. Bilderschüsseln der röm. Töpfer von Rheinzabern. 1942.

M. & S. H. Mattingly and E. A. Sydenham, *The Roman Imperial Coinage* (1923 and later).

M.Z. Mainzer Zeitschrift (Mainz).

May, *Colchester*. Thomas May, *Catalogue of the Roman Pottery in the Colchester and Essex Museum* (Cambridge, 1930).

— *Silchester*. Thomas May, *The Pottery found at Silchester* (1916).

— *York*. Thomas May, *Catalogue of the Roman Pottery in York Museum* (1908–11).

Miller, *Old Kilpatrick*. S. N. Miller, *The Roman Fort at Old Kilpatrick* (Glasgow, 1928).

Newstead. J. Curle, *Newstead: A Roman Frontier Post and its People* (Glasgow, 1911).

Niederbieber. F. Oelmann, *Die Keramik des Kastells Niederbieber: Materialen zur römisch-germanischen Keramik* I (1914).

Norfolk Arch. Norfolk Archaeology (Norfolk and Norwich Archaeological Society).

Old Kilpatrick, Miller, S. N., *The Roman Fort at Old Kilpatrick* (Glasgow, 1928).

Oswald, *Figure Types. Index of Figure Types on Terra Sigillata*. Liverpool Annals of Archaeology, Supplement (1930–37).

Oswald, *Stamps. Stamps on Terra Sigillata* (1931).

O. & P. ⎫ F. Oswald and T. D. Pryce, *Intro-*
Oswald and Pryce ⎭ *duction to the Study of Terra Sigillata* (1920).

O.R.L. Der Obergermanisch-Rätische Limes des Römerreiches.

Ospringe. W. Whiting, W. Hawley, and T. May, *Report on the Excavation of the Roman Cemetery at Ospringe, Kent* (Society of Antiquaries, 1931).

Poltross Burn. Transactions of the Cumberland and Westmorland Antiquarian and Archaeological Society, xi. 446.

P.S.A. Proceedings of the Society of Antiquaries of London.

P.S.A. Scot. Proceedings of the Society of Antiquaries of Scotland.

R.C.H.M. Royal Commission on Historical Monuments, *Inventory of the Monuments of North-East Essex*, iii (1922).

Rheinzabern, see Ludowici.

Roman Colchester. M. R. Hull, *Roman Colchester* (Society of Antiquaries, 1958).

Rottweil. R. Knorr, *Die verzierten Terra Sigillata Gefäße von Rottweil*.

Smith, *Cat*. C. Roach Smith, *Catalogue of the Museum of London Antiquities* (London, 1854).

Stanfield & Simpson. J. A. Stanfield and G. Simpson, *Central Gaulish Potters* (Oxford, 1958).

Throp. Transactions of the Cumberland and Westmorland Antiquarian and Archaeological Society, xiii. 374.

T.N. Terra Nigra.

T.S. Terra Sigillata.

T.R. Terra Rubra.

T.E.A.S. Transactions of the Essex Archaeological Society.

Trans. Lond. and Middx. Arch. Soc. Transactions of the London and Middlesex Archaeological Society.

Walters, *B.M. Cat*. H. B. Walters, *Catalogue of Roman Pottery in the . . . British Museum* (1908).

West Stowe: *Proceedings of the Suffolk Institute of Archaeology* XXVI (i) (1952).

Wheeler, *Brecon Gaer, see Brecon Gaer*.

Whiting, *Ospringe, see Ospringe*.

Wilts Arch. Mag. Wiltshire Archaeological and Natural History Magazine.

Wroxeter. J. P. Bushe-Fox, *Excavations on the Site of the Roman Town at Wroxeter, Shropshire, in 1912, 1913, 1914* (Society of Antiquaries Research Reports I, II, IV); *see also* Atkinson.

Zugmantel. O.R.L., no. 8.

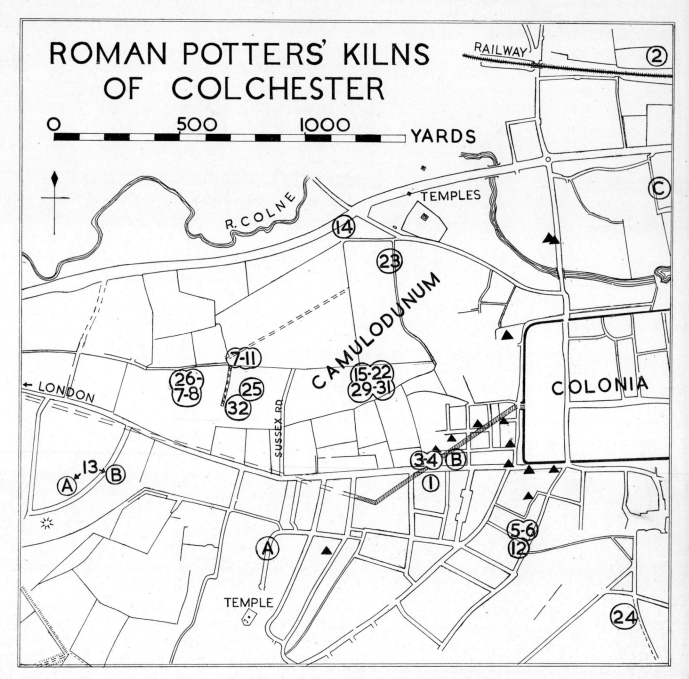

FIG. 1. Plan to show position of the Roman potters' kilns in Colchester

THE ROMAN POTTERS' KILNS
OF COLCHESTER

THE primary purpose of this report is the publication of the eight kilns found in the course of the work of the Colchester Excavation Committee in the summer of 1933, which include the first kiln for the manufacture of Terra Sigillata to be discovered in this country. At the same time the opportunity arises to publish other kilns found before, or since, including some already known, so as to bring under one cover as much as possible regarding the pottery industry in Roman Colchester. The prolonged delay in publication (this Report was prepared in 1935) has, however, enabled a further season's work on the site, in 1959, to be included.

KILNS FOUND BEFORE 1933

KILN 1

Mr. E. W. A. Drummond Hay has described[1] the discovery of a loaded pottery kiln found on the left-hand side of the road from Colchester to Lexden in 1819. The kiln was built of sun-dried bricks, one of which was $7\frac{1}{2}$ in. long, 5 in. wide, and $2\frac{1}{2}$ in. thick. Within it over thirty vessels were found 'standing on circular vents above the hollow chambers through which the heat was conveyed to them'.

are now in the National Museum of Antiquities of Scotland.[2] The position of the find is established fairly closely by the label on no. 1, which states that it was found 'upon a potter's furnace in preparing the foundation for the general hospital in 1819', and the entry recording their donation which tells us that 'these vases were found on their several stands[3] in a potter's furnace near the high road within the grounds of the Hospital'.[4]

The three pots we illustrate are from this kiln, accord-

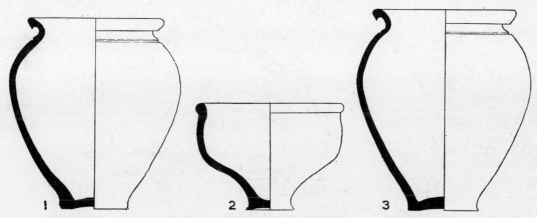

FIG. 2. Pottery from kiln 1 ($\frac{1}{4}$).

Of these vessels three have survived among twenty-four pots from Colchester, which were acquired by the Scottish National Museum in Edinburgh in 1827 and

ing to Roach Smith, and some of the others in Edinburgh may be. They are as follows (fig. 2):

    1. Jar of f. 277*a*, coarse bluish ware (fig. 2).

---

[1] In *Coll. Ant.* iii, 37–38, and ii, pl. XIII.

[2] We are very grateful to Mr. R. B. K. Stevenson for his ready assistance in providing all available information regarding these pots. *Arch. Scot.* iii, appendix, p. 115.

[3] 'on their several stands'. What does this mean?

[4] *R.C.H.M.* did not know the position, marking it near Gurney

Benham House (p. 72), but elsewhere remarking 'probably near St. Mary's Lodge' (now Vint Crescent), p. 29. This is due to the entry 'kiln' on P. G. Laver's manuscript plan (in the Colchester Museum) exactly in Vint Crescent. We do not know whether this is a kiln otherwise unknown or a guess at the site of kiln 1.

2. Bowl, f. 306, coarse reddish-brown ware, misshapen in firing (the rim is oval). It was found, Mr. Hay *thought*, 'near the furnace, with many broken vessels'.

3. Jar, f. 277*a*, like no. 1. This was 'taken from the furnace'; clay rather reddish; but one account describes both jars as bluish.

Mr. Hay adds that some of the vessels, all of which were of the same material, and nearly all of the same form and size, were less baked than the rest, and broke when handled without much care.

Dr. R. Sauvan Smith, and its garden formerly extended 55 yds. westwards along Lexden Road (see also p. 176).

KILNS 5 AND 6

In the mid-nineteenth century a row of houses stood north of Butt Mill and facing east on to Butt Road. They were known as 'Mill Place' and the field behind them was worked for many years as a sand pit. Being

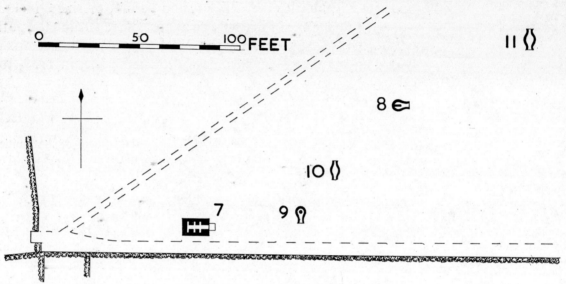

FIG. 3. Plan of kilns 7–11 found in 1877.

This is the only loaded kiln recorded in Colchester. The remains of the pottery which should have dated it are insufficient to do so. The 'sun-dried' bricks are, of course, the clay blocks we shall meet with again and again below (pp. 19, 150–1).

KILN 2

On 28 March 1845 Wm. Wire wrote in his diary: 'It has been stated to me that, some years since, a Roman pottery kiln was discovered near the brick kilns (sc. just east of North Station, and probably N. of the railway), when excavating clay.' We can add nothing to this record.

KILNS 3 AND 4

On 19 March 1855 Wire wrote in his diary: 'Mr. Thomas Fenton informs me that some years ago two potters' kilns of the Romans were discovered in the ground where Dr. Maclean resides immediately opposite the Hospital.' The house meant is that on the west corner of Hospital Lane, now (1961) occupied by

on a rich Roman burial ground the works received great attention from Wire. On 7 November 1843 he writes: 'About two years since a place about three feet square and two feet deep was discovered in the above field, filled with fragments of Roman amphorae[1] and mortaria of white earth. The construction of it I do not remember now, not taking sufficient notice of it at the time.'

This may or may not be identical with the following:

In Wire's *County Illustrations* there are two manuscript plans of finds made at Mill Place and in the field west of it, and on one of these plans is marked 'Kiln made of old materials, full of fragments'. There seems to be no mention of this in his text. The same plan has a mark under the middle of the front fence of Mill Place, on the west margin of Butt Road, against which is written 'circular cist nearly full of urns, most of which were broken by the workmen when taking down the bank'. The other plan adds—'all broken but two'.

There is perhaps the possibility of confusion with graves, but there was one undoubted kiln on the site

---

[1] Flagons are probably meant.

(12 below) and it seems most probable that we have here evidence that there were several.

It is very probable that other kilns were found in the next few decades, but we had no one to record them. The next discovery was made in 1877 by a Mrs. Kerry, who noticed pottery turned up by the plough on the north side of the top of the ridge north of Kingswode Hoe. Excavations carried out by Mr. George Joslin in March of that year revealed five kilns (fig. 3), all scarcely below the plough level.[1]

KILN 7 (FIG. 4)

Joslin's no. I. This was a large rectangular kiln and may perhaps have been intended for tiles rather than pottery, but it seems to have made the latter. After its excavation the Lord of the Manor, Mr. P. O. Papillon, had a brick building erected over it, which effectively preserved it, until the invasion scare of 1940, when it was broken open by troops when making a strong point and ultimately the kiln was deliberately destroyed by hooligans, who, after repeated attempts had been made to exclude them from the building, took down its east wall to gain entrance, and broke up the kiln with crowbars.

As found, the floor of the kiln remained intact, about 15 in. below the surface. Joslin says the side-walls and top of the furnace were 9 to 12 in. thick, and built of clay 'bricks' of various sizes. The floor is shown as 5 ft. 6 in. wide, pierced by thirty-one holes, 2 in. in diameter, communicating with the flues beneath. It was about 14 in. thick over the crown of the main flue. One thing clearly revealed by the destruction of the kiln is the method of construction with large rectangular clay blocks.

The building was again described by T. May, who found fragments of mortarium rims around the entrance and was inclined to believe they were made in this kiln.[2] This, however, need not have been so, though the mortaria were, no doubt, made in one of our kilns.

Under the floor the central flue, arched with tiles, was 2 ft. wide and 8 ft. long, but its floor extended another 3 ft. beyond the entrance, which Joslin says was broken, and must have been longer than he found it. (But there may have been a threshold, as there was to kiln 21, see below.)

The arch of the stoke-hole and the outside walls of the rectangle were built of tiles laid in clay. The piers dividing the lateral flues were inserted separately, and built of rectangular blocks of clay. There were two such piers on each side, 14 in. wide and 12 in. deep, forming three lateral flues of the same depth, nearly 12 in. wide, and raised 12 in. above the floor, with flat (not sloping) bottoms. Into each of these, four holes led through the floor above. A single row of such holes ran along the crown of the main flue, and two additional holes completed the row across the far end of the kiln, making thirty-one in all.

Joslin noted that in parts of the structure pieces of mortaria, pottery, and tile were built into the walls, and that large quantities of mortaria and 'pinched vessels' were near the entrance.

The plan of the next four kilns, made by Joslin, has long lain hidden in one of Wire's manuscript books in the Museum. It is reproduced in fig. 3. The hedges at the bottom and bottom left are the present hedges of the SW. corner of field 496.

KILN 8 (FIG. 4)

Joslin's no. II. A long pear-shaped kiln, with walls (presumably of clay) 10 in. thick, with the entrance turned to the east. The oven had been circular, 3 ft. 8 in. in interior diameter. Part of the floor remained supported on a wall running from the back of the kiln to the centre, where it was roundly expanded. Only two holes were preserved in the floor, and it can hardly have had more than four when perfect. It was 1 ft. thick over the crown of the flue, and the floor of the flue was 5 ft. below the modern surface. It was found full of fragments of pottery and wood ash.

KILN 9 (FIG. 4)

Joslin's no. III. Somewhat similar to the last, but with the walls of the stoke-hole curved inwards in plan. The oven was circular, 4 ft. 10 in. in diameter, with a circular central support 2 ft. 6 in. in diameter, which was made of fragments of pottery, tiles, and clay, and was only preserved to a height of 15 in. The oven floor and all above it had completely gone. The entrance was to the south, and the flue full of pottery, &c., as in the last.

KILN 10 (FIG. 4)

Joslin's no. IV. This is quite unusual in Colchester, being of the horizontal draught type (Grimes type B). The oven was circular, standing over an oval flue with an opening at each end, pointing north and south. The maximum interior diameter (E.–W.) was again 4 ft. 10 in. (5 Roman ft.). The bottom was 5 ft. from the surface, and though the walls stood about 3 ft.

[1] *T.E.A.S.* n.s. i (1878), 192 ff.; *J.B.A.A.* o.s. xxxiii, 230, 267; *Arch. Journ.* xxxiv, 302; *T.E.A.S.* n.s. v, 77; *R.C.H.M.* Essex, iii, 29; Grimes in *Y Cymmrodor*, xli, 66; May, *Cat. of Roman*

Pottery in Colchester Museum, pp. 173–4 and pl. LXX.
[2] *Catalogue*, loc. cit.

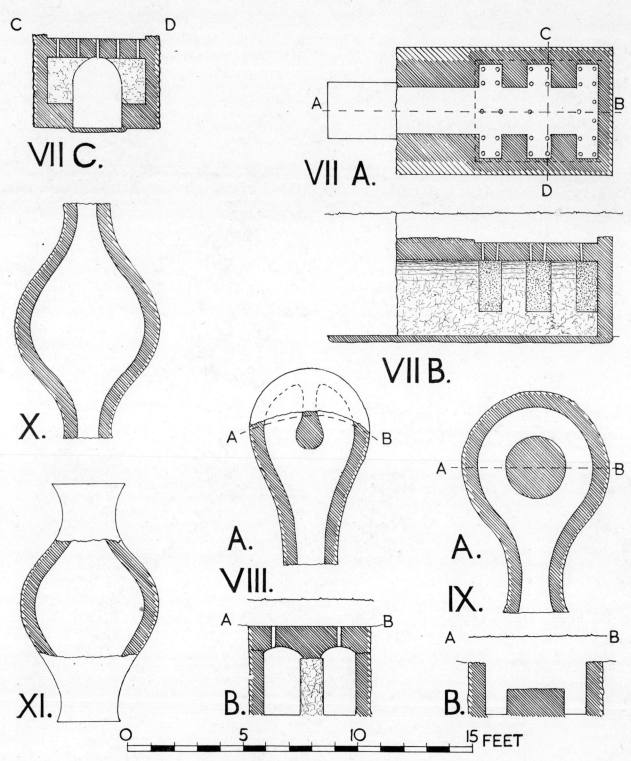

VII C.

VII A.

VII B.

X.

A.

VIII.

B.

A.

IX.

B.

XI.

0   5   10   15 FEET

Fig. 4. Separate plans of kilns found in 1877.

high there was no trace of oven-floor or central support. It was full of pottery and wood ashes.

KILN 11 (FIG. 4)

Joslin's no. V. This was another horizontal draught kiln, similar to the last, but better preserved, for the top of the two openings which again lay north and south, was preserved. The south opening expanded outwards, so was possibly the stoke-hole.[1] The sides were 2 ft. 6 in. high. Joslin notes that there was a second clay floor 9 in. above the lower one, indicating that the kiln had been restored at some time. The interior diameter in this kiln was 4 ft. 6 in.

In connexion with these kilns, but which one is not stated, it is recorded that parts of the upper structure were found made of clay as sections of a dome, with grass between the sections in order to facilitate removal after firing, and that one of the smaller kilns was built almost entirely of broken mortaria.

Joslin was of the opinion that further search might reveal more kilns, and Mr. P. G. Laver always held that more than five kilns were actually uncovered at the time (see pp. 8–9).

THE POTTERY FROM KILNS 7–11

The pottery (figs. 5 and 6) from these kilns was described rather more fully than usual by Joslin in *T.E.A.S.* loc. cit. with a large number of illustrations, which are not, however, adequate for modern purposes. Indeed they do not always suffice to identify the vessel. On his three plates, IV–VI, Joslin has mixed up first- and fourth-century vessels without order. With the former we are not concerned; any contribution they have to the history of the site has already been utilized in the *Camulodunum* Report. Of the rest his pl. IV, 10; pl. V, 2, 3, 15, 16; and pl. VI, 2, cannot be identified in the Museum.

In the catalogue of the Joslin Collection made by J. E. Price, F.S.A., F.R.S.L., in 1888 a few vessels are entered separately with a note that they came from these kilns. The fragments are entered in bulk under the number 980. There can be little doubt that the missing vessels were separately entered without statement of provenance.

The following is a summary of all the pottery (first-century wares excepted) which can now be identified as coming from these kilns. There is no doubt that it is only a fraction of what was found.

Sigillata. Joslin mentions platters and cups of the finer class. These must have been first-century. The only later fragment is a perfect roundel cut from a bowl f. Drag. 37, with part of the ovolo, and the hind-quarters of a running beast in free style. Probably Lezoux ware, Hadrian–Antonine. Graffito VAK on back.

Colour-coated. Fig. 5, 1 is the lower part of a f. 391 or 392,[2] probably the latter, in fine pale grey ware with red rind, mica-coated. No. 2 represents six bases of fine hard red-brown ware with dark chocolate coating. It was fluted above and the others may have been so. The form would be 406, and there is one such rim. Two have a groove under the base, the rest being smooth. One has no beading (as no. 1). Not all show rouletting. One is much distorted in firing.

No. 3 is part of the top of a fluted beaker f. 407 in the same ware; no. 4 is one of five similar tops all very distorted in firing. Beneath is shown one of three similar bases. The bead at the foot is very prominent, and the narrow band of rouletting deeply sunk.

Though not the tallest type of f. 407 these vessels clearly belong to a period later than that of the colour-coated wares so far found in our other kilns. They are paralleled by several found in the 'Mithraeum'[3] with a coin of Constans, and we shall note further contacts with this deposit.

No. 5 is a single pedestal base of a beaker, perhaps f. 395. It is a waster.

No. 6 is buff ware with a light red chocolate coating, rouletted and grooved on top, from a lid, f. 308. Probably Castor ware. Diameter *c.* 7 in.

There is also the base of a large urn, like f. 280, in fine but dingy red ware, very sooty, but the whole surface mica-coated. The base shows the mark of the wire which cut it off.

Buff ware. Not much of this survived in recognizable form. The mortaria must mostly be lost among the unmarked fragments in the Museum. The complete vessel, Joslin's pl. VI, 2, cannot now be identified and his drawing is inadequate, though it probably belongs to the f. 497 series. May, p. 172, attributes his types 332–3 (our f. 498) to these kilns, probably correctly. Joslin is definite that no stamps were found.

The most notable of the unidentifiable remains are two enormous fragments which are so unusual that they are useless for dating purposes, but otherwise of considerable interest. The first (fig. 5, 7) is represented by three fragments of a massive rim which measures $3\frac{1}{2}$ in. across the flat top. The vessel is said by Joslin to have been 8 ft. in diameter,[4] but we make it about $36\frac{3}{4}$ in. It is made of a good reddish-brown clay, with a darker surface which is well smoothed on the inside.

---

[1] But one would always stoke from the windward end.

[2] A reference list to the form-numbers used here will be found on pp. 178 ff., and small outline drawings of them on figs. 102–7 the end of the Report.

[3] They are taller than Gillam's f. 53 which is dated A.D. 240–320. *Roman Colchester*, fig. 70, 132, 133.

[4] Probably a misprint for 3 ft.

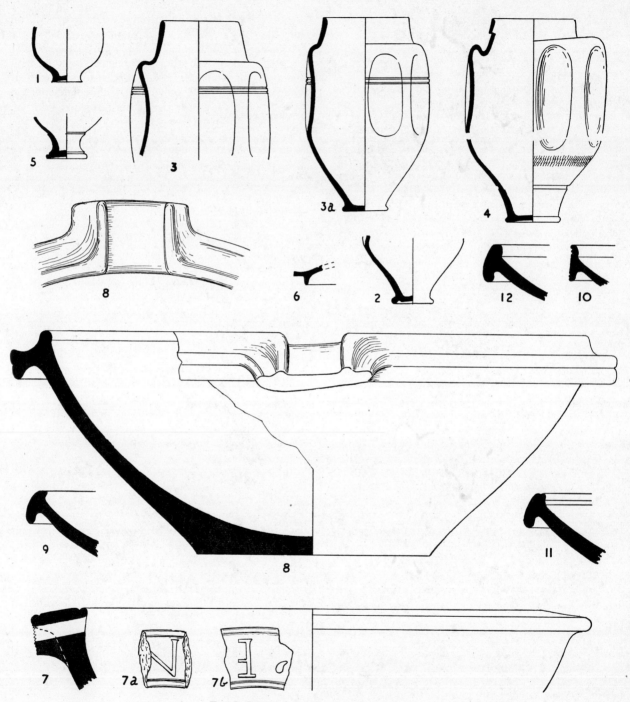

Fig. 5. Pottery from kilns 7–11 (рp. 5–8). (¼)

The wall is $1\frac{1}{2}$ in. thick. There is no grit on the inside. The clay contains a few largish pebbles.

The outstanding feature, apart from the size of the vessel, is that the broad, flat rim bears a band $2\frac{3}{4}$ in. wide, which has been coated with white paint or slip and which bore an inscription in raised letters $2\frac{3}{8}$ in.

been a special order for something in the nature of a bowl for a public fountain, which would account for the inscription. One fragment of the rim, nearly 5 in. long, shows no lettering, but the white surface has gone and letters may also have disappeared.

The second large example (fig. 5, 8) has been restored

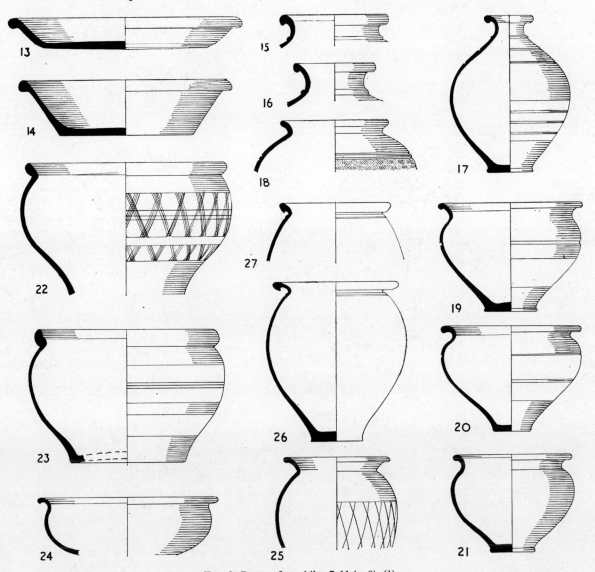

FIG. 6. Pottery from kilns 7–11 (p. 8). ($\frac{1}{4}$)

high. These were applied to the surface and the white paint ran over them. Only an E and an N and a leaf-stop remain. A portion of the spout is, however, preserved. A round opening, parallel-sided and $1\frac{1}{4}$ in. in diameter, ran outwards from the interior just under the rim, and was continued outside as a snout or spout, but the outer end is broken off. This very exceptional vessel may well not be a mortarium at all. It may have

with cement. It is nearly 27 in. in diameter, and made of a hard, nearly white ware. There are very few sparse pieces of grit on the inside. The rim is of un-usual form and the spout very square in design. The affinities of this exceptional vessel are not clear (Jos. Colln. no. 910).

There are also two rims, nos. 9–10, the first of hard buff ware, f. 498; the second, of white ware, underfired, is f. 501. Nos. 11–12 are two rims found in the stoke-hole of kiln 7 in 1924. They place the emphasis on f. 498 for these kilns. It also occurred in the 'Mith-raeum' and I do not recognize it among Gillam's mortaria.

Of flagons we can say but little. Joslin's pl. v, 12–13, seem to have belonged to the first century (ff. 137 and 171?), and his 15–16, which should be fourth-century, cannot be identified. They were our f. 375, or very near it, and compare with one from the 'Mithraeum'.[1]

Grey (fig. 6). One large fragment of a normal f. 37 in the black polished ware should not be contemporary with these kilns. No. 13 is about half a platter, f. 38, in ware intended to be the usual black polished, but misfired a sooty brown. No. 14, in the same ware, lacks the bevel at the foot and has a slight offset inside the lip. The lack of bevel was observed both in this form and f. 40 in the 'Mithraeum', and may be regarded as a fourth-century feature, though bevelled examples were still common at the same time.[2] There are two or more rims like no. 13 and one large and heavy rim of f. 40, in diameter over 17 in., apparently with bevel.

Storage jars were undoubtedly made here and are represented by very large fragments. They to some extent resemble the late fourth-century handled jars of the Yorkshire Signal Stations and are similar in size, shape, fabric, and decoration, but lack the handles. Joslin, pl. iv, 4, shows the most part of one less the rim, the body having polished horizontal bands over vertical groups of three or four scored lines. This is no longer in the collection, but there are fragments with similar decoration. This is, however, confined to the upper half of the vessel (as in the Signal Stations; the scoring is also occasionally done, as there, by a back-and-forwards motion of the hand without raising the stylus). There is one rim, no. 15, in good brown-grey ware, with small cordon and undercut lip, which is our f. 280, to which we may ascribe all these fragments. They seem to have been fairly well bulged and not to belong to the tallest type of the series, but it is difficult to be certain of this.

There are also three rouletted pieces which should not belong to f. 280, but to the late type of f. 119, indeed one of them might come directly from the vessel, May, *Colchester*, pl. LXXXII, grave 58.[3]

No. 16, in grey ware, is of f. 281, of which there are five complete necks varying from 2¼ to 2½ in. diameter. A few body-fragments with a band of normal or of 'chessboard' rouletting belong to these, and there is one complete vessel, no. 17, in fine light grey ware. It

is not quite so tall as those found in the 'Mithraeum'. There is also no. 18, of unclassified form, with chess-board rouletting, cf. fig. 94, 1.

The S-bowl, f. 299, was made here in fine dark grey ware, and is represented by two restored bowls, nos. 19–20, and a variant with offset neck, no. 21.[4] No. 20 is unusually narrow-based, a feature which is not seen even in the 'Mithraeum' examples, which are exactly as nos. 19 and 21.

Nos. 22–23 are drawn from two large fragments, dark grey and brown-grey respectively. The great width and large rim with hollow for lid are the standard features of f. 307. The decoration is of burnished and scored lines, with or without multiple lattice.

No. 24 is an unclassified form, of thin grey-brown ware, polished outside.

No. 25 is the top half of a jar f. 278 in good grey ware.

The colour-coated beakers of f. 407 are paralleled by a restored waster, no. 3 *a*, and several fragments, in grey ware. These also occurred in the 'Mithraeum', but with much shorter neck.

The only coarse ware made was of f. 268, repre-sented by the almost intact waster, no. 26, and the upper part of another, no. 27. The clay is thin and hard, brownish-grey. These were made in great quantities, for I have myself picked up the rims in numbers from the surface all over the site, especially near kiln 7.

A fragment of a cylindrical neck, with fine scored lines, in very fine, hard, pale grey clay is of the bag-shaped flask, f. 286 (see May, pl. LXXXVIII, grave 104, the tall vessel). There were also three fragments of lids with incurved edge in the usual sandy ware of varying shades of red, exactly as May, pl. LIX, 285. A fragment of a crude and heavy clay ring is obviously connected in some way with the kiln, the inner lip formed by being pressed between two pottery vessels which the ring had luted together. Vessels were found to have been embedded in clay in kiln 24, and compare the entrance of kiln 20.

Finally, there is a small piece of Kentish ragstone which has been shaped and carved, but is too small to describe, and a small, well-formed barrel-shaped object of clay, reminiscent of a more crudely shaped one found unstratified in area Z in 1932.

In August and September 1939 the last trenches were dug on the large field 496. Besides searching for the road found in the earlier excavations it was decided to explore the area between the Joslin kilns in the SW. corner of the field and the hedge on the north side.

---

[1] *Roman Colchester*, fig. 62, 46.   [2] Ibid., fig. 67, 91.
[3] This particular form was represented also in the 'Mithraeum'. Ibid., fig. 64, 56 and 57.

[4] I hardly think this can be considered as f. 221 of the early period.

The two lines of trenches, dug at intervals, were carried north and south and about 50 yds. apart, the western one running north from near the brick building over kiln 7. These were completely barren except in the immediate neighbourhood of the kilns. It had been considered likely that more kilns might lie hereabouts, so four trenches were dug close, and parallel, to the footpath on the north side of Joslin's site.

No new kilns were found, but the trenches revealed a fairly deep topsoil, very black with soot, charcoal, and ashes, and there was much pottery of the sooty black or brown appearance characteristic of that found by Joslin. The finds can therefore simply be reckoned as supplementing those of Joslin, and the following catalogue of them is important because it is complete, whereas the Joslin fragments are certainly selected from a larger mass.

These trenches were numbered M1–M4, which numbers the fragments in the Museum bear.

M1. Gallo-Belgic. 1 frag. T.N.; 1 frag. T.R. 3 beaker; 1 frag. T.R. 4; rim and 3 frags. f. 113.
Buff. 1 frag. f. 161; ditto f. 163.
Fine grey. 7 frags., including ff. 231 and 204.
Coarse. 10 frags. native large; 5 ditto small, ff. 259, 266.
Also, one lump vitrified kiln-wall; one small frag. lead; one brown-glazed rim, recent. All the pottery is of the early period.
M2. Here is a different picture. Of 36 frags. only 2 are native; these are of ff. 270 and 44A (?). The remainder are all Roman grey, of Antonine date or later, all *worn*. Recognizable rims were: ff. 268A (3), 280 or 281, 38 (2).
M3. Gallo-Belgic. T.N. f. 5 and frag.; also ff. 119 and 270 and one frag. of Roman large coarse pot; also one frag. f. 161. Many frags. of one early f. 232, native; 2 more frags. f. 119, native; and 5 frags. which may be of the early period.
All the small coarse ware is Antonine or later; no forms were recognizable. There were also 1 frag. amphora; 2 of buff ware; a chip of mortarium; and one frag. of red-painted wall-plaster.
M4. The easternmost trench seemed to be cut in a wide ditch or pit. Here there was more pottery than usual, and nearly all was of the early period.
T.R. Most part of a f. 91A; rim f. 84; rim f. 91 (mica-gilt on white); rim f. 7. White, 16 frag. f. 113; 1 frag. f. 191; 1 frag. f. 187.
T.N. 10 frags. of one f. 2; rim f. 15; 6 other frags., one stamped [CA]RISSO/ [RI]TVSCIA[1] central; another, VIBIAV radial, both platters.
Finer ware: 13 frags. f. 115; 3 frags. include ff. 218 and 231.
Coarse ware, large: rims ff. 270 and 271, and 29 frags. all native.
Coarse ware, small: rim f. 265, 3 frags. f. 259; 5 frags. probably all f. 266, all native.
Also two heavy lumps of iron (?) slag.

KILN 12

A potter's kiln was found when the old windmill, which stood on the south side of Butt Road near the present Salisbury Hotel, was pulled down in 1890. In that year the Museum acquired 'a portion of the top of a Roman pottery kiln on which the vessels were set for baking';[2] the site is specified. Nothing further is known of this kiln, but there is a small fragment of a rim of a mortarium in the Museum marked 'Butt Road Kiln'. The outline is close to that favoured by Martinus and also to that found at the Abbey Fields kiln (24, p. 152, fig. 87, 1). It bears an imperfect stamp reading...MIM.. between ornamental borders (fig. 60, 26B). There is no similar stamp in the Museum.[3] The date of this rim should be late second century or possibly early third, though the latter date is rather late for legible stamps. Whether this is the same kiln as the one in Butt Road referred to on p. 2, described by Wire (*County Illustrations*) as 'Kiln made of old materials, full of fragments', cannot now be ascertained, but it is most improbable.

KILN 13 A and B

Although no actual kilns have yet been found in Fitzwalter Road there can be no doubt that potters were working there. The evidence lies in the remains collected, chiefly by Mr. P. G. Laver and Mr. D. W. Clark, during house building and pipe laying in the years 1923–9. Much of this is simply labelled 'Fitzwalter Road', but the two most important lots are better located.

The remains from Mr. Clark's garden (B on fig. 1) included some vitrified fragments of kiln wall and several large fragments of clay blocks of the sort used to build the central supports in kilns. There were also fragments of Roman tile, one of which was stamped L.L.S. (fig. 61, 52. C.M. 3713.18). If we omit certain sherds of mid-first-century date, the pottery is such as might well have been the produce of a kiln.

In the same year (1929) Mr. Clark collected another lot, from the garden of Alderman A. W. Piper (A on fig. 1). Here again were fragments of vitrified blocks from the central support of a kiln, also a large piece of a massive, crude tube of clay of about 8 in. diameter at the bottom and exactly similar to the remains of those found at the entrance of kiln 20 (see below, and pl. VA, 1–2). Another fragment may be from a distorted tube of the type used in Sigillata kilns (see p. 23); otherwise it is difficult to explain. The best mortar-rims are illustrated (fig. 8, 1–14);[4] also the rim of a bowl in brown-red, rough sandy ware (fig. 8, 15).

The following gives a summary of the pottery found in this area (figs. 7 and 8):

Sigillata (all fragmentary), f. Drag. 31, *misfired* a

---

[1] *Camulodunum*, p. 210, pl. XLVI, 66.
[2] Given to the Museum by H. Laver, Esq. (C.M. 55.1890).
[3] Mrs. Hartley points out a stamp which seems to read

AMMINVS (retro) (462.29). Source unknown, perhaps Bradwell-on-Sea.
[4] No. 1 is stamped by Messor; no. 5 bears the stamp fig. 61, 47.

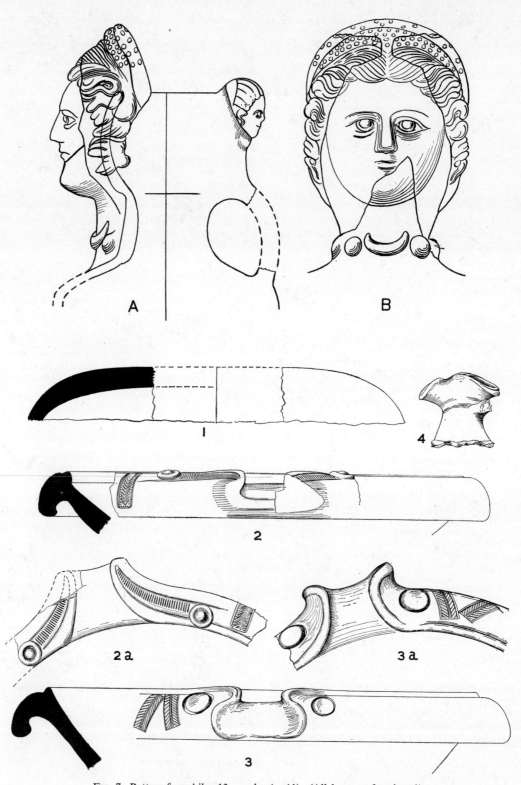

Fig. 7. Pottery from kilns 13 A and B (p. 11). (All $\frac{1}{4}$ except face jug, $\frac{1}{2}$)

chocolate brown; four f. Drag. 33. Two of these, in a good paste and coating, but rather bright red in the break, are stamped FIRMVS FE and MICCIO F. The former is the same stamp as Ludowici, *Rheinzabern*, i, 37 (B), and cf. ii, 30 (*d*); the second is apparently from the same matrix as our fig. 48, 26. The ware of both is identical. These may have been made locally.

Colour-coated. Two f. 391.

Buff. A quantity of f. 497, mostly misfired, including two stamps of Messor and Dubitatus; f. 501B is represented by several fragments, including misfired, and there is much of one f. 504. The rims of those from Mr. Piper's garden cover most of the series found in 1933 and are shown in fig. 8, 1–14. The many-moulded bowl-rim, fig. 8, 15, is from the same garden and is over-fired. Another similar was found at kilns 30 and 31 in 1959.

Exceptional are several fragments of at least two mortaria from Mr. Clark's garden; they are of a soft buff ware, probably underfired. They are decorated with cross-hatched bands and moulded bosses (fig. 7, 2, 2*a*), and bear the herring-bone stamp, fig. 61, 50. The same stamp has been found at St. Mary's Hospital.

Nos. 3 and 3*a* represent the rim and spout of a huge vessel typical in rim-outline and ware of the products of our kilns. It was collected by the boys of the late Mr. Chisnell's school and we do not know from what source. It is perhaps more likely to have come from the 1933 excavations than anywhere else.[1] The buff ware is the same as that of kiln 13 and kilns 15–22. The diameter is about 22 in. On each side of the spout is a deeply impressed circle and beyond this, on the one side preserved, the herring-bone stamp, fig. 61, 47, is impressed twice. Fig. 7, 4 is of rough red ware.

There are also a number of fragments (C.M. 4531.23) of soft yellow-buff ware which are underfired and to be classed as spoilt ware. They come from one or more handled vessels bearing a large female mask on the mouth.

This class of vessel is well known,[2] with a small female face on the side of the mouth and a small imitation handle on the opposite side. There are complete examples and fragments of at least thirty-two examples in Colchester Museum. The faces are in various styles, sometimes excellently rendered, and often have the details of hair and features picked out in paint. The largest and finest example is 3½ in. high from chin to crown.

The present example is of the same size, but there are remains which show that it was quite exceptional in having a real handle (or handles) surmounted by a small male head set on the rim.

The fragments are few and very badly broken. The drawing on fig. 7A and B has been made with some difficulty from what is preserved. The bulbous shape of the mouth of the jug, which is characteristic of these vessels, is plainly recognizable on the fragment with the head-dress and again on that with the handle and small head, which makes it probable that the two fragments, which are identical in fabric, belong to one vessel. There is also a second small head, in the same fabric, which suggests that there were two such handles, the heads being exactly similar. Other fragments preserve the base of a handle, and a large part of the neck, with chin. Round the neck is a necklace of large round bosses representing beads, with a central crescent-shaped ornament.[3] The head-dress resembles a bandeau of material rather than a tiara, apparently formed of two folds of cloth. The decoration of impressed circles may represent spangles or similar adornment. The hair seems to have been parted in the middle, soon running into a series of curls which end just beneath the ear.

The fragment with the base of the handle shows an abrupt angle in the wall of the vessel which is quite foreign to the type of jug with which we are dealing.

Grey. One rim f. 266 is probably from an earlier date; f. 268 is represented by at least 35 rims (fig. 8, 18, 20–26*a*), other forms are 277A (no. 19), 278 (3), 306 (fig. 8, 16, 17) (4), 389 (2), and platters f. 37 (5), fig. 8, 27–29 (28 is a variant), ff. 38 (much of one), and 40 (2). Fig. 8, 30, 31 are unclassified rims of rough grey ware.

From Piper's garden come two fragments (or possibly fragments of two examples) of a remarkable object like a shallow bowl of rather sandy dull red ware, very thick and heavy. In one case the outer surface is polished all over; the other piece has been so heavily fired that it is cracked and the surface destroyed. The inside is not smoothed, so that we are dealing with a cover of some sort, but whether an enormous lid, or some form of cover for a kiln cannot be said (fig. 7, 1). The diameter is about 17 in. as it is now without the rim.

KILN 14

This is the unexcavated tile-kiln lying just east of the former Sheepen Farm buildings. The brick-built furnace arch was exposed in 1931, see *Cam.*, p. 71, and pl. v, 2. It belongs to the period A.D. 50–61.

---

[1] This piece actually was shown here by mistake, but we think it deserves to retain its place.

[2] Our fig. 82, 1 illustrates the common type.

[3] Cf. Ludowici, *Rheinzabern*, iv, 244, K.25.

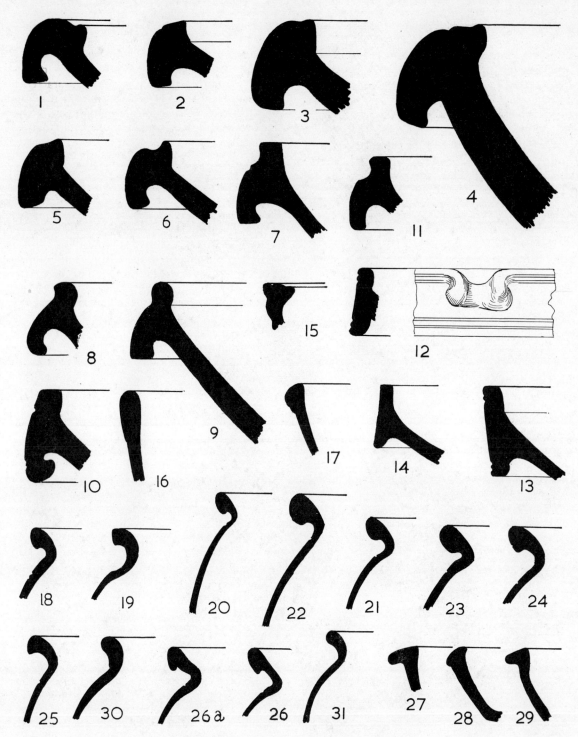

FIG. 8. Pottery from kilns 13 A and B (p. 11). (½)

THE KILNS FOUND IN 1933 (PLAN, FIG. 9)

The fourth season's work of the Colchester Excavation Committee on the site of Camulodunum had to be diverted from the main objective to the exploration of a series of kilns of the second century, in the course of which several other extraneous discoveries were made. These lay in area C and the adjacent part of area Y, fig. 9 (cf. the general plan in *Camulodunum*, pl. CXII). Part of them appears on the larger scale plan of region 5, ibid., pl. CX. They were of such importance that they almost monopolized the work of that season. They include the first kiln for the manufacture of Terra Sigillata to be found in this country.[1] The other kilns are notable for the quantity and variety of their products. Several of the small objects appear to be unique, and while some show that the whole establishment worked as one firm, making all the various classes of ware, others bear on technical methods and may have to wait some time for a proper understanding.

The kilns are situated on the southern slope of the hill south of Sheepen Farm, which formed the major portion of the site of Camulodunum, scattered relics of which were found throughout the area. The field, in the east end of which they lie, is no. 1074 on the O.S. 25-in. map, Essex N. XXXVII, 2, and was the property of Capt. J. L. Lockhart, to whose unfailing kindness and generosity we are deeply grateful for permission to excavate and for his continual interest in the work. Eight kilns were found, the first four set about singly and without order, the rest in a walled enclosure. Others may remain under the soil. There was no fixed orientation, and the structure and shape of the kilns was very varied. Other remains found around the kilns are described later under site C4 (pp. 139 ff.).

The subsoil here is a soft yellow sand, with hard yellow gravel never far away. To the south lies a small damp valley where clay would be available, but there were no visible signs of its having been worked. Another source of supply might have been the frequent layer of cheesy glacial loam, locally known as 'pug', which overlies the sand in many places. Such pug was found, disturbed as though it had been worked, in the area west of the kilns, and here and there we found patches of a white clay which must have been brought from some distance. Near the enclosure there were heaps of very stiff brown clay which were clearly remains of the potters' stock. Much of this had been thrown into the filling of the enclosure, and similar

clay was used to pack the back and sides of the Sigillata kiln.

The figure in brackets after the kiln-number is that by which the kiln was known during the excavation, and which is marked on much of the pottery.

KILN 15 (I) (PL. 1*a* and FIG. 11, 1)

1. This, found on the east edge of area Y, was the most westerly, and the ground west of it was so thoroughly explored that it is most unlikely that further kilns lay near in that direction.

The body of the kiln was circular, with an outside diameter of 5 ft. The sides were of clay fortified with pieces of tile and broken pottery, including pieces of imported T.S. dishes and local mortarium rims, and stood to a height of 20 in., at which level, only a few inches under the turf, the plough had removed everything. The interior diameter was 3 ft. 5 in. and the rectangular central block of burnt clay which had supported the floor remained in position. The stoke-hole or flue, approached by a small hollow in the surrounding yellow sand, was 2 ft. 4 in. long by 14 in. wide. It had been arched with tiles, some of which were still in position when uncovered (pl. 1*a*).

The interior everywhere presented a vitrified, glassy, greyish surface, and the whole was buried in a debris of broken clay from the dome and floor, mixed with sherds of buff and grey vessels, all compacted to a very hard mass. The flue opening was to the west.

The products of this kiln were probably grey (fig. 76, 5–6) and buff wares. No local T.S. or colour-coated ware was found incorporated in the kiln wall. Possibly this is the earliest kiln in the series.

KILN 16 (II) (PL. 1*b*)

2. Forty feet SE. of kiln 15, on the east edge of the first-century ditch, I, B, lay the much damaged remains of another, which was only identified with difficulty. Although the structure had been so much destroyed it is safe to say that it had been of a much lighter and inferior construction to any of the others. The photograph shows how irregular the remains were, and the floor of the furnace, which remained, showed that the original outline of the interior had been of no regular shape. The clay walls were eked out here and there with pieces of tile, and in one place a large thick tile,

---

[1] Interim accounts appeared in *Germania*, xviii, 27, and the *Illustrated London News*, 20 Jan. 1934, pp. 96–97.

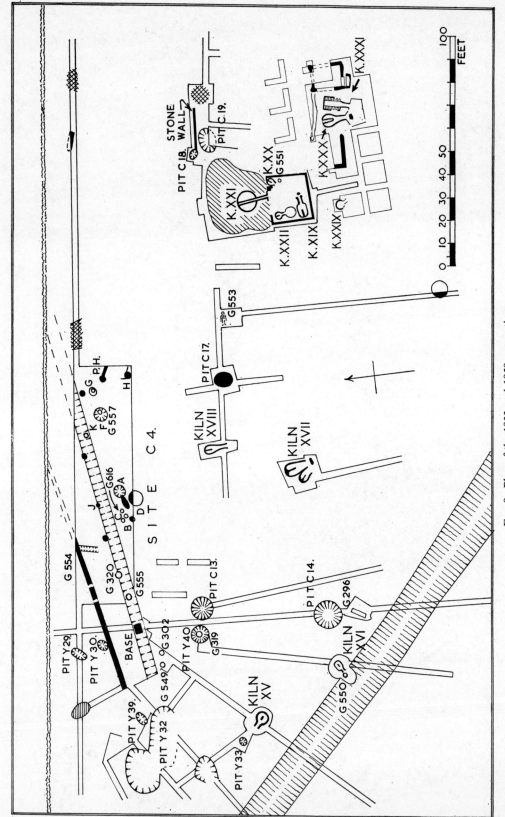

FIG. 9. Plan of the 1933 and 1959 excavations.

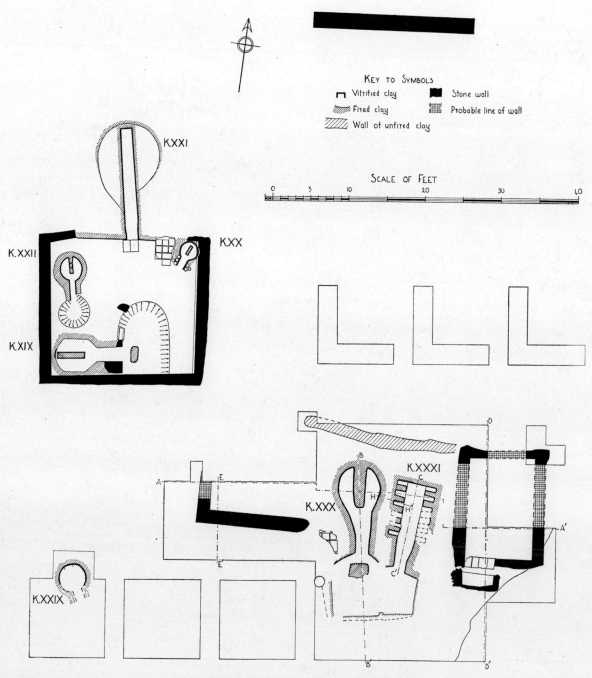

KEY TO SYMBOLS

Vitrified clay   Stone wall

Fired clay   Probable line of wall

Wall of unfired clay

SCALE OF FEET

0   5   10   20   30   40

K.XXXI

K.XXII   K.XX

K.XIX

K.XXXI

K.XXX

K.XXIX

A   E

B

C

D

H

C'

A'

E

B

D

FIG. 10. Plan of the 1959 excavations (pp. 34–43).

placed on edge, formed all there was of the wall, having no clay behind it. Possibly this had been a repair. The lower part of the central support remained in position.

The remains of pottery found included only one base of local red-glazed ware, no colour-coated or buff, but same type built against its west side. These were the only kilns found with the oven floor preserved. Most of the holes through the floor, for draught, are visible in the photograph (pl. 1c). The axis of the larger kiln was almost due north and south, with the entrance to

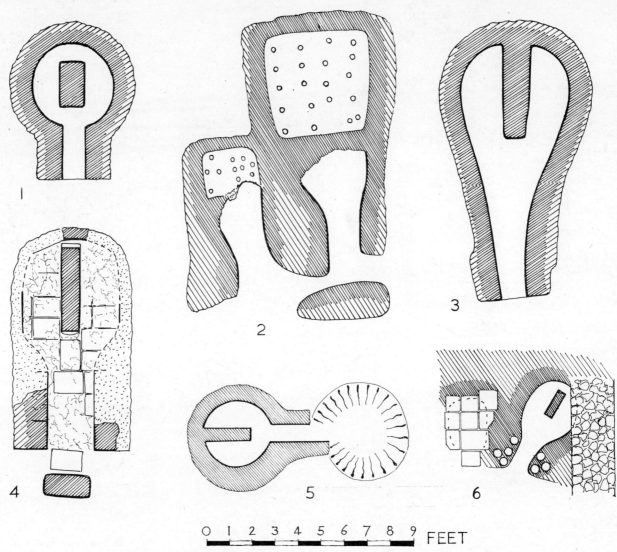

FIG. 11. Separate plans of the 1933 kilns. (1–4, kilns 15–19; 5, kiln 22; 6, kiln 20.)

a large amount of grey ware, chiefly of f. 268; there were also numbers of ff. 37, 277 (over-fired), and large 246 (fig. 73, 2, 3).

KILN 17 (III) (PL. 1c and FIG. 11, 2)

3. This was a twin kiln, lying 30 yds. east of kiln 16. A large kiln of well-known type, bottle-shaped in plan, with a central rib supporting the clay floor on arched flues of hand-puddled clay, had a smaller kiln of the

the south. A strong transverse block of burnt clay stood in position across the mouth of the larger kiln, a provision probably made to assist the control of the draught when required. No doubt, if not invariably, at least occasionally, it was necessary to close the entrance of the flue. Thus a kiln at Weisenau, near Mainz, was found with the entrance closed by a rectangular slab of sandstone (M.Z. vii/ix, 128, Abb. 5); another kiln on the same site is illustrated ibid. vi, 141, Abb. 1, also with a stone closing the entrance. The former was of late-first-century date, the latter much earlier. The absence of large slabs of stone in our district would necessitate an alternative method, the simplest of which would be to use heaped sand or earth. To have a large part of the necessary heap already in position, in the form of a permanent block, would assist speedy closure. Compare also the deposit of yellow sand left in the entrance to kiln 24 (p. 150), and the large rectangular tiles at kiln 32 (p. 168, note 1), which could have been used for this purpose.

The overall length of the larger kiln was 11 ft. 6 in., without the clay block, the width 7 ft., and the walls were of clay, 10–18 in. thick. The smaller kiln must have been about 7 ft. long, but was much broken about the entrance.

The support in the small kiln was not central. In some cases, especially with one row in the large kiln, the holes through the oven floor began over the support and had to be bored obliquely to reach the flue. The floor itself was well-preserved, though only a few inches below the turf, and it was possible, from the extent of the vitrified surface, to recover the plan of the ovens which stood upon them. These had been roughly rectangular, measuring inside the larger 4 ft. 6 in. by 4 ft. 9 in. and in the smaller 2 ft. 3 in. by 2 ft. 6 in. The stoke-hole of the larger kiln was only 1 ft. wide, and that of the smaller was probably the same.

The block at the entrance measured 4 ft. 3 in. long by 11 to 20 in. wide. It had not seen much use, for it was not much burnt, and the inner face was not vitrified as it was in kiln 24 (q.v.).

The amount of broken pottery found in excavating this site was vastly greater than at kilns 15 and 16. It may be summarized as follows:

T.S. Four frags. of one f. 18/31 and one of f. 33, imported; three frags. of one rouletted cup (fig. 46, 21) and a biscuit[1] rim f. 37, Colchester ware.

Colour-coated. This was in very great quantity, chiefly ff. 391–2, and some of 396, many fluted, all rough-cast or smooth, with no rouletting. There were also quite a number of fragments of mica-coated ware from flagons, &c., including rims of beakers f. 391.

Some fragments are vitrified, suggesting that this kiln was the source of the wasters in pit C17 (p. 141).

Buff. There were many mortarium rims with body-fragments in proportion. Over thirty rims were of bead-and-roll types; only two were wall-sided. Many have 'herring-bone' stamps: two at least are stamped by DUBITATUS. There was a huge quantity of fragments of the pedestal-based vases (f. 207) and of cup-mouthed flagons (f. 156).

Grey. There was not much of this; the remains included platters of ff. 39 A and B and 38, and jars of ff. 268 and 269.

Kiln-material (see description of kiln 21, p. 20). There was quite a number of fragments of tubes, but all very small. Possibly the tubes were fired in this kiln.

KILN 18 (IV) (PL. IIa and FIG. 11, 3)

4. Forty yards east of kiln 15 lay the lower part only of a long, pear-shaped kiln, which had been ploughed down until only 6 in. of the wall remained, which was about 8 in. thick and made of clay. The overall dimensions were 12 ft. by 6 ft. 6 in.; the central support 4 ft. long; the stoke-hole 15 in. wide. There were places where the inner face, which was, as usual, vitrified to a glassy grey colour, had been patched with handfuls of clay plastered into hollows where the surface had fallen away.

Here no pottery was found which could be said to be associated with the kiln (the level of the surviving wall would be below the Roman ground level), and the few sherds found belong to the general litter of the site. They included pieces of tile and kiln-wall.

THE KILN ENCLOSURE (PL. IIc)

The greatest discovery of the 1933 season was first encountered in a long trial-trench driven eastwards from kiln 18, passing the enclosure on its northern side and just cutting the north edge of the great spread of rubbish. From here eastwards the trench produced pottery in unprecedented quantities. From the edge of the rubbish layer (shown shaded on the plan, fig. 9) were recovered the first fragments of Sigillata moulds and most of the few fragments of the bowls made from them. The great quantity of burnt clay indicated the proximity of a kiln, and we soon had numerous fragments of pottery tubes and rings which we knew from continental finds to be characteristic of the special kilns used in making red-glazed ware (Samian) usually referred to as Terra Sigillata. The evidence for the near presence of such a kiln was now beyond doubt.[2]

A trench cut to the south proved to be in the right direction. It showed the deposit extending for some 50 ft. The amount of pottery, all firmly embedded in a mass of broken kiln-structure, had to be seen to be

---

[1] The term biscuit is here used of Sigillata fragments which have no coating; see p. 33.

[2] Attention was turned to the provenance of the fragment of mould which had long been in the Museum and which clearly was of the same manufacture as those now found. It was given by Mr. P. G. Laver in 1914 and entered as found in the 'Potter's Field' (Mus. no. 2896.14), which means that in which lay region 3 and the north part of region 5 of our published Report. But Mr. Laver recalled that he had some pottery about that time from a spot just north of the hedge in the next field to the east, that is about due north of the kiln-enclosure, so that we now regard this fragment as probably from there. Even so it is the most outlying sherd found.

believed. Digging in this was necessarily slow and laborious. As the time passed and the work was extended there seemed to be no bottom to the mass, and we had yet to find anything in position.

The first definite structure was encountered in what proved to be the SW. corner of the enclosure, when the top of the central support of kiln 19 was uncovered. The depth was then nearly 6 ft., and it was found that there was still 2 ft. to go to the lowest level of the deposit. The prospect was only slightly relieved much later when the true floor of the enclosure was found. The discovery, in this corner, of the scanty remains of the footing of the retaining wall enabled the outline of the enclosure to be followed systematically along the south and east sides.

When the entire filling was cleared it amounted to over 100 cu. yds., without the filling over the Sigillata kiln. The quantity of pottery was enormous, and the student helpers who tried to keep pace with the necessary washing, sorting, and listing cannot be too highly praised for their efforts. Some worked from 6 a.m. to 7 p.m. Even so, the cruder mass of mortarium fragments had to be left for later work.

At length the enclosure was cleared; three kilns and an oven had been found, but there still remained about 28 ft. of the red filling extending northwards from the north side of the enclosure, and on examining the exposed face a stoke-hole entrance was revealed, about the centre of the side, of larger size than any yet encountered. The excavation of this largest kiln (21) involved the removal of a further great bulk of filling and pottery.

The individual kilns are described below. We will first describe the enclosure in which they lay (pl. II c). An approximately rectangular area had been excavated into the sub-soil, which was soft yellow sand, with a flat bottom, so that the depth from the Roman surface on the north (uphill) side was about 7 ft. 6 in. and on the south side about 4 ft., the depth from the present surface being about 8 ft. and 5 ft. respectively. This was surrounded by a retaining wall of which only the slight footings remained, with no foundation trench, consisting of small irregular pieces of Kentish rag, laid in a poorish mortar, and about 18 in. wide. The wall had been (apparently) continuous on all sides except the north, where it was interrupted by the clay face of the Sigillata kiln (21). On each side of this there was but a small length of wall near each corner. That on the west had one course of rather better-shaped stones, and this may have been the first course of the actual wall. It can be seen behind kiln 22 in pls. II c and IV a. The eastern part of the face of kiln 21 was partly covered by a small oven (pl. III c, right centre).

The space enclosed by the wall was irregular, measuring 19 ft. wide on the south, 18 ft. on the west,

17 ft. on the east, and nearly 20 ft. on the north. There was no indication as to where the entrance had lain, but the only convenient place must have been about the middle of the east side. The floor was of soft yellow sand.

Within this space four kilns had been operated, of which two were sunk in the floor, and two stood upon it, or at its level. These are kilns 19 and 22, and 20 and 21 respectively.

Between the latter two, built against kiln 20 and backing on the clay of kiln 21, stood the platform of an oven. The top was tiled over, neatly, and evenly, and was 2 ft. square. The substructure was of seven courses of tiles, cemented with clay and reddened by heat. In front (the south) of this platform another smaller one projected, of less careful construction. The top was of two pieces of tile, level with the former, with two courses of tile beneath. Below these the right corner was of irregular stones and a mortarium-rim, while the rest of the face consisted of a large piece of septaria stone. The height was 13 in., width 14 in., and depth 10 in.

Our only conjecture as to the function of this structure is that it was the base for some sort of oven. It may have been used to bake bread in the heat of the kilns, or for some minor purpose connected with the work of the site. At any rate it seems it was designed to utilize the heat of the adjacent kilns.

Forrer was confident that the Heiligenberg potters worked under a roof. Fragments of tiles were abundant enough in the filling of our enclosure, but not so deposited as to suggest that they had fallen from a collapsing roof. This does not mean that a roof did not exist. It may have been removed, or at least the tiles salvaged, before the enclosure was filled in. The continental evidence is that such an enclosure would have a roof. The single large stone found almost exactly in the centre of our space (pl. II c, centre) may possibly have acted as a base for a central support. On the other hand, it may have been of some other service to the potters (see on kiln 24 below).

As the clearing of the filling progressed the vertical faces were watched for useful stratification. From them it was clear that the ruins of kiln 19 had been spoiled and covered over with debris during the time kiln 21 was in use. The outline of the sooty layer from the stoke-hole of the latter made this certain. After the disuse of kiln 21 the hollow was filled up with clay (the remnant of the potter's stock?), broken kiln, and mortar rubble from the robbing of the wall. West of kiln 19 lay the rubble remains of the retaining wall; and the face of the earth which it supported, consisted mostly of natural yellow sand and disturbed topsoil. The line of the top of the rubbish filling made it quite clear that the filling did not actually fill up the hollow to the level of the surrounding surface at the time, but that the top of the filling varied in level.

No variation in pottery content could be observed in the several sections of the filling, which must have been deposited over kiln 19 not long before kiln 21 shut down, and the next part of the filling followed at once, with no intermediate layer. Thereafter there was a layer of 'muddy earth' which may represent a period when topsoil accumulated. But whatever caused it, it had promptly sealed the loose rubble below, in which no snail-shells were found. Above it there was a later levelling of a foot or more of red rubble and pottery, from the potter's waste-heaps, and into this an inhumation burial had been inserted.

Well above kiln 22 the skeleton of an adult male lay extended with head to south and arms by the sides. There was nothing with it, but a grey jar stood upright in the ground just a little east of it. It was a large jar f. 268, with hollow for lid (fig. 75, 6).

Another jar of the same form, but not hollowed for a lid, was found upright in the filling over kiln 20. It contained only earth.

KILN 19 (V)
(PLS. II*b*, *c*, III*b* (top) and FIG. 11, 4)

5. This was a large kiln of almost rectangular form lying in the SW. corner of the enclosure, and, together with the sunken pit for stoking, occupying nearly all the south side. It was sunk 18 in. into the floor. It presented the appearance of having been dismantled by the potters themselves. The central support was almost intact, measuring 2 ft. high by 10 in. thick and nearly 4 ft. long. It was built of roughly rectangular blocks of clay about 5 in. square by 8 in. long. The line of the missing interior face of the flues could be followed by the colour of the burnt clay floor. They had together measured 4 ft. 2 in. wide by about 5 ft. 6 in. long, with a stoke-hole 2 ft. wide flanked by piers built of tegulae laid in clay, of which only that of the south was well preserved. The exact shape of the kiln could not be recovered with certainty.

A cross-block of burnt clay, as in kiln 17, stood across the entrance, at a distance of 1 ft.; the space between was occupied by a building-tile laid as a floor or threshold. The block measures 2 ft. by 1 ft., the height being uncertain, for the top was broken. It may also have extended a little more to the north.

The kiln had been stoked from a large boat-shaped hollow cut in the yellow sand subsoil. A tegula lay against the side of this near the kiln, and close to it, on the edge of the hollow, a large partly dressed block of Kentish rag, set as if to serve for a seat (but see pp. 17–18 above).

The pottery found was in huge quantities, but as the kiln had been demolished and cleared, the whole of this, even from low down, had almost certainly nothing to do with it, but was part of the general filling. In fact, the whole of the stone wall had been robbed before most of this pottery was deposited. It will therefore be described in the general report on the pottery.

KILN 20 (VII)
(PLS. III*b*, *c*, IV*b*, and FIG. 11, 6)

6. This was an interesting little kiln tucked into the NE. corner of the enclosure against the retaining wall. On the north side part of the clay wall was preserved against the clay of kiln 21 to a height of 3 ft. 3 in. from the floor. The central support was of clay blocks and measured 15 in. long by 5 in. wide and 12 in. high. The oven floor had completely disappeared. The structure of the stoke-hole was of interest. In the main it consisted of three heavy cylinders or tubes on each side, filled with clay, and in one case containing a smaller tube (C size), set upright on the ground and embedded in clay. (For the tubes see p. 22.) The tubes, or some of them, were continued upwards by columns of faulty colour-coated beakers inverted one upon the other (see pl. IV*b*.) The uppermost vessels were shattered, and there was no indication of how this arrangement was finished at the top. The whole was luted together with clay, most of which had fallen away.

The floor of the flue had broken away in use, and when found consisted mostly of loose yellow sand, on the same level as the general floor of the enclosure. The internal dimensions were quite small, the diameter being only 2 ft. 5 in., and the entrance only 10 in. wide.

In this case it is clear that the kiln had not been dismantled and cleared away, and to some extent the pottery found in immediate association probably belonged to it. This was in very large amount, chiefly colour-coated. Much of it was in large fragments, freely fitting together, but these may have come from the beakers used in building the entrance. No Sigillata wares were associated.

Inside the flue were fragments of ff. 391–2 and 396, i.e. the common forms of beakers, some lacking the colour-coating. Outside the kiln lay a great quantity of this ware, including red-coated flagons. There was also much buff ware; some lay inside the flue. The small amount of grey ware included f. 268.

Material from kiln 21 was found both inside and outside the flues. This would belong to the final filling, as would some fragments of the Claudius–Nero occupation.

KILN 21 (VIII)

(PLS. IIc (back centre), IIIa, c (left), and FIGS. 10, 12–13)

7. This without any doubt was the main discovery of the season, in which the great quantity of red-coated (terra sigillata) ware recovered was fired. It occupied the central position on the north (uphill) side of the enclosure and the main flue or stoke-hole was cut horizontally into the hillside like the adit of a mine.

The entrance was paved outside with two large tiles measuring 11½ by 17 in. These lay at the ground level of the flue, which level could be traced all round by a 4-in. layer of soot and charcoal from it. This was not less than 4 ft. from the Roman surface.

The sides of the entrance and flue were thickly built of clay, which included some tiles here and there. One of these was set flat and upright in the right-hand face, where it can be seen in pl. III a. The corner of another shows in the broken angle at the top on the left-hand side. The flue was 17 in. wide and a heavy clay cylinder lay almost horizontally across it at a height of 15½ in.[1] This was 6 in. in diameter and the walls continued another 15 in. above it, curving in slightly, as if to form a pointed arch. They were entirely of clay and were burnt red to 8 in. thick, behind which the clay continued, unburnt, as packing.

The destruction of the kiln had been so complete that only the lower part of the flue remained. It ran back, 17 in. wide, for 13 ft. 3 in. and was standing 2 ft. high at the far end. The whole interior surface, where it remained, was vitrified to a glassy grey colour.

The position and approximate size of the main body of the kiln was well indicated by the bowl-shaped hollow which was left in the clay packing after we had cleared away the rubbish filling it (pl. III c). The sides of this were simple to trace, for they were burnt brick-red, and as we have seen that this colour only penetrates the clay for about 8 in. even in the flue itself, we may conclude that the missing face did not carry much of the wall with it when it fell. The diameter of this hollow when cleared was about 7 ft. 6 in. The base of it had been much disturbed, as though there might have been something there which robbers thought worth abstracting. They had left it full of a loose red rubble of fragments of burnt clay, no doubt the broken remains of the fabric they had destroyed.

A kiln of this size must have had lateral flues opening from the main one, but the sides of the flue showed no traces of any such. This is evidence that they did not occur below the level of 3 ft. from the ground in the first 6 ft. of the flue, nor below 2 ft. in the remainder of the flue. Comparison with continental examples will show that there is no difficulty in this.

The original construction of this kiln will be discussed later when describing the structural remains from it (p. 26).

KILN 22 (IX)

(PLS. IIc (left), IVa, and FIG. 11, 5)

8. The last kiln found lay in the NW. corner of the enclosure and was sunk in the yellow sand of the floor. It was quite small, and irregularly circular. The central support, of crude clay blocks as before, was 2 ft. 1 in. long by 7 in. wide; the sides of baked clay 8 to 14 in. thick, reinforced with pieces of tegulae. The fire-hole was served by a small pit in the general floor level. The diameter of the kiln was 2 ft. 9 in. and the sides stood to 18 in. No trace of the dome remained, and of the floor only a small patch near the front. The stoke-hole was 10 in. wide and 2 ft. 8 in. long on the west side, but only 2 ft. on the east side.

The pottery found inside the furnace may well belong to it, for it contained a quantity of fragments of unguentaria, especially of the lip-rims, which had jumped off in firing, and which were rarely found in the rest of the rubbish filling the enclosure. There were no colour-coated fragments. The buff ware included ff. 156, 287; the grey ware, about fifty sherds, included a very large waster f. 268. There was also one fragment of kiln-tube, and some burnt fragments of *imbrices*.

The only T.S. found were some fragments of a very large f. 35, over-fired.

THE STRUCTURE OF THE SIGILLATA KILN (21)

Before going further we must now consider the remains of the Samian kiln itself which, in very fragmentary state, were found in great quantity throughout the filling of the enclosure and for some distance around it. They include a vast bulk of fictile fragments of very varied nature, few, or none, of which would be found on the site of an ordinary pottery-kiln. Most striking among them are the heavy and carefully made rings, which are as sure an indication of the presence of a sigillata-kiln as is a quantity of moulds. Besides these there is an almost incredible quantity of pottery tubes of different diameters, of clay luting, obviously used in conjunction with them, curious stoppers and discs which fit to them, small objects like small chimney-pots, and other pieces,[2] all of which we now proceed to describe.

---

[1] Compare a kiln found at Haltern in Germany, where the long cylindrical neck of an amphora f. 181 had been used in exactly the same position. *Germania*, xvi, 114, Abb. 2 (left).

[2] Forrer, pp. 70 ff.; Hermet does not discuss tubes; Déchelette, *Vases ornés*, ii, 341; Chenet, *Argonne* 52; Knorr and Sprater, *Blickweiler*, Taf. 103, 1, 2, 3.

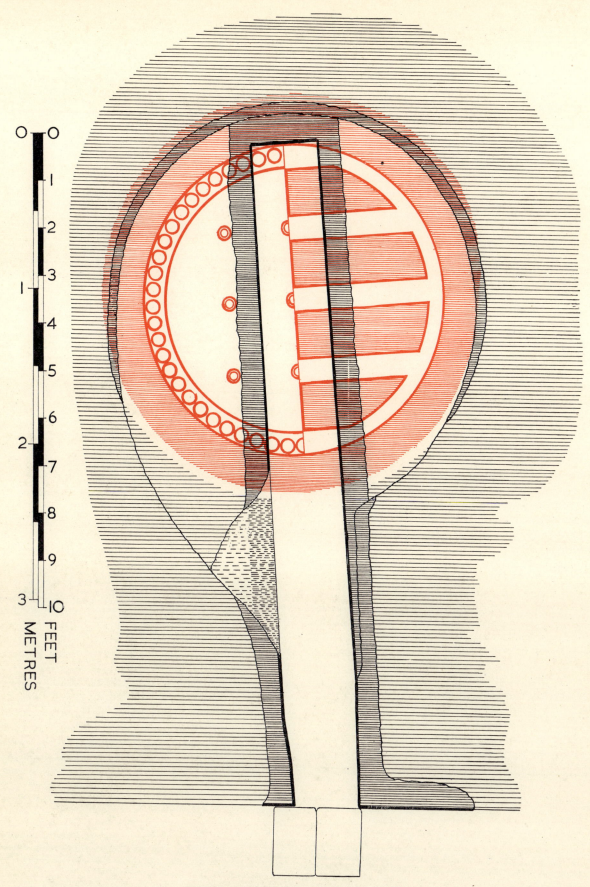

O
1
2
3
4
5
6
7
8
9
10 FEET
METRES

0
1
2
3

FIG. 12. Plan of Samian kiln (No. 21) (p. 26).

THE TUBES (A, B, C) (PL. V *a*)

There are probably two different classes of tubes. Those of the two largest sizes (pl. V *a*, 1, 2) were found built into the walling of kilns 20 and 21 (pl. III *b*) and their fragments were not sufficiently numerous to suggest that they had formed part of the interior system of the kiln.[1] The only complete (?) example was that spanning the entrance of kiln 21, which was not taken out, but was at least over 17 in. long. The remains of the tallest in kiln 20 (pl. IV *b*) stand nearly 14 in. high. They are made of a hard, sandy clay, and are nearly $1\frac{3}{4}$ in. thick, slightly tapered on the outside towards the top, a fragment of top showing the diameter reduced to $4\frac{3}{4}$ in. with a rounded lip. The thickness of the wall is reduced greatly upwards, so that the interior diameter increases. The outer surface is covered by bold horizontal grooves set $\frac{1}{2}$–$\frac{3}{4}$ in. apart. There are also remains of a few slightly smaller tubes, quite plain on the outside, and much resembling modern chimney pots. One of these stood almost intact in the entrance of kiln 20 (pl. III *b* (front), IV *b* (right), VI *b* (back)) with a beaker reversed in the top.[2] It is $10\frac{3}{4}$ in. long, 6 in. wide at the base, and $5\frac{1}{2}$ in. wide at the top. The thickness varies from $\frac{7}{8}$ in. at the base to $\frac{5}{8}$ in. at the top. The ends are both cut off square. There are fragments of a few others similar, but with the upper lip sometimes almost rounded. One fragment shows the complete length, $10\frac{1}{4}$ in.

The other class comprises thinner tubes, in much more broken condition and in such quantities that it is clear that they were in use in the kiln itself and subject to frequent replacement. They are not accurately cylindrical and can only roughly be sub-divided into groups according to diameter, for, though there can be no doubt, as we shall see, that they were designed for use in a system requiring several different diameters, they were casually thrown on the wheel to approximate sizes and of varying thickness. Thus any large number of diameters measured provides a continuous run, whether external, internal, or both dimensions are taken. We can, however, fairly assume that the tubes were used in three main sizes, the first of which, A, required an average external diameter of $4\frac{3}{4}$ in. (12 cm.), corresponding to the beading of the large rings; the second, B, had to be small enough to pass through the rings, and are about 4 in. (10 cm.) in diameter; the third, C, had to pass inside B. In no case has the complete length of any one of these been preserved, for we regard the complete piece (pl. V *a*, 7) as only part of a normal unit.

The material is the same as that of the largest tubes, and it may be fired red, by repeated heating, or soft white, in which case it seems to be underfired. The majority of the B-tubes were horizontally grooved on the outside, sometimes very closely, but there are also several smooth examples. None is truly cylindrical, for there is always a tendency to taper to the top, which is more or less rounded off, whereas the bottom edge is cut off square.

There is very little difference in the quantity of fragments of A and B, those of C are comparatively scarce, usually smooth, less burnt, and thicker (inasmuch as no tube had to pass inside them). They are markedly tapered near the top, with a slight final expansion.

The fact that these tubes, though fitting within one another, are not truly cylindrical, makes it impossible that they were used alone to form self-rigid columns. They are quite unsuitable for such use.

There are also many fragments of sub-units, or fractional parts of these tubes, which must have been used to make-up any series of tubes to some required length. A selection is shown on pl. V *a*, 4–14. They are mostly of A size, but some are of B. They vary greatly in length, from $\frac{1}{4}$ in. upwards, and correspond exactly to Forrer's Taf. VIII, 11, 12.

HEAVY CLAY RINGS (E)
(PL. VI *a* and *b*, 2–7)[3]

These have been explained by several writers as potters'[4] wheels, but they were recognized as used in the kiln by Dr. Meunier and Forrer. The wheel theory cannot be maintained against the fact that these rings are only found where Sigillata ware was made. As potters' wheels they should have been found in similar numbers on the many sites where coarse wares were made, but they never are. It is clear then that they belong to some technical process connected with Sigillata. Hermet attaches much value to the fact that a few have been found bearing the owner's name inscribed with a stylus, the argument being that they were thus not buried in the oven, but used in the open and valued by the owner. But in a great factory like La Graufesenque there would always be a number of piles of these rings standing to dry, and it would be natural for the owner to put his name on the top one. It would be of importance that he used his own, knowing exactly how

---

[1] Tubes of our size A (below) were used structurally in a kiln at Rheinzabern (Ludowici, iii, 144, fig. 15), being set all round the circular oven, embedded in the wall and filled with clay. The kiln was of ordinary type, not for Sigillata, at least so far as we know!

[2] This beaker, which we had left in position, was stolen one night.

[3] Forrer, p. 69, Taf. VIII, 6–9; Knorr and Sprater, *Blickweiler*, Taf. 103, 4; Hagan, *Sinzig*, in *B.J.* 124 (1917), Taf. XXXII, 15, 16.

[4] A summary will be found in Hermet, *La Graufesenque*, p. 215, who still clings to this view; see also Déchelette, *Vases ornés*, ii, 338.

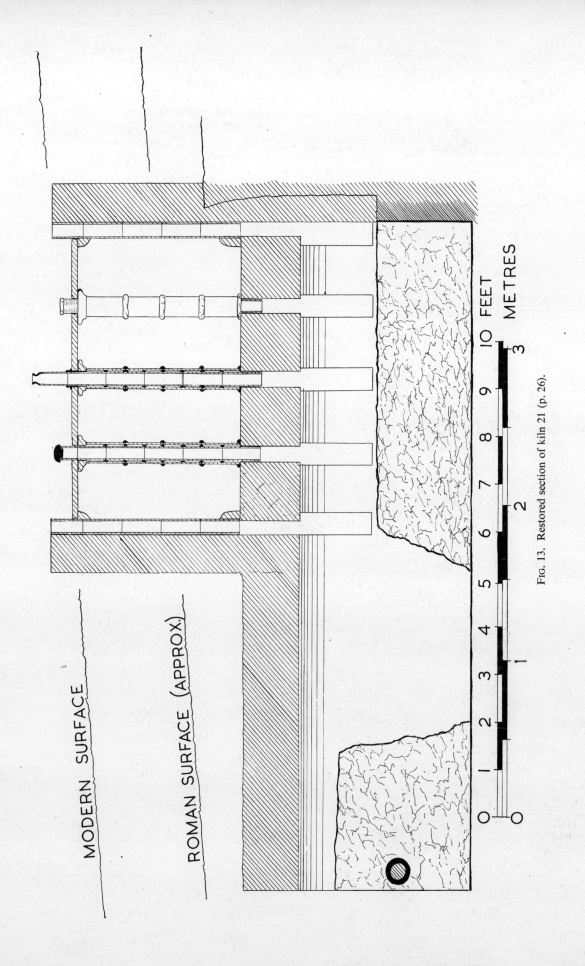

MODERN SURFACE

ROMAN SURFACE (APPROX.)

FEET

METRES

Fig. 13. Restored section of kiln 21 (p. 26).

long they had stood to dry. We hold that these are not wheels, and that wheels must almost universally have been made of wood.

Thirteen rings are fairly well preserved, and there are over a hundred fragments of others, plus thirty more found in 1959. The general outline is that of a thick ring, flat on the upper side, but with a stout, raised beading round the central opening, which is sometimes parallel-sided, but often bulged or splayed to some extent (as Meunier noticed). The flange is stout, of varying thickness, with rounded edge. The under (?) side is less carefully finished. The rim of the central hole is flat and broad, usually retaining the marks of the wire which cut it from the wheel. From this rim the flange drops away in a concave curve, usually deep, but there is great diversity here.

The following table shows the dimensions of the best thirteen, in centimetres.

	Ring	Hole	Rim	Height
1. Intact, hard buff, cracked in firing.	21·3	9·3	13·0	4·7
2. Intact, misfired, red-buff, containing white flecks, faulted.	22·5	10·5	12·7	5·2
3. Imperfect, waster, ring complete but edge of ledge jumped off; buff with very fine black and white grit.	23·4	9·5	11·6	6·1
4. In two pieces, edge jumped as last, but fragments present; clay as last (these two rings are of like clay and unusual form).	24·2	9·3	11·8	6·5
5. In two halves; good buff.	22·9	9·5	12·0	5·5
6. Restored; good buff; frags. differ in colour.	23·2	9·9	12·9	5·1
7. Restored; hard red-buff.	21·9	9·5	12·6	4·7
8. Restored; red-buff with black core.	22·7	8·7	11·0	5·4
9. Restored; red-buff.	22·9	8·4	11·4	5·5
10. Restored; good red-buff, frags. differ in colour.	23·6	8·9	11·3	4·9
11. Restored; as last.	22·0	8·6	11·3	4·9
12. More than half, in one piece, yellow-buff.	20·1	9·3	11·9	5·2
13. More than half, in four frags., hard grey-buff.	21·1	8·5	11·1	4·2
Average of the above dimensions.	22·4	9·2	11·9	5·3

Half a dozen or more of these rings had perforations in the flange[1] (pl. vi b, 2–7). The complete ring (no. 2)

has four such holes, made horizontally through the flange with a pointed stick or bone at equal distances (indicated by the match-sticks). They must have been made while something solid occupied the centre, as is clear from the way in which they stop at the inner face. These holes could not have been used to nail the ring to a wooden axis. Their making bulged up the soft clay across the face of the flange. Two other fragments have similar holes. One (no. 31)[2] of buff ware has two holes 5 mm. diameter and 2 mm. apart centre to centre, vertically through the flange slightly oblique to the radius. Another hole, 5 mm. diameter, runs horizontally through the flange (and collar?) at a point 9·3 cm. (measured round the circumference and centre to centre) from the first pair. No. 32, from a very thick buff flange, has one hole, slightly tapering, about 4 mm. diameter, vertically through the middle of the flange. No. 77, similar, but not, we think, the same ring, has two holes about 4 mm. diameter vertically through the flange near the middle and 4·1 cm. apart. No. 16, a small fragment, bright red, has one hole horizontally through the flange, tapering from 6 mm. diameter outside to 3 mm. at the inner end. Surface bulged above.

These perforations were not noted at Heiligenberg, but some are mentioned by Hermet, op. cit., p. 216, at La Graufesenque, without detailed description. He says that nearly all the rings there had them, and believes they were used to secure the disk of the potter's wheel to the top, or the ring to its wooden axis. They may have been actually intended to let out steam while firing,[3] but seem very carefully made and widely spaced for this purpose.

One fragment has three bold flutings on the flat side of the flange (pl. vi b, 5), and two more such were found in 1959.

One fragment alone is fused to the melted remains of a tube, which has fallen across the concave side of the ring. The diameter of the tube, which was a plain one, cannot be estimated.

Finally, we cannot emphasize too strongly the importance of noting the occurrence of these rings on any site. They may have been passed over (especially if fragmentary) in time past, since there has been no description of them previously published in English. So far as we know at present they are definitely evidence of the manufacture of Sigillata, and are easily recognized.

FINIAL FITTINGS (CHIMNEY-POTS?) (F, G, H)

F. Pl. v a, 15–16. We have only thirteen small fragments of objects shown by Forrer, Taf. viii, 1 and 4.[4]

---

[1] Hagen, op. cit. Taf. xxxii, 16.
[2] These numbers refer to those written on the actual fragments.

[3] Some of those found in 1959 have scattered jabs of no depth which are almost certainly intended to let steam out.
[4] And cf. Blickweiler, Taf. 103, 19; 104, 2, 2a.

These appear to have been upper terminals for the A tubes, to which they correspond in diameter, material, and thickness. They lack external grooves. The lower part of the wall is vertical, the height varying from about $\frac{3}{8}$ to $2\frac{1}{2}$ in., at which point the wall slopes inwards, conically or curved, and is perforated by triangular apertures cut out with a knife. The narrow mouth is finished by a beaded rim. The best-preserved is 2 in. (5·1 cm.) over the rim and $\frac{7}{8}$ in. (2·3 cm.) wide in the mouth. The openings may also be cut in the upright part of the wall or (?) in both. The clay never shows evidence of great heat. Another fragment had an internal diameter of $1\frac{1}{4}$ in. (3·3 cm.) and triangular openings spaced at intervals of $1\frac{5}{8}$ in. (4·3 cm.).

G. Tubes of some length, of size B, were narrowed at the top, with an angular shoulder, incurved to a stoutly beaded rim, which surrounded an opening much smaller than the diameter of the tube. The fragments of these very distinctive objects are not numerous, about fifteen in all, and include two large pieces (pl. v *a*, 17–18), both broken at the bottom, so that the original length is unknown. The first has a present length of $10\frac{1}{8}$ in. (25·7 cm.) with a body diameter of $3\frac{1}{4}$ in. (9 cm.) at the shoulder; the opening at the top is $1\frac{1}{4}$ in. (3·4 cm.) and diameter over the rim $2\frac{1}{2}$ in. (6·4 cm.). The second lacks the rim, but must have closely resembled the first; the body, of diameter $3\frac{1}{4}$ in. (8·4 cm.), is almost cylindrical. The internal diameters are $2\frac{1}{2}$ and 3 in. (6·4 and 7·5 cm.) respectively. Both are of fine buff clay, reduced to a very brittle state by great or protracted heat, but not vitrified and not made bright red. The whole, except the beaded rim, is covered by close horizontal grooves, exactly as in most tubes of size B. The other fragments conform exactly to this description and include a complete top, shoulder diameter $3\frac{1}{4}$ in. (8·5 cm.), opening $1\frac{1}{4}$ in. (3·3 cm.), rim diameter $2\frac{3}{8}$ in. (6·0 cm.). Measurements of the other fragments are closely similar.

H. A similar purpose was clearly attained by adding a small finial of the same pattern as the top of the tubes already described to the top of an ordinary tube of size B. These are of similar outline, but are of thicker clay and much cruder workmanship, with the grooves more widely spaced (pl. v *a*, 19–20).[1] Two are preserved intact and have an external diameter of $3\frac{1}{2}$–4 in. (9–10 cm.) with internal diameter about $2\frac{3}{4}$ in. (7·0 cm.), but are misshapen. The diameter of the small mouth is $1\frac{5}{8}$ and $1\frac{3}{4}$ in. (4·2 and 4·5 cm.) respectively, and the height $2\frac{3}{8}$ and $2\frac{5}{8}$ in. (6·0 and 6·7 cm.). The other fragments are similar in dimensions. The clay is soft, and whiter than that of G above.

There remains a complete top which may have belonged to either G or H. The clay is an intermediate soft buff, the shoulder more rounded, the maximum body diameter apparently $3\frac{5}{8}$ in. (9·2 cm.) with a top opening of $1\frac{1}{4}$ in. (3·3 cm.).

Fourteen further fragments suggest that the purpose of the objects just described (G, H) could be, and was, attained by using narrow rings in place of the shouldered finials. These vary in height from 1·7 to 4·0 cm. ($\frac{5}{8}$–$1\frac{1}{2}$ in.), and most have horizontal grooves round the outside. The base is flat, but the top is always rounded, distinguishing them from the 'fractional' tubes. Most are of size C, but six are of B. There is one example of the smaller size intact (pl. v *a*, 21).

CLAY PLUGS OR STOPPERS (K, L)

Pl. v *b*, 1–3. These are to be differentiated as clearly as possible into two groups, distinguishable by the shape of the impression they bear. We are here concerned only with those which were used in conjunction with tubes, and which show the shape of the end of the tube to which they were affixed. Others which show the impress of the base of a kiln-prop had no constructional function.

It is clear that on occasion the potter took a ball of soft clay and with it plugged the end of a tube. The interior diameter of these tubes was 2 in., rarely slightly more (5·0–5·5 cm.) and the outer about 3 in. (7·5–8·0 cm.), corresponding to tubes of size C. In four cases the back of the plug remains hemispherical; two burnt very hard red-brown, two soft white. Eight others, all in hard red-brown clay, are flattened on the back, where they have been fixed against a flat surface, probably a tile. Another white one may belong to this class, but the back is broken. Compare Forrer, Taf. IX, 1–3; *Blickweiler*, Taf. 103, 6, 7.

There are also cases where the potter has taken a flat disk of clay, pressed it on the end of a tube, and then set another tube upon it (pl. v *b*, 4–7, 9). These are all of hard-burnt red-brown clay. The impression on one side (the upper?) is of the size C, that on the other (lower ?) is nearly always slightly larger, but hardly as large as size B (e.g. upper diameter 4·0 (one only) to 5·0 cm., external *c.* 7·0 cm. or more; lower, internal 5·0–5·5 cm. (once 4·7, once 6·8 cm.) external uncertain, but about 8 cm.).

CLAY LUTING

(Fig. 14.) It is clear that the various 'prefabricated' parts which have been described were fitted together in the kiln and secured or stuck together by clay luting, which the potter applied by hand, and which bears numerous marks of his fingers. The quantity of

[1] Cf. ibid., Taf. 103, 9; Forrer, Taf. VIII, 2, 3.

fragments of this is very great, but most of them are small owing to the extreme brittleness produced by the severe heating. Most are of hard-burnt red clay, some of it well-levigated, some coarse and sandy, some muddy buff and full of paler streaks and spots as if from the boulder-clay, and some soft white.

Most striking are the remains of bands of luting which joined the ends of two tubes and rested, on the inside, against an inner tube, from which they usually preserve the impress of the horizontal grooves (fig. 14, 2, 6). These correspond to Forrer's fig. 37 and Taf. VIII, 13 ff., *Blickweiler*, Taf. 103, 8 (but see p. 30 below). Most of these fit exactly over the tube (pl. v*a*, 17) which has an outside diameter of 3 in. (7·5 cm.); very few are slightly larger, still fewer are smaller. About one-fifth of the total fit to a tube of nearly 4 in. diameter (*c*. 10·0 cm.).

Cases like Forrer's fig. 38, where a smaller tube is luted upon a larger, are rare, but a specious appearance of this is very common, and is caused by inaccurate centring of two tubes of the same size.

A few fragments (fig. 14, 17) have luted together two tubes of size B side by side.

Many fragments come from the joint of an A tube upon the rim of the flat side of the rings E (fig. 14, 1, 5). It is uncertain whether we have any showing the joint of such a tube to the *other* side of a ring. The uncertainty is due to the amount of 'skid' made in the clay by the end of the tube. Impressions wide enough to be those of the broad rim of the ring might equally well be a skidded impress of the end of a tube. This is regrettable because the point is very important as we shall see.

Some of these pieces of luting show a further joint or joints, and it is clear that they were not only in contact with tube and ring, but also with tiles laid horizontally, and even occasionally, vertically (p. 30 below, fig. 14, 4, 5, 13, 14, 15).

There are lutings which have been crudely moulded ridges running up and down the side of a tube, in this case of size B or C, but always with horizontal grooves. These ridges sometimes show that they had a vertical tile laid against them (fig. 14, 13, 14).

THIN SHEETS OF CLAY

There remains a great quantity of fragments of sheet-clay, very red and coarse-sandy in texture. The pieces are very much broken, somewhat over $\frac{1}{8}$ in. thick, but under $\frac{1}{4}$ in., thicker in places, and some pieces are altogether thicker. They are even and sandy on one side, as if rolled out on a bed of sand. The other side is sometimes the same, sometimes smoother, as if it had been smoothed down with the hand, or with a trowel or a piece of wood. All are more or less undulated and many show that they have been brought up to round or square objects and tucked in to fit closely to them. Some bear partial circular impressions, probably from vessels.

Forrer noted similar remains from his kilns, Taf. IX, 16–19, but in his case one side is covered with small impressions which he interprets as made by hobnails in the sandals of the workmen. The same is shown on *Blickweiler*, Taf. 103, 5.

Finally, there remains a body of fragments of burnt clay which includes lutings, the purpose of which cannot be hazarded, and large lumps which show no recognizable form.

THE RECONSTRUCTION OF THE KILN
(FIGS. 12, 13)

Having thus reviewed the materials available we may now proceed to consider how they may have been utilized in the working of the kiln. In this problem, despite the great number of Sigillata potteries[1] which have been identified and, in greater or lesser degree, excavated (see the map in Oswald and Pryce, to which many additions could now be made), we find help from only three published accounts. The first is Forrer's excellent and painstaking account of the Heiligenberg and Ittenweiler sites.[2]

This incorporates the work of Schweighauser, a pioneer of 1824, to whom we are greatly indebted for observations and drawings which have preserved for us some details of the one Sigillata kiln (Heiligenberg II) which has been adequately described. The value of these is so great that the lack of details, which we so much desire now, must be forgiven to so early a pioneer. His work has been ably continued by Forrer's masterly analysis of the remains found in the refuse-tips of the Heiligenberg potters, which form a series almost completely parallel to ours. The third account is of the kiln found at Eschweiler Hof, published by F. Sprater in 1927.[3] It is very brief, but none the less useful, and includes restoration drawings. These are the only sources to which we may look for help or corroboration, and it is essential in considering our remains to bear in mind those found at Heiligenberg and Eschweiler Hof, and the interpretation of them given by these writers.[4]

---

[1] For example, 160 kilns at Lezoux, reported by Plicque; *Bull.* and *Proc. verb. Soc. d'Emul. d'Abbeville* (1884), 52.

[2] Forrer, *Die römischen Terrasigillata-Töpfereien von Heiligenberg-Dinsheim und Ittenweiler im Elsaß*, 1911.

[3] R. Knorr and F. Sprater, *Die westpfälzischen Sigillata-*

Töpfereien von Blickweiler und Eschweiler Hof, pp. 112 ff.

[4] Since the above was written we have a circular kiln with tubes all round the walls and four flues under the floor. Chenet, p. 49.

There is no doubt that our kiln was circular and that it was of the type of those mentioned above. We accordingly may disregard the many other types which have been found on Sigillata sites. Of these many do not differ from the ordinary potter's kiln, though they may have performed some minor function in the preparation of Sigillata. Others are circular, but do not seem to have had the internal apparatus of tubes, rings, &c. Yet others are large and rectangular, elaborately constructed, especially as regards the floor and the holes through it, but these also lack evidence of the use of tubes, &c. Indeed, it would appear that there were at least two methods of firing Sigillata, for in the extensive and widely excavated establishment at Aquincum no circular kiln of our type, and no tubes, rings, &c., were found at all. Since this alternative method, whatever it was, was not used by our potters (so far as we know), there is no point in discussing it further here.

The first of our parallels is described by Schweighauser as semicircular, and his plan shows as if it were one half of a circular kiln with lateral flues at right angles to a main flue, which is parallel to an even larger flue resembling our central one. The illustration gives the impression that this kiln was not fully uncovered. However this may be, the plan is strange, but this kiln undoubtedly made use of tubes and rings.

The third kiln at Heiligenberg (Forrer, fig. 8) is so like the first that it is only after careful consideration that Forrer concludes that it is not the same one reopened. In any case only a small part of it was uncovered and it does not aid the investigation.[1]

The two kilns Heiligenberg II and Eschweiler Hof are very similar, and both have the floor preserved, with a few of the tubes. Otherwise the remains of these kilns have only been found in the potters' waste heaps. Our own waste heap must have been near the kilns, for its contents were used to fill in the enclosure.

Forrer's analysis of the objects found in the refuse, with some additional remarks by Sprater, corresponds with our own observations to a remarkable degree. Such differences as there are may be ascribed in part to different schools of technique, possibly also to a different stage in the experience of the industry as a whole. But the remarkable parallelism in detail, as already noted, indicates an established technique in which the potters of the several places were thoroughly versed.

THE SUBSTRUCTURE

All three plans consist of a long flue with a circular oven built over the farther end. There is, unfortunately,

no scale with Schweighauser's plans, but his flue must have been about 13 ft. (4 m.) long and 16 in. (40 cm.) wide. Eschweiler Hof was slightly shorter, about 12 ft. 6 in. (3·9 m.) long by 19 in. wide. Ours was 14 ft. (4·2 m.) long and 17 in. (43 cm.) wide at the entrance widening to 19 in. (48 cm.) after the first foot. The first 3 ft. of the flue still stood 3 ft. high and nearly completed a pointed arch, which must have been originally 3 ft. 6 in. high (1·07 m.) or slightly more. This was the form throughout the length at Heiligenberg and Eschweiler Hof, but in the former the height increased under the oven, we are told, so that a man of ordinary stature could stand upright, and Schweighauser's sections show a minimum height of about 4 ft. (1·22 m.), which increases to 5 ft. 6 in. (1·67 m.) opposite the lateral flues. The height of the pointed arch at Eschweiler was nearly 1 m., and somewhat greater opposite the flues, and was, therefore, much lower than that at Heiligenberg, though approximating to ours, which lies between the two.

Under the oven our flue-walls remained only 2 ft. (61 cm.) high, and 4 ft. of the west wall were completely gone, so that we had no trace left of the lateral flues. The presence of these is, however, amply attested by the other examples. Sprater shows four on each side, with a small space at each end over the main flue. They are about 14 cm. (5½ in.) wide, divided by walls about 32 cm. thick. They begin 26 in. above the floor of the main flue and slope up to 46 in. against the outer wall, where they are only 2 in. below the under side of the floor.

Schweighauser does not give a plan of the flues, but it can be seen from his plan of the floor of the kiln that the holes through it are in four lines, indicating four flues, and indeed he mentions three dividing walls. Yet he shows two sections each taken along a row of holes. One (Forrer, fig. 11) shows the holes in the floor communicating with a transverse flue in normal manner, the other (fig. 12) is quite different, showing the holes connected by (apparently) sloping tubes or pipes which run through solid masonry from the main flue to the base of the opening through the floor. In this section, also, the tubes of the outer wall are shown sloping inwards! It is further remarkable that the flues shown on each side in his fig. 11 have sharply upcurved floors.

In both kilns the lateral flues opened into a circular flue which ran all round the interior of the outer wall and served the continuous ring of tubes which lined it. We may confidently assume that our kiln had such flues, both lateral and circular. The latter was only 4 in. wide and 8 in. high at Heiligenberg (10 by 20 cm.) which seems rather small, and the tubes ran down

---

[1] A round kiln at Rheinzabern, Ludowici, ii, fig. 7, had been entirely surrounded within by tubes of 12 cm. outer diameter (approximating to our A-tubes), but there is no information as to the arrangement of the flues. The internal diameter, within the tubes, was 1·5 m. (c. 5 ft.). Another, without tubes, was 2·2 m. in diameter. Ibid., p. 164, fig. 4, 6.

through the floor to it. At Eschweiler the flue was similarly narrow, but extended to the top of the floor, the tubes standing partly on the floor and partly over the flue. The substructure at Heiligenberg was of stone, at Eschweiler not stated, and at Colchester clay.

THE FLOOR OF THE OVEN AND ITS SURROUND

Our floor had completely gone, but we have some guide to its size inasmuch as it must fit within the diameter of the circle of burnt clay which is all that remains of the wall. At Heiligenberg the floor was 8 ft. 2½ in. in diameter (2·5 m.), and it was bounded by a wall of tubes embedded in clay and fragments of brick, which was 20 cm. thick and stood directly over the circular flue, with which the tubes connected. When found it was standing 2 ft. high, but about one third across the front of the kiln was missing. The floor was quite flat on top, nearly 32 in. (80 cm.) thick, except over the main flue, where it was only about 12 in. (30 cm.).

At Eschweiler the floor was 7 ft. 6 in. wide inside the ring of tubes in its clay wall, which was nearly 10 in. thick. It is possible that the clay in which these tubes were embedded was simply to secure them and did not extend to any great height. Sprater's section (Textbild 39) seems to show that it was finished off as a chamfer a little above the floor. Schweighauser, too, says (Forrer, p. 35) that the clay wall holding the ring of tubes did not seem ever to have stood higher than it was when found. His drawings show it varying from 20 to 30 cm. high (8–12 in.). Yet Sprater, in his reconstruction, carries it through from bottom to top of the oven.

Besides this copious provision for lateral heat, ducts were also made through the floor, leading to flues beneath (the exception of Schweighauser's section, Forrer, fig. 12, has already been mentioned). Their number would vary with the size of the kiln and the judgement of the potter. The Heiligenberg kiln had four rows of holes, still containing their tubes standing about 1 ft. high above the floor.[1] The holes were three in the front row, then 4, 5, and 3 again respectively, 15 in all. The Eschweiler kiln had 12 holes in four rows, arranged 2, 4, 4, 2, on one of which part of a tube still stood. The floor was 12 in. thick (30 cm.) and stopped short of the outer wall by 9 cm., thus forming the circular flue. The holes were placed at a minimum spacing of c. 18 in. (45 cm.) centre to centre. With tubes of 5½ in. diameter standing on them this space is reduced to nearly 1 ft., and the largest space avail-

able on the floor would accommodate a dish of about 22 in. diameter.

In making our reconstruction we begin with the circular flue, the outer edge of which must coincide with the end of the main flue and must fit within the burnt clay walls. It must have been about 6 ft. 6 in. in diameter (1·98 m.). This makes a small kiln, for the wall of tubes would not be less than 6 in. thick, and more probably about 12 in. thick.

The internal diameter at floor level would therefore be 5 ft. 6 in. as a maximum, and perhaps only 4 ft. 6 in. We have allowed 5 ft. 6 in. in our drawing and three flues beneath, with nine holes through the floor. Dishes as large as 18 in. diameter could be set in such a kiln.

THE SUPERSTRUCTURE OF THE OVEN (FIG. 12)

The question of what stood upon this floor is the most engrossing and complicated of this inquiry. Apart from the tubes found in position by Schweighauser, and those recorded by Sprater, we are entirely dependent upon our analysis of the functions of the rings, tubes, and other objects which clearly belonged to it. Forrer's very careful study resulted in his fig. 39, which gives in diagrammatic form his theory of how all these varied parts may have been fitted together for use. Sprater (Textbild 40) gives a complete theoretical restoration of a kiln on much the same lines, and on the basis of these two diagrams, together with certain observations of our own, we give figs. 11 and 12, a conjectural restoration of the Colchester kiln.

It was desirable (but see p. 32 below) that vessels having a fine, glossy red finish should be fired in an oven in which they were protected from any contact with flame, smoke, or fumes. In an ordinary kiln they would be exposed to all of these, unless placed in closed saggers.[2] In the Sigillata kiln they were protected by conducting the heat from the flues through the oven in tubes.

The outer, continuous, wall of tubes would provide a great heat, and it was increased by certain tubes through the floor, up to fifteen in number. Some of these, at Heiligenberg, are close to the wall. Forrer further finds evidence that other tubes stood on the floor acting as supports for the roof and not conducting heat.

Now, as we have already outlined, once what we may call the 'live' tubes were in position on the floor the area was so subdivided as to leave only a limited space for large vessels, and, if we suppose further tubes to be placed among them, there would be only room for small vessels. It is therefore questionable to

---

[1] It is one of the minor catastrophes of archaeology that a fête was celebrated in a neighbouring village and the elevated participants enthusiastically demolished all the tubes exposed,

during Schweighauser's absence from the site.

[2] There is no evidence that saggers were ever used in Roman kilns.

what extent this may have been done, for vessels of 1 ft. in diameter (f. Sb) were made in quantity. We shall return to this question later.

It is next necessary to point out that none of the continental evidence shows double tubes in use, but Sprater found remains of a smaller tube fused within a larger, and so arrived at the first mention of double tubes. Further, the discovery of one tube in position on the floor at Eschweiler Hof confirms Schweighauser's drawing. The isolated tubes were of the smaller size, either fixed in the floor or standing on it, with, as Sprater conjectured, the larger ones slipped over them. The joints were arranged not to coincide, and thus each column received added rigidity and gave better protection against smoke.

We learn nothing from Schweighauser about the use of small and large tubes, but Sprater says that those in the circular wall were of the large size. Seven were preserved in position and did not have small ones inside. The evidence as to the isolated tubes does not support Forrer's hypothesis that the large rings lay on the floor as a base for the large tubes, and, as Sprater rightly points out, the only useful purpose of these would be to provide a broad seating for the roof at the top of each column.

These columns would not be very tall. The height would be determined by that of a reasonable pile of vessels arranged for firing. With unfired vessels the strength of the clay and weight of the pile would be a limiting consideration, and stability was always a problem as we can see from the numerous pieces of clay which were used to steady them in position. It has been suggested that more vessels might be packed in by using the tubes as supports for large tiles upon which further nests of vessels could stand; a method closely approximating to modern practice. This could well have been done, but if so, it is curious that it was never done in the case of the coarser wares, for the tubes are only found where Sigillata was made. On these grounds it has been reasonably argued that the interior height of the kiln would not be more than about 3 ft. Forrer suggested, and Sprater has followed him, that the roof of the oven was of flat tiles. If tiles of normal size were used (i.e. about 18 in. by 12 in.) the supports for them would have to be at an appropriate spacing centre to centre, but if some of the supports stood on the floor, and have disappeared, the plan of the holes in the floor gives only part of the plan of the supports. Of course, larger tiles, say 2 ft. square, might have been used, but no excavator has noticed the presence of any such tiles of unusual size. At any rate, it would be quite possible to lay a flat roof of tiles about 18 in. by 12 in. (45 cm. by 30 cm.) on parallel lines of 'live' supports all spaced at 45 cm. (of the Eschweiler Hof plan), with dummy supports, in

the same lines, where necessary. This would leave lanes about 1 ft. wide to receive vessels.

The 'live' columns must pass through the roof and yet support it, hence the necessity that they should carry a broad ring on the top, on which the tiles could rest. The tiles Forrer conjectured would be covered by gravel or sand to keep in the heat, or there may have been a double roof of tiles held apart by small clay pillars made for the purpose (Forrer, figs. 34–36).

Forrer's diagram on fig. 39 is unconvincing. It is not to scale, but he has not realized how limited was the room left when the columns were all in position. The evidence before him, since confirmed by Eschweiler, shows that the large rings were not used on the floor, as he had supposed. The fact that he only shows tubes of large size used in the 'live' columns may or may not be an error. We know he had tubes of at least two different sizes, and he conjectured that these were used in the dummy columns, which would be reduced in diameter upwards. Yet in this diagram he shows his dummy columns built of the large tubes alone. At the top he merely used a ring of luting to secure the last tube to the edges of the tiles, placing the large ring *on top of the tiles*, where it is useless except as a stand for his small chimney.

Sprater, though not mentioning the rings of clay luting, has found a much more convincing solution. If one so arranges the lowest tube that it is firmly embedded in the floor and projects for half its height above, one can then pass a large tube over it, then add another small tube in the centre, then another large over it, and so on, building a *double* column. His idea is that this would increase rigidity, and so it would, if the tubes were accurately made and fitted tightly. He then puts a ring on top of the last large tube, on the broad rim of which the tiles rest, while the smaller tube continues through the roof. This he finishes off flat, continuing the outer side-walls over it as a dome with a central vent.

Having thus reviewed prior attempts at reconstruction we may now proceed with our own. As our kiln is the smallest of the four we have allowed only three lateral flues. We make our floor about 1 ft. thick, level with the top of the pointed arch of the main flue, and we stop it short of the outer wall by about 4 in. to provide the circular flue. The large quantity of fragmentary tubes found would scarcely be accounted for by their use as free columns only in the kiln. From this, and the evidence of the other three kilns, we feel obliged to provide a ring of tubes around the wall. If this were 1 ft. thick, our oven' floor would only be 4 ft. 6 in. wide. We have, therefore, made it rather less than 1 ft. The only remains of it of which we have evidence are one or two small pieces of clay which joined tubes of size B side by side (fig. 14, 17). It may have been quite thin for there is some suggestion that it had received a facing of flat tiles held upright by clay luting (fig. 14, 14). Both continental kilns had part of the ring of tubes remaining, and they seem to have been single. We cannot say whether ours were so or not.

The main columns on the floor start with a B tube embedded in the floor. Outside it we build a column of A tubes, and here we come to a point which the

side, and the impress left by them is unmistakable; his appear to have been smooth. It should, however, have been noted that, after the luting was in position, the builder could not reach it to smooth its interior. That such double tubes were commonly used at Colchester is certain, and sometimes triple ones were used; cf. fig. 14, 7, 8. Short lengths of tube of each size were available (pl. v a, 8–16) to adjust the length of the columns to fit them to the roof.

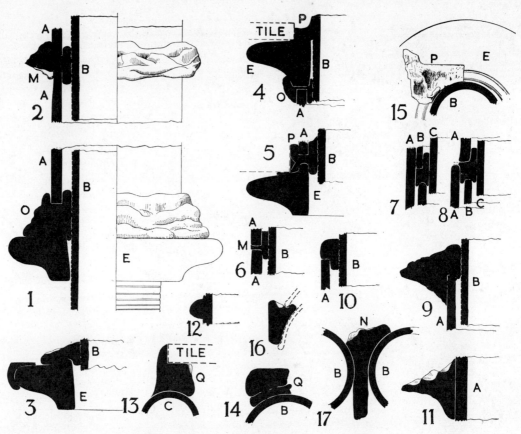

Fig. 14. Sections of kiln-tubes (see pp. 25–31). (¼)

previous writers have omitted. These outer A tubes were luted together with rings of soft clay, the use of which they have correctly appreciated, but we can add that beyond question these lutings were bedded against the outside of B tubes, leaving an interval of ⅛ to ¼ in. between the two tubes (fig. 14, 2). Thus our columns would not be much more rigid for being double, but would have a cavity wall. It is a remarkable fact that no lutings (out of a very large quantity) come from the joints of the B tubes. It seems possible that this point was missed by Forrer, for on his Tafel VIII he shows lutings exactly like ours, and his nos. 13–15 certainly looked as if they had backed against a smaller tube. Our B tubes are nearly all horizontally grooved out-

Besides the many fragments of lutings used in this way there are others as fig. 14, 1. These fit to the flat side of the large rings and show that a B tube passed through the ring while an A tube ended against its inner rim. Now this did not, we have decided, happen at the base of a column, so that here we have the arrangement at the top—unless indeed these rings were used at intervals up the columns to support tiles which would then act as shelves for vessels in the oven. This latter is an entirely new suggestion, and it is difficult to see how it can be substantiated, even if true.

Other lutings show the rings connected to a flat surface (fig. 14, 3), and some show that the ring was fixed

to an opening between tiles (fig. 14, 4, 5, 15). The imprint of the tile is certain. The drawings are probably the right way up, otherwise a support would have to be found for the tile.

Here then we have evidence for a ring placed at the top of a column, and supporting the tiles of the roof, to which it is luted. In all cases the ring is the same way up. The position of luting like that shown in fig. 14, 4 (beneath) is, as has been observed, doubtful, but we feel they must have existed so, and we feel justified in assuming that this was the manner in which our draught tubes passed through the roof and at the same time supported it. The luting, fig. 14, 5, could have been used in this manner.

Lutings like fig. 14, 5 may have been fixed to a 'chimney' F on the roof over the end of a column.

Other lutings (p. 30 above) show that some tiles at least were set vertically within the oven, almost certainly against the B tubes of the circular wall (fig. 14, 14).

Our dummy columns seem also to have been double, for we do not find luting for single tubes. But we do find the disks (L)[1] which luted together small tubes (B or C) inside these columns, and we must conclude from this either that the columns were triple, or that the outer tube was size B. We have, however, found no lutings for size B in such a position, so these columns may have been triple; cf. fig. 14, 7, 8.

When the columns reached the roof they ended in clay plugs (K),[2] and had been reduced to a single tube, C, to which alone such plugs fit. These latter backed on the tiles of the roof, but we cannot show them marked with the joint of two tiles as Forrer could.

Reduction in tubes in the column is proved by luting such as fig. 14, 10 and 9 (reducing from A to B size). It is also occasionally shown by the disks (L), and rarely by the ordinary luting of a joint. Fig. 14, 9 and 10, if inverted, could also come from the base of a column at floor level; cf. Chenet, pl. III, 10.

It seems that tubes of size C had been used, at least sometimes, in the circular wall, for fig. 14, 13 shows that a tile has been supported vertically by a ridge of clay against a C tube. Fig. 14, 14 shows the same with a B tube. Such tiling can hardly have been continuous, for we have not sufficient lutings. It is possible that they were arranged sometimes, possibly experimentally, as saggers.

We have still to notice certain lutings such as fig. 14, 3, where a B tube passes through a ring and is luted in position without an A tube. This may have occurred at the roof, but there is no mark of a tile. There are also plain, circular lutings which passed round A tubes where there was no joint, and which bear no mark of contact with anything on the part preserved

(fig. 14, 11, 12). These may have had something to do with our suggested tile-saggers.

At the roof it is clear that a tube of any size might stand in the final position, those of the draught columns passing through the tiles and bearing a chimney of appropriate size. Sometimes, but only in the case of C tubes, the last tube was plugged with a ball of clay (K).

We feel that Forrer's suggestion of a flat tile roof, followed also by Sprater, is the only satisfactory one. In one case he had evidence of distance-pieces for supporting a second layer of tiles, forming a cavity-roof to retain the heat; in the absence of this he suggests that sand would be laid on the roof for this purpose. Sprater, however, continues his outer walls as a dome over the roof, with a small central opening. While this is confirmed by ancient representations, in which kilns are domed like bee-hives, we need not feel compelled to follow them, as none is known to represent a Sigillata kiln. It is difficult, indeed, to see how Sprater's dome could have been built, and if we accept it, then all discussion of our so-called chimney-pots and plugs for the top of tubes to control the draught is ruled out, for the vents in the roof would be inaccessible.

There is no doubt, from the study of these remains, that one of the greatest difficulties of the Sigillata potters was to prevent the entry of smoke and fumes into the oven. All the fragments attest their endeavours to secure this end. The objects discussed above are peculiar to Sigillata kilns, and have not been found in any of the hundreds of ordinary kilns which have been excavated. The great difficulty was that their parts were 'prefabricated' and already fired, while the luting which joined them in the kiln, no matter how copiously applied, was liable to shrink and crack as the kiln heated. Hence our double and even triple tubes. These thus became cavity-tubes and must have seriously reduced the heat, and it is noticeable that most of our wasters are underfired. Thus it is probable that our potters were continually experimenting. Many different arrangements would be tried, and rarely, if ever, would the construction of the kiln be uniform throughout. Each time it was opened and cleared, some part would be judged sound enough to remain, but much would require replacement.

Often a new supply of tubes, rings, &c., would have to be made for this rebuilding, and very soon the various parts would differ, both in the manner of their fabrication and in constructional arrangement. It is improbable that any reconstruction we might make could properly show all the different objects we have discussed simultaneously in use in all the different ways which have been suggested.

[1] See above, p. 25.

[2] See above, p. 25.

THE FIRING OF TERRA SIGILLATA

It is certain that the attainment of the right firing temperature was a source of trouble to our potters. The clay itself may have presented difficulties; it was, however, capable of good results, as many examples show, though the vast bulk of our sherds is badly underfired. An effort to secure the necessary high temperature may have resulted in the fused mass of dishes (pl. XVIII b). Indeed at one time we thought the Sigillata kiln had been over-heated to a point of collapse, but, had this happened, we should have found fused tubes. The tubes are made of much coarser clay than the vessels, and designed to withstand heat, but the question is to what degree. It is significant that only one fragment was found fused, and that seems to have happened after breakage. The remainder show no undue traces of heat, and no soot or vitrification due to the action of wood ashes.

Reference has already been made (p. 27) to the fact that there seem to have been at least two different methods of firing Sigillata, which differed widely. In the one the kiln was kept clear of smoke and gas by tubes. The other system seems to have relied solely on the use of a very clear fire. M. G. Chenet's great work *La Céramique gallo-romaine d'Argonne du IVe siècle* has recently become available. On p. 50 he remarks that a roof was not necessary for a Sigillata kiln except to keep off the rain, the reason being that the firing was an oxidizing process.

We are greatly indebted to Miss H. Pincombe for the following explanation of the conditions in firing, and how the red and black colour of the majority of ancient pottery is produced. It is due to the presence of iron, whether in the clay or deliberately introduced; by firing in an oxidizing flame red is obtained, and in a reducing flame black. Thus we have often seen that of two pieces of a vessel which fit together perfectly one is red the other black.

The atmosphere in a kiln is oxidizing when there is plenty of air, and it is quite clear. Sufficient oxygen is then present to secure complete combustion. In the absence of impurities this will produce a clear red colour in the ware. If the air is shut off and the atmosphere smoky, a reducing condition is caused and the result is that the carbon draws oxygen from the iron in the ware, which becomes black according to the amount of iron present and the extent of the reduction. Thus many shades from grey and brown to black result.

It would, therefore, appear that Sigillata ware could be made:

(*a*) In a closed kiln (or muffle) provided carbon was

excluded: and it is clear that our tubes were solely for the purpose of excluding smoke and gas. If a supply of air could be provided to the vessels, without lowering the temperature, it would be beneficial.

(*b*) In a kiln of ordinary pattern if the fire was bright and smokeless with plenty of air in the draught. The stoking in this case would call for much experience and skill, for it is obvious that each addition of fuel would temporarily bring about reducing conditions.

This is summed up by Miss Pincombe as follows: 'It is therefore not necessary to have a muffle. But open firing requires right fuel and considerable care. A muffle, by keeping the products of combustion from touching the wares, ensures a clean oxidising firing under most circumstances.'

M. Chenet's work is limited to kilns of the fourth century, when the potters, though still using the traditional kiln-props or stands, and other instruments, dispensed with the muffle kiln almost completely. Only at Les Allieux B were tubes and rings found, and then (it appears) in such small quantity that one wonders whether they may not have been relics of an earlier kiln on the site.[1] But, as already remarked, as early as the time of M. Aurelius the Aquincum potters were operating without a muffle, while in East Gaul both methods seem to have been in use up to the invasion of the Alemanni.

It is perhaps remarkable that there is no direct evidence that Sigillata ware was ever fired in saggers.

METHOD OF MANUFACTURE

Only an experienced potter could write an authoritative treatise on the various processes and technical details of the manufacture of Terra Sigillata, and so far such a man is lacking. We can make no pretension to more than a general account here. Ludowici, who was a brick and tile manufacturer, has published some technical observations on the technique of the ancient potter in his report on his discoveries at Rheinzabern, but an exhaustive account backed up by experiments and practical tests and prepared by an experienced scientist is long overdue. The red 'glaze' has several times been analysed and a number of attempts have been made to reproduce it, without complete success.[2]

The clay was finely levigated by successive washings, so that when fired it became very hard. A good clay was necessary for this, because extreme levigation can lead to loss of strength. The finest continental wares are of a characteristic pinkish-red colour, which may or may not be due to some addition to the clay. Later fabrics are decadent, the clay is coarser, and in some East Gaulish fabrics, as notably in our own, fires to a bright, almost tile-red, colour.

---

[1] Chenet, p. 53 and pl. III.

[2] See now Mavis Bimson, *Antiq. Journ.* xxxvi, 200–4.

The clay was thrown into the required shape by the potter working it with his bare hands on the wheel. The latter might be of wood or pottery (p. 22) and was mounted horizontally on a vertical spindle which had a flywheel at the base which could be rotated by the potter's foot or by a slave. Wheels were mostly of wood, for traces of them are scarcely ever found.

When thrown the pot was cut off the wheel by drawing a wire through under the foot. This left the curious semi-spiral mark, somewhat resembling a gigantic thumb-print, so often seen under unfinished bases (e.g. always in f. 268). Normally the pot was next set upside down on the wheel and the base neatly finished and the footring (if any) added. The skill with which this is done is a direct index of the skill of the potter.

The vessels were next set out on racks in a store which must be open to the air, yet shielded from both sun and rain. The long, low, roofed but open sheds in which bricks are so stored in brickfields are familiar enough to most of us. Here the soft clay slowly dries and becomes of leathery consistency.

At a suitable stage the vessels are brought out for colour-coating and firing, at which time the surface is in the best condition to receive finishing touches such as polishing, grooving, or scoring.

The subject of the nature of the various glazes used by the Romans still awaits much research. There is confusion in terminology, if not in thought, in describing superficial finishes; the common terms such as 'glaze', 'varnish', and 'slip' have been used in several different ways. The subject has been discussed by Walters, *B.M. Catalogue*, pp. x ff.; May, *Silchester*, pp. 2 ff.; and by other archaeologists in this country and, in particular, many attempts have been made both here and abroad to reproduce the Sigillata finish, particularly in Germany, but the results are either unpublished or widely scattered.[1]

A glaze may be defined as a coating of glass fused over the surface of the vessel, but it is possible to obtain a finish like burnished metal ('lustre') in other ways, and it is now known that the Sigillata 'glaze' is not a true glaze, but a clay slip with alkaline base. The subject is too wide to be discussed here, but this much has been said to introduce the next stage in the manufacture.

The 'glaze' was a clay slip; the vessels would be dipped in it in the 'green' or unfired stage, and would only be fired once. A clay slip would not adhere to a pre-fired pot. In all cases also there is the consideration that a glaze or slip which contracted more or less quickly than the clay supporting it would, in firing, crack and flake off.

Certain it is that Sigillata vessels were dipped in a liquid slip; the workman dipped the vessel into it upside down, holding it by the footring, around which the prints of his four fingers and thumb can usually be seen.

In the case of the large Arretine platters the vessel was often not submerged far enough to let the glaze into the centre of the footring. In the case of vessels with narrow mouths an air-lock often formed inside, in which case the interior surface was not coated.

At Colchester, if we omit the wasters which were over-fired and fused, the spoilt ware consists of underfired vessels. On all of these the coating is flaking off (e.g. pl. XIII *a*), and the ware itself is soft, varying from nearly white in the softest, through pale red, to the correct, but still too soft, dark red. The white pieces are often so soft that no coating remains, and when it does it is a matt earthy coating like a bad paint, often of uniform black colour. On the others it is red, but darker and browner than the desired colour, and often of a peculiar soapy texture.

The above observations agree with the supposition that the coating was an alkaline slip containing iron, and that the vessels were dipped into it in the 'green' stage. We assume, therefore, that fragments lacking 'glaze' have lost it, for they are all excessively soft. Moreover, there are soft pieces with remains of 'glaze', and obviously if they had come thus soft from a biscuit stage they would have been discarded and not dipped in the 'glaze'.

A scientific treatise on this subject is much to be desired. It is indeed difficult to believe that the marvellous surface on the early Sigillata could be produced by a clay slip.

As many vessels were packed into the kiln as possible, by stacking them one within the other, usually upside down, but not always so (pl. XVIII *c*). As the clay dried it shrank considerably[2] and often cockled, so that the piles were liable to lose balance and collapse. To guard against this they were often propped in position by lumps of clay. The piles themselves were often supported (in the case of the Sigillata) on specially made supports. These were hollow and funnel-shaped, with a prominent beaded rim (pl. V *b*, 12–17), and are exactly paralleled at Heiligenberg (Forrer, fig. 44, and Taf. XI, 25, 26).[3] They were firmly fixed to the oven floor by being forced hard down into a ball of soft clay (pl. V *b*, 10), and were suitable for supporting small vessels such as form Drag. 33 in an inverted position (not upright as Forrer shows his). Forrer further had cushion-like lumps of clay used to support piles of forms 18/31 and 37, but here these do not seem

---

[1] But see p. 32, note 2 above.
[2] The total shrinkage in bricks made of local clay is about 12 per cent. For this information we thank Mr. J. Everett.

[3] And Chenet, pl. III, 5–9; pl. IV shows 45 examples bearing owners' names!

to have been used. He also had small twists of clay used to secure the rim of the lowest vessel of a pile firmly to the floor. These also are not found here. On the other hand, we have small cushions of clay into which the base of a f. 33 has been pressed (pl. v *b*, 10–11), exactly as shown in Forrer's fig. 41A. A few pieces of the clay sheeting show the imprint of the rim of the lowest vessel of piles of platters (pl. v *b*, 8). Occasionally a separate piece of clay was used to level-up such a pile. A plain, flat disk, somewhat wedge-shaped in section, may well have been used to level-up a flat tile as a stand for vessels. It is clear that, as convenient, clay would be used to secure these piles to the walls, or even to the roof, cf. fig. 14, 16, supporting vessels of f. Sb.

When the vessels were securely stacked, the dome of the kiln was completed over them and the furnace kindled. The task of the operator now was to bring the heat of the kiln up at a steady rate until the vessels were glowing hot, and to keep it so for some 48 hours, without either overheating or cooling. Great experience must have been necessary for this, for a wood fire can vary in heat excessively and very quickly. Some measure of control could probably be exercised by using tiles or sand partly to close either stoke-hole or chimney-vent, the latter particularly simply in a Terra Sigillata kiln (p. 31). Closing the vent in an ordinary kiln would smother the kiln. The difficulty of getting the right temperature without thermometers was doubtless surmounted, as now in brickworks, by watching the colour inside the oven through the vent-openings. It was easy to spoil much ware by overheating or by under-firing.

The kiln had to cool gradually, then the dome was opened and the vessels which had cracked or distorted too badly for sale were thrown upon the rubbish-dump.

The plain vessels were often stamped by the potters, usually in the centre of the upper side of the base. This was done by incising the name deeply, backwards (right to left) on the edge of a fragment of pottery. When this edge was pressed on the soft clay the name appeared in relief in a sunk label, reading left to right. Often the maker forgot to cut his stamp in reverse, so that it appears reversed (retrograde) on the vessel. None of these matrices was found.[1]

None of our decorated bowls was stamped. When this was done the stamp was impressed (as a rule) among the decoration in the mould. Thus it emerged finally in its original (negative) form. The moulds themselves (not ours) were sometimes signed by the maker, in a totally different manner, for he wrote with a stylus in the plain surface just below the decoration. The mark emerged in relief on the finished bowl, but was often removed or blurred when the footring was added.

Since the above was written an extensive new site has been explored at Mittelbronn, which lies about half-way between Sarrebourg and the Col de Saverne. Air-photographs revealed a large area of occupation, which was confirmed on the ground by tile-scatter. Here there seem to have been several *officinae* making samian (and other) ware, and about 120 sq. yds. of the site were explored in the years 1953–5 and 1957.[2]

The main kiln found was of the same plan as ours but larger; the flue was 0·8 m. wide and 7 m. long. The circular oven had been 3 m. in diameter. Immediately behind this kiln there had been a large building, either workshop or warehouse, which had two periods. In one it had been supported by uprights set on stone bases, which gave dimensions for it of 14 by 8 m. The other, set on practically the same lines, had narrow stone foundations, perhaps for a wooden building. It extended farther than the other towards the kiln; far enough, in fact, to include half the diameter of the circular oven, but whether the two are contemporary or not I do not know.

Here, too, the potters seem to have been concerned with drainage, and a conduit is shown leaving the flue at a point near the perimeter of the oven.

The date of this establishment, as also the products, seem to have been much the same as ours, but there are some notable differences. It seems there were kiln-rings, but no tubes; this needs verification. There were (or are as yet) no moulds for decorated Samian.

THE EXCAVATIONS OF 1959

In 1933, hoping to be able to return to the site, we only filled back the kiln-enclosure sufficiently to cover the kilns from frost. However, it was decided that attention must continue to be devoted to Camulodunum,

---

[1] For examples see Ludowici, *Rheinzabern*, ii, 105–6; iii, 84–85.

[2] *Annuaire de la Soc. d'Hist. et Arch. de Lorraine*, liv, 1954, 75–96; and *L'Officine céramique Gallo-Romaine de Mittelbronn* (*Moselle*), in *Gallia*, xvii, fasc. i, 1959, 101–59.

and so it remained to the outbreak of war. Thus it has not been possible to return to this very important site until 1959. It may be stated with confidence that there still remains much of importance to be explored.

In 1955 several people began to dig on the site, in particular Mr. H. C. Calver, who kept the Museum informed of his finds, and finally presented all, or most of them. He soon reported that there were three more unexplored kilns and gave up his interest in the site to the Museum. He had found many important additions to our knowledge of the pottery, all of which have been incorporated in the present report.

In 1959 it was decided to go forward with the publication of the Research Report on the work of 1933, and it seemed worth while to promote an excavation to add these three further kilns to the 25-year-old report. The Marc Fitch Trust generously provided a grant of £250 for this purpose, and the work was carried out in August and September by students and other volunteers under the immediate direction of Mr. Bryan Blake of the Museum, and the general supervision of the author. We take this opportunity of thanking all those who assisted with the work, and further thank the Ministry of Works for permission to excavate, and the Colchester Corporation as owners of the ground. All objects found, being the property of the Corporation, are in the Museum.

Since the position of the three kilns was known, the excavation was made in boxes 10 ft. square.[1] Great labour and delay was caused by the large amount of earth disturbed by previous diggers, which had to be removed before undisturbed strata were reached. This was worst in the area immediately south of kiln 29. The whole area had, of course, formed part of Camulodunum, but traces of that phase had been largely obliterated by the kiln-workings, and chiefly remained as the contents of very large pits or excavations, possibly originally gravel-workings. These large pits, one south of kiln 29 and another south of kilns 30 and 31 in particular, had by the late second century become shallow depressions, the uphill bank of which provided the potters with points very suitable for cutting kilns into the side of the hill. The material from these pits was all of Claudian-Neronian date and has been fully covered by the account of the small finds in our report on Camulodunum.

KILN 29 (PL. VII a)

This was found in a sorry state; it was uncovered in 1955 by Mr. Calver, who found it was circular and complete. He left it exposed but not excavated; in his absence some other enthusiast came along, and thinking, no doubt, that it was a well dug a shaft in the

middle of it. As we found it there was nothing left but the northern half of the circle. This consisted of a wall 3 ft. 6 in. high, made of clay blocks, pre-shaped and built into position unfired, with wet clay used to bond them together. After firing it had become quite solid. All the furnace entrance, floor, and central support had been destroyed; the mark of the latter showed red-orange on the vitrified grey of the back wall, against which it had fitted with a straight joint. The stoke-yard area and the top levels of the first-century pit below had been so much disturbed in 1955 that its limits could not be traced; indeed, very little was found undisturbed, though layers connected with our potters' activities remained as levels 9 and 9a in section F–F' (not published).

Most of the vast mass of fragments found hereabouts belonged to mortaria, and Mr. Calver says he found great quantities of these around the kiln. We, for reasons stated, could find no pottery connected with the kiln, but the mortaria we found were, no doubt, those disturbed by Mr. Calver and others.

This kiln had been cut into made earth which contained pottery of the period of the activity of our potters. This is probably debris from the kilns of 1933, farther up the slope, so that our kiln 29 should be later than those in the enclosure, or at least later than some of them.

KILNS 30 AND 31 (FIG. 10)

Some distance east of kiln 29 two kilns were found in juxtaposition, lying north to south like kiln 29. The western was pear-shaped in plan, the eastern rectangular; both were fired from the south using a common stokeyard. The northern slope of an underlying pit had been used for both. These two kilns proved to be the most complicated of all those found so far.

KILN 30

The history of this kiln can only be explained as a series of complicated phases, some of which have to be correlated with the several stages of the adjacent kilns—for kiln 31 proved to have another kiln under it which we have called 31 a.

The earliest structures of this group were kiln 30, phase I, and kiln 31 a (fig. 15, phase I). Kiln 30 was pear-shaped, 7 ft. wide and 11 ft. long. The walls and floor were of clay blocks laid in a raw state; floor and walls were then faced with a rendering of clay up to 1½ in. thick. The blocks used in the floor were roughly standard at 15½ in. by 10½ in. by 3 in. thick; those of the walls, however, were much rougher. Where protected from the heat and so not fired hard, these blocks could not be distinguished from the unshaped clay of

[1] See fig. 10, p. 15 above.

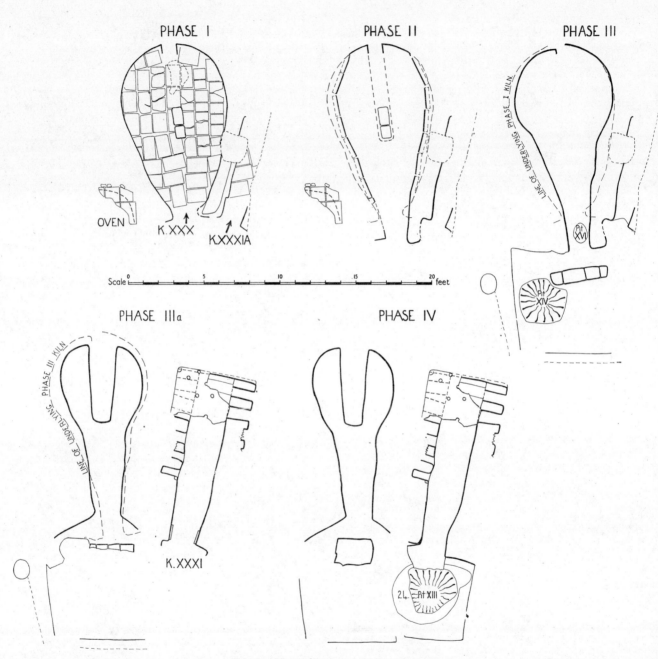

PHASE I

OVEN K.XXX K.XXXIA

PHASE II

PHASE III

LINE OF UNDERLYING PHASE I KILN

Pit XVI

Pit XIV

Scale 0   5   10   15   20 feet

PHASE IIIa

LINE OF UNDERLYING PHASE III KILN

K.XXXI

PHASE IV

24. Pit XIII

Fig. 15. Plans: the phases of kilns 30 and 31.

the structure. The floor blocks ceased just short of the mouth, where they may have existed but had perished with use, for here was the heaviest wear upon them. The remains of the central support for the oven floor consisted of a single line of blocks laid directly upon the floor-blocks and attached to the back wall; it had extended at least 6 ft. southwards; with its rendering of $1\frac{1}{2}$ in. of clay its total thickness was $11\frac{1}{2}$ in.

This tongue was so slender that it left a flue 3 ft. wide on each side of it, over which the oven floor had to ride. No trace was found of voussoirs or fire-bars, but the kiln had been so much repaired and rebuilt so many times that this was not to be expected.

In the final phase of this kiln (fig. 15, phase IV) the overall width was less—5 ft. 3 in., and the tongue 1 ft. 9 in.—but even so a wide space remained open for the flues. The walls were standing in most places to 3 ft., but showed no trace of a ledge or sockets for bars or of springing for voussoirs. There were occasional traces of the outermost of the holes through the floor. The span was probably arched with puddled clay.

KILN 31a

This was contemporary with kiln 30, phase I, which it adjoined on the east (fig. 15). It shared a common floor of clay blocks with kiln 30, although at front and back its floor was of puddled clay. The final surface of the floor was missing.[1]

This kiln had almost been destroyed by the construction of the deep central flue of kiln 31 which replaced it. It appeared to have been small; the back, mainly removed by a pier of kiln 31, was just traceable. Its height may be partly indicated by a vitrified face, which may belong to it and which is preserved because kiln 31 was built against it. As it had been cut away almost completely at the back by a rebuilding of kiln 30 it was not too certainly in position, but the general impression gained gave reason to suppose it was so (fig. 16, sect. H–H').

The only alterations during this first phase were in the front part of the common wall between the kilns. The mouth of kiln 30 after heavy use, which vitrified the wall, was narrowed on the west side; a relining of the west side of kiln 31 a had been done before it was much affected by firing. An odd feature of this relining was that the wall had an offset at the front which stopped 6 in. from the floor and left the mouth the same width as it was in the next phase (fig. 15, phase I).

OTHER FEATURES OF THIS PHASE

To the west of kiln 30 was a small oven floored with tiles (cf. the oven west of kiln 20 in the enclosure,

p. 18). Little of it remained, but it was possible to follow the rounded form of the oven wall by the different colouring of the floor where it had stood. It most probably was contemporary with phases I, II, and possibly III. Once the clay façade of phase III was erected it must have been difficult, if not impossible, to gain access to the oven.

PHASE II

There was little basic change in this period, which hardly amounted to a rebuild. The plan was altered so that the width became 5 ft. 9 in. and the length 12 ft. 6 in. This was done by lining the inner walls with blocks of clay measuring $15\frac{1}{2}$ in. by $3\frac{1}{2}$ in. and probably 11–12 in. in height. These had been made in wooden moulds. The grain of the wood was visible on the faces of the blocks, which were irregularly set, and indented at the corners, as if by clumsy or careless fingers when the shuttering was removed, or when they were set in position. They were not prefired, but laid in a green state, and their backs are fired no harder than the clay in which they were bedded. At the back of the kiln they had been made longer to fit the existing walls. The front, where blocks could not be used, had been lined with clay by hand to produce the desired shape. The mouth now lay slightly to the east of the earlier one, which had necessitated the partial destruction of the earlier east wall.

KILN 31a

Little appears to have happened to this kiln in phase II, except for an adjustment to the front; as the mouth of kiln 30 had been extended southwards by 15 in. on the west and 20 in. on the east, the west wall of kiln 31 a had to be advanced a similar distance. The old offset had been filled in after it had been fairly hard-fired, and the new wall was offset by 9 in. towards kiln 30. This would allow the stoker easier access to the stoke-hole. Even so the angle must have been awkward for his work.

PHASE III

The alteration which marks the beginning of this phase was more drastic. It involved the reconstruction of kiln 30 to a new plan. The walls of phases I and II were cut away to within a foot or 6 in. of the floor and much of their backing clay with them. In their place rose the new wall of phase III, but on a new plan and in such a way that in some parts the last few inches of the earlier work were left projecting like a rough step, while at others the new wall stood upon the old floor.

[1] In all the kilns the floors were very cracked and friable; where no rebuilding had taken place they remained, for the most part, in position; but where a kiln had been rebuilt above them they were usually missing.

The rough step was rendered over, like a crude quarter-round moulding of a tessellated floor, and this feature was added where necessary, so that it was continuous all round the furnace (fig. 16, sects. A–A′, B–B′). At the north end of this section (B–B′) the joint of the central support to the kiln-wall should show. But as this had been destroyed, the gap has been filled in our drawing by the complex of walls and floor-levels east of the tongue at the back of the kiln, which have been shown (projected westwards) in the section.

This kiln had a long life, and during this phase and phase III *a*, the floor was raised three times, the last one equalling the level of the top of the step. It must have already had a long life as kilns go, and the sole remaining part of the original phase I kiln must have needed replacement now. Just how and when the support was rebuilt has been obscured by the last rebuild of the kiln, and by activities of spoilers of the site both past and recent. The latter put a trench across the back of the kilns, obliterating much detail of the relationships between the various features. Another investigation, earlier by at least 50 years (it was sealed by the plough level and ploughing ceased about 1930) had done even more damage. A pit had been cut so as to reduce the west wall of the kiln to 18 in. and so as to remove nearly the whole of the central support (fig. 16, layers 11 and 13). With it had gone most of the details of its connexion with the rear of the kiln; all that could be gleaned was that the final tongue, like the first, was probably one with the rear wall, and not built on with a straight joint as in kiln 29. Reference to the rear of kiln 30 as shown in fig. 15, phase III, shows it to have assumed a most unlikely shape. This is because the western side of the back wall has been shown in the position it had assumed by the end of the third phase, and the other corner is that of the tongue and wall at the beginning of the phase, i.e. the tongue it inherited from phase II. The construction of the final kiln and robber activity had removed the connecting links on each side, leaving the plan imperfect.

The main alteration was at the front of the kiln where new features appear. The façade was again advanced and this time was much more imposing. Once away from the mouth where it was clear of the fiercest heat, the façade was formed of clay blocks, approximately 6-in. cubes. These faced the front for 2 ft. 9 in. and then returned south to form the west side of the stokeyard. This area was delimited by a wall of blocks and re-used fragments roughly and crudely laid in wet clay. The wall was subjected to enough heat, either deliberately or accidentally, to harden it.

The construction of the façade was linked with the abandonment of the oven, which appeared to have initiated a slipping movement of the bank downhill. Clayey soil, probably in wet weather, had washed down into the stokeyard. To combat this the NW. corner of the yard had been blocked off by a rather fine tile-and-block wall which was one of the characteristics of phase III *a* (see below) (fig. 15). In the final phase IV, the façade was, for the first time, moved northwards. Much of the bank and the oven was dug away and clay with pottery and tile debris was packed behind a retaining pillar of tile (pl. VII *c*) at the end of the clay façade. Even this did not solve the problem, and by the time the kiln was finally abandoned so much clayey soil had encroached upon the yard that only its southernmost 2 or 3 ft. were visible on this western side.

When the stokeyard wall had been constructed there was set into the back of it the upper part of an amphora (f. 188) with the mouth downwards and sealed with lead. It was full of ash, pieces of tegulae, and colour-coated ware; there was no clue to its purpose (fig. 15, phases III and III *a*). The rear wall of the stokeyard was of very rough construction, being merely a plastering of clay several inches thick against a shallow step. This had been barely heated.[1]

Across the front of the kiln and only about 1 ft. from it was a plug of clay blocks, measuring 4 ft. long by 10 in. wide (pl. IX *b*). The original height of this feature and of its successors was not indicated, for all were much damaged, but it was assumed that they might possibly have been as tall as the arch of the flue, or nearly so. Whatever the function, this plug remained through the ensuing phases. Like the stokeyard it may have existed before this phase, but if so the building of phase III had removed all trace of it.

At the end of this phase two pits were dug in the kiln area. Pit XVI, in the phase III mouth of kiln 30 post-dated the kiln. It was sealed by layer 26 (sect. B–B′) and was filled with ash and pottery, mainly large sherds of colour-coated ware (rough-cast beakers). Exactly the same story may be told of pit XIV, which had been so cut as to avoid the plug of phase III, but was again sealed by layer 26 (sect. B–B′, fig. 16).

These pits must have been dug during a period of disuse of kiln 30. Work could hardly have continued with the pits open, or even recently filled.[2] They were so placed and their contents were such as to rule out the idea of rubbish pits. Their filling consisted of large fragments of pottery and black ash, so that the most reasonable explanation is that they were 'soak-aways' for surface water, in which case the filling had to be of readily permeable material. Water would have tended to collect in the depression of the stokeyard, the floor of which was largely trampled clay. Pit XVI was deep, but stopped at the sand after passing through the

---

[1] Heat here could come from hot ashes raked from the kilns.

[2] The disuse could be short; firing would be seasonal, and the kiln would not be in use for much of the year.

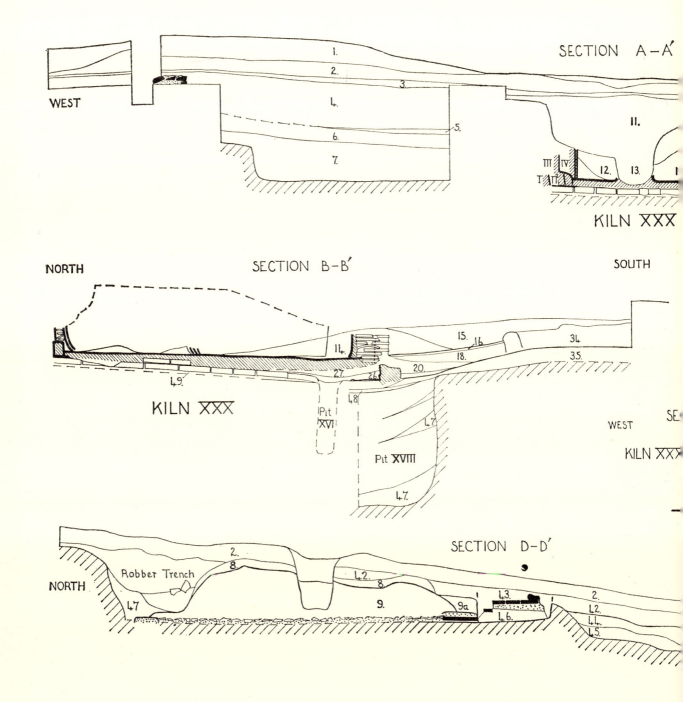

SECTION A–A'

WEST

1.
2.
3.
4.
5.
6.
7.

II.

III IV
T   12. 13.

KILN XXX

SECTION B–B'

NORTH   SOUTH

15. 16.   34.
14.   18.   35.
49.   27.   26.   20.
                          Pit
                          XVI   48.
KILN XXX   47.
                          Pit XVIII
                                      47.

                                      WEST   SE

                                      KILN XXX

SECTION D–D'

2.
8.
Robber Trench   42.
                      8.
NORTH   43.   2.
47   9.   9a.   46.   42.
                                        44.
                                        45.

FIG. 16. Sections of the 1959 excavation

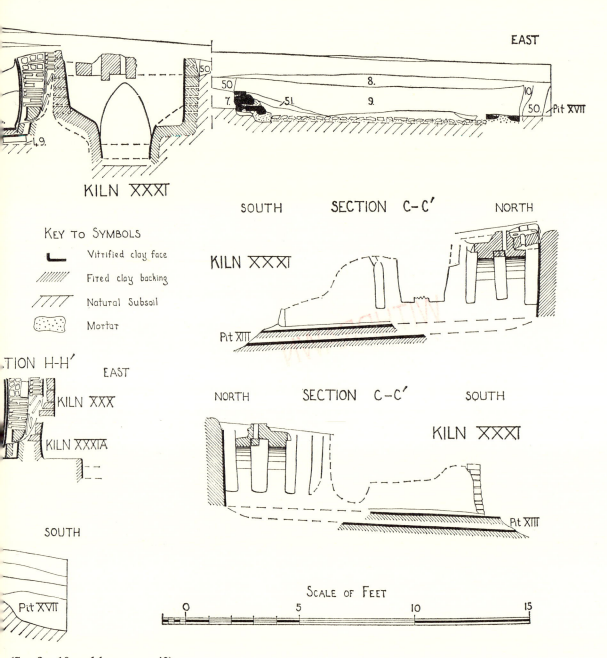

EAST

KILN XXXI

SOUTH   SECTION C-C'   NORTH

KILN XXXI

Pit XIII

KEY TO SYMBOLS

⌐ Vitrified clay face

///// Fired clay backing

//// Natural Subsoil

Mortar

TION H-H'

EAST

KILN XXX

KILN XXXIA

NORTH   SECTION C-C'   SOUTH

KILN XXXI

Pit XIII

SOUTH

Pit XVII

SCALE OF FEET

0   5   10   15

(See fig. 10 and key on p. 43)

filling of the first-century pit; pit XIV was cut in that filling on the northern side, but into natural gravel on the south. Actually the sand in pit XVI was merely a patch in the filling of the earlier pit.

It is probable that work had been transferred to the eastern side of the stokeyard, for layer 26 would appear to be the ash from kiln 31, which had now been erected upon the remains of kiln 31 a. The mouth of the latter had been plastered over, and all that was left to indicate its presence was the top of the buttress between kilns 30 and 31, a phenomenon which remained a puzzle until these two kilns were dissected.

Drainage of the area must have been in the mind of the potter when he constructed his new kiln. All the original structures and large rebuilds had a bedding layer of sandy gravel below the clay floors and backing (see fig. 16, sects. B–B', A–A', phase I, kiln 30; that of kiln 31 does not show in section). This was due to the fact that the fronts of the kilns were set upon pit XVIII and not upon the natural gravel, so that the natural drainage was impaired.

KILN 31

The central flue was deep and lined with crude clay blocks, as was most of the rest of the kiln, though in many cases they were not discernible (as where sect. A–A' cuts the lower levels). To the east and west of the central flue side-flues were built at right angles (plan, fig. 15). Their floors were at a higher level than that of the central flue. In the western series the floor was sloping at an angle of about 30 degrees, but those on the east seemed to have been built with a horizontal floor. Later, possibly when the kiln was refloored, these also had been sloped.

The kiln had had only one rebuild, which was confined to a reflooring of the main flue, a patching of the side-flues and arches at various points, and a new front. The early front was narrow (fig. 15, phase III a), merely of plastered clay, and was found slightly north of the later one.

Soon after the kiln was built the cheeks of the mouth appeared to have been wearing badly; to remedy this grooves 3 in. deep were cut in the floor against each wall, and in them a tile was set vertically and luted into position with clay. This lasted until the floor wore through. The second and last floor was laid on a thick bedding directly upon the detritus of the first one. Much pottery was embedded in it to give it strength. At the front a rendering of clay covered the earlier façade on the west, but on the east an elaborate wall of clay blocks had been built (pl. IX a). This had been united with the east side of the arch of the flue (foreground, pl. IX a), and proves that at least this part of the kiln needed rebuilding at this time. The façade

had not been carried high enough and material had fallen from the top of it, so clay, reinforced with mortaria sherds, tiles, and re-used clay blocks, had been piled on top of the wall as a retaining structure (see pls. VII d, IX a). At the end of this façade the eastern side of the stokeyard returned to the south. If a wall had existed before this date it had been swept away in this rebuild. It was considerably cruder than that to the west and was merely a layer of white clay plastered against the rather steep bank. After running south for about 4 ft. 6 in. it returned to the west to meet the earlier wall. The small projection at that point may have been the remnant of an earlier eastern wall. The stratification at the back of the stokeyard was very confused. It appeared as if the final working in the area had been carried on when very wet conditions prevailed. The strata had the appearance of having been trampled upon while very muddy, churning the ground and the wall into a shapeless mass.

The oven floor of kiln 31 had no apparent rebuild, but had been repaired several times. Thin surfaces, 1–1½ in. thick, of soft clay had been laid upon the existing floor from time to time and fired hard with the pottery loaded in the kiln. This was shown by the impressions of 'herring-bone' mortarium stamps impressed into the floor (pl. VIII a) from which it is evident that, in this case at least, mortaria were balanced upon their rims and not stacked in a pile.

Only a small part of the oven floor was preserved, in the NW. corner of the kiln (pl. VII d and fig. 15, phases III a and IV). It was supported on arches which ran across the kiln from east to west, rising high over the main flue (sect. A–A'). They consisted of a double row of clay voussoirs (seen in pl. X b where part of the arch has fallen). The plates also show the rendering of clay over the whole interior of the kiln. As it had been put on by hand it preserved the impression of the potter's fingers as he smeared the clay evenly. All this kiln was very heavily vitrified, the fired surfaces being grey and brittle. The plates cannot show the thick, bright green glaze that had formed on these surfaces, even at points far from the greatest heat.

The oven floor was pierced by the usual holes 2–3 in. in diameter and there were vents also at the ends of some of the side flues; repairs to the floor had made alterations in these, and in sect. C–C' the glaze in the flue can be seen going above the level of the bottom of the floor.

The central part of this kiln had suffered badly at the hands of intruders. A large pit had been cut through the floor, removing the arches and flues, and into the furnace floor below. On the west side another had cut away two arches (centre of pl. VII d) and removed much of the structure between kilns 30 and

31 (the small hole at the top centre of pl. IX *b* is its base).

The west wall of kiln 31 (sect. A–A') had cut into the wall of kiln 30. The horizontal roofing tiles at the top were placed there in phase III when the phase I wall was cut back and the broken face rendered smooth with soft clay reinforced with tiles. Against this smooth vertical face, which curved down to the top of the phase I and II walls, the blocks of the phase III wall had been placed (see fig. 16, sects. A–A', H–H').

LATER PHASES OF KILN 30

Possibly kilns 30 and 31 were sometimes fired simultaneously, but it seems certain that sometimes they were not. Thus kiln 30 could not be fired while pit XVI, which cut its floor, was open. This pit probably served as a soak-away for kiln 31 and was sealed under a layer of ash which most probably had come from kiln 31.

After this had accumulated a new floor was laid. Layer 27 (sect. B–B') was the lower part of this, which had never fired hard, but remained a soft red. At the front it was of one build and incorporated plug II, built of tiles. At the back of the kiln it was possible to trace three floors, all of which pre-date the final floor. It was impossible to correlate these floors directly with any one stage of wall, but the lowest belonged to the beginning of phase III, and the other two (which lifted the floor-level until the step at the foot of the phase III wall was hidden) pre-dated the construction of phase IV. Even the top level of the furnace floor could not be traced the length of the kiln, as it had been broken by the heat and repatched many times.

Phase III *a*, as shown on fig. 15, is, therefore, only an intermediate step in the alteration of the structure. It does not mean that the kiln was ever fired when its parts were as shown, or indeed, that all the features shown were contemporary. The kiln is almost the same as it was at the beginning of phase IV. By the time plug II was erected the phase III walls had been demolished, as the truncated façade had been incorporated with plug II which is actually set in the mouth of phase III. The walls of phase IV must already have been erected, and are contemporary with, or later than, this plug.

In this figure also is shown the curving wall in the NW. corner of the stokeyard, which was intended at the end of phase III to keep the corner clear of soil. The addition to the stokeyard and the earliest phase of kiln 31 is also shown, though it must not be supposed that this and phase III *a* of kiln 30 were contemporary.

KILN 30. PHASE IV (PLS. IX *a*, X *a*)

Fig. 15, phase IV shows the end of the phase, fig. 15, phase III *a* the beginning. (Phases of kiln 31 do not directly correspond, although we show them on the same plan.)

The final rebuilding of kiln 30 was severe. The second plug (phase III *a*) was the first one of this fourth phase. The floor level was lowered and the existing walls were cut back where necessary to obtain room for a wall-backing. In most places in the main body of the kiln this phase did not interfere with the lowest levels of the earlier one, which remained undisturbed for the most part. The phase IV walls are, indeed, in some places so far inside the earlier walls that they have cut through the three floors mentioned above (phases III and III *a*) and left them preserved as rings between the step of phase III and the back of the phase IV wall. (This occurs mainly to the south of sect. A–A' on the west side of kiln 30.)

In many places most of the phase III wall had been removed and a new backing of broken tiles inserted behind the rendering of the wall-face. In sect. A–A' this is shown at the east side, where one block of phase III remained at a low level, and the tiles of phase IV were laid above. The step of phase III had here broken away, but the phase II block, which was below the step, remained in front of the earliest phase I wall (see also sect. H–H'). Pl. XV *a* shows the wall in process of dissection. The clay rendering of phase IV shows on the right, but has been stripped away elsewhere; the block of phase II shows behind the vertical scale; at the level of the top of the scale the remnant of the phase III wall can be seen below the overhanging tiles of the phase IV backing. On the west side of the kiln (in the section referred to above) may be seen the other method of walling, in which only the top of the phase III wall had been removed and the rendering was merely on the front of the backing, which had been placed directly against the earlier wall.

As with kiln 31 the clay rendering was finger-moulded, and in some places showed the impression of the coarse weave of the potter's garments where he had pressed against the wet clay. The vitrification here showed a bright green colour near the mouth and some way up the flue.

If the walls with their glaze and rendering did not bear witness to the long life of this phase, its three plugs would do so. Plug II was broken down and plug III of tiles laid in clay was built upon it, but slightly more to the north. A re-rendering of this formed plug IV of the period when the kiln was last fired. As may be seen from pl. IX *a* most of the earlier structures had been well buried by this time. In the last working of phase IV the ash had been left blocking the flue arch to a height which must have made stoking most difficult.

On the east side of the stokeyard, sealed by the trampling of the last working surface of kiln 30 (layer

16, sect. B–B′), was pit XIII. It had cut through the front of the furnace floor of kiln 31, showing that the final working of that kiln antedated the final working of kiln 30 (pl. IX a). The position and contents of this pit were such that it appears similar in type to pits XIV and XVI. Pit XIII is a recutting of an earlier one of which layer 24 is the only remaining portion. It had been filled with mortaria fragments in black ash.

THE STONE STRUCTURES (FIG. 10)

The wall lying to the west of kiln 30 is difficult to explain. It did not enclose anything, and is essentially a retaining wall, finely built of dressed Kentish rag-

yellow mortar standing on the subsoil. Above the offset at the top of the footings there were remains of one course of tile and five of stone, the joints of which had been struck, apart from the lowest which was of fragments roughly laid. This wall might have been built in phase III of kiln 30, for prior to this the oven stood at the point where the wall strikes the kiln. The building of the wall may have destroyed the oven.

While it is clear that this was a retaining wall, it is not clear why it should have been built. It might have been a loading platform, but had no prepared surface to the south of it, nor any road leading to it. It may have been intended to support a levelled area upon

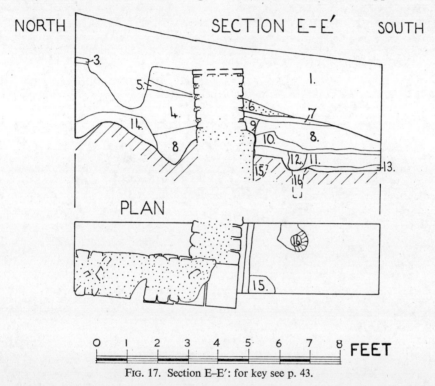

FIG. 17. Section E–E′: for key see p. 43.

stone with tile courses (figs. 10 (p. 15), 16, sect. A–A′; pl. VII b).

It was best preserved at its SW. corner, where it had a short return to the north; here one course of stone remained above the tile course. Three feet to the north it ended in a square face, but at a higher level there was a shapeless continuation for a few feet consisting of stones and mortar, hardly to be described as 'built'. Eastwards of this SW. corner the wall was more broken at the top, especially where it ran into the side of kiln 30 in an irregularly shaped trench. Elsewhere it had been built against a face cut in the natural slope of the hill, with a slight batter uphill.

An offset low down may be just below the old ground-level. The footings consisted of 10 to 12 in. of

which to erect a shed for drying or storing vessels, but no evidence of a building above it was seen, for this area had been very completely churned up by amateur diggers in 1955.

A short section cut to the south of the wall is shown in fig. 17, sect. E–E′. This section (see plan, fig. 10) runs N.–S. across the wall. It confirmed that the wall was in existence during the period of kiln-activity. There was no indication of the date of its construction.

The layers 8–14 through which the wall cuts, contained pottery none of which need be later than A.D. 50–60. No pottery was found in the small foundation-trench (layer 9). The abutting layer (7) and the mortar above it (layer 6), contained material contemporary with the kilns. Layer 7 contained evidence of occupation

—oyster shells, food-bones—and had every indication of having been a surface during the kiln-period. The mortar above it was loose and broken, and seemed rather to have accumulated during the decay of the wall than during its construction. The layer was quite thick, perhaps denoting a much higher wall than that which now remains.

The small pit contained early material and was cut by the wall footings. Layers 16 and possibly 12 may have been a small post-hole and from the stratification appear too early to have been connected with any structure of the kiln-period. This need not be so, however, if layers 10 and 8 are interpreted as material from north of the wall thrown to the south when the bank was cut back for the wall. The foundation trench would naturally cut through this material. Against the complete acceptance of this theory is the fact that 11 is unlikely to have been a surface-layer, while 10 seems much more likely to have been so.

To the east of kiln 31 stood a small building just under 9 ft. by 13 ft. (figs. 10, 16, pl. x d). It was not symmetrical and was very close to kiln 31; it appeared to have been deliberately destroyed and the building material removed (to go into the wall just described ?). The rubble of the demolition covered the remains of walls and floor, but had been cut into along the line of the north wall, where the foundations had been robbed some time after the demolition.

The walls appear to have been similar in construction to that farther west. Between two faces of coursed dressed stone (Kentish rag) was poured a mortar and rubble core. The mortar was yellow, the stones small, wedge-shaped, with a face about 3 in. square. A few pieces of septaria were used where they would not show. The footings showed little care; their width was uneven, usually 18 in., but varied on the south and west sides. The tiles in the SW. corner formed the base of a door-sill (sect. D–D').

The floor was of beaten clay on a mass of broken stone and mortar; its level was that of the threshold, but only a small part of it remained. Much of the rubble overburden consisted of mortar and plaster fragments with some stone chips. The plaster was mainly thick, painted white, but with traces of red pattern. Insufficient labour was available to remove more than a small part of this rubble. At one point a shallow pit had been dug into it, and in this stood a small, coarse, grey vessel (f. 268) with a perforated base, which had been covered by a flanged dish f. 316B, which exactly fitted as a lid. This vessel stood at an angle, not upright. The two vessels were not made on the spot and are of fourth-century date (fig. 92, A, B).

Sections A–A' and D–D' cross this building. At the north end of the latter can be seen the robber-trench in the rubble; it contained unburnt clay, but mostly dark soil with potsherds and fragments of burnt clay. One would conclude it had been cut while the kilns were active, or soon after.

Across the doorway of the building a trench had been cut, partly into the rubble of the building, and in this was laid a foundation or basis of broken tile on mortar, with an area about 4 ft. 6 in. long and 1 ft. 3 in. wide. We may imagine that something stood upon this, for it was surrounded by a low kerb of stone and tile on the south, east, and west sides; on the north there was only soil.

Layer 9a of sect. D–D' was slightly different to the main body of 9, in that it had a slightly higher soil content. The rubble covered the remains of the walls and a later levelling may have deposited layer 9a, which was cut by the trench for the base just described.

Under the SE. corner of the building was pit XVII, cut into the natural gravel and antedating the structure. The pottery contained was late second-century.

Across the back of the kilns ran a most unusual feature. A wall of stiff clay 15 to 18 in. wide and at least 3 ft. high had been slotted into the natural sub-soil of sand and gravel. It runs from the NW. corner of the stone building to a point 12 ft. north of the east end of the L-shaped wall, and may well never have risen above ground level. It stops short at both ends with no returns (pl. x c).

The top of this clay wall had been burnt to some extent, presumably by the heat from the kilns, though it is not clear how this could happen. When the kilns were opened much very hot clay was no doubt spread around, but whether this could cause such an effect is uncertain. It is also to be noted that the clay wall may have run farther east. If so it had been removed by the robber-trench or the north wall of the stone building, in the filling of which there was some clay, which could have come from a disturbed part of this feature.

The only purpose of a barrier of this nature is as an impervious wall across a slope down which water flows. This may have served to keep water off the lower part of the slope, but a more usual use of such a barrier would be to collect the water on its upward side in order to lead it away to a water-supply. In our case the clay wall does not go down deep enough; there is still sand and gravel under it so that it could not trap water. Its only function, therefore, would seem to be to prevent water running downhill into the kilns. There are two difficulties here; in the first place this sand and gravel is perfectly permeable and allows storm water to sink away instantly, so that there would be little or no downhill flow beneath the surface; secondly the walls of the kilns themselves were of clay and no less resistant to any water which might come than this clay wall put in with such labour. Up to the present no other possibilities occur to us.

Key to the numbered levels in section E–E′

1. As 1 below, plus 1955 disturbance.
3 and 4. As 3 and 4 below.
5. Black trampled layer.
6. Mortar spread, containing oyster shell and pottery. Builder's debris from repairs, or debris of frost-damage.
7. Grey soil containing a small amount of oyster shell and sherds. This is an old surface level sealing the construction trench.
8. Clean grey, sandy soil.
9. Construction trench to the south of the wall.
10. Yellow-grey soil, less sand, more clayish with a few distinct sand patches, and some flecks of charcoal.
11. Cleaner than 10, more consolidated.
12. Cuts 11 and a little more grey in colour, charcoal flecks.
13. Stones in a clay matrix coloured whitish, charcoal flecks.
14. Similar to 13 but cleaner.
15 and 16. Pits projected into the section, see plan. Darker in colour than soil adjacent, otherwise very similar in texture.
16. Possible post-hole, the bottom of 12 perhaps.

Key to the numbered levels in the other sections

1. Spoil heap of 1933 excavations.
2. Humus or plough-soil.
3. Yellow sand with small stones. Common on the site at the base of the plough-soil.
4. Grey-brown soil with small stones, contains sherds.
5. Spread of oyster shell with some charcoal.
6. Grey-brown soil, becoming sandy, with a few oyster shells and flecks of charcoal.
7. Cream-coloured clayey soil at the top, changing to sand and gravel at the bottom of the layer.
8. Brown soil with many lumps of fired clay and specks of mortar and wall-plaster with a few pieces of tegula and imbrex.

9. Mortar and stone rubble with wall-plaster, little soil.
9a. As 9 above, but containing slightly more soil.
10. Wall trench.
11 and 13. Recent disturbance which removed floor support of kiln 30.
12. Fill of the kiln cut by 11 and 13, fired and vitrified clay.
14. Black ash.
15. Ashy soil trampled all over the area south of the kilns.
16. Working surface of the stokeyard, of trodden fired clay.
18. Some soil, black ash and fired clay with much pottery.
20. Below 18 but probably more or less contemporary with it, fired and unfired clay containing few sherds.
24. Black ash with mortaria fragments.
26. Ash—black to the south of plug I, white to the north of it.
27. Red clay—the unvitrified under-portion of the kiln-floor.
34. Brown soil containing some ash and much comminuted pottery.
35. Clayey white soil under 34 and on natural subsoil. Contained Claudian-Neronian pottery and represented surface before the kiln-period.
42. Brown soil with pieces of red clay in places. Contained sherds but no building material.
43. As layer 42 above. This is the filling of the foundation trench of the stone base.
44. Sandy soil.
45. Sand.
46. Very stony brown soil.
47. Gravel.
48. Oyster shell.
49. Sand bedding of kilns.
50. Grey humus becoming sandy at the base, lying on natural.
51. Clayey soil with burnt clay and sherds. A spread from the west after the demolition of the building and before the rubble was levelled.

THE POTTERY FROM THE 1933 AND 1959 KILNS

THE MOULDS FOR DECORATED SIGILLATA

AND THE REMAINS OF THE VESSELS MADE FROM THEM

(PLS. XIa, b, XII, and FIGS. 18–37)

Moulds for decorated sigillata ware, were with the exception of those for special purposes (e.g. decorated flagons), made in one piece. They were stout-walled bowls of a fine buff clay, the interior taking the form of the exterior profile of the form of vessel required, usually forms Dragendorff 29, 30, or 37. The mould only extended upwards as far as the limit of moulded decoration, finishing, in the case of forms 30 and 37 with the ovolo or its substitute. Downwards they were

rounded, the footring, like the rim, being added later.

After turning, and before drying, the smooth interior was decorated with the design required by impressing upon it the separate units of the pattern with small stamps or punches, which could thus be used again and again in any combination or order. Stalks or scrolls, and wavy lines were added with a stylus. Bead rows were probably done with a wheel, as also perhaps the ovolo, though ours appear to have been made by repetition of a single stamp.

Though most of this was done by eye the potter often made light guiding lines on the wheel which served to keep his lines horizontal. Such a line can be seen through the rosettes at the bottom of the York mould, fig. 19, 2.

The impression was taken by placing the mould on

the wheel and spinning soft clay into it, pressing it into the pattern and finishing off the interior as required. The mould was then set aside, with its contents, and as the soft clay dried it shrank and pulled out of the negative portions, so that it could in the end be turned out. In case a slight push was necessary a small hole was left in the centre of the bottom of the mould to

ring. A footring is usual, and generally carefully made; it would help when fixing the mould on the wheel.[1]

At Colchester over 400 fragments of moulds have been found. Some more, found in the NW. corner of the enclosure, among clay, were apparently still in the 'green' state and unfired; these could not be preserved. They differed in no way from those now to be described.

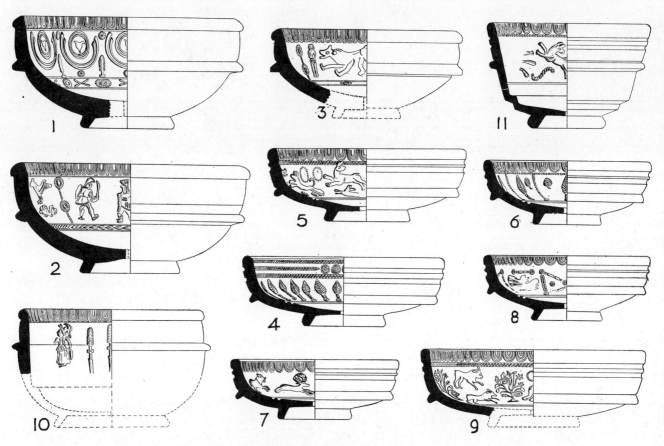

FIG. 18. Sections of Samian moulds. (See p. 43.) ($\frac{1}{4}$)

facilitate this. The green impression—the cast bowl in the positive—was then placed on the wheel and the footring and the rim added to it.

The exterior profile of the moulds varies a little according to the place of manufacture. Ours are shown on figs. 18 and 35. They may be compared with those at Rheinzabern (Ludowici, iii, 282 and v, 293) which mostly have the same ledge as ours, but no grooves above, but some (Ludowici FS5) have an upright collar round the top. We find the same outline at Heiligenberg-Dinsheim (Forrer, pl. XVIII), except in the case of f. 30, where, as at Aquincum, the general form is conical, like a modern flower-pot, without foot-

Many of the fragments are very small, or from the base of the mould, preserving no decoration.

The fragments are easily classified into two very distinct groups by outstanding differences in shape, clay, and style of decoration. They are clearly products of two individual potters, neither of which, unfortunately, has signed his work. Inasmuch as quite a number of the type-stamps used are shared between them, and the clay, though very different, seems to have been prepared from the same natural bed, it seems certain that they both worked on this site. There is no evidence to show to what extent they were contemporary. They may have been all the time at Colchester, for the

---

[1] Cf. The curious mould for goblets made at Autry-Lavoye and the many disjointed patterns employed. *Pro Alesia*, n.s. v,

1919, 130 ff.

Sigillata industry here can only have covered a short space of time.[1]

For convenience we have named the maker of the first group of moulds 'potter A'. His paste is thick and, at its best, hard, with a good polish on its interior surface. But the majority of the fragments have weathered or otherwise perished so that the surfaces feel finely sandy, often quite soft and decaying. The colour is pale buff, reddish in the break, but strongly inclined to yellow on the surface (pl. XII, 1, 2).

In shape the moulds of potter A are quite distinct (fig. 18, 1–3, 10 and fig. 35, 1, 2). The vessel is regularly thicker than those of potter B, and, in the case of f. 37, deeper, with a heavy beaded rim and a strong ledge 1 or 2 in. below. There is a strong, carefully made foot-ring, with a small hole in the centre. No mould of f. 30 could be reconstructed. Fig. 18, 10 is from a fragment (fig. 26, 7) and the base is restored in drawing from a fragment of another; a second outline is given, fig. 35, 2. The rounded shape as compared with the angular moulds of potter B will be noticed. Over fifty fragments of moulds of potter A have been numbered and listed, and there are many more small fragments.

The moulds of potter B amount to over 100, and are better preserved. They are in larger fragments with cleaner breaks, and more could be restored than in the case of the more numerous fragments of A. Possibly this might indicate that B is the later of the two.[2]

The shape of the moulds of potter B is different. The main difference lies in the plain lip with no beading and the two (sometimes three) very wide and carefully made grooves on the outside, below which comes the pronounced ledge (fig. 18, 4–9, 11). The moulds for f. 37 are wide and shallow, and those for f. 30 are conical, with two carinations at the base, the upper of which may be more rounded than the one drawn.

The paste, always much more finely levigated than that used by potter A, yields a much finer surface both inside and out, and stands better. The colour is normally dark brown, tending to red in the break, with occasional tell-tale pieces of chalk, presumably from the boulder-clay.[3] Variations in colour occur and are chiefly bright reds or golden yellow—whether due to accidental firing after fracture, or to original misfiring must remain uncertain. A feature of these moulds, due to the style of decoration, is the deep, finely cut groove or grooves which close the decorated zone at the bottom.

All have the central hole in the base. In 1959 several more fragments of moulds were found, in addition to some important pieces found in previous years by Mr. H. C. Calver. These are illustrated in figs. 35 and 36. The only new evidence among them is a small fragment, fig. 35, 4, of a small mould for an ovoid jar or beaker of some form resembling Déch. 67. It is decorated with two rows of impressions of a small satyr. The clay is perhaps more like that of potter B than potter A.

OTHER MOULDS FOUND IN BRITAIN

The discovery of an undoubted Sigillata manufactory in this country, even though of limited life and success, calls for a revision of our attitude to this question. The literature of Sigillata has become so immense that an exhaustive review of what has been said on this subject is impossible, but it has been repeatedly stated in the better known and accessible works that the ware was not made in Britain. The general attitude is excellently summed up by Oswald and Pryce, p. 10. 'They [the centres of manufacture] were all confined to the Continent and, notwithstanding the discovery of isolated moulds in the country, there is, at present, no evidence of this fabric in Britain.'

The Colchester discovery has swung the pendulum the other way, and we read in Prof. I. A. Richmond's *Roman Britain* (p. 37) that Sigillata ware was made at Colchester, York, and Pulborough.

The evidence at the latter two places consists of fragments of moulds, and there are good reasons for adding London to the list. At York there has been in the Yorkshire Museum for many years a large fragment of a mould for a bowl of f. 37 (fig. 19, 2). There seems no doubt that it was found at York, though it might well have been found at Lezoux, for it was made by potter X–3.[4] The decoration includes a figure holding a shield, Oswald 692A, but larger, and the Sphinx, Oswald 855, Déchelette 498, both Lezoux types, the former Trajanic, the latter perhaps Hadrianic. The bust is not in Oswald. The ovolo has corded tassels with small eight-pointed stars, too minute to draw in detail. The astragaloid bindings on the festoons and fronds are confused by overlapping, but there were perhaps two punches used. The style of the whole belongs more to the Trajanic period than any other. The reader is referred to Pryce and Birley, 'The First Occupation of Roman Scotland,' in *J.R.S.* xxv, 59 ff. where the same lower band of rosettes occurs on a bowl by DONNAVCVS (ibid., p. 64, fig. 15, and pl. XIV, 3). Our frond and astragaloid binding is their pl. XIV, 12. The very fine and small bead-rows of the York mould also fall into this class of ware. From this article we also learn that the Lezoux connexions are much less

---

[1] Reference to a possible third potter will be made later.
[2] See notes on his style later.
[3] Similar white flecks and streaks occur in all the clay used for

coarse work in the kilns.
[4] Stanfield and Simpson, p. 16, pl. 16, 206; R.C.H.M., *Roman York* (1962), p. 63 b and pl. 31.

strong than those with Luxeuil and Vichy (ibid., p. 67). The date lies between A.D. 100–120, but whether our piece belongs to the period before or after the loss of the Ninth Legion we do not presume to decide.

It is worthy of note that in 1956 Mr. F. Erith cleared a large pit in the area of the Roman pottery kilns at Ardleigh, five miles NW. of Colchester. It was full of charcoal and ash and broken wasters. Among these lay nearly all the fragments of a samian bowl f. 37; it has been restored. Mr. Erith recognized the pattern of the York mould, and close examination showed that the new find might well have been from the York mould, only the pattern differed in having one small leaf added. That it is from a mould of potter X–3 is certain. The wasters found in this pit were of Trajanic date.

At Pulborough in Sussex, in 1909, three fragments of moulds for bowls of f. 37 were found. They are described and illustrated in *P.S.A.* (ser. 2) xxiii, 127, with fig. 5. The fragments are small, but two of the figure types have connexion with Lezoux. The danseuse is like Déchelette 216 and 217, and Oswald (*Figure types*, 354) identifies it with the latter, which is of Lezoux, Hadrian–Antonine. The other figure most resembles Oswald's 368, a danseuse with a tambourine, not Minerva as suggested in the published account, and indeed Oswald identifies it with his figure, which we would hesitate to do. It is again Lezoux and Trajan–Antonine. It is also connected with the style of Butrio. The ovolo is larger than that at York, with double margin, otherwise similar, but wavy lines are used instead of bead-rows. There was, curiously, nothing found in association with these to suggest the presence of a pottery on the site, but a renewed investigation is most desirable.

There are at least two suggestive finds from London. The first is a name-stamp of Cerialis, said to have been found in London and now in the Guildhall Museum. Then there is, in the British Museum, a fragment of a waster of f. 37, found when making the extension of the Metropolitan Railway at Aldgate. It is illustrated by Walters, *Catalogue*, M1546, p. 292. It was assigned by Déchelette to the fabric of Nouâtre, but Walters says the style is of Lezoux. We should attribute it to a later and poorer fabric, judging by the illustration. At any rate it is suggestive of a factory in London.[1] Such are the small evidences for attempts by experienced potters to make Sigillata in Britain.

There were also attempts by others who lacked experience, or tried out new methods.

Fig. 19, 3 shows the section of part of a mould in the Yorkshire Museum, presumably from York, with an impression from it. The decoration seems to have been of the incoherent style of the late second century (or later), but the technique is strange, for the base of the vessel is included in the mould.

Fig. 19, 1 and pl. XIII b, shows a mould in Hull Museum,[2] the source unknown except that it was acquired from a Mr. Dack of Peterborough, in which town it was picked up on a rockery. It is of brown-grey clay, hard and heavy with dark grey, smoothed surface. The pattern is not impressed in the usual way, but cut out by hand with V-shaped gouges, in exactly the same manner as are the soft steel moulds for imitations of cut glass at the present day. The ovolo presented great difficulty for this treatment, but was regarded as essential. This strange technique, and the continuation of the mould above the ovolo attest the work of potters unacquainted with the methods of Sigillata potters.

One is left to surmise that, in the case of the genuine moulds, and perhaps the London fragment, the coarse ware found at the same time may have included pieces of rings and tubes, which would have been conclusive evidence for a manufactory. Unfortunately no such evidence has survived, but it seems very probable that it will turn up in the future, not only at these places, but at others.

As long ago as 1895 Dragendorff remarked that of 675 different stamps of Sigillata potters found in Britain 'only' 250 were unknown on the Continent, and of these about 60 were illegible or useless. The figures are vastly greater now, so that we have not attempted to count them, but the critical point is not whether a stamp (or decoration typical of any given potter) is found on the Continent, for we know how the potters moved from place to place, and a potter might very well produce much ware on the Continent before moving to Britain. In this respect it is intriguing to find in how many cases of well-known continental potters Oswald's list shows many more records for Britain than for the Continent. We do not press this point further, for it is very possibly due to lack of records from Gaulish sites. Moreover, were there anything in it, it would imply the existence in Britain of one or more first-class manufactories, which could scarcely have escaped observation thus long, and which should have been able to continue in production without the interruptions to which those on the Continent were subjected. No evidence exists of any such continuation. On the contrary, it is remarkable how the importation of Sigillata terminated at the end of the second century, without any obvious reason, and there seems to have been no serious attempt to seize the British market. Possibly it is to this period that the curious moulds of inexperienced potters belong.

---

[1] See Simpson, 'The Aldgate Potter', *J.R.S.* xlii, 68–71.

[2] We are indebted to Mr. Fay for kindly submitting this to us for study and drawing. Fragments of others have now been found in kiln A at Water Newton (1958).

In the following description of the moulds found it should be noted that, to facilitate comparison, all drawings of moulds have been reversed, so as to show the design in the positive.

5. Quarter of a mould. Similar ware, but darker and polished all over. Decoration expanded, fig. 30, 3.

6. Fragments making half a mould. Clay fine, leathery brown, polished. Two grooves under base. Decoration expanded, fig. 29, 3 (pl. XII, 3).

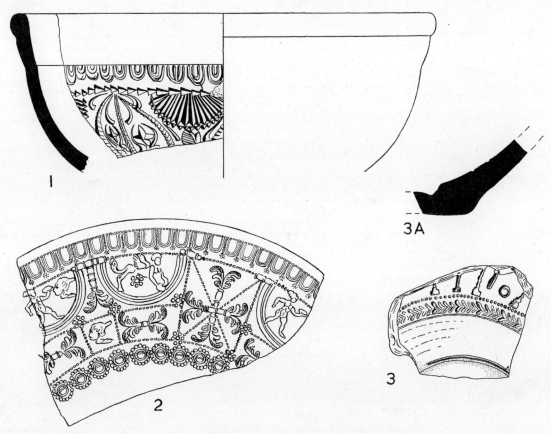

FIG. 19. Moulds from other sites (pp. 45–46). ($\frac{1}{2}$)

MOULDS OF POTTERS A AND B
(FIG. 18)

1. Several fragments of a large mould found in the kiln enclosure, normal yellow buff ware, in good condition. Decoration shown expanded on fig. 20, 3.

2 (and pl. XII, 1). Half a large and heavy mould, yellowish-grey buff, good condition. Decoration expanded, fig. 20, 1.

3 (and pl. XII, 2). Several fragments making more than half a mould. Ware as last. Decoration expanded fig. 20, 2.

These three moulds are of potter A. The chief peculiarities have been noted. We further remark here on the greater depth and rotundity aimed at in the finished bowl as compared with those of potter B, and the slant of the inner wall at the top where it carried the ovolo.

4. Several fragments making half a mould. Clay fine, red-brown with grey core, the surface well finished and partly polished. The pattern, expanded fig. 37, 1, is remarkable for the three lines of cable (103) interspersed with groups of rosettes (70) in place of the ovolo.[1]

7 (and pl. XI b). Fragments forming complete mould. Clay as last. Decoration expanded, fig. 28, 1.

8. Fragments which restore a mould of bright red-brown ware, distorted probably in firing. Decoration expanded, fig. 28, 2. Unusual.

9 (and pl. XII, 4). Fragments making more than half a mould. Light red-brown ware, finely finished and polished. Decoration expanded, fig. 29, 2.

The above six sections are the best preserved of the moulds of potter B. They tend to be wide and shallow, and the workmanship is better than that of potter A. The exterior ledge always points downwards, and all grooves are large and bold.

10. Restored drawing of a mould of f. 30 of potter A. The upper part from a fragment, fig. 26, 7, and the base from another fragment. Other pieces confirm this reconstruction. The clay is similar to that of the three moulds nos. 1–3.

11. Section of a mould of f. 30, of potter B, drawn from two fragments probably of the same mould. Other fragments agree. The form is more conical and angular than that of potter A. The ware is the same as that of other moulds of potter B, fig. 31, 6.

[1] For figure-types see figs. 39–41.

Fig. 20. *Moulds of potter A*

1 (and pl. XII, 1). Half a mould in two pieces, quartered by upright wavy lines and rosettes; types,[1] gladiators 5, 6; cocks and cantharus 57, 58, 66, and 16, 21, 22, 56, 62, 63, 68. The continuous band of chevrons, 105, is characteristic of the majority of this potter's work.

2 (and pl. XII, 2). Half a mould in several pieces, quartered as last, but wavy line under ovolo and the lower band is two raised lines with widely spaced rosettes. Types 5, 6, 17, 22, 33, 35, 40, 42, 68.

3 (and fig. 18, 1). Several fragments of one mould. Unusual decoration of festoons. Lower band as last with addition of opposed chevrons. Types 59, 68, 72, 85, 88, 89, 105.

Fig. 21. *Fragments of moulds of potter A*

1. The continuous large rosettes in the lower band are a common feature, usually between two lines. Panelling of the main band with wavy lines is common. Types 5, 6, 24, 68, 72.
2. Similar types, Minerva 3, 64, 68, 72, and part of an unknown, possibly the new winged figure, no. 112 below (fig. 41).
3. Types 6, 7, 16, 68.
4. Types 5, 68, 72, 95 and parts of unknowns.
5. Similar to no. 3, types 7, 8, 68, 72.
6. Apparently animals only, types 48, 49, 52, 68.
7. Circus scene, types 17, 30, 40, 68.
8. Similar, found near the stone wall, types 40, 59, 68.
9. Compare pl. XII, 2, types 7, 8, 68, 72.
10. Probably evenly divided by the leaf, types 40, 68, 83, and an unrecognizable forepaw.
11. Types 10, 11, 72.
12. Complete base, mixed rosettes in lower band, panelled, types 7, 8, 22, 62, 68, 72.
13. Lower band of rosettes on a faint setting-out line, types 44, 72, and part of an unknown.
14. Similar, with types 14, 33, 72. There are at least thirteen other similar fragments with lower band of the rosette. Most are very small and none gives any new detail.
15. Lower band of branched ornaments 78, not often used. Types 30, 56, 72, 78.

Fig. 22. *Fragments of moulds and vessels of potter A*

1. Several small fragments of one bowl f. 37. The drawing is made from three partly overlapping pieces, which prove the regular pattern of the decoration. Diaper pattern of types 85 and 87, with band of 68. Surface soapy chocolate-red.
2. Small fragment of bowl f. 37, similar ware and coating. Types 14, 68, 72; note joint in ovolo.
3. Two fragments of a bowl f. 37. Free style. Types 9, 10, 26, 40, 68, 72.
4. Similar fragment, but panelled. Types 11, 33, 37, 68. Soft red ware with soapy red-brown coating.
5. Two fragments of a bowl f. 37. Free style. Types 9, 51, 53, 72.
6. Similar fragment. Types 3 (?), 72, 83, 85, and part of the unknown group 28. Soft white ware, with traces of coating like thin red paint, mis-fired.
7 (and fig. 27, 1). Five fragments of one bowl f. 37. Free style. Types 1, 5, 6, 7, 8, 59, 72. Soapy chocolate-red coating.
8. Small fragment f. 37, found on the site of the Technical College in 1914 and therefore a marketed piece. Decorated zone very narrow, reticulated with wavy lines enclosing leaf 86. Compare figs. 24, 4, and 25, 3. Red ware, matt red glaze.

9. Small fragment of a bowl f. 37. Types 11, 17, 48, 68, 78. White paste, coating burnt black.
10. Fragment f. 37, compare pl. XII, 1 and 2. Types 35, 38, 59, 68. Good ware, good matt finish of correct red colour.
11. Small fragment of mould. Double ovolo divided by a wavy line.
12. Small fragment f. 37. Types 2a, 24, 72.
13. Many small fragments of one bowl f. 37. Very unusual diaper pattern. Types 65, 71, 85. Soapy chocolate-red glaze. Fragments of the mould from which this bowl was made were also found.

Fig. 23. *Fragments of vessels and moulds of potter A, with continuous band of chevrons beneath, and moulds of potter B*

1. Fragment of bowl f. 37, panelled in quarters. Types 35, 37, 51, 52, 53, 64, 68, 105.
2. Fragment of mould, potter B. Types 12, 13, 70, and part of an unknown.
3. Two fragments f. 37. Pale paste with very dark glossy coating. Types 5, 16, 47, 49, 105.
4. Two fragments f. 37. Pale buff biscuit ware. Types 51, 53, 68, 105.
5. Fragment of mould potter B; unusual. Types 79, 92, 100.
6. Fragments of a mould. Types 33, 35, 59, 64, 88, 90, 105.
7. Fragment of bowl f. 37, nearly white ware, traces of coating like red paint. Types 62, 63, 105.
8. Base of f. 37, pale paste with soft dark red coating, thin in places. Types 7–10, 17, 30, 94, 105.
9. Fragment of bowl f. 37, pale buff with traces of colour-coating. Types 68, 94, 105.
10. Two fragments of f. 37. Pale pink paste with faint traces of yellowish red glaze. Probably quartered by leaf 83. Types 5, 17, 40, 94, 105.
11. Fragment f. 37. Fair glaze. Types 43, 47, 48, 52, 59, 105.
12. Large fragment of mould of potter B. The best example of scroll-decoration found. Types 67, 74, 77, 95. The stalks are scribed in the mould with a large, rounded point, with which type 67 might have been formed freehand.

Fig. 24. *Fragments of vessels of potter A*

1. Base of f. 37, white paste, poor thin coating, mostly gone. Types 7, 14, 16, 17, 33, 105.
2. Fragment f. 37. Types 40, 53, 72, 94, 105.
3. Several fragments of a large bowl f. 37. Coating thick, brown-red, soapy. Types 7, 8, 9, 33, 43, 59, 72, 94, 105, and an unknown.
4. Two fragments f. 37. White ware, underfired. Panelled and reticulated with wavy lines. Types 78, 85, 105.
5. Four fragments of one bowl f. 37. Coating thick, brown-red, soapy. Straight line under ovolo. Types 2, 5–9, 94, 105.
6. Two fragments f. 37. Types 19, 63, 64, 65, 88, 105.
7. Fragment f. 37, soft red ware, underfired. Types 22, 85, 105.
8. Fragment f. 37. Good red ware with dark red coating. Types 47, 51, 72, 105.
9. Fragment f. 37. As last. Types 26, 32, 72, 105.
10. Fragment f. 37. Panelled with wavy lines. Types 9, 10, 11, 72, 86, 105.
11. Fragment f. 37. Types 13, 17, 30, 47, 105.

There are many more fragments of moulds and bowls, all f. 37, with the straight chevron-band, mostly quite small. All worthy of illustration are given on figs. 23 and 24 with one or

[1] For figure-types see figs. 39–41.

two others elsewhere. Those not shown contribute no new types or arrangements.

FIG. 25. *Fragments of vessels and moulds of potter A, in various styles*

1. Several fragments of one bowl f. 37. Coating thick, chocolate-red, soapy. Diaper pattern of rosettes 68 in a circle 90. Type 72 in field and two setting-out lines below (pl. XIV, 1).
2. Four large fragments f. 37. Good red ware, dark red coating, but one fragment fired white with black coating. Types 68 and 85 in continuous rows.
3. Several fragments f. 37. Good red ware and coating (drawn out on fig. 27, 2). Saltires of wavy lines with types 59, 78, 86, 105 (pl. XIV, 3).
4. Small fragment of mould. Circles 89, 90, the inner one done with the stylus.
5. Small fragment of mould. Types 72, 87, 90 (?).
6. Small fragment of mould, like no. 4, adding type 72.
7. Small fragment of mould. Types 68, 89.
8. Fragment of same mould (?), adding type 87.
9. Small fragment of bowl f. 37. Types 59, 83, 87.
10. Fragment of mould. Types 29, 68.
11. Ditto. Types 68, 72, 85, 90.
12. Ditto, possibly the same mould.
13. Ditto, possibly the same as no. 9.
14. Ditto. Types 53, 85.
15. Fragments of bowl f. 37. Hard red ware with smooth red coating. Type 26.
16. Two fragments f. 37. Yellowish paste with poor thin coating. Types 47, 49, 85.
17. Fragment f. 37. Pale buff ware with traces of faint coating like red paint. Types 1, 68.

FIG. 26. *Fragments of vessels and moulds of potter A, mostly of f. 30*

1. Much of one bowl f. 30. Pale paste with thin, paintlike glaze, somewhat glossy. Types 11, 33, 37, 49, 68, 72, 83 (pl. XIII*a*, XIV, 4).
2. Fragment of a mould f. 30. Panelled with wavy lines. Types 43, 68, 94.
3. Two fragments of mould f. 30. Types 11, 48, 49, 68.
4. Fragment of mould f. 30. Types 5, 6, 68.
5. Large fragment of bowl f. 30. Soft red ware (underfired), with traces of brown-red soapy glaze. Types 4, 85, 94.
6. Small fragment of bowl f. 30. Red ware with dark red glaze. Types 59, 85.
7. Fragment of mould f. 30. Types 3, 59, 85.
8. Two fragments of mould f. 30. Types 28, 83, 85 (pl. XIV, 2).
9. Several pieces of one bowl f. 37. Red paste with dark red soapy glaze. Panelled by rows of circles 90. Types 5–8, 72, 86.

FIG. 27. *Vessels by potter A*

On this fig. are shown the most complete outlines which could be obtained of vessels of ff. 30 and 37 by potter A. The decoration no. 1 is displayed on fig. 22, 7, that of no. 2 on fig. 25, 3; no. 3 is the same as fig. 26, 5 and no. 4 as fig. 26, 1 (pl. XIII*a*).

FIG. 28. *Moulds of potter B*

1. Fragments making the complete mould, fine, light brownish-red ware. Smoothed and almost polished. Outline fig. 18, 7. Quartered by leaves 95. Types 39, 43, 44, 47 (pl. XI*b*).

2. Many fragments making a restored mould. Fine light golden-brown ware. Distorted in firing. Decoration unusually geometrical. Type 97 (sheaf) is rarely seen; the impressions are not clear. Other types 23, 44, 47, 53, 79, 106, 110.

FIG. 29. *Moulds of potter B*

1. Several fragments of one mould. Quartered by bead-rows. Field sparsely filled with types 34, 54, 55, 70.
2. Fragments making half a mould, light, warm, red-brown, polished. Quartered by tree 82. Types 36, 41, 44, 47, 107, 109. Outline fig. 18, 9 (pl. XII, 4).
3. Fragments making half a mould, similar ware but browner and darker. Panelled with 79 and 104. Types 77, 83. Outline fig. 18, 6 (pl. XII, 3).

FIG. 30. *Moulds of potter B*

1. Several fragments of one mould. Dark brown ware. Rosettes 70 instead of ovolo. Quartered by cable 103. Types 24, 41, 79, 83, 95.
2. Many fragments from more than one similar mould. That illustrated is of very bright orange-red ware, burnt soft, with a light blue-grey core. Decoration free. Types 12, 15, 20, 27, 60, 61, 69, 93.
3. Large fragment of mould, dark brown-red, fine. Cable 103 under ovolo. Free in field are types 36, 48, 50, 77, 107.
4. Fragment of mould similar ware. Same use of 103. Free pattern of types 23, 70, 74, 82, 92, 95.

FIG. 31. *Moulds of potter B*

(All in fine brownish ware.)

1. Leaf 78 used instead of ovolo. Types 23, 24 (?), 82, 84, and an unknown.
2. Similar, but bead-row added. Types 39, 50, 95.
3. Leaf 78 set obliquely as ovolo plus a small impression resembling 79, but unclear. Types 18, 101, and an unknown.
4. Probably quartered by cable 103. Types 23, 74, 76, 83.
5. Begins a series with bead-row under the ovolo. Types 12, 13(?), 111, and an unknown.
6. Form 30. Types 48, 93, and something like 32 upside down.
7. Large fragment with attempt at scroll. Types 5, an imperfect dolphin left, 74, 95, 101, 103.
8. Types 60, 70, 79, 93, 106, 111.
9. Two fragments of one mould, orange ware. Types 54, 70, 103.
10. Form 30. Curiously unconnected decoration. Types 70, 73, 74, 87, and an unusually large bead-row. The ovolo unusually spaced.
11. Band of overlapping wreaths 92, with 79, also types 48, 95.
12. Form 30. Small fragment with types 92, 100, and part of an unknown dolphin(?).
13. Large fragment f. 37. The most elegant example of a scroll found. Types 76, 80, 81, 95, 103.
14. Small fragment, f. 37, possibly from same vessel as no. 9. Adds lion 34.

FIG. 32. *Moulds of potter B*

1. Four fragments of one mould. Free style. Types 34, 46, 47, 70, 74, 84.
2. Similar. Types 31, 77, 82.
3. Possibly from same mould. Type 31.
4. Types 41, 70, 83, 97.

E

5. Types 37, 55, 76, 95.

6. Types 14, 24.

7. Types 44, 47.

8. Types 5, 6.

9. Large fragment. Types 12, 61, 70 and part of an unknown eagle (?).

10. Types 42, 47, 107.

11. Exceptional in the widely spaced ovolo and use of a cable like 103 but larger and without dots. Types 70, 77, 79, 95.

12. Small fragment with unconnected decoration. Types 54, 70, 80, 92, 109.

13. Types 34, 70, 111.

14. Types 56, 80, 103, 106.

15. Small fragment. Types 12, 104, 108.

16. Types 20, 70, 80, 95, 111.

FIG. 33. *Fragments of moulds and vessels of potter B*

1. Two fragments of a bowl f. 37. Thin, hard red ware with dull matt glaze. Types 48, 50, 70 (note different appearance on bowl), 93.

2. Fragment of mould. Types 18, 42, 70.

3. Ditto. Types 24, 47, 93, 104.

4. Ditto. Types 9, 44, 79, 92.

5. Ditto. Types 23, 44.

6. Ditto. The only occurrence of type 25.

7. Ditto. Types 70, 111. The cross made by hand.

8. Ditto. Types 2a (or b), 60, 82.

9. Ditto. Types 2a, 20, 93.

10. Four fragments of one mould. Types 13, 34, 81, 82.

11. Fragment of mould. Types 70, 93, 101, 109 (?).

12. Fragment of mould, with triple groove. Types 60, 70, 82.

13. Small fragment of mould. Types 77, 92.

14. Ditto. Types 70, 74, 84, 93.

15. Fragment of bowl f. 37. Good matt red ware. Types 46, 69, 82, and unknown.

16. Fragment of bowl f. 37. Good red ware and glaze. Types 50, 69, 79, 109.

17. Ditto. Thin red ware, matt glaze. Types 27, 70, 77, 79, 104.

18. Ditto. Types 2b, 82, 95.

FIG. 34. *Moulds found during 1954–9*

1 and 2. Displayed pattern of mould fig. 35, 1, by potter A. This provides the best impression we have of the danseuse; unfortunately the Mercury is not so good (pl. xi a).

3, 4, and 5. Fragments of moulds f. 37, by potter A. The winged figure on no. 5 (Victory?) is new and is added to the list of motifs, fig. 41, 112.

FIG. 35. *Moulds found in 1959*

1. Almost complete mould by potter A, f. 37, with six unequal panels filled with human and animal figures (displayed fig. 34, 1, 2 and pl. xi a).

2. Fragment of a mould f. 30, by potter A. Pattern displayed fig. 36, 1.

3. Fragment of mould f. 30, by potter B, with a new ovolo.

4. Fragment of a mould f. Déchelette 64(?). This mould is in fine hard clay which appears to be that of potter B. The only figure used is a small satyr(?) applied in two rows, which does not appear on any other fragment. This mould was a ring, in which was made the central decorated band of an ovoid beaker.

5 and 6. Fragments of mould f. 37, by potter A.

7. Fragment of mould f. 37, by potter B, using the motif 101 as an ovolo.

8 and 9. Fragments of moulds f. 37, by potter B. No. 9 is exceptionally large in diameter.

FIG. 36. *Moulds and ware found 1954–9*

1. Fragment of mould f. 30 by potter B (fig. 35, 2).

2, 4. Fragments of moulds f. 37, by potter A.

3. Fragment of mould f. 37, by potter B. We now have a complete outline of the lion seizing the stag, fig. 41, 31.

5, 6, and 7. Fragments of moulds f. 37, by potter B.

8. Fragment of ware by potter C.

9. Fragment of mould f. 30, by potter B.

FIG. 37. *Moulds and vessels of potter B*

1. Fragments forming half a mould of bright brown-red ware. Three bands of cable 103 in place of ovolo, with groups of rosettes 70 interspersed. Below, a continuous band of leaf 83 and 84 alternately, with 79. Outline shown in fig. 18, 4.

2. Four fragments of one mould. Types 55, 79, 83.

3. Fragment of a mould, found north of the hedge, in the 1938 season. Types 70, 89, and an unknown sea monster.

4. Another fragment found similarly. Types 46, 47, 69, 79, 107.

5. Small fragment of mould with part of stalky scroll and type 103.

6. Ditto. Types 70, 76.

7. Ditto. Possibly part of no. 5.

8 and 9. Two fragments of bowls f. 37 drawn out to show profile, the first by potter A, the second by potter B.

10. A fragment of a bowl f. 37 of very strange appearance, with dark red glaze and a lion with curled tail resembling Oswald's 1434–6.

At first thought possibly from our kilns (see ovolo and rosette like our 72); but neither is identical with ours. This bowl is from some unknown pottery. Found at the Essex County Hospital, 1935.

THE FIGURES OR MOTIFS EMPLOYED IN THE DECORATION

In 1933 no trace was found of the hand-stamps or punches which were used to decorate the moulds, but in the intervening period two of the actual punches have been found.[1] The first of these was found and given to the Museum by Mr. H. C. Calver, the second by Mr. J. Shaw.

The first is for the Triton (our no. 26) and is, in general form, of mushroom shape (pl. xvi a); the broad head (c. 2¼ in.) is slightly umbonate to fit the interior curve of a bowl of f. Drag. 37. It bears in strong relief the figure of a Triton blowing a conch, the figure being so disposed that it approximately fits a circular space (pl. xvi b, 1). The execution of the figure is typical of the Colchester potters, having at times a fine disregard for detail and accuracy. The hands are disproportionate in size and the eye is a simple pellet. There is a faint indication of a belt at

---

[1] And I have heard that there is a third in private hands.

Fig. 20. Moulds of Potter A (p. 48). (½)

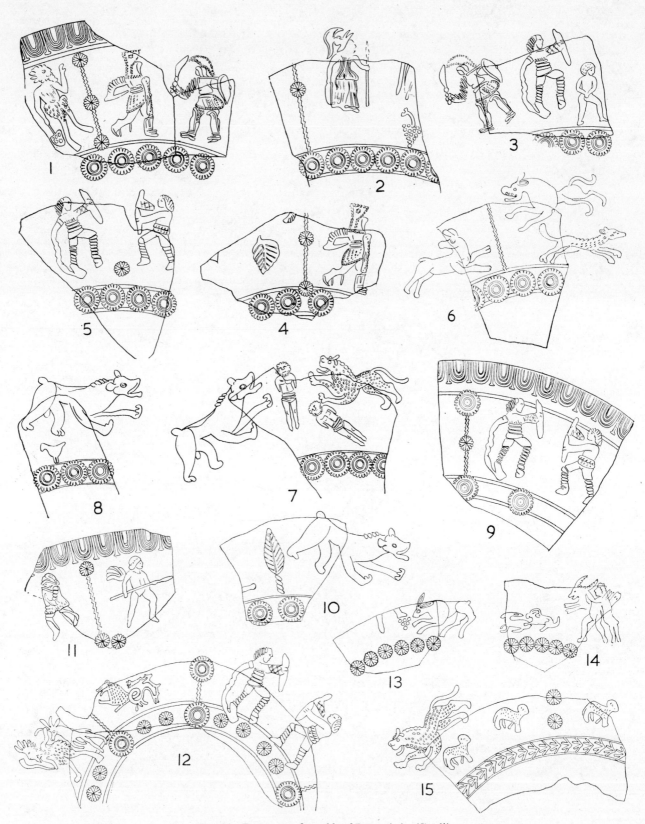

FIG. 21. Fragments of moulds of Potter A (p. 48). (½)

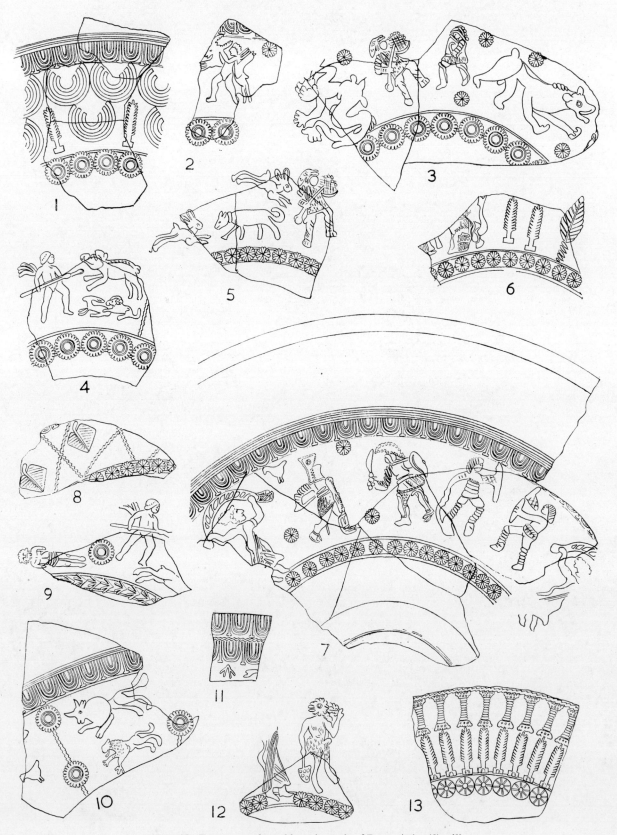

FIG. 22. Fragments of moulds and vessels of Potter A (p. 48). (½)

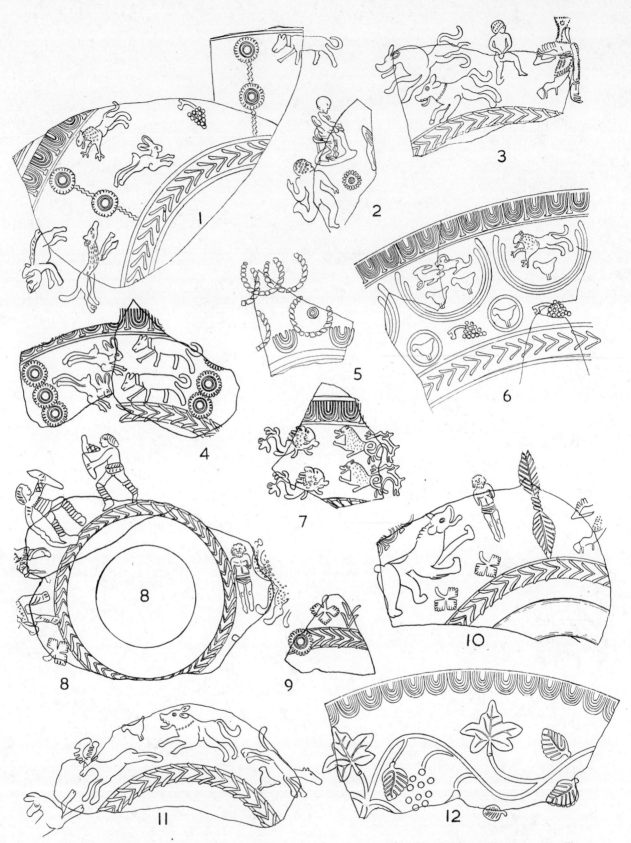

FIG. 23. Fragments of vessels and moulds of Potter A (1–4, 6–11), and moulds of Potter B (5, 12) (p. 48). (½)

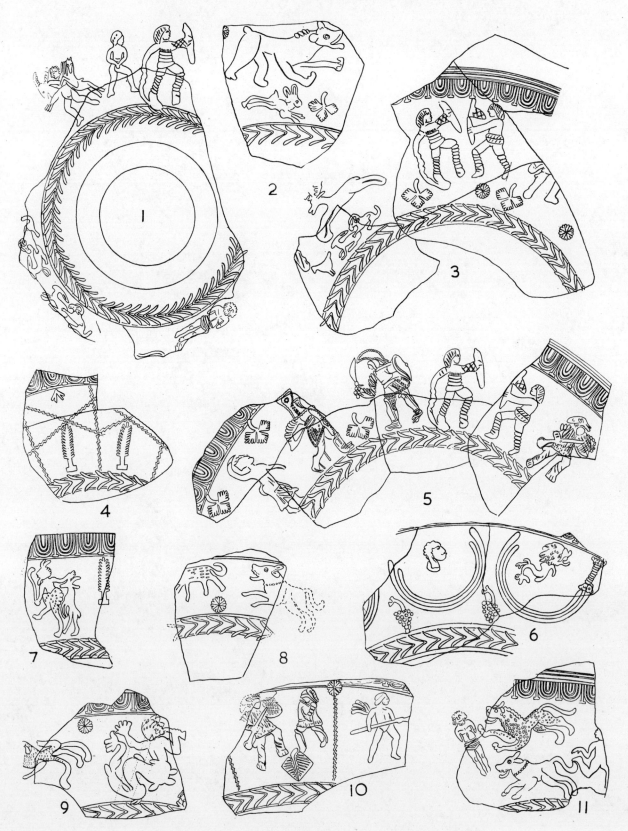

FIG. 24. Fragments of vessels of Potter A, in various styles (p. 48). (½)

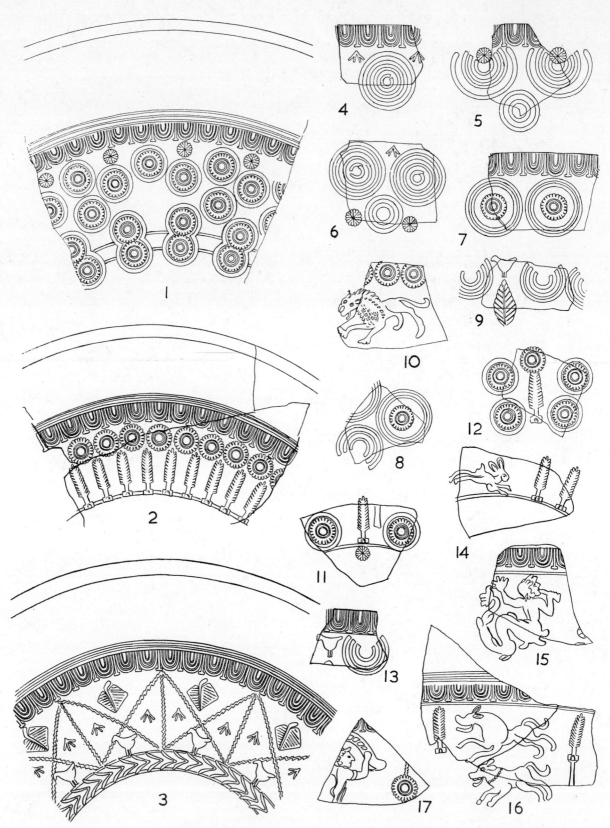

FIG. 25. Fragments of bowls and moulds of Potter A (p. 49). ($\frac{1}{2}$)

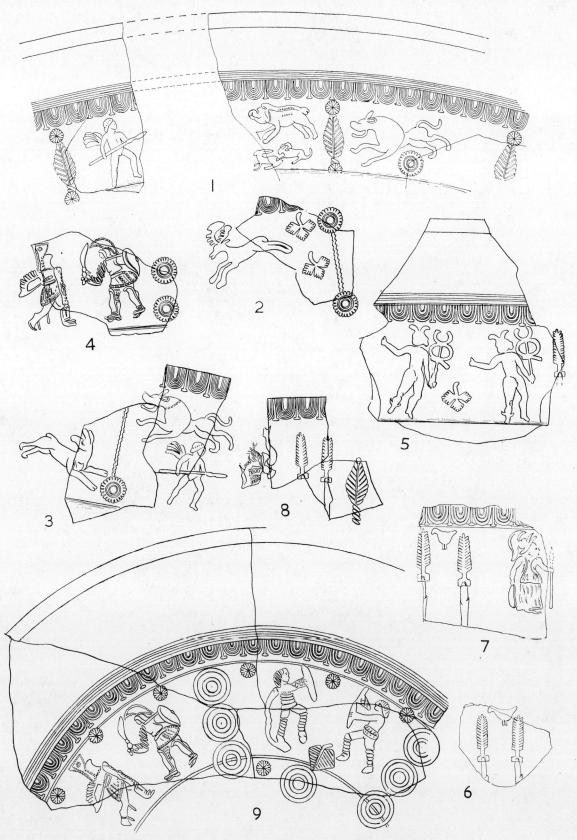

FIG. 26. Fragments of vessels and moulds of Potter A, mostly of f. 30 (p. 49). (½)

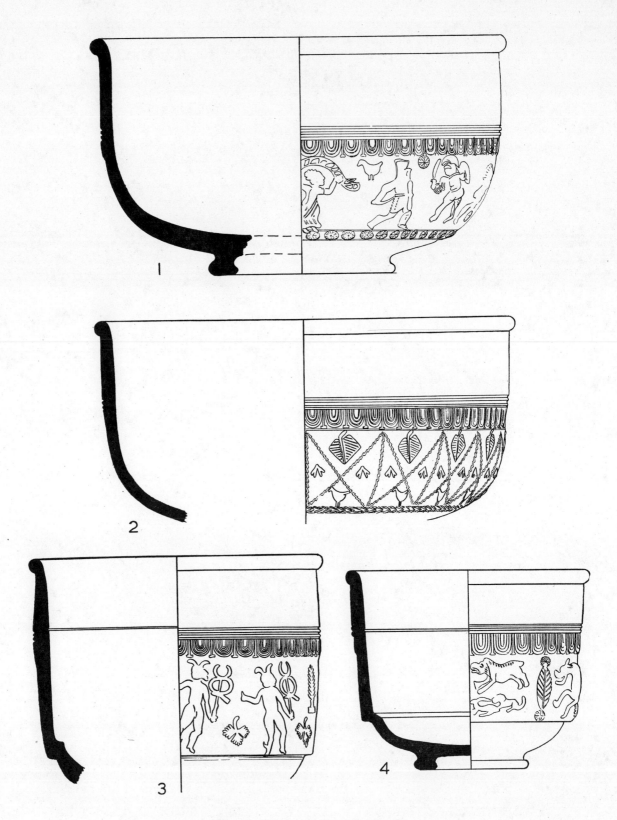

FIG. 27. Vessels by Potter A (p. 49). ($\frac{1}{2}$)

Fig. 28. Moulds of Potter B (p. 49). ($\frac{1}{2}$)

FIG. 29. Moulds of Potter B (p. 49). (½)

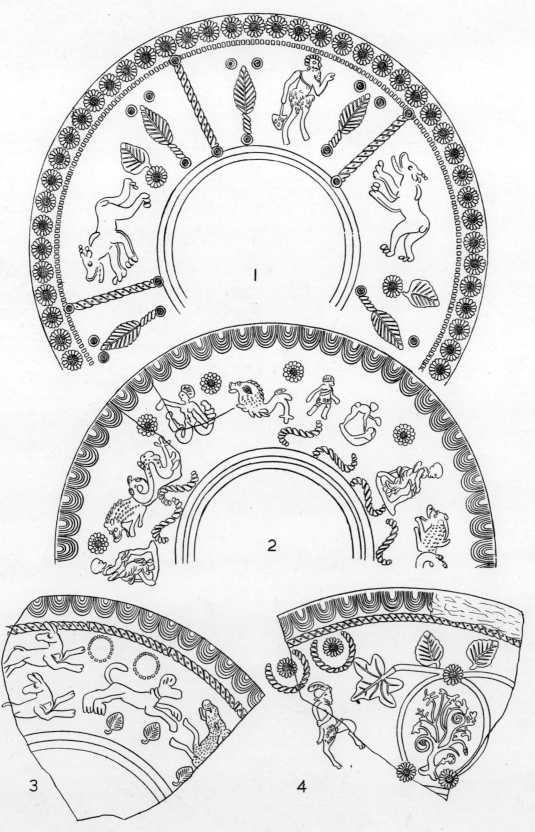

FIG. 30. Moulds of Potter B (p. 49). (½)

Fig. 31. Moulds of Potter B (p. 49). (½)

FIG. 32. Moulds of Potter B (p. 49). (½)

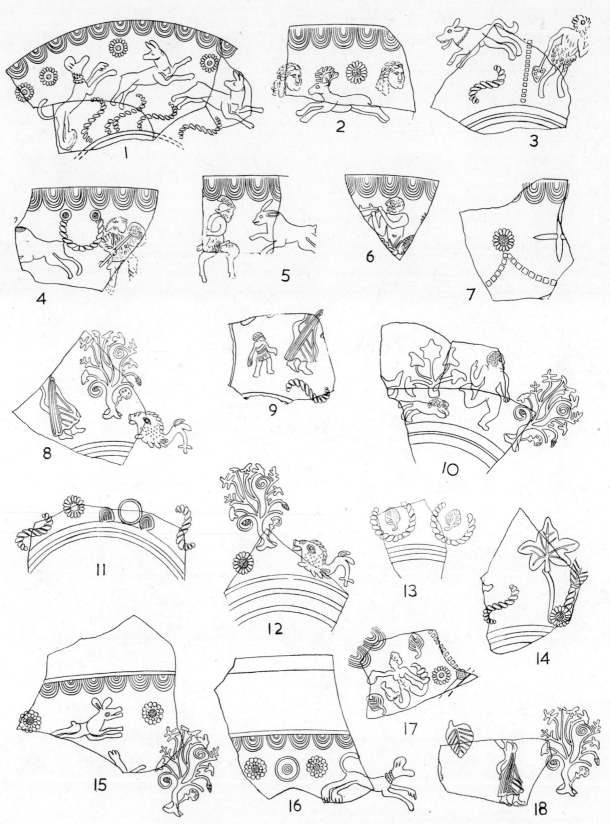

FIG. 33. Fragments of moulds and vessels of Potter B (p. 50). (½)

FIG. 34. Moulds found during 1954–9 (p. 50). (½)

F

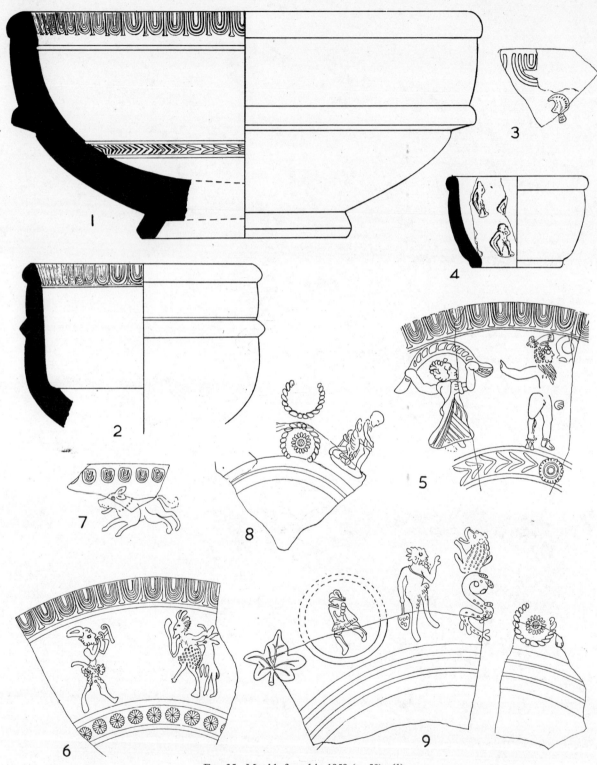

Fig. 35. Moulds found in 1959 (p. 50). (½)

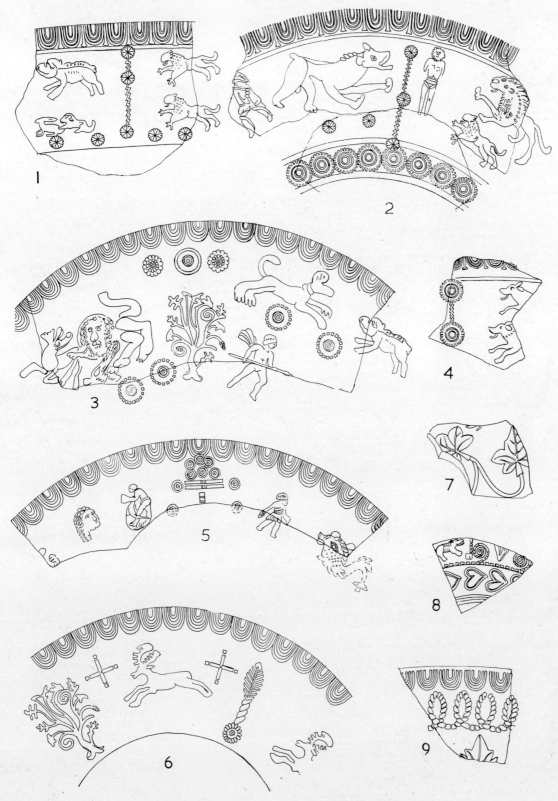

FIG. 36. Moulds and ware found in 1959 (p. 50). (½)

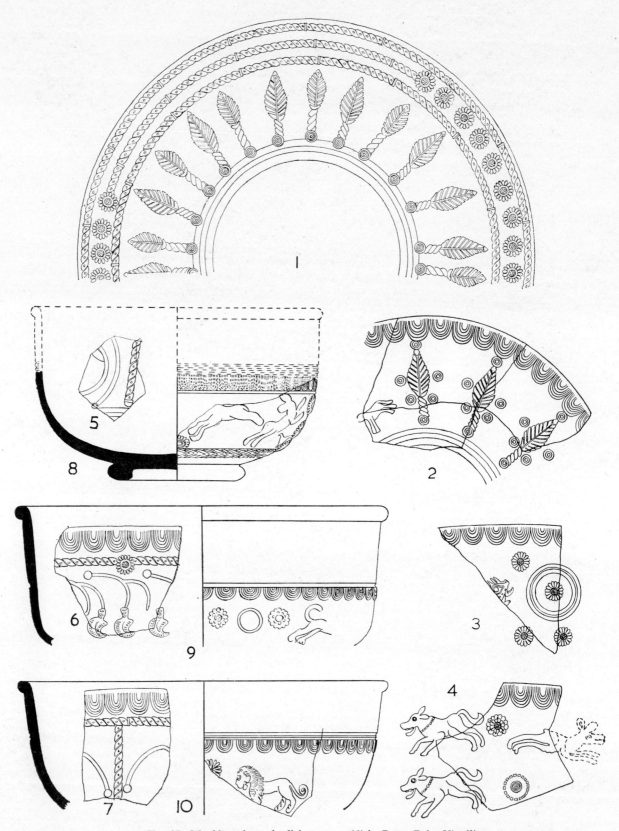

FIG. 37. Moulds and vessels all (except no. 10) by Potter B (p. 50). (½)

the waist, and numerous fins or flippers adorn the anguiform body, which bears a triple fish-tail. At the back there is a roughly cylindrical handle of $\frac{3}{4}$ in. diameter and $1\frac{3}{4}$ in. long; it, and the curve where it expands to the head, are shaped by whittling the almost dry clay with a knife. The material is the finest clay used on the site, of very fine grain, very hard, and of light, red-buff colour.

No fragment of mould bears this figure, but at least three pieces of the actual decorated ware bear it (pl. XVI b, 2, 3). All of these have the distinctive ovolo of potter A; one has also his equally characteristic band of chevrons closing the bottom of the decorated space. The degree of relief in these positives varies according to how deeply the stamp was pressed into the mould, and this in turn can vary the dimensions from side to side of the positive figure.

Great interest attaches to the amount of shrinkage, which occurs thrice in the manufacture of decorated Samian ware. The stamp is impressed in the very soft mould, which is then fired and must shrink considerably in the process. How much this shrinkage was at Colchester we cannot yet know, because we have no fragment of mould bearing this particular impression. Soft clay was then forced into the hard-baked mould and allowed to dry to a leathery consistency. In this process it had to shrink sufficiently to pull itself clear of the sunken negative pattern. The positive cast was then dipped in the engobe and fired, thus completing a shrinkage which should generally correspond (in sum of shrinkage) to that of the first operation. In this way the figure which finally appears as a positive on the decorated bowl has suffered two complete shrinkings, and in consequence is two degrees smaller in dimensions than the figure on the stamp used.

The percentage of shrinkage is of some interest, for though it may vary according to the clay used (and its humidity at the time of use), it should not vary beyond certain limits. This has a definite application, for it has been suspected, and may well prove true, that figures which for some reason appealed to the potter, were mechanically copied by taking impressions of them from a bowl of another potter, bought in the market. From such an impression a punch could be cast (in clay); both would have to be fired, and the resulting punch would be two shrinkages smaller than the positive figure which was copied. The argument that such piracy of types was practised rests on the observation that copied types do show progressive diminution in size, while preserving a suspicious degree of similarity amounting almost to identity.

Having now been able to study an original stamp I begin to doubt the theory, for the copied stamp would be in such shallow relief that it would be detected; on the other hand, on removal from its matrix it could, no doubt, be so trimmed up by hand, while still in a leathery state, as closely to resemble one originally cut by hand. With these few remarks we leave the matter to research, with the following observations:

The distance from the tip of the central digit of the upper hand to the tip of the central of the three fins on the belly is 52 mm. (obtained by slightly rolling the ruler over the bulge of the stamp). The same dimension on the two pieces of ware which preserve it is 46 mm. in each case. The distance from the forehead to a point on the outer edge of the figure, 8 mm. below the last flipper on the left, is 51 mm. on the stamp and 41·5 and 42 mm. on the ware. The total shrinkage therefore varies from 11·54 to 18·63 per cent., with an average of 15·94 per cent. Since this results from two distinct firings we must halve it to obtain an approximate figure of 7·97 per cent. as an average shrinkage in firing.[1]

FIG. 38. Hand-stamp for decorated ware ($\frac{1}{1}$)

The second is for the sheaf-like pattern, our fig. 40, 97, which had not survived to us in any clearly preserved example. Though it does occur on a mould (fig. 28, 2) it is ill-preserved and blurred. We now have the original stamp, with every detail. The clay is the same as that of the first stamp, but the form is oblong, slightly curved to fit to the mould whether applied vertically or horizontally, but only about $\frac{1}{4}$ in. thick, and with no handle or grip of any kind on the back. A detailed drawing is shown in fig. 38.

The punch measures 59 mm. by 24 mm., while the impression in the mould is only 43 mm. by 17·5 mm. This gives a shrinkage of 27·23 per cent. in one direction and 27·1 per cent. in the other—a very different result from that yielded by the first case! One may even suggest that our matrix is not that which was used on the mould.

[1] The Triton stamp was published, soon after its discovery, in *Antiq. Journ.* XXXVII, 222 ff.

FIG. 39. Figure-types of Potters A and B. (½)
(For no. 31 see also fig. 41.)

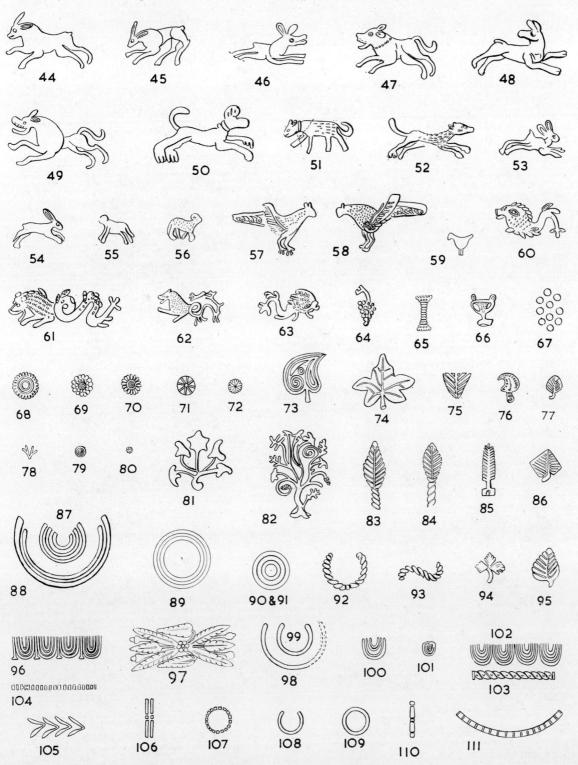

FIG. 40. Figure-types of Potters A and B. (½)

Published references to objects of this sort are deplorably scanty. Large numbers should have been found on French sites, but in Déchelette's great work we have only the brief remark—'All the punches we have found are of clay; some are partially glazed. We know of 49 bearing the name of the mould-maker or of the master potter who employed him.'[1] A note giving the names adds that nearly all those of known provenance come from Lezoux. Hermet says he only recovered two from La Graufesenque, one for a semi-circle, the other for a leaf, but he also illustrates one for making an ovolo by single impressions. The two shown are both drawn out behind into longish handles.[2]

The fullest account of these stamps will be found in Dr. Kuzsinszky's account of the Roman pottery quarter at Buda-Pest-AQVINCVM.[3] His figs. 156–230 illustrate a large number, and also moulds from which they could be produced in numbers, a detail so far not recorded elsewhere. His figs. 176, 177, 188 show stamps with long handles like ours; others have the small fingergrips like two small examples in the British Museum which come from Gaul.

The various figures used as type-punches by the Colchester potters are shown, half size, on figs. 39–41. Several have been added since the list was first published in *Germania*. Originally we divided them into three groups, as used by potter A, potter B, or by both A and B. Now, however, when further types have to be added, and also the number used by both increased, it has been deemed advisable to revise the order, grouping the figures by subject, and re-numbering.

The drawings are made from paper squeezes taken direct from the moulds and *reversed* so as to appear as they do in the finished bowl. In each case all the best preserved impressions have been employed to obtain the greatest possible accuracy in detail. Nevertheless, in some cases the complete figure could not be obtained (e.g. nos. 1, 2 *a* and *b*) and in others no impression had been preserved well enough to give the detail (e.g. no. 4). In a few cases the figures have had to be taken from the bowls. They are thus of a smaller size than the remainder, for the shrinkage in the firing of the bowl was quite considerable.[4]

This shrinking should always be borne in mind, as also the fact that it is not constant. The dimensions of impressions from the same matrix can vary considerably. A further difficulty in comparing them is that the larger ones were so applied to the mould that there is a certain amount of distortion owing to a twist of the potter's hand. Still further, the impression is often uneven, one part being much more deeply impressed than another. All these causes contribute to a variation in dimensions, so that it is rare for squeezes from two impressions of the same die to coincide exactly when superimposed.

The moulds show that the punches were very sharply and finely cut, in high, rounded relief. They are often picked out or enlivened by prodding, as if with a bone point, in order to represent hair or other details by raised points. A similar technique is well known on the figures in barbotine decoration. We shall refer to this similarity in style and technique more fully later when dealing with the barbotined ware.

One hundred and seventeen different types have been drawn, and there are fragmentary traces of a few more. Very few of them can claim direct derivation from continental sources, the majority being distinctly original in design. While the figures are Roman in character, the animals belong to the native style so well known to us from the 'hunt cups' of Castor and similar potteries. The leaves and scrolls, too, are more native than Roman.

Figs. 39–40

1. Dancing girl. An excellent example of this figure was found on the mould fig. 34, 2, in 1959. Oswald 358A.[5] Potter A only.

2 A and B. Dancing girl. Taken from moulds and good in detail. Potters A and B.

2. A very similar figure, taken from a bowl, but hardly the same. Potters A and B.

3. Minerva. Used fairly frequently by potter A, but face never clear, and tip of spear never preserved. Oswald 129B.

4. Mercury. Taken from a poor bowl and therefore without detail. Fragments of mould show that the figure shrank much in firing, and are too small or blurred to help with the detail. Another mould found later provides fig. 41, no. 4 *bis*.

5 and 6. Pair of gladiators, rarely used apart. The detail of these two figures has been taken very carefully from a number of good impressions. They are very good examples of the use of points to enhance the details, and confirm the impression given that these points are permanent, always occurring in the same place and number, i.e. that they are not added by hand in the mould. It should be understood that the average impression only reproduces part of this fine detail on the finished bowl. Oswald 1013 M and N. Potters A and B.

7 and 8. Pair of gladiators. Frequently used, apparently by A only. Oswald 1105D.

9, 10. A pair of gladiators. Oswald 1039A. Potter A only.

11. Spearman with flying cloak. Cf. *Heiligenberg*, fig. 116 (from Jebsheim, IVLIVS F), and *Blickweiler*, Taf. 76, 8, 9. Oswald 1074A. Potter A.

12. Seated figure holding a roll. Same figure as *Blickweiler*, Taf. 72, 2, but hardly from the same matrix. Oswald 138. Potter B.

13. Nude figure. Potters A and B.

14. Apparently a man holding a stag. The drawing is made with difficulty from several fragments of mould, all very imperfect and unclear, but probably Cyparissus and his stag. Our

---

[1] *Les Vases céramiques ornés de la Gaule Romaine*, ii, 337.
[2] *La Graufesenque*, pl. 115, A, 4, 5, and p. 217.
[3] B. Kuzsinszky, *Das große römische Töpferviertel in Aquincum* (Budapest, Régiségei, xi, 1932).

[4] About one-eighth linear in the manufacture of local bricks, for which I am indebted to Mr. J. Everett, a local manufacturer.
[5] Dr. Felix Oswald, *Index of Figure Types on Terra Sigillata*, 1937.

drawing cannot be far from the original outline. Cf. Oswald 1137A, La Madeleine, Hadrian. Cf. also Ludowici, *Rheinzabern*, v, 34, two examples by Cerialis. Potters A and B.

15. Unexplained group. Potter B.

16. Small nude, possibly a captive. Oswald 1158A. Potter A.

17. Captive. Potter A.

18. Mask. Oswald 1366A. Potters A and B.

19. Mask. Oswald 1314B. Potter B.

20. Small male figure. Potter B.

21. Pan playing pipes. Oswald 717B. Potter A.

22. Pan holding lituus and leading a deer by the horns. Potter A.

23. Ithyphallic Pan, wearing cap and feather (or merely horns?). The same figure as *Blickweiler*, Taf. 74, 12, but smaller, cf. Oswald, sub. 718, where several examples are quoted from Lezoux, Vichy, Trier. Potter B.

24. Pan or Satyr with bunch of grapes. Potters A and B.

25. Imperfect impression of squatting satyr playing the pipes. Oswald 724B. Potter B.

26. Triton blowing a horn. Taken from a bowl, all the impressions on moulds being too fragmentary. Potter A. The matrix of this has now been found. See p. 50.

27. Anguiped female. Same as *Blickweiler*, Taf. 71, 17, but smaller. Oswald 20A. Potter B.

28. Part of an unintelligible figure. Potter B.

29. Lion left. Oswald 1497N. Potter A.

30. Lion (or Leopard) left. Oswald 1497O. Potter B.

31. Lion seizing a deer. Oswald 1492B. Potter B. Another fragment found in 1959 gives us fig. 41, no. 31 *bis*.

32. Lion seizing a deer. Oswald 1492B. Potter A.

33. Lion seizing deer. Very small. Oswald 1492A. Potter A.

34. Small lion right. Potter B.

35. Small lion left. Oswald 1573E. Potter A.

36. Boar left. The bristles indicated by small points, which rarely come out clearly in the positive. Oswald 1696J. Potter B.

37. Boar left. No impression is really clear. Oswald 1696K. Potters A and B.

38. Bull charging left. Taken from a bowl and so on a smaller scale. Potter A.

39. Stag charging left. Complete figure not preserved. Potter B.

40. Bear right. Oswald 1633N. Potter A.

41. Bear left. Oswald 1633O. Potter B.

42. Stag left. Oswald 1822T. Potters A and B.

43. Similar stag. Oswald 1822W. Potters A and B.

44. Doe left. Oswald 1822V. Potter B.

45. Doe crouching left. Oswald 1822S. Potter A.

46. Dog (?) running right. Not found complete. Figure taken from a bowl and therefore on a smaller scale. Potter B.

47. Dog left. The raised points of the collar are often invisible in the positive. Oswald 2039S. Potters A and B.

48. Dog or deer. Same figure as *Blickweiler*, Taf. 79, 8, but much smaller, cf. also *Rheinzabern*, iii, 244, T246. Potters A and B.

49. Large dog (?). Oswald 2039P. Potter A.

50. Dog with collar. Oswald 2039T. Potter B.

51. Dog (?) with shaggy coat. Impressions are poor. Oswald 2039R. Potter A.

52. Cat-like animal with shaggy coat. Oswald 2039Q. Potter A.

53. Hare. Oswald 2140F. Potter A.

54. Hare. Oswald 2140G. Potter B.

55. Lamb (?). Potter B.

56. Sheep. Compare Forrer, fig. 82, *h*. Potters A and B.

57 and 58. Pair of fighting cocks. Oswald 2377A and B. Potter A.

59. Small bird. Potter A.

60. Dolphin. Potter B.

61. Sea monster. Various parts very carefully picked out with points. Much better work than those at *Blickweiler*, Taf. 71. Oswald 38. Potter B.

62. Sea monster with remarkable tail. Potter A.

63. Dolphin. Potter A.

64. Bunch of grapes. Potter A.

65. Pedestal. Potter A.

66. Cantharus. Potter A.

67. Berries. Potter B.

68. Rosette. Potter B.

69. Double rosette. Potter B.

70. Rosette. Potter B. In both of these last two the central florets of the disk are indicated by minute points in the mould, but do not register in the positive.

71. Wheel-like rosette. Potter A.

72. Very neat and regular rosette. Potter A.

73. Conventional leaf. Potter B.

74. Leaf. Potter B.

75. Half leaf. Potter B.

76. Curious sickle-shaped leaf. Potter B.

77. Small leaf. Potter B.

78. Branched ornament. Potter A.

79. Small concentric circles. Potter A.

80. Minute rosette of eight petals. Potter B.

81. Small tree. Potter B.

82. Tree. Compare these two trees with *Heiligenberg*, Taf. XXXVI, 4, Cerialis of Rheinzabern.

83. Leaf. Potters A and B.

84. Similar leaf. Potter B.

85. Leaf. The small U on the base rarely registers in the positive. Compare *Blickweiler*, Taf. 80, 35. Potter A.

86. Leaf. Potter A.

87. Double festoon. Potter A.

88. Large double festoon. Potter A.

89. Concentric circles. Potter A.

90 and 91. Small circles. Potter A.

92. Corded festoon. Potter B.

93. Corded S-shaped ornament. Potter B.

94. Leaf. Potter A.

95. Leaf. Potters A and B.

96. Ovolo of potter A.

97. Foliate ornament of poppy-heads. The few impressions are all very blurred. Compare *Blickweiler*, Taf. 81, 1–3. Potter B.

98 and 99. Festoons. Potter A.

100. Ovolo of potter B.

101. Very small ovolo-like ornament. Potter B.

102. Ovolo of Potter B as it usually appears. Potter B.

103. Corded band. Potter B. The row of points does not show on the positive.

104. Bead-row. Potter B.

105. Chevron. Potter A.

106. Ornament. Potter B.

107. Beaded circle. Potter B.

108. Horse-shoe ornament. Potter B.

109. Small circle. Potter B.

110. Astragaloid ornament. Potter B.

111. Segmented festoon. Potter B.

Fig. 41

4 *bis*. Imperfect impression of Mercury, no. 4 above, but from a mould. Potter A.

112. Winged figure, very blurred impression on mould. Fig. 34, 5.

113. Small satyr (?). Potter A. Mould f. 67, fig. 35, 4.

114. Figure of uncertain meaning on mould of potter B. Fig. 36, 5.

115. Ovolo used on mould, f. 30, of potter B. Fig. 35, 3.
116. Part of a large circle or festoon. Potter B. Fig. 35, 9.
117. Part of a leaf. Potter B. Fig. 36, 9.

6. Good ware, possibly imported, found in Colchester (not on the kiln site). The circles are Fölzer 827 and there are traces of the festoons with horses' heads, Fölzer 797 (C.M. 22.38).

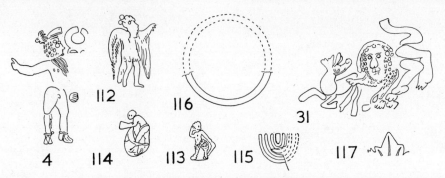

FIG. 41. Figure-types of Potters A and B. (½)

FIG. 42. *Potter C*

There remain to be described some twenty-five pieces of decorated ware, some of which have a very good surface and would be undoubtedly described as East Gaulish were it not for the fact that the remainder present, in every respect, the appearance of Colchester ware. All are bound together inasmuch as many are underfired and the ovolo is always the same, very distinctive in having no tassel and the outer edge partly beaded or corded. The details of the decoration have a limited range and are repeated again and again. The pieces are clearly of one potter, and his connexions are chiefly with Trier, where he would seem to have worked before coming to Colchester. He seems to have worked here, though no moulds have been found.

The best fragments are illustrated on fig. 42.

1. Ten or more fragments of one bowl. The larger portion with very good coating, some of the other fragments poor, exactly as Colchester wasters. The pieces were found in the rubbish dumps both near the kiln and at the east end of the stone wall. The straight line under the ovolo is probably a guide-line on the mould. The bead-rows are remarkably angular. The Diana is like Oswald 105, Trier, late Antonine, but probably not identical. The other group is like his 960, Chemery, Trajan–Hadrian, and 960A, Lavoye, Antonine, but not, we think, identical with either. The rest of the decoration is characteristic of this potter. The lower band is common at Trier (Fölzer,[1] Taf. XI, &c.) and the spirals also. On her Taf. XIV, 23 we have the lower band combined with our same ovolo and on no. 20 the same panels of spirals. The types are her Taf. XXXI, 779 and 138 (nearly), Taf. XXIX, 478, and perhaps 477 (on no. 11 below) (Trier) and the ovolo is Taf. XXXII, 950 (Trier).

2. Small fragment, apparently Colchester ware.

3 and 4. Two fragments of one bowl, with the appearance of Colchester ware. The lower band and bead row as before; new types are the three poppy-heads, bunch of grapes, and beaded circle. Compare Fölzer, Taf. XXXI, 747, 739, and 819, all Trier.

5. Good hard ware, possibly imported. The leg of the small figure is possibly Fölzer type 500. From filling of enclosure.

7 and 8. Two fragments of one bowl; a Colchester waster, the glaze very poor and very pale, all gone from the outside. The left figure is Fölzer 474.

9 and 10. Two fragments of one bowl, paste and glaze exactly as nos. 3 and 4. The boar is very like Fölzer 610, but is smaller.

11 and 12. Two fragments of one bowl; a Colchester waster. The clay is soft and soapy, glaze pale and nearly all gone. The Diana is Fölzer 477, and compare the animal with her 597.

13. A small fragment, similar ware, with part of the seated figure, Fölzer 470. From the enclosure.

14. Fragment in the Museum. Very good ware, perhaps imported. The small ornaments in the field resemble minute busts. Fig. 36, 8, another fragment of this potter's work found in 1959; compare no. 5 above.

IMPORTED DECORATED TERRA SIGILLATA

Every fragment found of sufficient importance to be illustrated is shown on figs. 43 and 44. All belong to the general litter over the site, most being found in the rubbish dump round the sigillata kiln (21), and in the filling of the enclosure. No. 14 was in the upper filling of ditch III at 3 ft. Most would normally be dated Hadrian–Antonine on their general style, and the majority of types used belong to such potters as Cintusmus, Cinnamus, Doeccus, Butrio, and Libertus, who are usually thus dated. The pieces may be contemporary with the local products, but are more likely to be survivals, and it is worthy of note that the plain band above the ovolo is generally much narrower than the average of that of the local bowls. An exception is no. 19 which also stands out as different in fabric, possible East Gaulish. Less than half the total are of East Gaulish character and it is doubtful whether any, except no. 19, would be regarded as certainly post-Antonine.

---

[1] Fräulein E. Fölzer, *Die Bilderschüsseln der Ostgallischen Sigillata-Manufakturen*, Bonn, 1913.

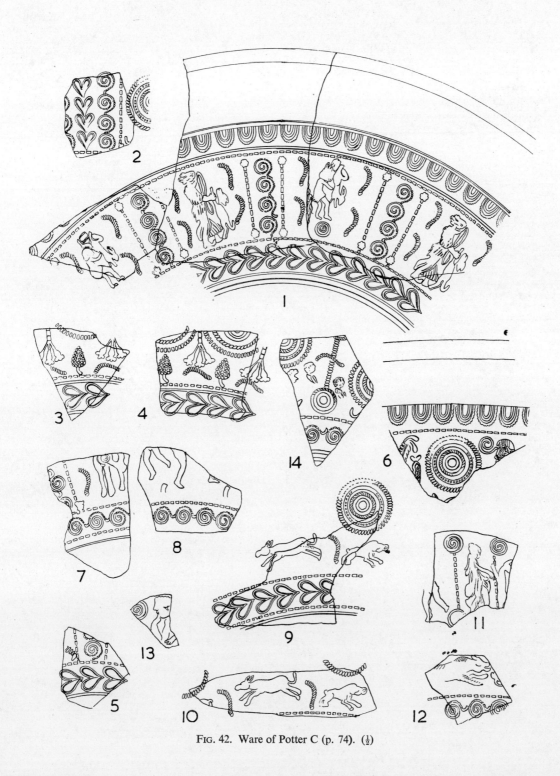

FIG. 42. Ware of Potter C (p. 74). (½)

FIG. 43

1. Form 30, good bright glaze; goat Oswald 1836, but smaller. Hadrian–Antonine, kiln enclosure, with another small fragment of same bowl.

2, 2a. Two fragments form 37, bright red ware, matt glaze; the masks are Oswald 1214, used by Paternus and Cinnamus.

3. Form 30, good dark glaze, Lezoux ware, with wavy line above and below ovolo; female figure used by Banuus, cf. Oswald 1142a but smaller, and bigger than his 1142, both Lezoux, Antonine and Trajan–Hadrian respectively. We may say Hadrian–Antonine for ours; the bear is like Oswald 1617, Lezoux, Hadrian–Antonine; figure with shield like Oswald 212, Lezoux, Trajan (?). Ovolo and lion of Paternus.

4. Several fragments of one f. 37, rather bright glaze, fine wavy line under ovolo; bear perhaps Oswald 1588, Lezoux, Trajan–Antonine; small bear exactly as on May, *Colchester*, pl. xxviii, 212. Style of Justus or Paternus.

5. Two fragments of one f. 37, thick ware with thin, dull glaze, sphinxes like Oswald 854 and 857–8, but smaller. Lezoux, Antonine; danseuse is Oswald 346, Lezoux, Hadrian–Antonine; cock somewhat like Oswald 1250, Vichy and Lezoux, Trajan. Cinnamus.

6. Form 37 (as are all the following), good ware with dark, matt glaze. Types not closely identifiable, but ovolo of Cinnamus.

7. Three fragments of one bowl, matt glaze, Lezoux ware. The Minerva is Oswald 126b exactly, Lezoux, Hadrian. The contents of the medallion are uncertain. Cinnamus.

8. Fair ware with soft, matt glaze. Danseuse Oswald 322, Blickweiler, Hadrian to late Antonine; faun Oswald 711a, Lezoux, Trajan–Hadrian. 322 occurs at Old Kilpatrick, pl. xiii, 16, and 711a on May, *Colchester*, pl. xxiii, 151. Several other fragments with same ovolo are probably from same bowl. From rubbish layer and stone wall. Cinnamus.

9. Small fragment of good Lezoux ware.

10. Similar fragment, with head of large Dolphin. Near kiln 19. Twelve fragments.

11. Good ware and glaze, Lezoux ware, vase like Déch. 1073 also on May, op. cit., pl. xxv, 181 (fits to no. 18 below). Vase of Jullinus.

12. Good ware and glaze; the deer is Oswald 1743, which occurs at Newstead (Curle, p. 225, fig. 17, stamped by Cinnamus).

13. Similar fragments, types not identifiable. Ovolo of Cinnamus.

14. Similar fragment; gladiator like Oswald 195a but smaller, the other gladiator very like that on no. 3 above. Lezoux.

15. Fair ware, of Lezoux quality, horseman like Oswald 245, but smaller (Trajan–Antonine), cf. *Newstead*, p. 225, fig. 7; small figure Oswald 688, *Rottweil*, pl. xx, 17, Cintusmus and several sites, Trajan–Antonine. Near stone wall. Cf. work of Advocisus and Jullinus.

16. Small fragment of Lezoux ware, cf. *Balmuildy*, pl. xxxiii, 28. From rubbish layer at end of stone wall. Cinnamus?

FIG. 44

17. Two fragments of one bowl, Lezoux ware. Horseman probably Oswald 258, Lezoux and Vichy, Trajan–Antonine and Blickweiler, Hadrian. The bear something like Oswald 1606, Lezoux, Hadrian; the deer difficult to identify.

18. Lezoux ware, glaze almost bright. Ovolo of Jullinus.

19. Two fragments of one bowl, light red ware (like Colchester ware) and glaze, latter poor, possibly East Gaulish; leaves and ovolo (?) exactly as Arentsburg, xxxvii, 31 and cf. ibid. xlii, 31. Style of Paternus?

20. Bright glaze. Lezoux ware, detail of decoration obscured by sandy accretion.

21. Form 30. Good ware, stamped CINNAMI (retro). The Cupid is Oswald 401, Lezoux and Vichy, Trajan–Antonine. Found with wasters in pit C17.

22. Large fragment, good glaze, the lion resembles Oswald 1373–4, Lezoux, Trajan and Antonine, and 1497M, Lezoux, Trajan. The figure, which is laid horizontally, resembles his 592–3, Lezoux, Blickweiler and Rheinzabern, Trajan–Antonine.

23. Two fragments of one bowl f. 37, the surface badly eroded so that the figures cannot be identified. Neat ovolo with small bead-row beneath. Probably Lezoux ware.

24. Form 37 or 30. The ovolo is very small and peculiarly confused as if overlapping. Rather bright red ware with poor glaze. Found in rubbish at east end of the stone wall.

25. Form 37. Bright red ware (like Colchester), with light red, matt glaze. The ovolo with only one loop, and knobbed tassel attached on the right, is peculiar. Figures not identified.

26. Form 37. Very hard and good pinkish ware with dark glaze (Lezoux). The lion is probably Oswald 1388, Lezoux, Trajan–Antonine; for the goat cf. Oswald 1834, Trier, late Antonine. Found in the upper filling of well V, probably of kiln date.

27. Small chip, f. 37, of good ware and glaze, with captive, Oswald 1142, Lezoux, Trajan–Hadrian. Found near the last.

28. Fragment of f. 30, pale red ware with light red glaze. Ovolo with ring-ended tassels; bead rows of alternate round and long beads. The siren on the right is probably Oswald 863A, Lezoux, Flavian–Trajan, but the style of this bowl is undoubtedly Hadrian–Antonine.

Thirty-two other fragments are not worthy of illustration. Two are Flavian and may be discounted; of the rest four are certainly East Gaulish, one bearing Oswald 322. The remainder are of better class and may all be Lezoux ware; recognizable upon them is the horseman, Oswald 245, Lezoux, Lubié, Rheinzabern, Trajan–Antonine, and a lion like Oswald 1447, but not identical.

The presence of the two Flavian pieces calls for comment. There was no apparent Flavian occupation of the site in general, but just east of it, around well V, an area which was not explored. We had reason to suspect that the well had been filled up mainly in Hadrianic times, and had presumably been in use for some long time before that. It seems, therefore, that our potters were not the first on the site, for the fused mass of flagons of the late first- to early second-century f. 154/5 (pl. xx a) was found accidentally near well V in 1936.

THE PLAIN OR SMOOTH FORMS

Fragments of the plain forms are present in very great quantity. As would be expected, they are mostly of the common and well-known forms of the period. But most of the forms which were never really common, but which are known to have been contemporary, are also represented. Of these the most remarkable is f. 27, which maintains its anachronistic reputation, already earned at other places such as Blickweiler and Heiligenberg.

FIG. 43. Imported decorated Sigillata (p. 76). ($\frac{1}{2}$)

The potters' names are found in the usual frequency on the usual forms, and not on those forms where one has learnt not to expect them, thus conforming to continental practice.[1] The stamps are reported in their own section, but it may be remarked that the proportion of fragments of imported plain wares is

numbers, and we cannot say whether our large quantity is above normal or not.

Remains found in the 1959 season were not numerous and give rise to only small modifications in the following text, which has been arranged in the same order (on the whole) as that followed in Oswald and Pryce,

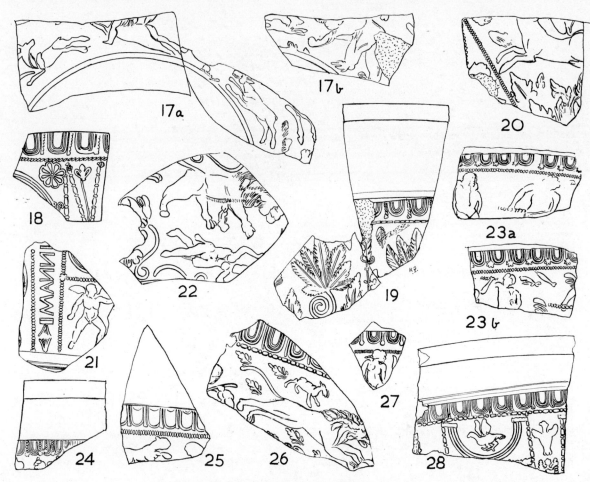

FIG. 44. Imported decorated Sigillata (p. 76). (½)

small; smaller indeed than that of imported decorated ware. It is possible that our plain ware was produced before decorated ware was attempted, and that it had a wider distribution, for stamps of Cunopectus have been found at Kettering, which is farther afield than the decorated ware has yet been shown to have spread.

There is no difference between the plain forms and their continental prototypes other than the very red paste (when correctly fired) and the fact that the vast majority are wasters. Wasters are scarcely mentioned by continental writers, but must have occurred in large

Introduction to the study of Terra Sigillata, but it has not been possible to keep closely to the same sequence in the figures. Fragments from the Claudius–Nero occupation of the site are omitted.

FORMS DRAG. 18/31, 31 AND LUDOWICI *Sb*

The fragments are innumerable, especially of f. 18/31; a selection of the outlines is given in fig. 45, nos. 1–8. No. 1 is overfired, almost vitrified, and stamped SENILIS FE. Like most, it has a rouletted wreath in

---

[1] But this only applies to the Sigillata ware. Entirely new is the use of the same stamp on Sigillata, colour-coated ware, and mortaria, see pp. 85, 91 below.

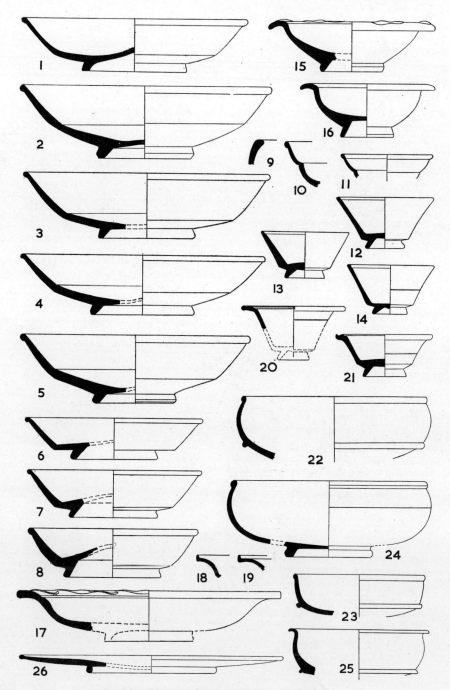

FIG. 45. Forms of Sigillata ware (pp. 76–85). ($\frac{1}{4}$)

the centre. No. 2 is good red ware, with excellent coating, stamped LITVGENVS F in a rouletted wreath. No. 3 is good ware, but the paste is fired nearly white (underfired) and the coating is fired black. No. 4 is of thin pale red ware, with hard red coating and rouletted wreath. No. 5 is underfired, causing the good blood-red coating to flake off. No. 6 is of fairly good dark red ware. No. 7 is soft and underfired. No. 8 is bright red, very soft, and powdery.

The imported fragments of this form were few. The local products have a tendency to be thicker (cf. no. 8).

Remains of a complete bowl f. Lud. Sb were recently found in the NE. cemetery: it is stamped GABRVS FE with our local stamp. Two more examples of this stamp were found in 1959.

FORM DRAG. 40

Three rim-fragments only, all in local ware and alike, save that one, fig. 47, 7A, has a light groove inside the lip.

FORM DRAG. 27

Fig. 45, 10–11. Three fragments of two rims only. Both are in very good local ware, which rules out the earlier period. This form occurred similarly rarely at Blickweiler and Heiligenberg. A rim found in 1959 is of a peculiar reddish-yellow colour.

FORM DRAG. 33

The quantity of fragments is very large and very varied in state and quality. The form is the normal one of the Antonine period. Many are not stamped, and many have the red-brown soapy coating already noted as the result of misfiring. The figures, fig. 45, 12–14, are typical, and there is little variation.

An unstratified base found in 1959 is stamped with the rosette (fig. 40, no. 70) of potter B.

FORM DRAG. 35

These were made in fair numbers, with and without ivy-leaf decoration. There are several vitrified and distorted fragments. One or two rims were rouletted on top. Fig. 45, 15 was found inside kiln 22. No. 16 is chocolate-brown and has no decoration on the small part of the rim which is preserved.

FORM DRAG. 36

The typical form as made in Central Gaul is only represented in local ware by a single fragment found in 1959. There are, however, several fragments, particularly of the one figured (fig. 45, 17), which may or may not belong to the same vessel. It has a large roultteed wreath and is underfired; the coating is

chocolate-brown. The upper part is overfired and distorted, almost vitrified. The rim has a broad shallow fluting at the outer margin and at the inner lip. It bears the usual ivy leaves in barbotine. There was another similar rim.

About half a dozen other rims are similar, but rouletted instead of barbotined, and most of them lack the shallow flutings. All rims found differ from the usual outline of the form in being flatter and cut-off to an upright face on the outside.

It must also be noted that these rims are overfired, so that none can be proved to have been intended to be Samian ware. They might have been intended to be colour-coated, but are included here on the balance of probability. All were found in the filling of the kiln enclosure.

FORM CURLE 15

There are at least two rims of this form: fig. 45, 18 is fine ware; no. 19 is a waster which has lost its coating. The form occurs at Newstead in the Antonine period and was made at Rheinzabern; the example from Pan Rock (O. & P., op. cit., pl. LVI, 14) is of a different form.

FORM LUDOWICI TQ

These were very scarce. Fig. 46, 7 is drawn from about a quarter of a dish with matt coating almost like red paint. Another rim found in 1959, the coating fired brown, was from the lower filling of kiln 30, and another, vitrified, was from the lower filling of kiln 31.

FORM FORRER HEILIGENBERG PL. XIII, 6

Two fragments, perhaps of one rim, fig. 47, 19, resemble Forrer's figure. The ware is local, thick, and poor, with traces of a fairly good coating. The size was large, not less than 12 in. in diameter.

FORM DRAG. 44

There are fragments of between fifty and sixty vessels of local ware, and three imported rims. Our fig. 45, 22–23 are good examples of the local product. It is noteworthy that all fragments of this form are of good quality, the majority being really good ware with a fine orange-red coating. No. 22 is from the stone wall; no. 23 is unusually small and has a darker coating than usual. Another example, fine red, is shown in fig. 47, 18. Only two more fragments, both local, were found in 1959.

FORM WALTERS 81

Only a few small fragments were found. The largest is shown in fig. 45, 25, and is of excellent local ware; the

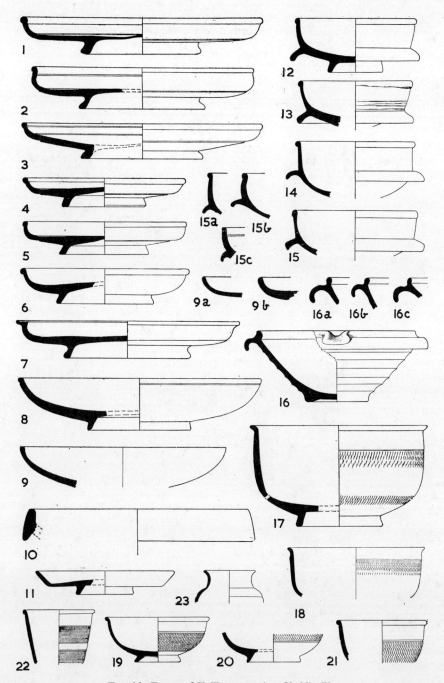

FIG. 46. Forms of Sigillata ware (pp. 80–83). ($\frac{1}{4}$)

same applies to a rim, burnt black, found unstratified in 1959.

FORM UNCLASSIFIED

Fig. 45, 24 illustrates a fine bowl with orange-red coating and resembling f. 44 without the exterior ledge. There is a fine sharp groove on the beading of the rim and another at the greatest diameter. The base, though not actually fitting, almost certainly belongs. Found scattered in the filling of the kiln enclosure. Another almost identical is fig. 47, 17.

FORM DRAG. 32

There are a number of rims of this form varying much in diameter and degree of curvature. All are apparently local. Fig. 46, 8 is a large example in soft, bright red ware (underfired) with no trace of coating. The rim is flat on top and has a groove outside. Compare *Niederbieber*, Taf. I, 5*b* and O. & P., pl. VIII, 3. There is another similar rim in hard ware, coating burnt brown and black. No. 9 has a similarly flat rim and is also underfired and without coating. Two shallower rims, both in good well-coated ware are shown, 9*a* and 9*b*; the latter was about 9 in. in diameter: another rim was found in 1959. Top layer, kilns 30 and 31.

FORM LUDOWICI TY

There were only two or three fragments. Fig. 46, 11 shows one from the kiln enclosure. It is underfired. Another larger rim, without coating, was found near the stone wall.

FORM DRAG. 38

The total fragments probably do not represent more than forty vessels, with the addition of one or two imported pieces. Four vessels and three rims are illustrated on fig. 46, 12–15 and 15 *a, b, c*. All are local ware of good quality, except 15*a*, which is not coated, and 15*b* which is poor. No. 13 is carelessly finished outside. Only two rims were found in 1959, one local, one imported.

There is a single fragment from an exceptionally deep and thin ledge like O. & P., pl. LXXII, 12, but larger, the ledge measuring 1½ in. from top to bottom in elevation.

FORM CURLE 21

The Antonine form of the mortarium with barbotined rim is sparsely represented; fig. 46, 16 is the only complete section obtained. It is of soft whitish ware, with good coating and might be either local or imported. Three other rims are given, 16 *a, b, c*, which

are local, some misfired. Possibly as many as ten vessels may be represented in all.

FORM DRAG. 45

One rim only was found, fig. 46, 10. The paste is very pale, the coating matt red, like paint (underfired). Diameter *c.* 10⅛ in. Found near kiln 19.

HEMISPHERICAL BOWLS, ROULETTED

For these see O. & P., pl. LXXV. They were not common, and it is noticeable that they are all in the very best local ware, which is really good, and the work is fine and neat. Fig. 46, 19 is the only complete section obtained. Nos. 20–21 furnish another base and a deeper form, compare O. & P., pl. LXXV, 1, Hadrianic; and Chenet, *Argonne*, p. 70, fig. 21, examples of second- and third-century date.

HEMISPHERICAL BOWLS WITH EVERTED LIP

These were scarce, and tended to be large and coarse in comparison with the preceeding. The rouletting is spaced in bands, and on the larger bowls is done with a very coarse wheel. Fig. 46, 17 is drawn from much of a large bowl from kiln 19; it is soft red, underfired. The base, which may not belong, is of good local ware with yellowish-red coating. No. 18 shows a smaller, thinner form with very fine rouletting in soft local ware. There are fragments of others, and an overfired rim like no. 17 was found in the phase IV floor of kiln 30.

CONICAL BEAKERS, ROULETTED

For this form see O. & P., pl. LXXV, 13–17. There were only one or two fragments, of which one is almost certainly imported. The other, fig. 46, 22 is of local ware, fired almost white, the coating reduced to a red paint.

BARREL-SHAPED BEAKER

Fig. 47, 11–16 represents these vessels, of which three fragments were found in 1933 and a fourth in 1956. There are four other fragments in the Museum, and a fifth was found in the rampart of the Town Wall in 1951.

This form is scarcely known in Samian ware outside Colchester. It does not appear in Oswald and Pryce. In other ware we find a single rim at Niederbieber (Oelmann, p. 42, Abb. 20, 1). That is colour-coated, and a complete example in Koblenz Museum, of the same fabric, is illustrated (ibid. 2). Another at Zugmantel (*O.R.L.* 8, Taf. XVII, 15) is decorated in barbotine.

The only one Oelmann can quote in Samian ware is *Zugmantel*, Taf. XIX, 36.

All the above are reduced in diameter over the parts which are horizontally grooved; two parallels for the smooth curve which our vessels display are illustrated by Oelmann, loc. cit. 3 and 4, but both are handled. No. 3, from a grave at Remagen, dated *c.* A.D. 100, has two handles. No. 4 has one handle, and I cannot see a reference to it in the text.

On fig. 47, 11–16 we illustrate the Colchester examples:

Fig. 11. Two joining fragments, one given by Mr. P. G. Laver, from 'Sheepen' (no doubt from our kiln-site), the other with no provenance. The ware is thin and brittle, but good, and fully comparable with the other rouletted Samian from our site.

Fig. 12. A base almost exactly similar, without provenance, again given by Mr. P. G. Laver and therefore local. The ware is brilliantly good and would pass as Lezoux ware, but it is obviously by the same hand as the last.

Fig. 13. Base of rather different character from the others, from the site of the Playhouse in St. John's Street. The ware is of continental appearance; the coating is a fine red with very high gloss, and there are only small splashes of it inside, whereas all the others are evenly coated inside.

On these three bases it is the highest part of the groovings which is sharp.

Fig. 14. Base found on our kiln-site in 1933, very good ware, which could pass for continental. A second base is identical, also from our site, but the ware has the usual rather brick-red appearance of our local ware, which it surely is. The two are clearly by the same hand.

Fig. 15. Base with no record; very good ware, of continental appearance.

These three bases have the grooves clear and sharp and the high-points rounded.

Fig. 16. Two fragments of one rim from our kiln-site in 1933. The ware is good with a matt coating, and quite certainly local.

VESSELS DECORATED IN CUT-GLASS STYLE

There are imported fragments of one or more of Ludowici form VSe (or similar), in the style of O. & P., pl. LXXVII, 4, and another fragment more elaborately decorated than any on that plate.

No fragments in local ware were found, but an elaborately decorated piece found at St. Mary's Hospital in 1935 seems to be of local manufacture.

FORM DÉCH. 72 AND SIMILAR

There are only two rims. One like O. & P., pl. LXXIX, 6 is in fine imported ware. The other, fig. 46, 23, is probably of local make. There is a groove on the shoulder. A third fragment has a double groove. The clay of these two is soft red with deep red matt coating. One or two bases also occur.

FORM WALTERS 79 AND 80

The great quantity of fragments of this form, in perfectly normal outline (as O. & P., pl. LVIII, 1, 5, 7, 8) and all sizes, is of some chronological importance. For this is without doubt a standardized form, the principal dated deposit of which has hitherto been the 'wreck' on the Pan Rock (*c.* A.D. 190). We may look for it in vain on the Antonine Wall, which was abandoned about A.D. 180. It does not occur at Niederbieber (occupied from A.D. 190–260), but is found at Rheinzabern and Trier. Oswald and Pryce describe it as of Antonine date, but much will depend upon the dates at which it was made at Lezoux, and these we do not know. However, six of the names given by O. & P. as stamping this form at Lezoux occur in the list of dated potters in Stanfield and Simpson, all working between A.D. 150 and 190, with a slight emphasis on the later part of this period.

The fragments include some good pieces of imported vessels—including a base stamped ADVOCISIO, found in 1959—but the majority are of local ware of various qualities and defects. Five complete sections are given, fig. 46, 1–5. No. 1 is from half a platter of good local ware from the kiln-enclosure; no. 2 is of good ware; no. 3 has a good matt-red coating, with rouletted wreath (found with no. 1); no. 4 is black, overfired and is stamped SENILIS FE (as are many); no. 5 is from the stone wall.

No. 6 we place here as rather a f. 79 without offsets than a true Drag. 18. It is in good local ware.

VARIOUS TYPES

Several fragments exist of a large platter or lid, with a foot-stand or cordon of almost round section, which does not look like a foot-stand. A fragment of another has an exactly similar cordon; the outline is otherwise nearly flat, so these are probably lids. The ware is good, local, but the coating is misfired a soapy chocolate-red (fig. 45, 26).

Fig. 45, 20 is the rim of a cup in fine hard local ware, related to Ludowici Bb and Bc, also to our form *Cam.*, pl. LIII, 53.

Fig. 45, 21. Cup in good local ware, variant of the same form, found at the Royal Grammar School; stamped by CUNOPECTUS.

There is also a single fragment, fig. 45, 9, of a thick incurved rim; good ware with rather thin and yellowish coating. The only parallel seems to be Haltern, Type 6.[1] This rim seemed local, and, indeed, three more were found in 1959, the best shown on fig. 47, 7 and 7*a*.

Fig. 47, 1–3 are from the ornamented rims of bowls of approximately f. 39. Nos. 1 and 3 may be from one vessel, and nos. 2 and 2*a*, with scored pattern, may be from another. A shattered rim of this form found in 1959 in the upper filling of kiln 30 is of local ware (fig. 47, 5). Since the diameter seems to be at least 18 in. it may come from an oval dish. No. 4 is the rim of a similar vessel, and no. 6 a small flat handle with scored pattern.

[1] Loeschcke, p. 145, Abb. 3, which is, of course, much too early for us.

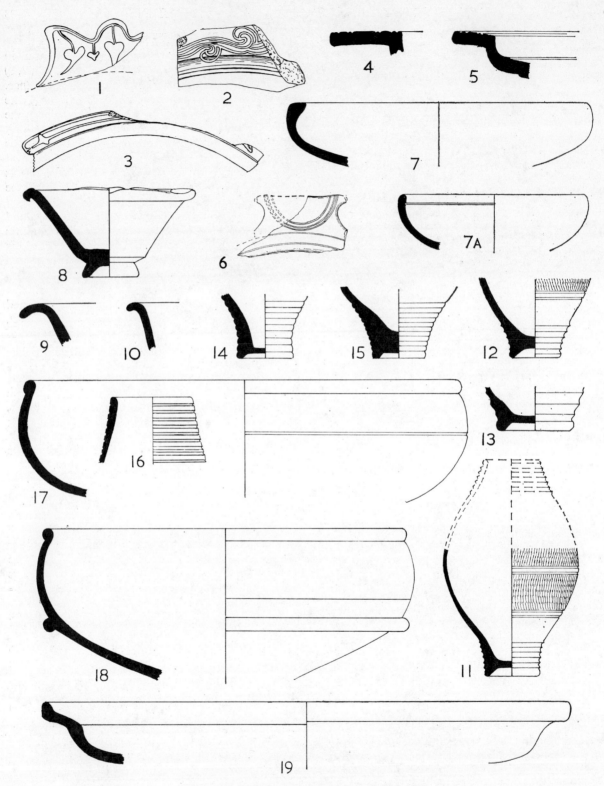

FIG. 47. Odd pieces of Sigillata (pp. 80–85). (½)

Fig. 47, 9, 10. Diameter 5½ in. and uncertain respectively, show that vessels of the type of Curle 23 were made here, though not in quantity.

Fig. 47, 8. Barbotined cup found at St. Mary's Hospital; local make; compare O. & P., pl. LIX, 12, from the Pan Rock.

POTTERS' STAMPS ON TERRA SIGILLATA

The great number of stamps found is made up chiefly of those, many times reduplicated, of the potters who undoubtedly worked on the site. There are also a certain number of stamps on imported ware and a few single examples of which it is not possible to state with certainty whether they are imported or local.

The local potters are identifiable (*a*) by the character of the ware upon which the stamps appear, (*b*) by their frequency. Usually a Colchester potter is at once recognizable by the number of stamps found, among which most are on spoilt ware. It will be noted that the stamps listed as certainly continental (i.e. imported) each occur singly. Doubt only enters when a single stamp occurs on pretty good ware which lacks the characteristic pinkness of the continental paste. In some cases the paste is so exactly like our local product that the name is included in the Colchester list.

In working over these names we have often been struck by the fact that so many which still evade reasonably close dating (we refer to those with such attributions as 'Trajan–Antonine' in Oswald's list), have a disproportionately high distribution in Britain as compared with the Continent. This may be largely due to inaccessibility of, or lack of, foreign records, but quite possibly may be due, in some part, to their having worked in this country.

FIG. 48. SAMIAN POTTERS' STAMPS
(**Colchester potter: † possibly Colchester*)

*1. ACCEPTVS.F There are 18 examples, all from the same matrix. Seven are on bases f. 18/31, with 'kick', and no rouletted band; 8 more are on bases of f. 33; another is on the outside of a colour-coated 'hunt-cup' with barbotined decoration, fig. 50, 1; a second and much better fragment of a hunt-cup with this stamp has since been found by Mr. Calver on the slope opposite the kilns; and an 18th is on the rim of a mortarium of f. 501B, fig. 64, 5. All those on red glazed ware are of local ware and none are overfired. It is noticeable that this potter did not stamp ff. 79 or Lud. Sb.

Oswald, p. 2, assigns Acceptus to Rheinzabern in the Antonine period and records 6 examples only, all ACIPTVS (save one from Arentsburg (ACCEPTVS.F)), Echzell, Mainz, Rheinzabern, Friedberg, Jagsthausen; but Ludowici, *Rheinzabern*, iv, lists four stamps ACCEPTVS F, and more, v, 207, 210. Even if there were any evidence that this is the same man as ours, there is no evidence for date in these locations other than 'pre-260'. It is peculiar that our stamp is not recorded previously in Colchester.

2. ADVOCISIO on f. 79. The paste is rather pale, but the

'glaze' looks like that of Lezoux. This potter worked at Vichy Lezoux (?), and Lubié. Dated Hadrian–Antonine by Oswald (p. 50) he is now more closely dated by Stanfield and Simpson to A.D. 160–90. This is a very common form of his stamp.

3. AISTIVI.M on f. 31. Lezoux, Hadrian–Antonine. Oswald, p. 6. The ware looks imported (Lezoux style), but the records have a remarkable British bias. This form of the name (AISTIVI.M) has 8 British records to 3 Gaulish, while a summary of all records gives 45 British (including 2 Pan Rock[1] and 1 Castlecary) to 19 continental. It is therefore not impossible that Aestivus worked in Britain (c. A.D. 150–90).

4. ALBVCI OFIC on f. 18 or 31, Lezoux. A.D. 150–90. Oswald, p. 11. The ware looks imported. But again the records are surprising. The exact form of the stamp does not occur, but the summary of all forms gives 92 British (including Birrens and Balmuildy) to 77 continental.

†5. AMANDIN Presumably Amandinus; only one stamp was found, on f. 33, with every appearance of being local ware. In addition to this the name is not previously recorded.

6. ARICI M on f. 33. Oswald's Aricus ii of Lezoux and Lubié, Hadrian–Antonine (p. 351). Omitting records beginning with OF as belonging to Aricus i, we have 14 British records to 7 continental.

†7. ATTI..S.FE Occurred only once on f. 18/31 which was built into the wall of kiln 15. There is hardly room for ATTILLVS.FE and no recorded stamp of Attillus ends with FE. If Attius is the name we are probably dealing with a Lezoux potter of the Trajan–Antonine period whose numerous records include 16 from Britain, none farther north than York and Wilderspool. The same form of the name occurs at London, York, Caerwent, Colchester, and Holt (f. 27!). Probably again two potters are involved. The ware of our example is not good, and may be of local manufacture.

8. AVNVS F in *tabula ansata*. There were at least two potters of this name. C. Aunus of Lezoux, Vespasian–Trajan, always wrote his name in the genitive (O., p. 35). Aunus ii is attributed by Oswald to Rheinzabern and dated Antonine. Our stamp is on a rounded base with a footring of square section and a glaze like that of Lezoux. It agrees with those of Aunus ii, two of whose stamps have been found at Wroxeter (O., p. 356). The lettering is remarkably large and fine, with careful serifs.

9. BELINICIM (retro) on f. 18 (?). Lezoux, Trajan–Antonine. The same stamp is recorded from Richborough, Wroxeter, London (4), and Newstead II (ours is much abraded, but seems a different and shorter matrix). Altogether there are 48 British records to 58 continental.

10. BORILLI.OFFIC on f. 33. This is Borillus i of Lezoux, dated Trajan–Antonine (O., pp. 46 and 371), but Stanfield and Simpson date him c. A.D. 150–90. There are 14 stamps recorded in this same form, of which 11 are British, 3 of them from Scotland.

11. (C)ASVRIVS F on f. 33. Lubié, A.D. 160–95. The beginning of the stamp is very lightly impressed and the C may just not have registered. The same form is recorded from London and Corbridge (f. 37) and from Compiègne, Lubié, and Saalburg. There are 14 British records (including Pan Rock) and 20 continental.

11a. CINNAMI (retro), f. 30 (fig. 44, 21) of Lezoux and Lubié, A.D. 150–90. There were also two fragments of f. 37 with the same stamp in pit C17 with the wasters. So well known as to need no remarks.

†12. CINTVGN.F Once only, on f. 18/31. The same form of the name is only recorded from Mainz and Zugmantel, but Ludowici, *Rheinzabern*, iv, records ten examples of

[1] If the Pan Rock find is really from a wreck the stamps should be counted as continental.

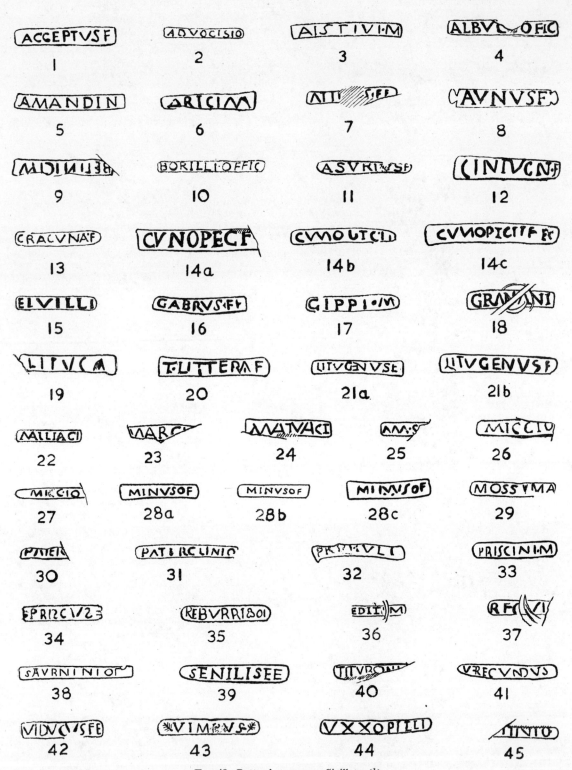

FIG. 48. Potters' stamps on Sigillata. (½)

CINTVGNATV in caligraphy like ours. The ware is typical of the Colchester fabric. Our man seems to have been of peripatetic disposition, for he is alleged to have worked at Lavoye, Ittenweiler, Heiligenberg, and Rheinzabern; and now possibly Colchester. Oswald, p. 78, dates him Trajan–Antonine.

13. CRACVNA.F f. 18/31, bordering on 31. He worked at Lezoux and Pont des Rêmes and is dated Hadrian–Antonine (O., pp. 93 and 378). This is the common form of his stamp.

*14. CVNOPECTVS (?). The 17 stamps are from 3 different matrices, but 4 are too fragmentary to identify other than that they cannot be a.

   a. CVNOPECF... (Large well-formed letters). Once only on f. 79. There is part of another (CVNOP...) probably from the same matrix in the Museum, without provenance.

   b. CVNOPTCII (N and P reversed). Thrice on f. 18/31 or 31; twice on f. 79; five times on f. 33.

   c. CVNOPICIIFEC (N reversed). Twice only, on f. 79 and f. 33.

   According to Oswald the stamp occurs twice at Kettering (CVNOFECTI and CVNOPECTE), which suggests that our potters' wares were marketed to some distance at any rate.

   The mortarium stamp CVNOPI (Colch. Mus. Rep., 1928, fig. 2, 5) may, on the analogy of what we have seen with Acceptus, be attributed with confidence to this same potter; see also the stamp (Roman Colchester, fig. 9, 1).

†15. ELVILLI Only once, on f. 33, possibly of local fabric. In support of this stands the paucity of his records, in which British sites predominate: Kettering, Littlington, Silchester, York, Cirencester, Corbridge, Margidunum, Wroxeter, Leicester, Richborough, Colchester (2), London, Westbury, but abroad only at Amiens, Bavai, Boutae, and Etaples. He is attributed to Lezoux by Oswald (p. 114) in the Antonine period, though no stamp is recorded from there, and he may have moved from there to Colchester, possibly with a stay somewhere on the way.

   Since the above was written Prof. Atkinson's Wroxeter Report has appeared. My account published in Germania was provisional, and I have, in this final account, revised my views on the names in the second group in Germania (rare names on 'clearly' local ware). My revision does not fit in with Prof. Atkinson's suggestion (pp. 140–1) that all names in the second group save one should be attributed to the Continent. This is due to the fact that they are ordered according to the nature of the ware. The two main groups were definitely on either local or imported ware; the third group in that report included those pieces of ware on which I hesitated to pronounce. If there was a place on the Continent which made ware indistinguishable from the local ware here, then several of our names would become very dubious.

*16. GABRVS.FE The 26 stamps of this potter are all from the same matrix. Twelve are on f. 18/31 and 1 on a flat base of uncertain form, 11 more are on f. 33. Like Acceptus, Gabrus did not stamp f. 79.

   In 1959 the most part of a Lud. Sb was found with this stamp, and a complete bowl of the same form was given to the Museum by Lt.-Com. Farrands; both are local ware.

   Oswald (pp. 129, 388) attributes Gabrus to Lavoye and Trier. His first 3 stamps listed for Colchester are all from our matrix and the total has since risen to 5; the forms are 33 (4) and Sb. There is as yet no evidence that our stamp, with only the middle bar to the E, has been found outside Colchester. GABRVS I from St. Albans stands alone. GABRVS.F is quoted from London and four continental sites. GABRVS from Ilkley and York, and at least 9 con-

tinental sites. A few less-certain stamps are added, all continental.

   This potter is well attested to the Hadrian–Antonine period, and if indeed there was only one of this name, we may set him down as a certain immigrant from Trier.

17. GIPPI.M on f. 33. Lezoux, Antonine. With the exception of G.IPPI at Bordeaux we have only (G).IPPIM with 6 continental records and GIPPI.M with 13 British (including Pan Rock) to 4 continental. There seems to be little evidence that he worked at Lezoux. Found west end of site C4.

†18. GRAN..NI (possibly Graniani). Once only, on f. 33. The break through the middle leaves a doubt whether to read GRANANI or GRANIANI, but GRANIANI is recorded from Cirencester, Cambridge, Southfleet, and Aldborough, and from Rouen, Riegel, and Vichy in Gaul. GRANANI occurs in London (B.M.), GRANA... at London, GRANIAN at Rouen, and GRAANIAN at Riegel. Oswald (p. 138) attributes him to Lezoux, although no stamps are recorded there, in the Antonine period.

†19. LIPVCA One example, form uncertain, on ware which may be local. Oswald, pp. 165 and 396, assigns him to East Gaul in the Antonine period. As LIPVCA F there are 9 continental records and 1 at Colchester; as LIPVCA simply there are 8 continental and 2 in Colchester Museum, 1 on local ware, both of the same matrix as this from the kiln. The form is 31. The name also occurs in Wire's list c. 1850.

*20. T.LITTERA F. There are 4 stamps, all of the same matrix and all on local ware; the forms are 79 (2), 31, 33. Another was found at the Colchester County Hospital, f. 31 (?).

   The stamp is not recorded previously. It is unlikely to be connected with the well-known Littera of Lezoux, whose period was first given by Oswald as Flavian and later amended (in the Appendix) to Flavian–Hadrian. Either dating is much too early for us.

   Nor is it likely that our Titus, who made mortaria, is to be connected with this stamp!

*21a. LITVGENVS F, length 25 mm., in small letters; five examples, all on f. Sb, or possibly twice on f. 79.

*21b. LITVGENVS F, length 32 mm., in larger letters; two examples on f. 33 and one on f. 31.

   The records of this potter were already more numerous at Colchester than anywhere else. Oswald (p. 166) records him from Bavai and Amiens, with MA or M. and LITVCIN (sic) from Bonn. To his one record from Colchester, LITVGENVS F (in the B.M.), is to be added another in his appendix, and two published in Colchester Museum Reports, 1929, p. 17, no. 16; 1932, p. 14 (our matrix a, complete). There is a third on f. 31, from the Hollytrees drain.

   Oswald hesitates, not without reason, to attribute this potter to Lezoux. He seems more certain of a Hadrianic date, which is on the early side for us.

*22. MALLIACI The one example is on a base f. 33 in local ware. Other records for Britain comprise London (several), and six other places, including Balmuildy (different matrix). The continental records are 22.

   Oswald (p. 180) places this potter at Lezoux in the Trajan–Antonine period.

23. MARCI... on f. 18 (fine). This name may be MARCIANVS (of which there were two) or Marcius, or Marcus (of which there were three). In the absence of facsimiles it cannot be identified.

*24. MATVACI There are 2 stamps reading MATVACI from one matrix, and possibly a third. The forms are 18, 31, and Sb.

   Oswald (pp. 196 and 404) places him at Trier and in the

Antonine period. The records are scanty and the readings varied. Most are from Trier, and all, except MATVCVS from Shefford, are from East Gaul.

25. MA.S... (Mansuetus ii) on f. 33. Lezoux, Hadrian–Antonine, Oswald (pp. 183 and 401). British records 26, chiefly London; continental 18.

*26. MICCIO.F There are six examples of this stamp, four on f. 18, and one each on ff. 33 and 38 (?). The matrix seems always the same; all are badly preserved and only one is complete. The matrix is not the same as at Heiligenberg or Blickweiler, but the caligraphy is similar. It is different also from the Newstead stamp.

This is probably Oswald's Miccio ii (p. 205), Trajan–Antonine, whom he assigns to Lubié. The stamp has been found at Alchester, Colchester, Crococalana, Newstead (II), Corbridge, Chesterford, Enslow, and Caerwent, and there are 11 continental records.[1]

27. MICCIO on f. 33. Oswald makes three potters of this name. Miccio i of S. Gaul, Flavian (?); Miccio ii of Lubié, Trajan–Antonine; and Miccio iii of Blickweiler, Heiligenberg and Reinzabern, Hadrian-Antonine. With an imperfect stamp and no facsimiles we cannot identify our man confidently. He should be from Lubié. Miccio ii has 26 British records (including Newstead II) to 31 continental. Miccio iii has only 4 British records, but 2 of them are from Colchester! Ours is not the same matrix as the Newstead stamp. See also Atkinson, Wroxeter, pp. 142, 170, 261.[2]

*28. MINVSOF There are 28 stamps of this potter, from three different matrices. All read the same, and are to be understood as Minuso fecit.

(a) The first matrix is 21 mm. long and appears on five bases of ff. 18 or 31 with high kick, and on the centre of a flat base possibly f. 79. It occurs seven times on f. 33, and, with the exception of one or two of these, always on bad ware.

(b) The second matrix is 18·5 mm. long and the M is square. All ware is comparatively good. The stamp occurs five times on f. 33 and ten times on ff. 18 or 31 (two of the latter are almost illegible).

(c) The third matrix is 22 mm. long, with slanted S and two dots (?accidental) under the centre. It occurs once only on ff. 18 or 31.

Oswald (pp. 206 and 406) attributes Minuso to Pont-des-Rêmes (Florent), and calls him Antonine, on what evidence he does not state. The records are very scanty and may be reproduced here in full:

MINVSO F f. 31 Mainz, Ruckingen, Trier, Zugmantel, 32 Zugmantel, 33 Mainz, Vechten, Andernach, Bonn.

MINVSO f. 31 London (L.M.), 33 London (B.M.), Rheims, Rouen.

MINVSSO Rheims.

MINVSA f. 37 Chester, Corbridge (MIN...).

MINVSV... Tongres.

MINVSO F ff. 18/31 and Curle 15, Trier, 32 Bonn, Trier, 33 Colchester, Bonn, Trier.

MINVSO f. 32 Trier.

MINVS... f. 33 Colchester.

MINVSVS F Colchester (May, Colchester, p. 216).

29. MOSSIMA on f. 18. Lezoux and Lubié. Vespasian–Hadrian. This same form of the stamp has not been previously recorded, but is the seventh record at Colchester. Altogether there are 50 British records, none of which is from Scotland. The continental records are many.

30. PATER . . . f. 33. This might be one of quite a number

of potters but the form and ware show that it does not belong to the time of activity of our site, so that there is no need to pursue a probably fruitless investigation further (site C4, east end).

31. PATERCLINIO f. 33. Lezoux, Hadrian–Antonine (O., p. 230). This same form of the stamp is only recorded once, from Corbridge.

32. PRIMVLI f. 31. This is Primulus ii, of Lezoux, Hadrian–Antonine. Apparently from the same matrix as at Old Kilpatrick (Miller, pl. XVII, A, 6). There are 11 other British records (including Pan Rock) and 13 continental.

33. PRISCINI.M on f. 33, Vichy, Trajan–Hadrian. The same form occurs at Ashstead, Carlisle, Littlington, London, Silchester, Chester, and at eight places on the Continent. There are 4 other British records and 6 continental.

34. PRISCVS f. 33. The glaze is foreign, and this can only be Priscus ii of Blickweiler and Eschweilerhof. Dated Hadrian–Antonine (O., p. 252).

*35. REBVRRI OF. There is one stamp only, on f. 33 in local ware. This is Oswald's Reburrus ii of Lezoux (pp. 259 and 415). The numerous records of this potter may be summarized as follows: Britain 42, Gaul 16, Holland 1, the particular form we have occurring in Britain 17, Gaul 7 times, and in Holland once. There is, therefore, good reason to believe that this potter migrated to Britain after working some time in Gaul. There are five examples of this same stamp already in Colchester Museum.

Reburrus ii is attributed to Lezoux and dated Trajan–Antonine by Oswald.

36. ...EDITI M on f. 33. Almost certainly REDITI M. Lezoux. Trajan–Antonine. Occurs in the same form at London, Cirencester, Corbridge, Melbourne, Wroxeter, York, Richborough, Colchester, Devizes, Mendip; British records 14, continental 15.

*37. RECVI... (?) One stamp only, on f. 33, local ware. The second and third letters are damaged by the inscribed circle, the rest of the stamp is missing. It is probably REGVLVS, for Regulianus of Lezoux (?) has only 5 records, all Gaulish save 2 at Wroxeter, and Regulinus of Rheinzabern is, with one exception (from Colchester!) only recorded from Gallia Belgica.

Regulus of Lezoux (?) has 20 British records, 16 Gaulish, and 6 Dutch and German. His date is given as Trajan–Hadrian, which seems early for us. Regulinus of Rheinzabern, Hadrian–Antonine, is another possibility.

38. SATVRNINIOF on f. 33. Saturninus i of Lezoux, Hadrian–Late Antonine. A very well-attested potter. See Oswald, pp. 283 and 418.

*39. SENILIS FE This was the most prolific of the Colchester potters. His stamps are all from one matrix and number over 50. There are 12 on f. 33, 6 on Lud. Sb, 7 on f. 18/31, and no less than 28 on f. 79. The stamp SENILIS FE was already twice represented in Colchester Museum (f. 33); the only other record is from Chesterford in the same county. All other records are from the Continent and are chiefly East Gaulish. SENILIS F (retro) from Rheinzabern may indicate that our man came from that direction.

This is Oswald's Senilis iii, Rheinzabern, Antonine (p. 419, an excellent correction of p. 292).

40. TITVRON(IS...) on f. 33. Lezoux, Antonine. This potter has a heavy British record; 47, to 18 continental. This is his fifth at Colchester.

41. VERECVNDVS on f. 18/31. Verecundus iii of many places in East Gaul, Trajan–Antonine. The name is very com-

---

[1] These are not necessarily all from our matrix.

[2] The two stamps nos. 26 and 27 are here handled quite

separately because the former is regarded as local and the latter as imported.

mon in Germany, but is only recorded from York and Richborough in Britain. This is not the same stamp as at Heiligenberg, nor Forrer, ibid., fig. 55, nor Blickweiler, nor Rottenburg, but the caligraphy is similar.

*42. VIDVCVS FE The only example is on a rounded base; the ware is local.

Oswald lists three potters of this name, but in the absence of the necessary facsimiles it is hardly possible to feel confident about the allocation of the stamps recorded. Among the many variations in the form of the name ours occurs but seldom and is placed under his Viducus ii, attributed to Lavoye and Pont-des-Rêmes (Florent) under Hadrian. The records are five only and show a stop before the FE, they are: f. 33 Rouen, Bonn, Neuss, and Groesbeek, Nijmegen. Other forms of the name, however, have been found in Britain in numbers, as well as on the Continent, except those attributed to his Viducus iii, who is allocated to Heiligenberg and Rheinzabern, Hadrian–Antonine. If we go by Oswald's list our potter is his i (Lubié, Domitian–Trajan) or ii, but this can only be decided by facsimiles, and it must be admitted that the caligraphy of our stamp much resembles that of Viducus of Rheinzabern, that is Viducus iii, whose date also suits us better.

*43. VIMPVS Again only one stamp is present, on f. 18 in local ware. It is from the same matrix as Blickweiler, p. 111, no. 30a (compare Eschweilerhof, ibid., p. 107, almost identical, and *Cat. Bingen Mus.*, Taf. 10, 11, 9a).

Oswald (p. 336) dates Vimpus, of Blickweiler and Eschweilerhof and Lezoux (?), Vespasian–Trajan, which is too early for us. Form 27 at Heddernheim and Heidelberg and 31 in Hofheim II and the earth fort at the Saalburg cannot be our man. Two potters are therefore stipulated and only facsimile stamps will enable us to distinguish them accurately. The form VIMPVS is recorded from London and VIMPVS F at Cirencester. There is a VIMPS reported from Colchester (not there now) and a VIMP... from Cirencester; otherwise all records are East Gaulish.

44. VXXOPILLI on f. 38 (?). Lezoux, Antonine. This is the first record of this form of the stamp in Britain. There are 15 British records to 25 continental.

45. There is also the following imperfect stamp. .....TINIO or ...SINIO on the plain band above the ovolo of f. 37. This is possibly PLAVTINIO. Lezoux, Hadrian.

The evidence of the following table for the date of our Sigillata industry and these potteries as a whole is at variance with that from other sources. The broken lines show the dates ascribed by Dr. Oswald, the firm lines the continuation of these which we may now regard as fairly certain. We have not presumed to carry on any continental name not found to be working at Colchester. Dr. Oswald has had to date widely, for chronological evidence in the second century is not so good as in the first. We find that these difficult names have, in many, if not most, cases, a greater incidence in Britain than on the Continent, and some at least worked at Colchester about A.D. 190.

Here we see that they certainly knew their trade—some of them at least had passed their apprenticeship, and must have come here from the Continent. Some

of their ware is good, but on the whole the local clay may have proved unsuitable. The adventure may have bankrupted them all, but it is much more likely that we shall find that this was not the only such enterprise

SUMMARY OF POTTERS' STAMPS

	Trajan	Hadrian	Antonine	Pan Rock
i. *Continental*				
Advocisus			———	
Aestivus		-----------	-----------	*
Albucius			———	
Aricius		-----------	-----------	
Aunus			-----------	
Beliniccus	-----------	-----------	-----------	
Borillus	-----------	-----------	-----------	
Casurius		-----------	———	*
Cinnamus	-----------	-----------	-----------	
Cracuna	-----------	-----------	-----------	*(?)
Gippus			-----------	
Mansuetus ii	-----------	-----------		
Miccio ii or iii	-----------	-----------		
Mossius				
Paterclinus			———	
Primulus ii	-----------	-----------		
Priscinus	-----------			
Priscus	-----------	-----------		
Reditus	-----------	-----------		
Saturninus i	-----------	-----------	-----------	*
Tituro	-----------			
Verecundus iii	-----------	-----------		
Uxopillus				
ii. *Colchester*[1]				
Acceptus			———	
Cunopectus			-----------	
Gabrus		-----------	———	
Littera			———	
Litugenus	-----------	-----------		
Matuacus	-----------	-----------	———	
Malliacus	-----------	-----------	———	
Miccio	-----------	-----------	———	
Minuso			———	
Reburrus ii	-----------	-----------		
Regulus (?)	-----------	-----------	———	
Senilis	-----------	---- ---- ----	———	
Viducus		-----------	———	
Vimpus	-----------			
iii. *Possibly Colchester*				
Amandinus			———	
Attius	-----------	-----------	———	
Cintugnatus	-----------	-----------	———	
Elvillus			———	
Granianus			———	
Lipuca			———	

that they, or others, undertook in this country, and that the date of their records, and of others similar to theirs (of which there are many in the pages of Oswald) will be considerably clarified by future discoveries, not

[1] The dating of Oswald for continental potters with these names is shown.

only in this country but in the neighbouring parts of the Continent.

Since the above was written Stanfield and Simpson's book on the second-century potters of Lezoux has appeared, and has produced some of the evidence we forecast. The only four names in our table which also appear in theirs (they only deal with makers of decorated ware) are Albucius, Borillus, Casurius, and Cinnamus, and all four are now known to have worked late. This is supported by the analysis of the imported decorated Samian, for all the potters who have to be considered as possibly concerned in the production of the vessels are now given similarly late dates by Stanfield and Simpson.

These potters who worked at Colchester can hardly have been active earlier than in Antonine times. The graph for such names as Malliacus and Miccio must be halved, unless we are to suppose more than one man of the same name. To what extent the same adjustment is called for in the case of the continental names is not yet clear, for these names may be survivals on our site. It is comfortable to observe that not one of the Colchester potters' names appears at the Pan Rock; quite properly, for if they worked here they could not be represented there, if that find was indeed from a wreck.

While the decorated ware only gives slight connexions with the Continent at Lezoux, Trier, and Blickweiler, the names of our potters connect with an embarrassing number of continental sites. More are attributed to Lezoux than elsewhere, but most sites are represented. This fact and the originality of the decoration, suggests that our firm came here from some intermediate site, possibly in the low countries or North Gaul, which has not yet been discovered.

'GINGERBREAD' MOULD (FIG. 49)

The object which we include here is exceptional; in the first place it must be said that it exists in the Museum with no number or any other identification, and that, while this undoubtedly allows that it may not have been found locally, the vast majority of our ancient pottery is of local provenance.

An illustration in the report on the Roman potteries of Buda-Pest—AQVINCVM first suggested the possibility that here we had part of what has been called a 'gingerbread' mould.

The object is part of a shallow, circular mould of a dark, sandy buff clay, designed to produce relief decoration on a disk. It is closely paralleled by much more complete examples found at Buda-Pest and Trier. I would expect to find that they are known in Gaul.[1]

The illustration, fig. 49, shows the negative fragment on the right and a drawing of the positive apposed on the left arranged to complete the diameter which was just under 5 in. The device seems to show a genius in a vineyard.

FIG. 49. 'Gingerbread' mould (right) and impression therefrom (left). ($\frac{1}{2}$)

There is nothing to connect this piece directly with our Colchester kilns, but it is at least worth recording that it exists.

COLOUR-COATED WARES

Fragments of colour-coated wares were found in very large quantities, not only in the filling of the enclosure but littered all around the site, and particularly associated with kilns 17 and 20. The quantity was no less in 1959, which extended the association to kilns 30 and 31. There were also several vessels from contemporary and later graves, and this discovery leads to reconsideration of certain vessels in the Museum. In addition there is an important deposit from the Sussex Road building site, which we will discuss below (see pp. 168–9). A most interesting deposit was found in the small rounded pit C 17, which was filled with fragments of overfired beakers, f. 391, the majority more or less vitrified, including several large masses consisting of piles of beakers which had collapsed and fused together as they stood stacked in the kiln; a good example is shown on pl. XVIII, c. There were no beakers of large size in this deposit, but there were a few fragments of over-fired Samian, and an important fragment of f. 30 stamped by Cinnamus (pp. 76, 85, fig. 44, 21).

It will be noted that painted decoration, such as

[1] Cf. now the Silchester mould, *Antiq. Journ.* xxxviii, 237–40 and pl. xxv.

white on colour-coated ware, does not appear. It is to be presumed that it had not yet come into fashion (in Colchester at least). Other similar negative conclusions may perhaps be inferred from this report.

Though quite a variety of forms were produced in colour-coated ware (in which, properly, Samian ware should now be included), some were produced in much greater numbers than others; the number of beakers of f. 391 represented by the fragments is so great that it cannot be accurately estimated. Certain differences are noticeable between the finds made in the two seasons' work: in 1933 we had colour-coated flagons, in 1959 scarcely one sherd, except those mica-coated, and these were very few. This fact is noted under each type or form where it occurs.

The ware varies greatly in colour and quality, but, as in the case of the Samian, this is due more to differences in firing than deliberate intention. There was, however, some considerable variation in finish and form. Some vessels show magnificent potting and design, among them some finished a fine shining black; others are a deep, slate-grey. These finer vessels commonly have multiple grooved bands among the decoration (e.g. figs. 57, 9 and 58, 3–5). Some of the smaller beakers (cf. fig. 58, 15) could be described as 'egg-shell' ware and are every whit as fine as the best of the first century (cf. *Camulodunum*, p. 228, sub f. 64). In all cases the colour-coated vessels are remarkably light in weight.

As in the Samian, under-firing can result in the ware being white, yellowish, or red, and as soft as blackboard-chalk. Correct firing produced as a rule a fine hard ware of brownish-red colour. The coating applied to this may be bright red, chocolate, dark chocolate to purplish-grey or even black. A metallic effect is sometimes seen, but is infrequent and probably accidental.

The decoration used included various forms of barbotine-work; rouletting; sanding or rough-casting; and the sides of the vessel are often 'folded'. Folding was not used (in these kilns) with barbotine or with all-over rouletting. Normally we deal with the decoration under each form of vessel in the description, but the barbotine decoration is of sufficient importance to demand a section to itself, which, also, can conveniently deal with some of the more remarkable objects which were found.

VESSELS DECORATED IN BARBOTINE
AND ASSOCIATED OBJECTS

There are several outstanding pieces which call for special notice:

Fig. 50, 1. A small fragment of a beaker f. 391, of good local ware, with a greyish-chocolate slip, almost metallic. Traces of barbotine decoration remain, and the impression of the normal Samian stamp of Acceptus is applied perfectly clearly just below the offset for the rim. So far this would appear to be the only known example of a signed colour-coated beaker. It is sufficient proof in itself that our potters made barbotined wares, and that those stamping Samian also engaged in other work.

Figs. 50, 2 and 52, 4. A single mould was found in the form of a stamp or punch similar to those used in making Samian moulds, but negative, i.e. for making a figure in relief. It is of fine reddish-buff clay with a light red surface. The shape is triangular, about $2\frac{1}{2}$ in. high by $1\frac{3}{4}$ in. wide. The back is convex, bevelled round the edges, and has a flat, tall, projecting handle. The face of the mould is concave, corresponding to the convexity of the back. The curvature would fit the bulge of an average sized beaker of f. 391 or 392.

The figure is that of a gladiator armed cap-à-pie, and is executed in exactly the same way as the impressions in the Samian moulds, with the same use of points for detail. The whole, however, is less sharp, though this may be due to wear. On the other hand, no example of this figure has been found on a piece of pottery, and, indeed no evidence that pottery so decorated was made on the site. If figures could be made in this mould and applied to vessels there would be finger-marks on the inside wall; moreover, the design on the mould includes bead-rows, which could not be transferred in this way. The only conclusion is that it was prepared for use and not used, or, possibly, prepared to order for another pottery and not sold.

A close parallel is afforded by a very similar mould, for a somewhat similar figure, found in the debris of the Louis-Linz Strasse kilns in Trier;[1] it is bigger (height $4\frac{1}{2}$ in.), equally curved to fit a vessel, and somewhat lacking in sharpness, like ours.

The purpose of a not dissimilar stamp or mould found at Gt. Bedwyn, but bearing a purely native scroll-device, has also not been ascertained; cf. *P.S.A.*, 2nd ser. xix, 188; *Wilts. Arch. Mag.* xxxv, 406, fig. 26; *Cat. Devizes Mus.*, p. 202, fig. 34.[2]

A vessel covered with figures in relief is illustrated in *Trierer Zeitschrift*, v (1930), 9, Abb. 6, and a small beaker in Colchester Museum has isolated stamped groups of small figures. No doubt a number of such examples could be collected, but we know of none bearing our stamp.

There is also a fragment of a large flat mould of fine reddish-buff clay, similar to the preceding, and resembling that of the moulds of potter B. The original shape is unknown; the piece is nearly $\frac{1}{2}$ in. thick, and has a lug or handle nearly 3 in. long and 1 in. high, projecting from the back. The figures,

[1] *Trierer Zeitschrift*, i (1926), 12, Abb. 11a and b.

[2] Wrongly here placed under North Wraxall.

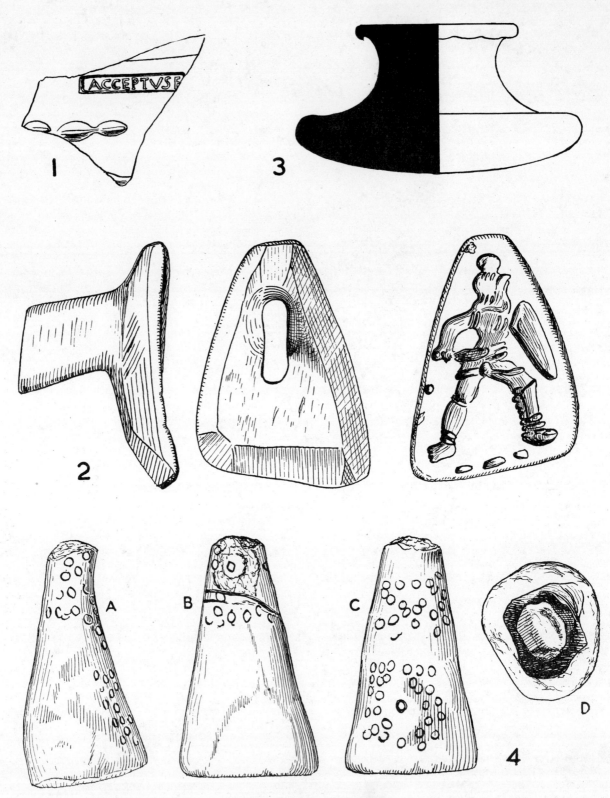

FIG. 50. Various small finds. (⅓)
(See pp. 85, 91, 108–9, 141.)

partly preserved, show a gladiator, which strongly resembles figures on fig. 51, facing a figure of which very little remains (fig. 52, 3). In this case there would appear to be less doubt that the purpose was to make figures for application to colour-coated beakers, especially those of the large variety such as figs. 51, 3 and 53, 8. Presumably such a process would only be employed in the case of elaborate products. The most outstanding of such vessels in the Colchester Museum are shown on fig. 51 and are described below. Many more could be collected: for example, there is a fine one from Colchester in the British Museum (Walters, M. 2479, pl. XVI) and another with phallic quadrigas (not, we think, made at Colchester) in Saffron Walden Museum.

Figs. 52, 1 and 56, 23. The most part of a small flagon of f. 156 was found in pit F on site C4 (p. 139). The ware is fine buff, with a thin slip coating varying from dark chocolate below to light red in the upper part. The handle was flat and three-ribbed. The body, unusually (?) oblate, is decorated with a barbotine band, which partly overlaps its double de-marking grooves. Below is a single line of applied scales. The three animals are well-executed in high relief, and it is unnecessary to point out their similarity in style to that of the other fragments here illustrated. A small fragment of another similar flagon, found close by, was the only evidence of any other similar vessels.

Fig. 52, 2. A large fragment of a lid, probably for f. 308, and if so perhaps the first to be recorded with barbotine decoration. Such lids are normally rouletted. The bear strongly resembles the Samian types 40 and 41; the stag also is familiar. This fragment seems overfired; the paste is very pale grey, and the surface purplish grey, resembling the mildly vitrified pieces.

Fig. 52, nos. 3 and 4 have been described above.

Fig. 52, no. 5. Several fragments of a beaker f. 392 in local ware; the decoration is in a different style from our other fragments and is unusually crowded.

Fig. 53, 9. The most part of a wide bowl f. 308 in thin, hard, dark grey ware, bearing a band of spirited animals alternating with trees, the whole executed with a charming elegance and freedom of style. The similarity in the drawing of the animals and trees to that of the motifs on the Samian ware is striking. This bowl has been restored but has no base. One or two bases found are *sui generis*, and one has been used to complete the restored drawing (fig. 55, 2). Fig. 54, 3–5 are from similar bowls.

On figs. 52–54 we show a selection from the fairly large quantity of local barbotined work. We have not as a rule chosen fragments of the normal scroll-work and hunt-cup type, but those which show more ambitious designs.[1] Taken in conjunction with other similar examples in the Museum collections they show that there is a comparatively unexplored field awaiting the study of these contemporary representations of Romano-British costume and pursuits. What is the strange appendage on the shoulders of the fig. 51, 4? How widespread is the use of points in the decoration to represent fur and feathers, as on fig. 51, 4, 5 and fig. 53, 2, 9? The large bird on fig. 53, 2 is out of the ordinary. The small feathers are indicated by points, the flights by continuous lines.

Only four or five fragments are from very large beakers like fig. 51, 3, 8 and fig. 53, 8, 13. In addition to figured barbotine there are over 100 fragments of beakers and bowls covered with overlapping scales (see fig. 58, 24, 25).

Fig. 53 includes a phallic piece (no. 1) and examples of the rendering of animals. No. 11 with animals in two zones divided by a bead-row is novel.

Fig. 53, 13, represents a number of fragments from a beaker f. 391 well fired and chocolate coated; it was found by Mr. Calver in 1955. The subject seems to consist of a single scene; the figures are placed in the lower loops of a large scroll of grape-vines. They are unfortunately marred by patches where they have become detached from the vessel. One figure stands out as the most important; he is bearded and wears a radiate head-dress, with crossed braces over his chest; with each hand he grasps either a branch or the scroll itself. We have remains of three of his companions, two of whom carry a curved stick or carnyx: both appear to have been bearded; one beard is long and pointed. Of the third figure only the head remains; the chin, though long, is smooth and the hair is drawn back into a bun: presumably therefore a woman.

The attention of all the figures seems to be devoted to the vines, which are laden with fruit. A curious feature is that the artist has gone to considerable trouble to show the leaves and tendrils on top of the limbs of the figures. This can only be to emphasize the fact that they are actually among the vines. It seems that we have a representation of a ceremony connected with the vintage—a most interesting ray of light on Roman Britain. The grapes are clearly by the same hand as those on fig. 53, 9, as are the leaves of the vines and trees on fig. 54, 3–5.

Fig. 53, 14 is a small fragment, nearly flat and very thick, from a vessel of great size; it is slightly underfired. To judge from the size of the arm, which is armoured like those of the figures on the Colchester vase (fig. 51, 3), the figure must have been about 9 in. tall. On the left we have possibly a fore-arm protected by bandages or wrappings, as on fig. 53, 8 and again on the Colchester vase.

The fragments shown on fig. 54 are all from the

---

[1] A normal hunt-cup, almost complete, is shown on pl. XX *b*.

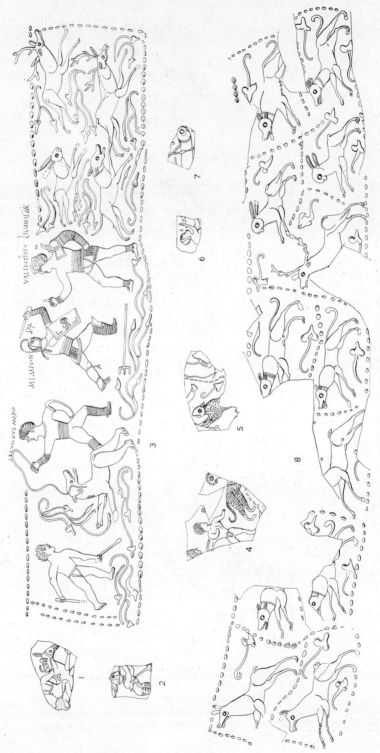

Fig. 51. Barbotine decoration (pp. 93, 96). (c ¼)

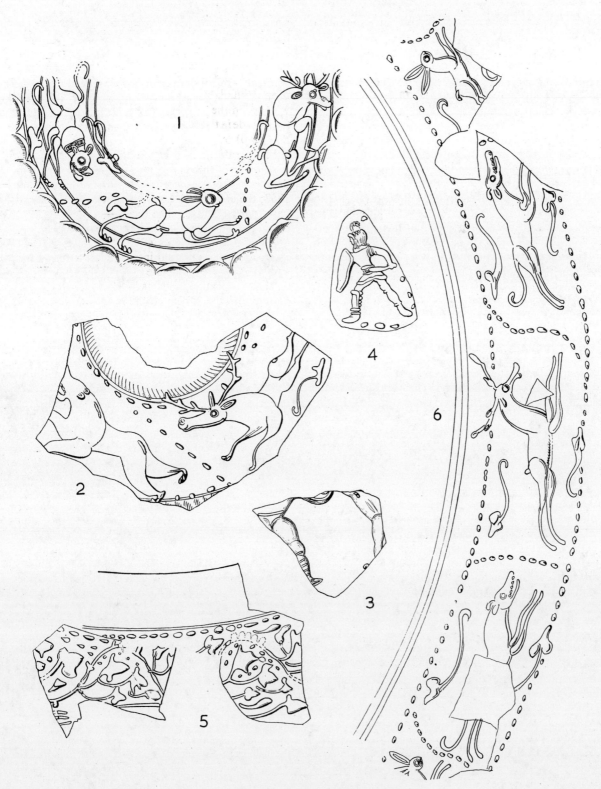

FIG. 52. Barbotine ware (pp. 91, 93, 102, 106). ($\frac{1}{2}$)

1959 excavations. No. 1 is new to us; it represents a few sherds of a large vessel of thick buff ware with a thin, matt-red coating with a simple, frilled rim and with slight remains of barbotined leaves and stalks on the neck. It drew attention to the fact that there were other fragments among the remains of heavy buff jugs which had had a similar red coating, which was very evanescent.

The outline of this vessel is unusual[1] and not paralleled on the site, so that we may fairly assume that most of the other red-coated fragments are from vessels of more usual form.

Fig. 54, 2 is a reconstruction of a beaker f. 392 in our local ware but with a much darker coating than usual, and with an almost metallic finish. It is perfectly made and must either have cracked in the kiln or been accidentally broken. It is decorated with phalli arranged horizontally in threes, each with a tail-like appendage. Other phallic sherds are shown as nos. 6–11.

Nos. 3–5 are fragments of another bowl like fig. 55, 2 equally fine and almost certainly by the same artist. There is another good fragment from a third bowl.

Nos. 12–16 are illustrated because we cannot determine what they try to portray. They are shown with the throwing-marks horizontal, but we cannot be sure which is the right way up. The device on them resembles most the sinuous curves of a sea-monster, but no fragment preserves enough evidence to settle the question.

Such is the description of the barbotined ware found and certainly manufactured on the site. In order to complete the picture the following vessels found in Colchester are described, for it now seems probable that they also are of local manufacture.

The *Colchester Vase*, displayed on fig. 51, 3, was found in grave 136[2] at West Lodge in 1848, accompanied by a T.S. platter of f. 36 exactly as our fig. 78, 1, a flagon f. 156 like our fig. 79, 9, and a mortarium of f. 501, like our fig. 64, 3. The f. 501 is a waster, and unfortunately is not stamped. The group is clearly contemporary with our kilns, from which all the vessels might have come save the Samian dish which looks like Lezoux ware. The Colchester vase is pre-eminent among these vases with human figures, but our potters have been shown to be capable of such work, and the ware, fine brown-red with dark purplish-chocolate coating, is not essentially different from the local ware. The decoration speaks for itself. The extension of the design has necessitated some dis-

tortion of the pattern, but this does not affect the individual figures. The inscription, which has received much attention in the past, reads SECVNDVS MARIO MEMNON SALVIIII VALENTINV LEGIONIS XXX. The fourth word may have been intended for SALVINI or SALVILLI. The thirtieth legion was stationed at Xanten on the lower Rhine, and the vessel could have been made in the Rhineland (cf. Ludowici, *Rheinzabern*, iii, 244–5) but equally well here, for the inscription is simply scratched upon it by the owner.

Another of these large beakers, fig. 51, 8, is without detailed history, except that it was found by Joslin in 1867; the colour is the normal chocolate-brown at the base, darker above. The decoration consists entirely of animals in panels, and could well be local.

Fragmentary remains of a third large beaker, fig. 53, 8, are of exceptional interest. The red-brown clay, with fine purple-chocolate coating, is probably local, and the decoration, with its hooded figures, is perhaps unique. It differs from all the ware so far described in the use of colour. The shield, harness, and breeches of the right-hand figure are picked out in white. So are the puttees and shoe of the leg on the left (top): so also the right leg of the dog behind and its teeth, while the rest of the dog is painted a light red-brown. The hooded figures, which seem to be shown as dwarfs, resemble figures of the *genius cucullatus*, and they seem to be pursued by an almost naked hunchback armed with a stick.[3] A small bronze in Trier Museum, figured *Coll. Ant.* iv, pl. xxiv is very similar to these dwarfs. The fragments of this vase were found from time to time in the grounds of St. Mary's Hospital, which seems to have been the rubbish dump of the Roman town.

Fig. 51, 2, 4–6. Four fragments from another beaker. The main figure is nude save for a loin cloth and a curious projection behind the shoulders which may represent a cloak. The attitude seems pugilistic. Others are represented by legs, one of which seems to have been breeched, and there are traces of a whip, as on the preceding and on no 3. The head on no. 4 has an interesting conical head-dress. The animals are of an unusual style, but the use of points to represent fur is familiar enough. The relief is high and no colour is used. The ware is brown-red with a purple-black matt coating. Found at the Essex County Hospital, 1924. Nos. 1 and 7 are isolated fragments.

Fig. 53, 12 is from a very large vessel in similar ware to the last, but very thick; coating purple-black inside and dark to light chocolate outside. In high relief are the horses of a quadriga and the hinder part of a bear.

---

[1] In some respects it resembles *Roman Canterbury*, no. 5 (1946–8) (=*Arch. Cant.* lxiii, 105), fig. 13, 59, brown, with cream or buff coating.

[2] May, *Colchester*, 293 and pl. xcii, 14.

[3] For the *genius cucullatus*, see J. M. C. Toynbee, 'Genii Cucullati in Roman Britain', *Collection Latomus* xxviii (1957), 456–69.

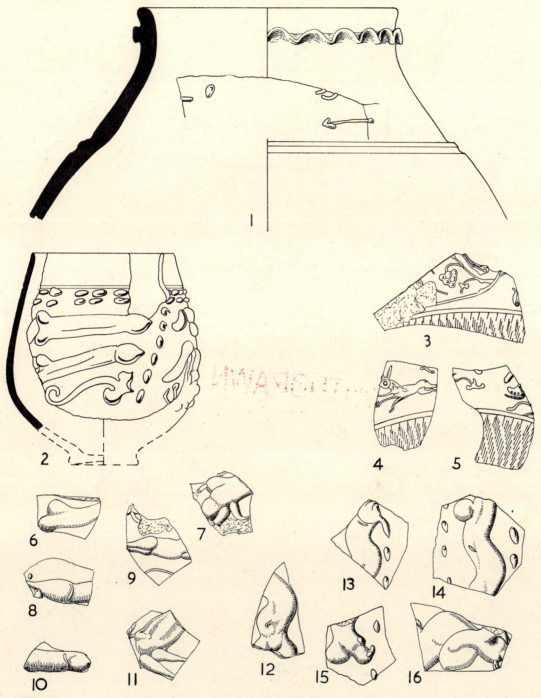

Fig. 54. Barbotine ware (pp. 93, 96, 102). ($\frac{1}{2}$)

The incomplete figure top right is unidentified. (Joslin Collection, Colchester.)

No doubt a lengthy list of such beakers with human and other figures upon them could be collected, beginning with the fine example in Saffron Walden Museum which shows four phalli yoked in a quadriga. The circles, presumably done with a compass, containing rouletted stars. The outside is surrounded by rouletting in lines like the ray-florets of a sunflower. The other is a fragment from an ovoid beaker with decoration of vertical and crossed raised lines applied to the surface. The style is fairly common on the Continent, and has

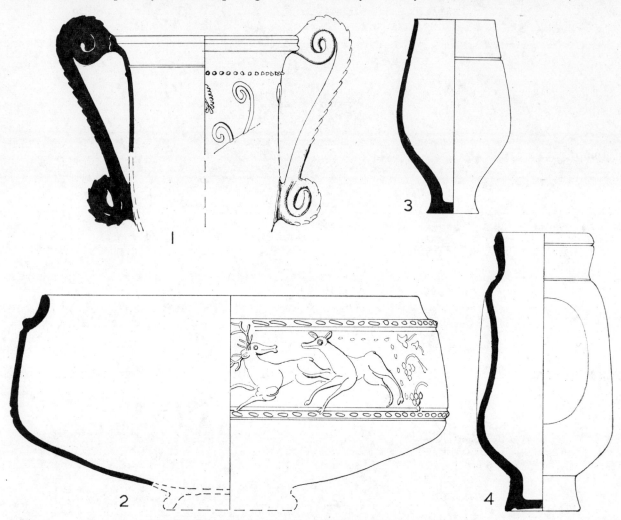

FIG. 55. Various colour-coated vessels (pp. 93, 98, 105–6, 140). ($\frac{1}{2}$)

subjects are nearly always gladiatorial or connected with wild-beast shows or hunting. It is worthy of note that allusions to Graeco-Roman mythology scarcely appear at all, for example, Hercules and Hesione on a Castor fragment.[1]

Before leaving the subject of decoration we have to mention two fragments which appear to be of local manufacture and which are exceptional. One, apparently from the side of a large beaker, is of reddish-buff paste with red coating. The decoration is of large

been occasionally found on fragments in Colchester (see also kiln 32, p. 169). In 1959 a very few fragments were found with decoration of barbotined straight lines and/or circles.

Finally, we have to describe the scanty remains of the very fine cantharus, fig. 55, 1. It is of thin, fine bright yellow-buff ware, with a brilliant, glossy black glaze, which has worn off all the high parts. The thin handle, of nearly round section, was coiled to a spiral at both ends, and its outer side decorated with overlapping

[1] Coll. Ant. iv, pl. xxiv.

scales. (This technique is found on some of our local handles.) The fragment of the lower spiral does not fit on, and its position on the drawing is conjectural. The decoration shows a floral scroll, with part of a rather elaborate leaf showing top left. The bead-row is small and carefully made. The rim is upright, grooved on the outside, hollowed inside, and there is a slight groove lower down. Two somewhat similar fragments were found near kiln 32 (fig. 96, 5, and 6 a–d).

These fine black-glazed wares require a historian. They seem to have come from Gaul, certainly from the Continent, and examples are scarce. I have seen a small fragment of a carinated vessel of this ware from Binchester. A bulbous beaker of this class is from Caistor-by-Norwich,[1] and resembles one from Ospringe, Kent.[2] The piece from Binchester was of the form illustrated by Reginald Smith, speaking of the Pan Rock,[3] from that site and from Bath, with references to examples found at Old Ford,[4] and at Hoo Street, Werburgh, Kent.[5]

There are two examples of this ware in Colchester Museum. One is a handled pannikin,[6] with a rosette stamp in the base. The handle bears moulded decoration. The other is part of a small, narrow, cylindrical vessel decorated with a very finely executed vine-scroll in high relief.

THE FORMS OF THE COLOUR-COATED VESSELS

FLAGONS

The cup-mouthed flagon, f. 156, already described p. 93, is unique in this ware. On the form see p. 124 below. Other flagons were not numerous, but the scanty remains are of great interest. There was evidence that mica-coated ware was made in kiln 17, in which fabric there are three general forms of flagons:

Form 361A. With short neck, fig. 75, 8, is certainly of local make, but may not have been made in these particular kilns, for all the necks found are longer, though the ware is the same. It is in the Joslin Collection (no. 618). B, Probably quite similar, but with taller neck (fig. 56, 1–4).

We illustrate four necks, which show that the form is a copy of the bronze flagons such as that which contained the hoard of *denarii* and *Antoniniani* deposited A.D. 231–5.[7] The body was probably oblate, as in the prototype. The neck is long in comparison with A and

carries a pressed-out cordon without any offset from the shoulder. The lip, masked in the drawings by the spout and handle, is usually simple, but fig. 56, 1 has a double groove. The spout is the outstanding feature. In the original it is tubular and there is a hinged lid; in the copy the spout is semi-tubular and the lid is not attempted. A single fragment from the top of the handle found in 1959 has the two upstanding lugs representing the hinge of the lid. Red ware, probably intended to be mica-gilt.

Fig. 56, 1 is of sandy red ware with brown, micaceous surface, and there is another similar; no. 2 is of brownish ware and lacks the mica-coating; no. 3 is of sandy red ware with brownish surface with no mica; no. 4 is a neck found in the Roman town at the back of Sander's premises in Pelham's Lane. It is of hard red clay, fine ware, beautifully mica-gilt. There can be no doubt that those without the mica are wasters. The handle seems to have been fairly thick and broad, of D-section without grooving or ribbing.

Form 362A. A complete vessel is shown at fig. 75, 4. It was found, no doubt in a burial, in Creffield Road in 1906. It is in the same ware as the preceding, and no doubt local. The rather unusual shape suggests that the bodies probably varied as much as the necks which we are able to illustrate. The handle is three-ribbed (others are two-ribbed), and the base has four sharp concentric grooves inside the footring.[8] Another such base was found in 1959 (213) with a rim like our fig. 56, 6. These bases imitate the turned concentric rings under the bases of bronze vessels.

The fragments found are illustrated by several necks, fig. 56, 5–8, all from trench C28: another was from pit B, site C4. No. 5 was an attempt at a thin and elegant flagon which became badly distorted in firing. The clay is the usual sandy red-brown with a fine mica-coating. The widely spreading mouth has a groove inside the top and two grooves outside the rim. There are two more grooves at the shoulder, but that part of the neck which might have carried the cordon is missing. This is from kiln 17B. There is no doubt that the prototype is again bronze and must have closely resembled the fine flagon from the Bartlow Hills.[9]

No. 6 is of fine red-buff ware with mica-coating. The outline has been adapted to the clay medium. The handle is two-ribbed. No. 7 has a rim nearer the original but lacks the cordon. The ware is the same and the mica-coating good; handle of squarish section, two-ribbed.

[1] Atkinson, in *Norfolk Arch.*, xxvi (1936,) T. 4.

[2] Whiting, *Ospringe*, pls. xv, 123, lvi, where further references are given.

[3] *P.S.A.* (Ser. 2) xxi, 273, fig. 1.

[4] *Trans. Lond. and Middx. Arch. Soc.* iii, 207, pl. vii, 4, 13.

[5] *Arch. Cant.* x, 75.

[6] *Roman Colchester*, fig. 66, 83. These and others have now

been published by Miss G. Simpson, *Antiq. Journ.* xxxvii, 29–42 with pl. xiii, 35.

[7] The bronze prototype was also probably of local manufacture, for remains of similar necks have been found more than once locally.

[8] Compare *Niederbieber*, Abb. 27, 19a, e.

[9] *Arch.* xxvi, pl. xxxiv.

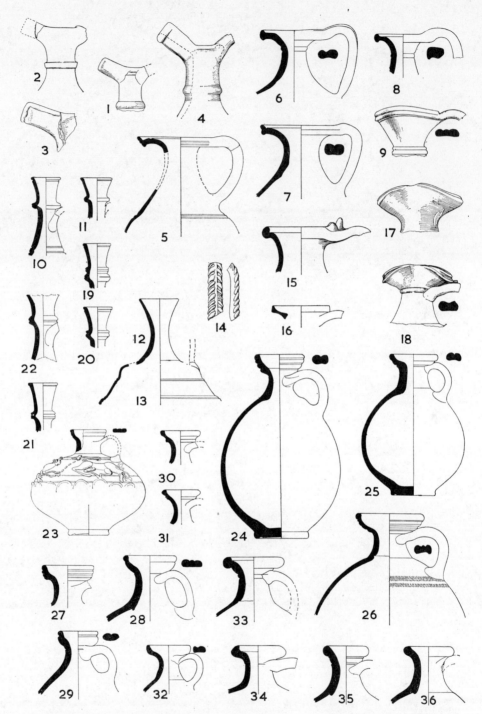

FIG. 56. Flagons of colour-coated and coarse ware (pp. 93, 99–102, 124). (¼)

No. 8 is similar to no. 6 but much smaller; the ware is the same. The handle is squarish in section and smooth on the outside. The other, from pit B, site C4, has a handle of rectangular section with four ribs and a wide central furrow.

Form 157. Fig. 56, 9. Flagon with short, cordoned neck, pinched at the top to form a spout. Found in pit A, site C4, and there is another handle from the filling of the kiln-enclosure. Ware and coating the same as the preceding (and f. 362A above). Cordon double and lip triply beaded. The handle is three-ribbed. A complete vessel cannot be quoted, but one from the 'Mithraeum', with a coin of Constans, is not very different, and, though thicker, is of the same or similar ware.[1]

The remaining fragments of this ware are not significant. Two more handles (plain), and a base with careful concentric grooves beneath cannot be assigned to definite forms. Fragments found in 1959 include several handles, plain, or with two or three ribs, also ornamental and severely plain bases, but add nothing to what has been said.

A Celtic origin for mica-gilt ware has already been suggested by Loeschcke (*Haltern*, p. 286) and May (*Silchester*, p. 114). It is confirmed by the presence of two magnificent flagons, f. 131, in a pre-Roman grave at Colchester (*Cam.*, p. 13, note 5, no. 1, with references). Approximately contemporary would be the gilded lip and shoulder of f. 114. Mica-gilt was also early in use on ff. 41, 95, 102, 166, and no doubt, others. Those mentioned were imported in Claudian times, but the two flagons can hardly be regarded as imports. At any rate the technique was soon in use with potters of the Roman period and continued so throughout. In the first century we find f. 17 occasionally mica-gilt (see p. 107 below), also the bowls resembling mortaria, f. 312, and spouted strainer-bowls, both of which last into the second and even third centuries. The late period is well furnished with this ware, from the time of our kilns onward, in the flagons of ff. 361–3, 366, and beaker f. 391.

There were two techniques, and both seem equally early. In one the clay is white, and the mica is laid on an under-coat of yellow or reddish paint (ff. 114, 166): in the other the clay is burnt to a reddish buff and the mica laid directly upon it, or on a scarcely perceptible reddish slip (ff. 41, 95, 102, 131, and all the later forms). The aim was, of course, to imitate bronze. In order to secure the fine surface the clay is usually very finely levigated. The gilt and polished surface must have been a fair representation of golden bronze. Occasionally a poorer clay was used (e.g. f. 366, with coin of Constans). Failures in firing became an unpleasant red-brown, and either lost their mica, or, if

wasters, never had it applied. The total fragments, though many, were not numerous in comparison to other wares. Though mostly from various flagons, besides f. 391 there were two rims of bowls, fig. 73, 28–29, and various bases, probably of flagons, some offset, plain beneath, others beaded with concentric grooves beneath, some incurved to a quite plain base. There was also one rim of f. 38, and one resembling f. 305. Most of these fragments came from kiln 17, where they were certainly made.

Form 363 (fig. 56, 10–11). Flagons in the more familiar colour-coated ware were well in evidence, but the remains are very scanty. There are 200 fragments of thin, fine red ware with a bright red coating which, in the best pieces, is very good, strong, and resembling samian in appearance. The colour frequently runs off to brown or nearly black. This is probably accidental in the firing. Sometimes the interior surface is a dark chocolate colour, exactly as the beakers of ff. 391–2, &c., but nearly as often it is the natural red of the clay.

None of these flagons could be restored. This is partly due to their brittle nature, but chiefly to the fact that nowhere were large fragments of any one vessel found together. It is clear that none had been made very recently when the works closed down. The only possible parallels in the Museum are certain flagons found in the lowest level of the 'Mithraeum' in 1929, with a coin of Constans, but these are not of proved local manufacture.

The ware is almost identical with that of a remarkable series of flagons which is undoubtedly local, but later than those from our kilns. Apart from the very distinctive forms (360, 364–5, 368) and treatment of the base, this series is distinguished by the red surface, which seems more closely united to the paste and really closely resembles the fine *terra rubra* of the first century. When picked up still moist it is easily mistaken for samian.

Nos. 10 and 11 are the only two necks which could be drawn. It will be noted that the mouth is wider at the top and has a groove at the lip. The ledge of no. 10 is grooved and there is a double groove on the long neck. The handle seems to have been long, and in this respect they differ markedly from the red-polished series. The bodies seem to have been oblately globular (below the long shoulder), on well finished, beaded bases, sometimes with a footring beneath, sometimes flat. About one-eighth of the body-fragments bear narrow bands of rouletting, but some of these could belong to beakers. The shoulder may be plain, or slightly cordoned, or curiously shaped as no. 13 below. It is important to note that not one recognizable fragment of these flagons was found in 1959.

[1] *Roman Colchester*, fig. 62, 46.

Form 364 (fig. 56, 12). Flagon with simple funnel-form mouth. The figure, set conjecturally upon an unusual shoulder (13), represents three fragments, none of which shows the position of the handle. Other examples in the Museum are not so wide at the top and are shorter. This neck, like most of the previous form, has a small air-vent at the base necessary to the very small opening.

A damaged and worn neck of this form is of almost white ware with a thick yellow-brown glaze, resembling Saint-Rémy ware, which indeed it may be, for it was unstratified, some distance from the kilns. On the other hand, it has the very narrow opening of these late 'oil-flasks'.

No. 14 is a handle with raised chevron pattern and central ridge; local ware with purplish-black coating. It is not known what form of vessel it represents, but compare the crater, fig. 55, 1.

BEAKERS (FIG. 57)

Forms 391 and 392. The larger, barbotined examples of these forms have already been described (pp. 93–98). The great bulk of the other fragments were the commonest colour-coated vessels on the site, possibly the most numerous of all types. The forms show little variation, except in size and decoration and in the firing. When correctly fired the clay is fine, thin, with only a slight gloss, and rarely or never highly metallic. Misfiring may make the clay soft and powdery or vitrify it to a purple-grey. More than a barrow-load of such vitrified fragments was found in pit C17. They are indistinguishable, except by form, from similarly over-fired samian vessels—a point worthy of note. The largest lumps of fused vessels were all of these forms (391–2), collapsed in stacks in the kiln (pl. XVIII, *c*).

Owing to the enormous mass of the fragments and the general similarity of the vessels it has scarcely been possible to piece together any of them, but several were found nearly intact in the entrance of kiln 20.

Form 391. 'Bag-shaped beaker' with cornice rim; the greatest diameter in the lower half of the vessel. Fig. 57, no. 1 is from the entrance of kiln 20. It is a waster only in colour, the coating having misfired a purple-black mottled with natural red. The rouletted bands on the body are typical of hundreds of examples. No. 2 is a similar beaker from near kiln 22, obviously a waster and very distorted. This accounts for its apparently shorter foot. No. 3 is a restored example from kiln 17. The ware is good and the coating a chocolate colour. The fine, sanded rough-casting is typical of the vast majority of the fragments. No. 4 is another restored example found around kiln 15, with dark chocolate coating. These were also occasionally made in mica-gilt ware (three rims from kiln 17 and one from kiln 24: none found in 1959).

On fig. 58 we show further examples found in 1959. No. 1 illustrates a few small fragments of a vessel decorated with small pointed dots, the only one of its kind. No. 2 is a scaled example with dark, purplish-chocolate coating. Nos. 3–6 illustrate the very finest vessels, very carefully made, with thin walls and fine rouletting divided into bands by double grooves. No. 3 is thin hard dark grey. No. 4 is thin hard dark red-brown with dark chocolate-brown coating. No. 5 is particularly fine ware, the surface a shining black. No. 6 is red-brown with black coating. No. 7 is a barbotined example (displayed fig. 52, 6), misfired, the paste orange-buff, with a chocolate slip. No. 8 shows another style of rouletting, the commonest, not using grooves. The paste is red, the chocolate coating almost metallic. Nos. 9–11 are typical folded and sanded beakers, representative of hundreds of fragments. Nos. 13 and 14 represent the smaller beakers, and show a difference in body-proportions. No. 16 is representative of a very few fragments bearing 'chess-board' rouletting.

Form 392. 'Bag-shaped' beaker with simple rim, diameter as f. 391. Though not uncommon this form is not present in such large numbers as 391, and it is rarely found with barbotine decoration.

Fig. 57, no. 5 is a complete example from the entrance to kiln 20 and is rough-cast. No. 6 is an over-fired waster, with surface purple-grey and quite smooth, not even rough-cast. No. 7 is another waster from kiln 22; the coating is dark chocolate-purple.

Later discoveries, besides the phallic pot shown on fig. 54, 2, are illustrated by fig. 58, 15, which is inserted as an example of the many small examples made so finely that the term 'eggshell ware' could fairly be applied to them. They may be sanded or smooth, usually the latter. The coating is chocolate to nearly black.

The history of these forms has been discussed by Wheeler in *Trans. Essex Arch. Soc.*, n.s. xvi, 24, on the evidence of continental finds. Since then evidence has piled up to show that whereas on the Rhine these forms already appear with unworn coins of Nero, Domitian, and Nerva, in Britain we have an unbridged gap between the disappearance of f. 94 and the appearance of ff. 391 and 392 which happened about A.D. 120 (*Halt-whistle Burn*, pl. v, 7; *Poltross Burn*, period I, pl. III, 25; *BirdoswaldTurret*, pl. XVI, 7 (a tall example in period I); *Throp*, pl. XXVI, 7, &c.; and examples at Brecon Gaer, Segontium, and Wroxeter fit in with this dating). I know of no definite record of these forms in the period A.D. 100–20. All records before 120 are ascribable to f. 94, e.g. *Newstead* type 31 and *Richborough*, i, 12.

From their inception the forms gained popularity very quickly and there is no doubt that their production reached its height from the middle to the end

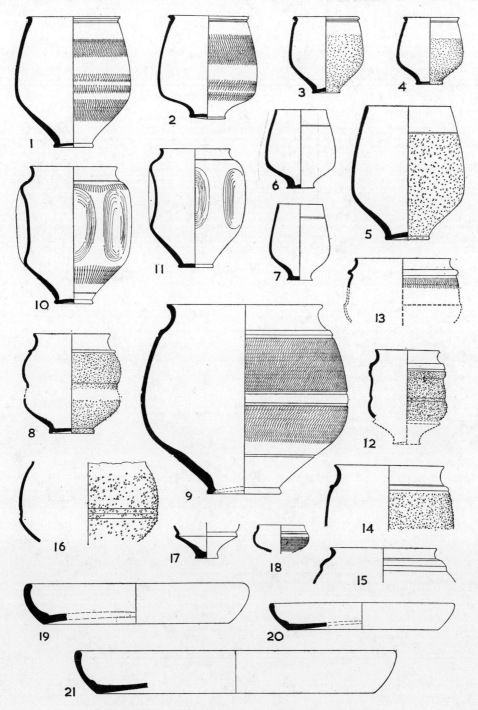

FIG. 57. Colour-coated beakers and platters (pp. 102–7). (¼)

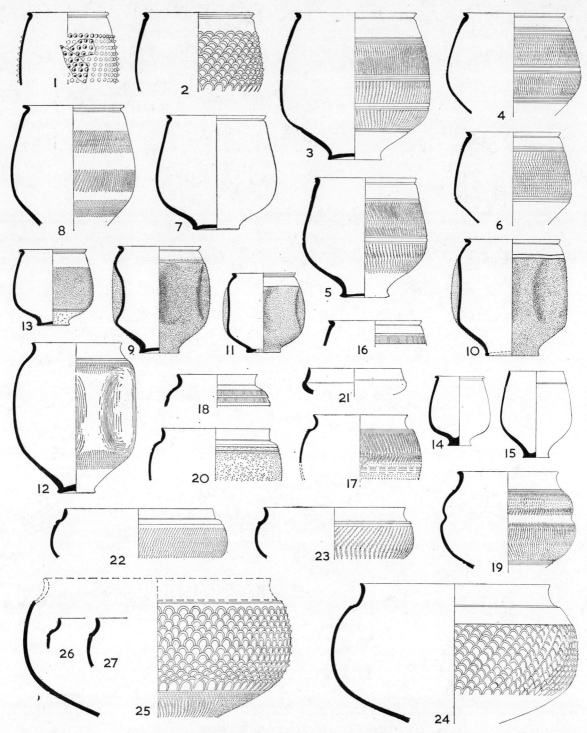

FIG. 58. Colour-coated beakers and bowls (pp. 93, 102, 105). (¼)

of the second century, but f. 392 continued to be popular (as observed by Oelmann, *pace* Wheeler, his sub-type 30*b*, *Niederbieber*, pp. 38–39) through the third century, and is still found here in the first half of the fourth century.

It is clear also both from the continental evidence already adduced, and from indications in Colchester, that both squat and taller forms (A and B, but not C) were evolved almost equally early. The squat form disappeared first. The tall form developed, in some cases, almost a carination where the lower part joins the upper (C). This is not noticeable in the mid-second century, becoming marked in the tallest, f. 391. It may prove to be a late second- and (early?) third-century characteristic, but it has disappeared in the fourth-century layers of the Mithraeum. Fig. 55, 3, a very tall example in plain orange-red ware, from site C4, could be of much later date than our kilns.

These beakers may be either fluted or not, both being common.

Form 396. Globular beakers with upright, simple outcurved rim.

These are much less common than the preceding. Ware and finish are exactly as before, but the decoration is nearly always rough-cast, rarely of applied scales. None could be restored but one was found complete, fig. 75, 7, and we figure a variant fig. 57, 8, which we call 397, with a constriction round the middle. It is of thin blue-grey ware (misfired) with dark red to brown coating, from kiln 18. This type of rim frequently goes with a double groove or false cordon on the shoulder. A pronounced cordon sometimes occurs on more pretentious examples.

Fragments of these rims were quite numerous, but the majority belong to beakers of fluted pattern like ff. 406 and 410 below. The reverse was the case in 1959 when fluted vessels with this rim were very scarce; we show one, fig. 58, 12.

There are many fragments of one of very large size, decorated with rouletted bands divided by double grooves (fig. 57, 9). Some of the smaller ones were similar.

In 1959 we found 'chessboard' rouletting on this type, fig. 58, 18, and some other interesting pieces are shown on fig. 58, nos. 17, 19, 20.

Form 397. Beakers with simple outcurved rim like 396, the body constricted several times, usually becoming more or less cylindrical thereby.

These were not at all numerous, nor are they generally so in Roman Colchester. We show seven examples, fig. 57, 8, 12–17, but of these nos. 13, 14, and 16 are quite exceptional. No. 14 is from kiln 17. These show great variety of outline. No. 12 is approximately standard. It is of thin, soft ware, rough-cast, from the kiln-enclosure. No. 17 is a base, not rough-cast, which

has been used in the restoration of no. 12. It has a very fine groove under the foot. No. 13 is a fine rim-fragment with black coating; the part indicated in broken line is taken from other fragments which seem to belong to the same vessel but do not fit. It is from kiln 17, where other similar fragments of unusual outline occurred, but which are not large enough for reproduction. Fig. 58, 19 is one of Mr. Calver's finds (1956), soft red ware with fine chocolate-black coating. Fig. 57, 14–16 are unclassified, all from kiln 17, and of thin red ware, red coated; 14 and 16 are rough-cast. There are a number of rims, bases, &c., in small fragments, which come from similar beakers.

Form 406. Tallish beaker with simple rim, like those of the preceding forms, the sides fluted.

Though actually the folded form of 396, these vessels are all taller, and many of them are rouletted below the folding exactly as in ff. 391 and 392, with a narrow rouletted band on the shoulder. Rouletting never occurs on the numerous rough-cast examples. Fig. 57, 10 and 11 represent a great quantity of fragments. The former is misfired, the purple-black coating peeling off the soft red clay. It was built into the entrance of kiln 20. Probably more than half the fragments were of similar dimensions. No. 11 shows a smaller beaker; fig. 58, 12 is from the 1959 excavations (pit 13).

This form was numerous in kiln 24, and it has a long life, in which it changes but little.

BOWLS

Form 308. Figs. 57, 18; 58, 22–27; 59, 1 and 2. Wide bowl with sharply inbent shoulder and upright rim. A well-known and widespread form, which, in its general outline and its possession of a large lid, is reminiscent of the popular and handsome bowls of the end of the pre-Roman Iron Age, f. 253. They are, however, much smaller and more fragile than these.

The form is a wide bowl, the foot of which, in our kilns at least, is indistinguishable from that of other colour-coated vessels. The chief feature of the body is that the sides have a more or less straight and vertical portion which is usually rouletted all over. Above this the shoulder bends in at a right angle and then again upwards to form the simple rim. This rim, with us, may be straight and slightly inclined inwards or thin and curved outwards, cf. figs. 58, 21–27; 59, 1, 2. Below, the wall is usually roundly curved, but (rarely in Colchester) may occasionally be carinated (Corbridge, *Arch. Ael.*[3] viii, pl. 12, 63). There was but one carinated example in the finds of 1959.

We have quite a number of recognizable fragments, but since the rouletted wall is slightly curved, fragments are not always distinguishable from those of beakers. None could be restored, even in a drawing.

So fragile are these vessels that we cannot produce a single drawing from the large collection in the Museum, though the form is common enough in fragments.[1] The Colchester lids are distinctive (fig. 59, 6–13), wide and flatly conical, with a stout, vertical rim and a beaded, grooved knob; they are usually rouletted in bands divided by deep grooves and/or

The elegant barbotined vessel, p. 145 and fig. 79, 3, is an exceptional example of this form. Another exceptional vessel is fig. 57, 18, in our usual local ware with dark chocolate coating.

LIDS

The colour-coated lids are of two distinct forms.

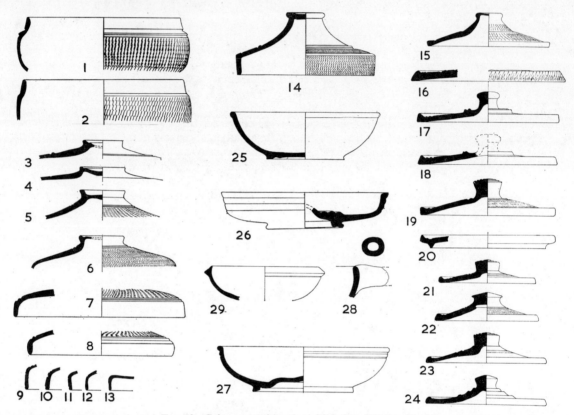

FIG. 59. Colour-coated bowls and lids (pp. 105–7). (¼)

cordons. The sections shown (fig. 59, 3–5), all rouletted, may equally well have belonged to the centres of lids or the base of bowls.

The lids attributed to the Castor potteries are of different form, larger, and better made. They were common also in Colchester, but only one lid in that fabric was found on our site (fig. 59, 14).

Form 308 does not appear to have been found on the Antonine Wall, but must have appeared about A.D. 180, if not earlier. But, as May remarks, *Colchester*, p. 161: 'The ware is very brittle and generally appears in small fragments which are often unrecorded.' (For the form see Artis, *Durobrivae*, pl. 49, 4; May, *York*, p. 43, pl. XI, 9; Walters, M.2732; *J.B.A.A.* iii, 331. It was not so popular on the Continent, Oelmann, *Niederbieber*, type 105.)

Those belonging to f. 308 have already been described. They vary greatly in size. Besides fig. 52, 2 and fig. 79, 3, there are two other barbotined fragments. Most of the fragments show a double groove round the central boss and again at the curve of the rim. The space between is rouletted. There may be other grooves on the outer face of the rim, which is only once rouletted.

The other form of lid is not so familiar, and we cannot say for what type of vessel it was intended. The diameter does not as a rule exceed 6 in. The best examples are shown on fig. 59, 15–24. The knob is very prominent and solid, sometimes with a double raised moulding round it, or just as often with two or more grooves. There are two main forms, either rounded on top (fig. 59, 17) or flatly conical (fig. 59, 22) and the latter often carry concentric grooves on top (fig.

[1] We must recognize our good fortune in having the complete section of the two *barbotined* examples, figs. 55, 2 and 79, 3.

59, 19, 21, 23); no. 15 is quite exceptional. The space between knob and rim is usually rouletted, rarely smooth, and runs in a concave curve to the rim where there are usually two grooves inside the thickened, upturned lip. The ware is the usual local colour-coated in all its variations. The remains are unusually well-preserved, so that we can illustrate quite a number. No. 20 is the only example with the rim projecting downwards, and no. 16 is the only one with rouletting on the outer face of the rim. A variant of the previous form in buff ware is described below.

BOWLS IMITATING HANDLED BRONZE PATERAE

We have seen flagons copying bronze prototypes (p. 101 and fig. 56, 1–9), and now we come to copies of the bronze paterae. Certain types of these vessels were traditionally in use in sacrificial ritual throughout the Roman Empire. The flagon used was our f. 362, its near relative fig. 70, 5, 6, and the squat form with the clover-leaf mouth, which does not seem to have been copied in pottery with mica coating. Bronze vessels are scarce in comparison with pottery, but we have, exceptionally, in the county of Essex a series of examples of the flagon and the patera found together in the tombs of the landed British gentry. It is not unreasonable to suppose that these persons, the 'county' aristocracy of the period, would be likely to have held the position of High Priest of the Emperor for the Province of Britain, and that these symbols of their calling were buried with them with ceremonial intent.

The best series comes from the Bartlow Hills[1] but there are also examples from Rivenhall,[2] Black Notley,[3] Heybridge,[4] and, outside the county, at Thornborough.[5]

Fig. 59, 26. Red-buff ware, with remains of mica-gilding; base with high kick and with three carefully made cordons inside; there are also cordons on the exterior wall and under the base. The high kick is particularly obvious in a bronze original found at Toppesfield.[6] The vessel is a distorted waster.

Fig. 59, 27. Bright-red ware, mica-gilt; two grooves under rim and one under base; base raised high in two steps.

Fig. 59, 25. Greyish ware with red rind, mica-gilt, finely made.

Fig. 59, 29. Fine grey core with light, reddish-buff rind, probably intended to be mica-coated.

Fig. 59, 28. Part of the rim of a bowl in the same ware, mica-gilt, with part of a stout tubular handle attached; this provides the clue to the original design and purpose of these vessels.

Fig. 73, 28–29. Two more rims, red ware, found 1933.

All of these vessels are of superior material and technique; the potter was evidently giving of his best.

[1] *Arch.* xxv (1834), 1 ff.; xxvi (1836), 300 ff.; xxviii (1840), 1 ff.; xxix (1842), 1 ff.; *J.B.A.A.* n.s. xix (1913), 249.

[2] Chelmsford Museum, unpublished.

[3] *Minutes Soc. Ant. Lond.* vii 89 (6/12/1753).

PLATTERS OF FORM 17 OR 39

A large number of fragments of platters were found of this common form. They are perhaps more like f. 17 than f. 39, but are quite remarkable and do not appear to have been found off the site. They are wide and shallow, with a curved side sloping outwards and no foot-ring. There is nearly always a thickening or bulge in the wall just above the angle of the base. The latter was probably intended to be flat, but is often much bulged in the middle. There are a few shallow concentric circles in the centre, quite different in style from those on the first-century vessels. It is possible that our potters were copying early fragments found on the site. Like the original Pompeian red series our series runs to some very large diameters; one waster is 15½ in. in diameter.

The ware is the usual colour-coated, but the surface has a browner colouring and a peculiar roughness. Three examples are illustrated, fig. 57, 19–21. Twenty-three more fragments were found in 1959, differing in no way from these described.

TETTINES

Two small pointed objects found in 1959 resemble the feet of tripod-bowls (*Cam.* f. 63), but such bowls are not known at the time of our kilns, and these objects have, moreover, a small hole made lengthwise through them. They must be spouts from tettines. One of several examples of these vessels in the Museum, found in the cemetery on the Abbey Field, is in colour-coated ware typical of our kilns.

We are not without further traces; there are two or three small fragments of thin, straplike handles, only about ¼-in. wide, clearly from very small vessels, and there is at least one side-fragment from a small, rounded, sanded vessel, with the mark of attachment of such a handle at the widest diameter. We assume these also to have been tettines.

BUFF WARES

The buff ware, including white and some red, formed the largest section in weight and bulk and much more than half of it is misfired in some way. Most red fragments are accidentally so, having been intended to be grey; some of the buff vessels seem to have had a whiter coating. We have found that some of the large white or buff vessels preserve traces of a mostly evanescent thin red coating. To a limited extent red painted decoration was employed.

[4] Colchester Museum, Price's Catalogue 1204, 1239.

[5] *Records of Bucks.* xvi, 29 f. and pl. ivb.

[6] *Arch.* xiv, 24 with illustration.

There is a great variety of vessels and other objects: indeed one might say that our potters made almost everything that could be made in clay. Before dealing with the standard forms of vessels made, there are several of the more unusual objects to be described.

AEDICULA (?)

A single fragment discovered by Mr. Calver, and not stratified, is part of a flat wall with a part-engaged column at the one end. The material is a good light buff clay and the wall is about ⅜ in. thick. A square ridge or skirting runs along the outer base of the wall. The fragment is about 6 in. high and 3 in. wide.[1] Against the outside wall is depicted a goat, in high relief, crudely modelled by hand, the head turned to look back over the shoulder (pl. XVII b).

This would appear to be part of an aedicula, but what part is uncertain, for the end with the column should be the front, and, if so, the interior would be exposed to view. But the inside (the back of the fragment as it lies in the photograph, pl. XVII b) is crude and unfinished, while the outside is finished. This is assuming that one sees the left-hand wall as one looks at the object. If it is the right-hand wall, then the inside is the finished side, and the goat is represented as inside the building.

There is one more fragment which was found unstratified in 1959 and which seems to come from the same or a similar object. It is in the same clay, and from a flat wall ⅜ in. thick. At the left-hand side it is broken along an angle; from the outer side (as shown by the curve of the angle) projects part of a long narrow object in relief over ½ in. high with deeply scored grooves, and with a kind of linenfold festooning at the base. This could best be explained as part of a draped figure. Once more we have to comment that what we might expect to find within the aedicula is found, on the contrary, outside it. I have no knowledge of any aedicula similar to this, nor indeed of any parallel at all.

MOULD FOR MASK OR BUST

A single fragment (pl. XVIII a) is from a heavy mould, in dark, reddish buff ware, for a life-size human face. It is beardless, and the indication of an ornamental head-dress makes it probably female. The modelling is done with the sure hand of experience. Nose and chin are boldly and accurately formed, but the eye is staring and round. There is, however, some damage to the higher parts of the mould here, which may cause a false impression. The little that remains of the eye-brow is deep and heavy. Part of the head-dress which is preserved seems to belong to an ornamental plaque hanging down before the ear. The inner (front) edge of this has a bold half-round moulding decorated by deeply impressed chevrons (embossed in the positive). The flat portion has moulded decoration the detail of which is now obscured. The angle of the plaque to the face suggests pendant ornaments rather than part of a helmet. The modelling of the face, though we have only one-half, gives the impression that the whole would be too narrow, when complete, to serve as a mask, and in a mask the mouth and eyes should be open.

The few parallel cases do not help greatly. First we have to mention that a fragment from a similar object was found when making the south bowling green in the Castle Park in 1935. It is of hard flower-pot red ware (pl. XVIII a top) and is from the hair, which is rendered by a triple series of bosses pressed out from the inside. These, while the clay was still soft, were incised with concentric circles and parallel curved strokes, giving an impression of complicated and careful coiffure. This piece is also of life-size.

Such things seem always to have been rare, and we have to choose between two possibilities. Occasionally large busts of goddesses were made. The remains are few, for example, one at Aquincum and another from St. Matthias, Trier, the latter having a broad, flat, ornamental head-dress.[2] The Aquincum fragment is almost exactly similar to ours.

But there is another possibility; a complete mask was found in the Trier kilns,[3] with the hair done exactly as in the Castle Park fragment. The eyes are cut out (which could be done after casting) and so is the mouth. It is doubtful whether ours could be wide enough for a mask, either to wear or to hang up, and a mask would not be likely to have an ornamental head-dress, nor does the mouth in our case seem to have been intended to be shown open.

The peculiar rendering of the hair by whorled bosses is seen on a vase decorated with busts of the gods of the days of the week (from Bavai or Mons, in the Cabinet des Médailles, Paris),[4] and a mould for making such busts was found in Trier.[5] The same can also be seen on the curious face-urn from the drain in Holly-Trees Meadow.[6]

AN UNNAMED OBJECT

On fig. 50, 3 we show a mushroom-shaped object of

---

[1] A further piece now makes the column c. 12 in. high.
[2] *Trierer Jahresberichte* II (1909), 20 and Taf. 1; *Budapest Régiségei* XI, 327.
[3] *Trier. Zeitschr.* ix, Taf. XXI, 2; compare also the bronze mask *J.R.S.* xxxvi, pl. VIII.
[4] *Rom-Germ. Korrespondenzblatt* viii (1915), 2, Abb. 2; *Germ. Rom.* v, Taf. XXIV, 6.   [5] *Germ. Rom.* ibid., no. 4.
[6] *Roman Colchester*, p. 131, fig. 59, 1.

soft (underfired) yellowish-buff clay[1] which seems to have had a white coating. The diameter is just over 3 in. and the height 1⅝ in. The serviceable part is the broad, rounded face; the knob or handle is less carefully made and was cut from the wheel with a wire.

Three of these objects were found at Aquincum, two of them exactly like ours.[2] It has occurred to me that they might be used to force the clay into a mould for decorated Samian and to secure a fine smooth finish to the interior surface. Otherwise one would expect them to have been found on sites of non-Samian kilns. It was found by Mr. A. F. Hall in the large pit C19, full of brown clay just south of the stone wall of 1933 (fig. 9 and p. 141).

Another Unidentified Object

On fig. 50, 4 we show an irregularly shaped cone of 1½ in. diameter and 2½ in. length, made of fine buff ware with a light red to chocolate colour-coating. The base is hollow with a central plug of clay which looks as if the whole, when soft, had been pressed upon the end of a tube (such as a bone). One face of the cone bears what is almost a rectangle of small circular impressions, with one impression in the middle. Higher up a band of impressions runs all round the small end, like a necklace, and in this, on the side opposite the rectangle, is the mark where some circular projection like a ring has been broken off. The small end itself is broken.

Pottery Palette (Pl. xix *a*)

In pit 14 was found a palette spoilt in firing; it had been intended to be just under 3⅞ in. long by 2⅝ in. wide and $\frac{5}{16}$ in. thick, but the clay has blown out hollow, and the paste is now a reddish grey with a red-buff surface, very hard and brittle, being overfired. The edge, finished nearly square, has only a very slight bevel. These palettes are usually made of some fine sort of stone, and are generally carefully made and finished. They occur from time to time on Roman sites, but never, so far as I know, under circumstances which might explain their purpose. Lehner, describing several found at Neuss,[3] says they are for rubbing down the ingredients of ointments, supporting this theory with an illustration of one found with a fitment of thin bronze which slides on the bevelled edges and contains a hemispherical receptacle for either the material or the ointment. With these he associates also the ends of two of the glass stirring-rods, broken off short, which he thinks were used as rubbers.

Lamps and Lamp-holders

Lamps do not occur in excavations with such frequency as might perhaps be expected. They figure rarely in the literature of Roman Britain in the last 60 years. Colchester has perhaps more than its share. Of 105 pottery lamps exhibited in Colchester Museum 28 are in groups from graves, and probably most of the others were found in graves if their provenance had been recorded. It is not surprising, therefore, to find that our potters made lamps, though only two fragments occurred in the many tons of pottery which have been examined. There are, however, the following objects:

Pl. xvii *c*. Mould for making a small lamp. It consists of a plaque of white-buff ware, flat on the back, about ¾ to ⅞ in. thick, and shaped as an irregular quadrilateral. The upper face has in the centre the recessed mould for the body of the lamp, which had a single nozzle and a small lug where the handle should come. There are four very crudely impressed hollows, one in each corner, for the keys centring the upper half of the mould. An additional aid for this is a sharply incised V on the flat upper end, which continued over the end of the upper part of the mould, forming a double check. This mould was found by Mr. Calver in 1956 and is unstratified; its length is 5 in. and width 4 in.

Two fragments of moulds for lamps were found in 1933 (pl. xvii *a*); both are of good buff ware.

No. 1. Creamy buff ware; part of the mould for a lamp of the 'firma' type (Wheeler, type III*a*).[4] A cast from it is shown. It has in each corner a projection to key it into position on the lower mould. Thickness about 1 in., width about 3¼ in.

No. 2. Dull white ware, rather underfired. This is thick (about 1½ in.), and the cavity for the lamp is not central. Though the right side looks broken we have the full width, 3⅜ in. The lamp has a round base which flares out hardly at all, but the nozzle is long and tapering, suggesting a bronze prototype.[5] A cast from the mould is shown beside it.

Both moulds have deeply cut lines across one end, like the first described. These moulds are very solid affairs and not easily broken. One might have expected more remains of lamps made from them to survive; these, however, are easily broken, but even fragments were not found.

The only good reference for lamp-moulds known to me is Kuzsinszky's account of the Aquincum potteries;[6] the moulds are described on his pp. 270 ff.

[1] It has been chemically hardened in the Museum.

[2] Balint Kuzsinszky, p. 64, fig. 44, 2, 3. He describes them as polishers or smoothers for pots.

[3] *B.J.* 111–12 (1904), 401 and Taf. xxv, 35–38, with Abb. 19.

[4] R. E. M. Wheeler, *London in Roman Times*, p. 63, and fig. 15. See p. 110 below, footnote 1.

[5] For the prototype see Loeschcke, *Lampen aus Vindonissa*, Taf. xxi.

[6] Op. cit.

His figs. 278–9 are those for 'firma' lamps.[1] Most of the Aquincum moulds are pointed ovals in shape, but fig. 295 is rectangular; all have the usual registering keys and the checking lines on the ends, see his figs. 293–5.

Lamp-holders. Lamps are frequently found in graves standing in a shallow dish of suitable size and shape to hold them, and furnished with a handle at one end and a spout at the other. These dishes are often found alone and much sooted, and it seems that they themselves often served as lamps.

Fig. 73, 31, fragment of soft brown-buff ware with grey core, almost certainly part of a lamp-holder, from the waste heap.

Fig. 73, 32. Hard buff ware, poorly smoothed and quite rough in the centre of the base beneath. The rim is flat on top. Kiln 21, one of a number found.

Fig. 73, 33. Thick brown ware lamp-holder, diam. 4¾ in. Near kiln 19; two fragments of another, kiln 17.

Three or four more fragments of lamp-holders were found in 1959.

CANDLESTICKS

There were about half a dozen recognizable fragments of candlesticks, most of which are illustrated, fig. 72, 23–27. They are all of very hard clay burnt red-brown to red. All were found near the kiln waste heap. No. 23 is shown with the finished side uppermost, but may, nevertheless, be upside down. It was made in two parts, one ending in a conical nose which fitted into the other part, which is missing. The flange of the grease-catcher on nos. 24–26 is broken. No. 27 has a hollow pedestal the floor in which has broken away, and which has a conical stopper set into the top which probably served to hold the candle.

THE MORTARIA

The remains of mortaria formed by far the largest bulk of the pottery found. This was so in both seasons, and it has not been possible to sort through the remains exhaustively for joints and for restoration. By far the largest part of the fragments are underfired, and very soft.

POTTERS' STAMPS ON MORTARIA

I. *Legible or lettered stamps* (figs. 60 and 61)

The stamps are normally impressed on the roll of the rim, near the spout, and frequently on both sides of it. Occasionally a different arrangement is encountered such as fig. 7, 2A and fig. 64, 8. Very rarely a name-stamp is found alongside a herring-bone stamp. The largest matrix of Martinus (no. 5) is curiously decorated with ogees, pyramids of dots, and a bird, all in

relief; and indeed this potter excels in the variety of his stamps. Acceptus is notable, as already observed (p. 85), as stamping T.S., colour-coated, and mortaria-wares all with the same matrix. The two names Dubetavus and Dubitatus are not only similar in sound but also in character of 'handwriting': one would suspect that one name was meant and that the owner was somewhat illiterate. All show preference for elaborate hatched borders, with or without *ansae*.

1. ACCEPTVS F (fig. 50, 1), stamped four times on rim and flange, twice each side of spout; fig. 64, 5; hard creamy white ware.

   Part of a second example, on this same form (501B), was found in 1959.
2. BARO Two examples on f. 497, fig. 66, 5. The label is semi-ansate.
2a. BARO F *In tabula ansata.* Fig. 61, 2a; very similar to the last; rim shown on fig. 68, 18; diameter 11½ in.
2b. BARO FI in plain label. Fig. 61, 2b; rim shown on fig. 68, 19; diameter 11½ in.
3. DVBETAVI (retro). Fig. 66, 7, 10. Eight examples.
4. DVBITATVS Two examples.
5. MARTINVS F... (I). Two examples. Fig. 66, 6.
6. MARTINVS F' (II). At least 25 examples and 6 more in 1959. Fig. 66, 8, 11, 12.
7. MARTINVS F (III). Six examples.
8. MARTINVS (IV). In Museum, not found in the excavations. Four more examples were, however, found in the excavations of 1959.
9. MARTINVS F (V). One example only.
10. MARTINVS F (VI). One example only.
11. M]ARTIN.. (VII). One example only.
12. MARTINVS.FE (VIII). Seven examples (in two cases this stamp is side by side with Martinus I).
13. MARTINVS (IX). Two examples. Fig. 67, 5.
14. MARTIN.... (X). One example. Kiln 8.
15. MARTINVS F (XI). One example.
16. MARTINVS II (XII). One example.
17. MESSOR (I). Fig. 66, 9. Creamy white ware with large mixed grit.
18. MES.SOR (II). Four examples.
19. MESSO(R) (III). Fig. 66, 15. At least nine examples.
20. MESSOR (IV). One example.
21. RIIGALIS (retro) (I). Fig. 64, 6. Four examples.
22. REGALI... Fig. 64, 2. One example.
22a. SC..PI (?). Fig. 61, 22a, rim fig. 68, 6. Once only on a very large rim f. 497 of at least 19 in. diameter. The vessel is spoilt in firing, so we may suppose the potter worked here. As for the name the faulted surface is so bad that the space of two letters is quite illegible. One might have SCIRPI, or perhaps SCARPI, but it is possible that SCARPFE or SCARPIF was intended.

   The name does not seem to have been found before.
23. TITVS FE. At least 12 examples, all from the one matrix, and two more in 1959. Rims are shown on fig. 66, 1–4.
24. VITALIS... One example.
25. MARIAVS FE (?) We had written this down as illegible; but Mrs. Hartley found another impression which looks very like MARIAVS FE; only the fifth letter remains very doubtful.
26a. This stamp is not from the 1933 site, but from kiln 24, see pp. 153–4. For 26b see pp. 9, 115, 120.

---

[1] The 'firma' lamp is so called because of the fashion of placing the name of the manufacturer under the base. The practice was soon abused, and minor firms commonly used the well-known names of the larger firms. This type of lamp (Wheeler IIIa and b) was in use from about A.D. 75 to 200.

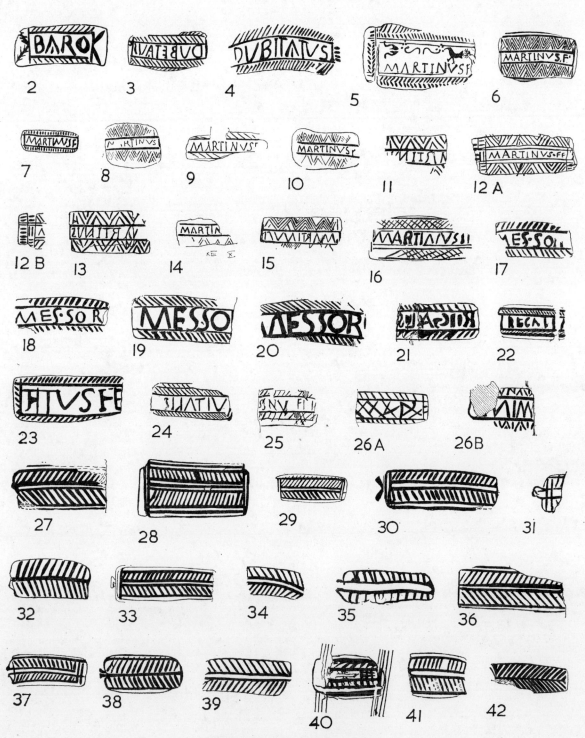

Fig. 60. Potters' stamps on mortaria.

Some eleven names are here represented, and, considering the bulk of the output, it is remarkable how seldom any of them is recorded elsewhere. We may fairly add Cunopectus to the list, for his name occurs on f. 504 in the Museum, and if we include him we

shown that the Colchester products have a very much higher calcium content than others. It would thus appear that our factory had, for a time at least, secured an army contract. This need not have been limited to mortaria; indeed the quantity of colour-coated drink-

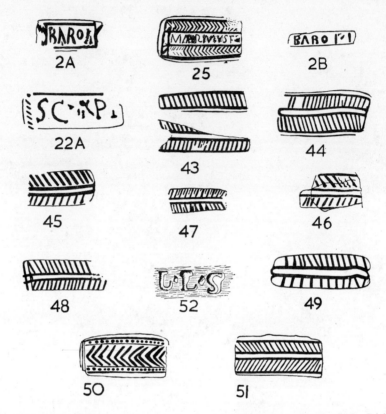

Fig. 61. Additional stamps on mortaria, save no. 52 which is incuse on tile (p. 9). (½)

have three Celtic names. The rest are Roman, though their owners were probably not.

A rim like fig. 66, 7, stamped by Dubitatus (4), from the Prittlewell cemetery at Southend is in the Museum there. A fragment in York Museum (f. 501B) is stamped MARTINVS F;[1] the same name occurs on f. 501A at Caistor-by-Norwich.[2] Regalis also occurs there on f. 497[3] in two different forms. MESSOR F occurs at Cadder[4] but none of these here named is from any of our matrices. Mrs. Hartley tells me that quite one-third of the Roman mortaria found in Scotland are proving to have come from Colchester. This information is partly derived from identifying the stamps, both named and herring-bone, and partly by analysis of the clay, experiments with which have

ing-beakers produced becomes understandable on the basis of such a contract.

As might be expected, our names do not occur on continental sites in *C.I.L.* xiii. The eight or nine stamps listed from Colchester in *C.I.L.* vii include none of our potters, but there are two from London, viz.: 1334, 27 DVBITATVS and 1334, 33 MARTINVS both quoted as C. R. Smith, *Cat.*, p. 16, and *R. London*, p. 89.

II. *Stamps of so-called 'herring-bone' pattern*

These are much more difficult to classify than the lettered stamps. The large matrix had to be applied to the rims of varying curvature with a rolling movement beginning from the beading. This was not always

[1] May, *York*, pl. xix, 14.
[2] Atkinson, *Norf. Arch.* xxvi (1936), 210, R 32 (...TINI, retro).

[3] Ibid., R 24–26.
[4] *P.S.A. Scot.*, p. 69, fig. 11, 11, on f. 497.

carefully done, and not only did the end of the stamp frequently not register, but the impress may be curved either to left or right. When it is further considered that the impress may be deep or shallow, and that the contraction of the clay in firing varied, it will be realized that it is very difficult sometimes to decide whether two stamps are from the same matrix or not. The stamps illustrated have been drawn over the best rubbings obtainable. Many of them are, perforce, composite from different portions of the same stamp. It is remarkable how different two imprints from the one matrix can appear, and we are in some doubt whether or not the outer furrows bordering stamps like nos. 27 and 28 may, in some cases, not appear in the impression, though the matrix is the same. It certainly would appear to happen, though it is difficult to see how. Some of the stamps, as will be seen, occur in combination with named stamps.

No. 27. Occurs with Messor (4), lacking lateral grooves, nearly 2¼ in. long, and complete at both ends. Two others with lateral grooves, but otherwise apparently the same, have the beginning preserved, and one of these provides the figure. Connected with kiln 17. No others are in the Museum, and no more were found in 1959.

No. 28. A large stamp with character, easily recognized by the double furrows in the centre and sides. It occurs on one vessel with no. 4. Of twenty-two examples examined only one was on f. 501, the rest were all of f. 497 with wide flange, squared or rounded beneath, never 'bunched'.[1] There are four other examples in the Museum, three of which come from St. Mary's Hospital. Three more found in 1959.

No. 29. This is drawn from a very clear impression. Three others are not so clear, and there may be a fourth. All are on flanges cut off flat beneath and with bead below the top. The association is with the enclosure. There are no examples in the Museum. None was found in 1959.

No. 30. This stamp is less characteristic, closely resembling nos. 27, 33, and 36. It is doubtful whether the marginal grooves always appear, and the ansa indicated in the drawing only appears in one case. The drawing we believe to represent the full-length. Sixteen examples were all on rims like those bearing no. 28, none on f. 501. The association is with kiln 17 alone. There are ten further examples in the Museum, two from within the town walls, others from Crowhurst Road, the County Hospital, and St. Mary's Hospital (two). Among these are three complete vessels, one of which is f. 501A; the other two are as fig. 66, 9. Two more possible examples were found in 1959.

No. 31. Fragment of a stamp only. Another similar was found in 1959.

No. 32. A very characteristic stamp on this site, with single centre rib and coarsely cut. There are six examples, associated with the enclosure and the stone wall. The stamp may have been actually straight, but is found curved, as shown, in either direction. The right end may be incomplete. Two others may also be this stamp; one is on a rim resembling those of Martinus (fig. 66, 11), the other on a fragment of an enormous rim, with an internal diameter of not less than 30½ in., which has been decorated with rows of small punctures and impressed lines (fig. 64, 7). This came from the enclosure. Two more examples were found in 1959. Another example was found in the Grammar School excavations in the garden of Gurney Benham House.

No. 33. Examples very numerous. The rims have the bead level with the top of the flange, or below, but never above. Six of the former are associated with the enclosure and the stone wall. Over twenty of the latter are all associated with the enclosure, especially around kiln 19. Some are of the 'bunched-up' form. All spouts are of normal type, and the lower edge of the flange may be cut off square or rounded. One of these stamps was found in trench G18 (in north part of region 5, *Cam.*, pl. cx). There are examples in the Museum, one from the Technical School, two complete vessels, one of which is in burial 163 with forms 391, 278, and 273. Twelve more examples and a possible thirteenth were found in 1959.

No. 34. Is the stamp on the whole vessel fig. 63, 4. There are at least five examples from the enclosure, and it is possible that some more may have passed as no. 27 or no. 39. All are on similar rims; none in Museum. Two more found in 1959, but see no. 39 below.

No. 35. Twelve examples of a very coarsely cut stamp, mostly on smallish rims, but some large. The association is with the enclosure almost exclusively. Four more certain, the three possible examples in 1959 all have a similar flange (figs. 65, 2; 68, 1 and 3).

No. 36. A large stamp similar to no. 27, with which it might possibly be identical. Three examples are definitely as this figure, from kilns 17 and 19, six others possibly the same as no. 27 (or even no. 30) are from the stone wall and the enclosure. Two others in the Museum are from Hollytrees Meadow and St. Mary's Hospital.

No. 37. Eight examples show the bead level with the flange, or the rim 'bunched' with the bead below the top of the flange. Of five spouts four were of our normal pattern and one had a very wide volute on each side of the inner end of the channel of the mouth. The association is with the enclosure and the stone wall; six more found in 1959. This stamp is usually easily recognizable.

No. 38. Only two examples of a simple stamp with single mid-rib. They are f. 501 and come from kiln 19. Three more were found in 1959. Two others are in the Museum from the Hollytrees Meadow and St. Mary's Hospital.

No. 39. A single specimen, from kiln 19. There are four examples in the Museum, one complete like fig. 63, 4, but the bead just rising above the flange; two are doubtfully identified. In 1959, however, twelve examples were found, and a possible thirteenth, and it became probable that no. 34 is merely a twisted and partial impression from the same matrix.

No. 40. A single specimen on f. 501, from kiln 19, fig. 64, 4.

No. 41. A single specimen from the enclosure; a possible second, found in 1959, is longer.

No. 42. Occurs on a fragment of a spout. f. 497 (?) fig. 64, 8, in combination with no. 28. It is small and narrow and is impressed twice, once *along* the flange and again on the broad margin of the spout. It appears again, in the same position on the flange on a fragment from kiln 19, and again in the Museum, on a rim f. 501B, from St. Mary's Hospital. Unfortunately none is sufficiently well preserved to give a clear and complete rubbing.

No. 43 A and B (fig. 61). Two fragmentary stamps found in 1959; very possibly they both belong to the stamp represented by no. 41 above.

No. 44 (fig. 61). This stamp does not appear to be identical with any of the foregoing. Found unstratified in 1959.

No. 45 (fig. 61). Three examples of this stamp were found in 1959; two could be from one vessel.

No. 46 (fig. 61). Two fragments of yet another stamp found in 1959. Matrix crudely fashioned and irregularly cut. Ware good and hard. Small rim resembling the preceding.

---

[1] By 'bunched' we mean compact or compressed in section, e.g. figs. 67, 2; 68, 8.

No. 47 (fig. 61). Two neat stamps, perhaps from one vessel.

No. 48 (fig. 61). A very clear-cut stamp on a complete vessel.

No. 49 (fig. 61). Closely resembling no. 35, but hardly the same.

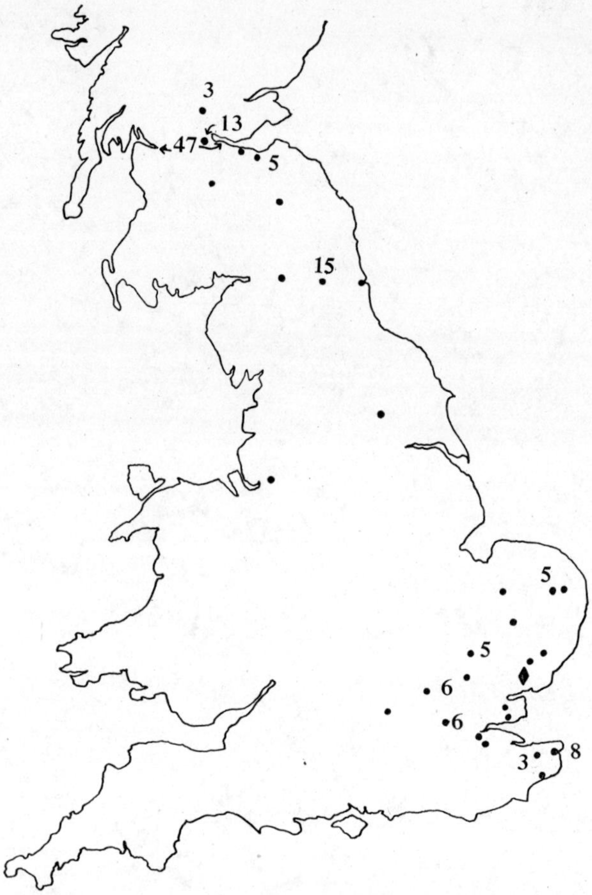

DVBETAVS	Bishop's Stortford; Corbridge; Great Chesterford and Verulamium.
DVBITATVS	London and Prittlewell, Essex.[1]
MARTINVS II	Capel St. Mary, Suffolk; Canterbury;

FIG. 62. Distribution of stamped mortaria from the Colchester factories. The total number (where more than 2) of stamps from each site is indicated.

THE DISTRIBUTION OF STAMPED MORTARIA FROM THE COLCHESTER POTTERIES

Mrs. K. F. Hartley has kindly contributed the following note.

Examination of mortarium stamps found at sites throughout Britain has revealed with notable clarity several interesting details of the markets supplied by the Colchester mortarium-makers in the latter part of the second century. The distribution of their mortaria for all sites, except Colchester itself, is shown in Fig. 62. The detailed list is:

CVNOPECTVS   Richborough and a site of uncertain location in Kent.

Corbridge (4); Great Chesterford; London (2); North Ash, Kent; a site of unknown location in Kent, and York.

MESSOR   *Scotland*: Cadder and Camelon; *England*: Caistor-by-Norwich; Hockwold-cum-Wilton, and London.

REGALIS   Brundall, Norfolk; Caistor-by-Norwich (4); Great Chesterford; Grimstone End, Suffolk (2) and South Shields.

TITVS   Great Wakering, Essex.

Herringbone Trade-marks   *Scotland*: Ardoch (3); Balmuildy (4); Bar Hill; Cadder (5); Camelon (13); Castlecary (3); Castledykes; Cramond; Inveresk (5); Mumrills (15); Newstead; Old Kilpatrick (7); Rough Castle (12). *England*: Birdoswald; Burgh, Suffolk (2);

[1] DVBETAVS and DVBITATVS almost certainly represent variations in the spelling of one potter's name.

Canterbury (2); Corbridge (10); East Cliff, Folkestone; Great Chesterford (2); Great Wakering, Essex; Hambleden, Bucks.; London (6); Richborough (7); Springhead; Verulamium (5); Wilderspool; York; Kent, exact provenances unknown (4), and Worthing Museum, provenance uncertain.

These details reveal two distinct markets, one confined to south-east Britain, the other embracing the two northern frontier-systems. The areas adjacent to Colchester, namely East Anglia, Kent, and such towns as London and Verulamium, would be natural markets for any successful industry based on Colchester, but the presence of Colchester mortaria in quantity in the frontier zone requires more comment, especially since they are virtually absent in the regions between these markets. There are 149 second-century stamped mortaria from the Antonine Wall forts. If those from Ardoch, Camelon, Cramond, and Inveresk are added, the total becomes 201. Of these, 34 per cent. are stamps assignable to Colchester by identification of the die or occasionally by such close similarity to definite Colchester products that they may be accepted without hesitation. At individual sites where there has been much excavation the proportion of Colchester stamps sometimes reaches 50 per cent., the rest being clearly from the midland centres and from unlocated centres in the north of Britain. The situation in Scotland may be summarized thus:

		Total of second-century stamps	Total from Colchester potteries	% from Colchester
Ardoch .	. .	12	3	25
Balmuildy	. .	31	4	13
Bar Hill .	. .	19	1	5
Cadder .	. .	10	5	50
Camelon	. .	26	13	50
Castlecary	. .	5	3	60
Castledykes	. .	4	1	25
Cramond	. .	4	1	25
Croy Hill	. .	1	—	—
Duntocher	. .	2	—	—
Inveresk .	. .	10	5	50
Kirkintilloch	. .	1	—	—
Mumrills .	. .	38	15	40
Newstead	. .	44	1	2
Old Kilpatrick .	.	18	7	39
Rough Castle .	.	24	12	50

Antonine Wall Forts are in italics.

Corbridge is the only northern site in England with a sufficient number of Colchester stamps to permit

useful analysis. There are at least 15 stamps, giving approximately 6 per cent. of the total of Antonine stamps. In East Anglia, excluding Colchester, they form 22 per cent. of the total of second-century stamps, which do not admit of close dating. In Kent, London, and Verulamium the proportion is unduly high, 25–50 per cent. because, at the main kilns supplying these areas after *c.* A.D. 140, the practice of stamping mortaria had virtually ceased.

The relative incidence in Scotland of stamps of different potters is interesting. Apart from two name-stamps all the Colchester stamps from Scottish forts are herring-bone trademarks. Those certainly identifiable are from the same dies as nos. 30, 32, 33, 37, 38, and 45 (figs. 60 and 61);[1] thirteen stamps are too fragmentary or too worn for the dies to be identified, but they are attributed to Colchester by the general characteristics of the stamps, forms, and fabric. Four herring-bone trademarks, from three dies, have also been attributed to Colchester in this way, although no stamps from the same dies have yet been discovered there.

It is of interest that MESSOR, the only Colchester potter whose name-stamps appear in Scotland, is also the only potter, apart from DUBITATVS, whose stamp has occurred on the same mortarium as herring-bone trademarks (p. 113). It may, moreover, be taken for granted that the potters using herring-bone trademarks belonged to one group, since the dies are so similar.

At sites in England, except in East Anglia where the proportion appears to be reversed, the trademarks predominate at a rate of two to one over the products of the potters using name-stamps; stamps from the same dies as nos. 28, 29, 30, 33, and 37 being the most common. Stamps of ACCEPTVS, BARO, and AMMINVS (fig. 60, no. 26 B), have yet to be found outside Colchester. Stamps of MARTINVS are far more common than those of any other named potter, and they get as far as York and Corbridge. It therefore seems curious that they do not appear in Scotland, if he was working at a time when the forts there were occupied. Stamps of REGALIS and DVBETAVS also reached the north, but only rarely, and again are not yet attested in Scotland.

The concentration of Colchester stamps in the frontier zone, combined with their rarity in the midlands and the north of England, may indicate military contracting, comparable to that already suggested for black-burnished ware and Warwickshire mortaria at military sites in the north.[2] The putative contract must, however, have been short-lived, for the mor-

---

[1] More than one die could be involved with the stamps similar to no. 32, as this is a particularly featureless stamp. The fabric and forms used, however, leave no reasonable doubt of the source.

[2] *Römische Forschungen in Niederösterreich*, Band III, pp. 64 ff. CRICO, working at another *colonia*, Lincoln, provides an interesting parallel with the Colchester potters, since he also had a considerable trade in Scotland.

tarium-types and stamps used are limited and cannot span a wide period. The distribution-pattern implies direct shipment up the east coast to the Tyne and Forth. That dispersal from Corbridge to Scotland is not in question is shown by the lack of Colchester stamps in Lowland Scotland, particularly at Newstead, where there is a large total of stamps. This must have been both cheaper and more convenient than land transport and it is, indeed, surprising that given this advantage the Colchester potters did not take more trade from the established midland potteries.

Dating evidence for Colchester stamps in the north is not abundant. However, an unpublished one from Birdoswald was in a deposit of Wall Period I and another at Corbridge was found in the late second-century destruction (A.D. 197, with an uncertain proportion of residual material: *Arch. Ael.* 4th ser., xxviii, fig. 10, no. 103, on fig. 81, no. 57). For those from Scotland the precise dating depends on problematic factors. However, a stamp from Mumrills comes from a deposit of the penultimate period, whether Antonine I or II. Furthermore, as Dr. K. A. Steer has recently pointed out (*J.R.S.* l, 90 ff.), the evidence for a third period of occupation of the forts is very much open to question, and any suggestion of a Severan reconstruction becomes correspondingly less likely. In fact the only fort in Scotland near the Forth–Clyde isthmus known to have been occupied in the third century, namely Cramond (Richmond, *Roman and Native in North Britain*, p. 96), has so far yielded only one Colchester stamp, and that could well go with the Antonine occupation. A high proportion of Colchester stamps is present at Rough Castle, where the timber barracks show only two phases (*J.R.S.* xlix, 104).

To sum up, it is certain that stamped mortaria from Colchester were circulating in the north before the end of the second century. So far there is no evidence for their use in the third century. In fact no certain third-century stamped mortaria are known anywhere in Britain. On the whole the evidence points to the period *c.* A.D. 150–200, but does not allow more precision.

THE FORMS OF THE MORTARIA

(FIGS. 63, 64, AND 65)

The forms of these vessels produced here fall into two groups, the bead-and-roll, or flanged type, which developed directly from our earlier ff. 192–5, and the wall-sided type which did not develop from the earlier f. 191, but was an innovation of the second century (at least in part).

The flanged rims include nearly every outline shown in fig. 19 in the first Wroxeter Report. Notably absent are the broad flat rims *Wrox.* 10, 14, 18 (our f. 195C),

[1] On the Hardknott mortaria in *Arch.* lxxi (1921), fig. 3.

while 22 to 46 are not numerous (our 195B, 196A, and 496 in that order): the rest occur in very great quantity, including some like 118, though never with painted decoration.

The diversity of outline among all these rims is much greater than it was in the first century. On the Camulodunum site the majority were of ff. 191 and 192; the numbers of 193–5 were never large.

From the end of the Camulodunum site we continue our series with the large number of early rims found in the *colonia* itself.

Here f. 191 does not occur, and if we segregate our earliest-looking rims we find few of f. 192 either, the bulk now consisting of f. 195 in three main forms, of which two are common and one scarce. Our f. 195C has a large, deeply curved flange, with a small beading at the inner lip, which is continued along each side of the spout as far as the outer lip, where it ceases abruptly. The spout is longer than in A and B. In f. 195B the flange is much thicker, shorter, and less curved while the beading is remarkably large. In these vessels the white grit is frequently carried over the rim. Though common on military sites farther north, the form is not at all common in Colchester. Form 195A has a broad, flat flange, only slightly curved and that mostly at the edge, while the beading is very narrow indeed, and occasionally evanescent. The spout is very short, only a stub. This is Newstead type 24, which shows clearly the pointed, low aspect of the spout of this early (Flavian) form as compared with the rounded view of the later f. 497 (Newstead type 25).

The period from about A.D. 100 to 130 should, according to the Wroxeter chart, and Collingwood,[1] be characterized by *Wrox.*, nos. 42–46, in which the flange of the rim bulges up to rise above the beading, and the curve of the flange varies considerably, appearing to be deeper in the earlier ones, as if continuing on f. 195A. Such rims duly appear in the series from the *colonia* but they are not numerous enough to compete with those characteristic of the site.

We now reach the period to which, approximately, our present series belongs. So great is the diversity of our rims that at first sight one feels that several different forms are to be listed, but longer acquaintance teaches that this is almost impossible. In the end we have decided to group nearly all of them under one form-number (f. 497).

Form 496. Mortarium with curved flange rising above the beading without altering profile of wall at beading. Collingwood,[2] fig. 52, 3 and 4; *Wroxeter* i, fig. 19, 46–66.

Fragments of this form were not numerous and were usually of small diameter. We differentiate them

[2] *Archaeology of Roman Britain.*

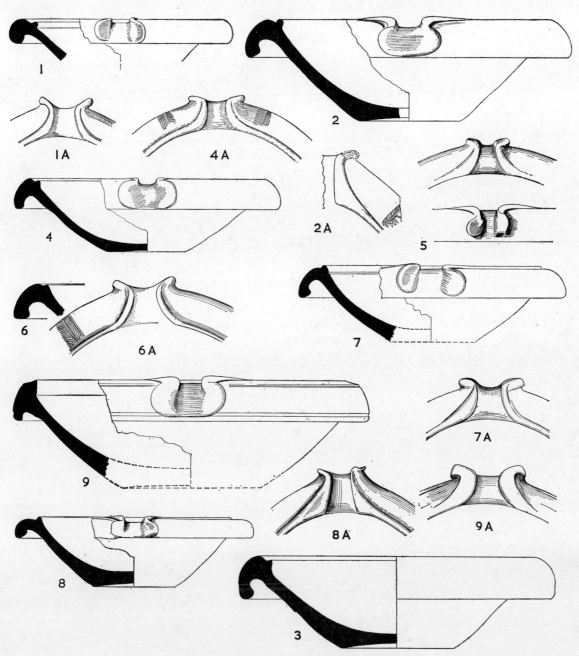

FIG. 63. Forms and outlines of mortaria (p. 119). (¼)

from those of ff. 195 and 497 in which the flange rises above the beading by two characteristics which are usually both present—the altogether narrower and less downcurved flange and the manner in which the beading (viewed in section) sits on the unbroken continuous curve of the wall; cf. fig. 65, 1, 3, 4. The distinction from f. 497 is not at all sharp, but the intermediate outlines like fig. 67, 7 (diameter 10 in., from the stone wall) and fig. 66, 2 (*Titus*, diameter large) are not numerous, and rims like fig. 67, 5, 6, 9, 10, are not easily confused with this form.

We have no stamps on these rims, and there are not more than half a dozen in the Museum. The form begins at the end of the first century and is characteristic of the Trajanic period but is recessive (?) after about A.D. 130.

Form 497. Mortarium with heavy, curved flange, which may be below, level with, or above, the beading; *the spout has sharply everted, rounded lobes.*[1]

In general the wall is fairly steep and slightly curved, the body fairly deep and conical, with rising base. The grit is white, or mixed. The rim outlines vary greatly, but the form is all one in that the spouts are all of one pattern, and, in the subdivisions mentioned below, we find one and the same potter stamping on varied rim-forms. The following subdivisions seem worthy of separate description.

(i) Beading usually overtopping the flange (fig. 63, 7, *Messor*, and 8; fig. 66, 3, *Titus*). The bottom edge of the flange may be flat, either horizontal (fig. 66, 1) or tilted (fig. 66, 2 &c.) or rounded (fig. 66, 5, *Baro*). The beading is often flattened inside and/or incurved and offset (figs. 66 and 67 *passim*). Grooves on the flange are rare. The size is usually large. Grit mixed.

Makers: *Baro*, 2 exx.; *Dubetavus*; *Martinus* (VIII), 2 exx.; *Messor* (I?, II, III), 5 exx.; *Titus*, 13 exx. Herring-bone stamps II, IV, V, VI?, VII, VIII, IX, 15 exx.

(ii) Beading almost obsolete, the groove defining it becoming a broad fluting or flat ledge (figs. 66, 11, *Martinus*, and 67, 1, also *Martinus*). This is the favourite form of this potter, and is usually of a finer, whiter clay than those of group (i); the outer lip of the flange is pointed and hooked; the size is smaller, and sometimes the flange has a groove above; less frequently another one, or more, lower down. The inner lip is usually deeply offset (fig. 67, 1).

Makers: *Dubetavus*, 7 exx.; *Dubitatus*, 2 exx.; *Martinus* (I), 7 exx.; (II), 26 exx.; (III), 8 exx.; (IV), 2 exx.; (V), 2 exx.; (VII), (IX), (X), (XII). Herring-bone stamps 28 and 30.

(iii) Rims similar to (i) above but the flange level with the beading or below it. Bottom of flange usually horizontally flattened, otherwise the same remarks apply as to (i). The slight difference is perhaps due to the fact that these seem to have been made almost solely by Messor and Regalis.

Makers: *Messor* (II), 2 exx.; (III), 7 exx.; (IV), 1 ex. with herring-bone stamp 33, also herring-bone stamps 30, 2 exx.; RIIGALIS, 3 exx., all small, soft, brown-white ware, also the illegible stamp fig. 61, 22*a*.

Form 498. Mortarium with the rim or flange flatly

compressed forming a steep collar rather than a rolled rim (fig. 64, 1 and cf. fig. 67, 8, 11–12).

There is no doubt these developed from f. 497 and that they are typologically later, though probably actually very little later on our site, where they are far from numerous. A transitional rim is shown on fig. 64, 1, with the same form of spout. The inner lip almost invariably projects inwards and may or may not be offset. All the stamps are of herring-bone type, being fig. 60, no. 28, no. 33, 4 exx., and no. 34, 4 exx.

Judging from the number of fragments in the Museum this form became more popular in later times; evidence for date is yet to be sifted. The specimens in the Museum are not stamped.

Form 501. Mortarium with steep collar-rim, with two grooves at top and bottom (normally). A, Rims steeply sloped, flat on top, with a small beading at inner lip. B, Rim almost vertical, often merely grooved on top.

501A is simply derived through ff. 497 and 498. Unfortunately our larger fragments (fig. 64, 2 and 6, *Regalis*) are not typical, and fig. 67, 8, *Martinus* IV or VI, has not the usual square and horizontally cut-off section of the lower edge of the flange. A rim of this form in the Museum (942.31, from St. Mary's Hospital) is stamped . . . VNOPEC FE, possibly our *Cunopectus*, or possibly another potter of the same name (see below).

501B is presumably developed from the preceding and represents the final form, being much more common. We illustrate (fig. 64, 3) one from grave 136 (which contains the Colchester vase already described, p. 96); fig. 64, 5, is stamped by Acceptus, and this appears to be the only stamp on rims of this form at Colchester, except one bearing *Regalis* II in yellowish-white ware, also from our kilns, and one with a herring-bone stamp, fig. 64, 4. In all about 160 rims were found.

Form 504. Mortarium with short downcurved flange and tall stout rim of more or less rectangular section, through which the spout is made by simply everting the rim on each side (fig. 64, 9, 10).

This is a later type (Collingwood,[2] pp. 220, 221, sub no. 12), and the few examples from our site show that it is just coming into use (see kiln 24 below). There are two rims of this form in the Museum, both stamped CYNOPE . . . (6377.31 from the Hospital, and 191.28 without provenance), which we may suppose to have been our *Cunopectus*.

We illustrate a fragment of a spout, fig. 67, 15. Fig. 67, 11, 12 are variants of f. 498, and 13 and 14 are rims as yet unclassified.

---

[1] Contrast the rounded lobes on fig. 63 with the pointed lobes on fig. 87.

[2] *Archaeology of Roman Britain.*

Description of Fig. 63

1. From kiln 3.
2. Pale buff ware, mixed grit, TITVS FE.
3. Mixed grit, H/B stamp 33, from stone wall.

8. Part of a spout bearing H/B stamp 28 and 42, the latter twice.
9. From waste heap.
10. In filling of enclosure, mixed grit; with H/B stamp 28; another of same outline has H/B stamp 36 or 39.

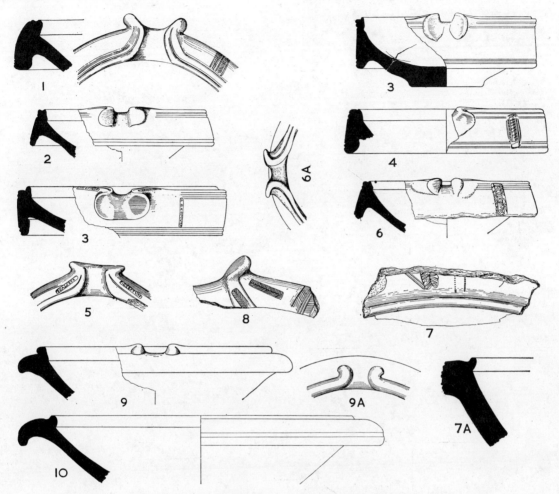

FIG. 64. Forms and outlines of mortaria. (¼)

4. Unstratified, H/B stamp 34.
5. Spout, MARTINVS 4.
6. Rim and spout, H/B stamp 30; from kiln 17.
7. Large mixed grit; MESSOR, creamy white ware.
8. Found between Trenches Y23 and 25 in top 2 ft.

Description of Fig. 64

1. H/B stamp 33.
2. From kiln 15; stamped REGALI(S).
3. In grave in Museum. No. P.C. 730.
4. H/B stamp 40. Hard white ware.
5. Hard creamy white ware, stamped ACCEPTVS F.
6. Soft white ware; RIIGALIS (21).
7. Part rim of a huge mortarium (section at 7A). Part of a herring-bone stamp can be seen impressed on the flange, with two parallel incised lines and two deeply impressed bead rows. Diameter (interior) over 31 in.

Description of Fig. 65

1. Form 496. Rough buff, sparse mixed grit; from pit 12.
2. Form 497. Hard buff, stamp 35. Grit mostly white; from grey ash, kilns 30 and 31.
3. Form 496. Buff; sparse mixed grit.
4. Form 496. Yellow-buff. Stamp fig. 60, 38; from pit 5.
5. Fine hard buff; from pit 15. One piece had been in a kiln-wall.
6. Poor buff ware, from lower filling of kiln 31.
7. Complete vessel, underfired. Stamp is no. 31. Found on east lip of stoke-hole of kiln 31.
8. Form 497. Good buff, grit mostly white. Stamp fig. 39, 60. Several other rims like this.
9. Buff, remarkably upright rim, another even deeper rim, both unstratified.
10. Unusual and small vessel, poor red-buff ware with white flecks. Distorted waster, from pit 7.

11. Form 501B. Good buff, no grit.
12. Form 501B. Fine buff, no grit.

Description of Fig. 66 (*Standard outlines*)

1. Form 497. TITVS FE, yellow-white ware, mixed grit.

12. Form 497. Same stamp, soft pale yellow, rather large mixed grit.
13. Form 497. Herring-bone stamp 37, diameter *c*. 11½ in.
14. Form 497. H/B stamp 32, white ware, mixed grit; another, smaller, is stamped TITVS FE.
15. Form 497. MESSOR (III).

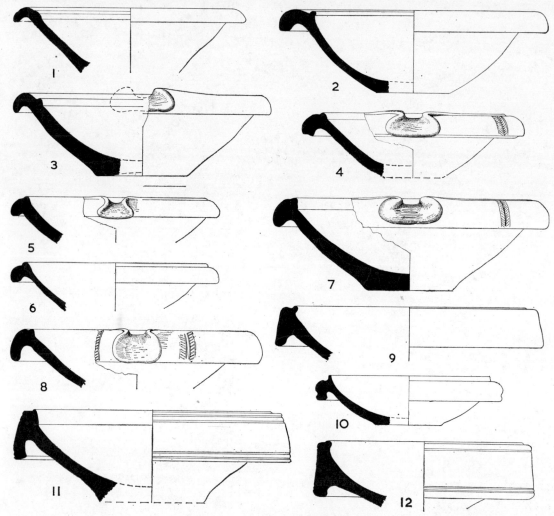

FIG. 65. Forms and outlines of mortaria. (¼)

2. Form 497. TITVS FE, hard buff, mixed grit. C.M. 52.40.
3. Form 497. TITVS FE, creamy white ware, mixed grit.
4. Form 497. TITVS FE, pale yellowish ware, mixed grit, two others similar with same stamp.
5. Form 497. BARO, dirty white-buff, small mixed grit. Two alike.
6. Form 497. MARTINVS (I), from kiln 20.
7. Form 497. DVBETAVIF, fine pale buff ware, small mixed grit, C.M. 395.29 from St. Mary's Hospital.
8. Form 497. MARTINVS F (II), soft yellowish-white, mixed grit.
9. Form 497. MESSOR (I).
10. Form 497. DVBETAVIF, yellowish-white, mixed grit.
11. Form 497. MARTINVS F (II), soft white, diameter large.

16. Form 497, ...MIM...., white. From Butt Road kiln, see fig. 60, 26B.

Fig. 67. *A selection of non-standard outlines*

1. Form 497. MARTINVS F (II) nearly white.
2. Unusual rim, compare nos. 13 and 14 below, has herring-bone stamp, possibly our 38.
3. Form 497. Variant, bears herring-bone stamps 28 and 29.
4. Form 497. Variant, herring-bone stamp 37, diameter 14 in.
5. Form 497. MARTINVS FI (IX). Nearly white with yellowish surface; two others are similar.

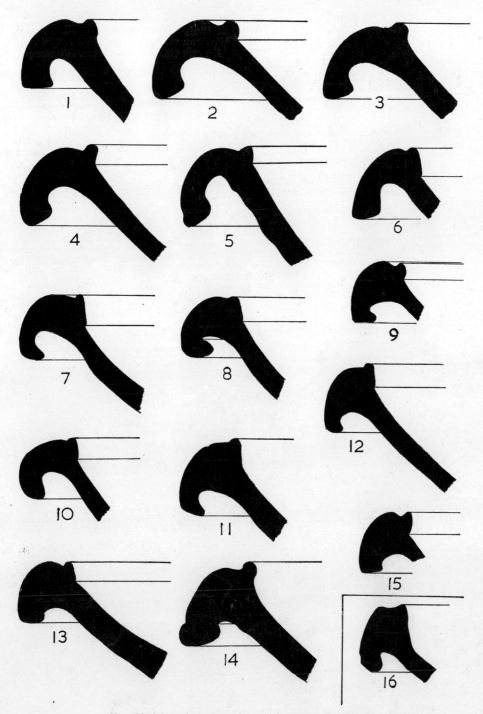

Fig. 66. Mortarium-rims. (No. 16 from Butt Road.) (½)

6. Apparently a variant of f. 497, having herring-bone stamp 28, but reminiscent of f. 195a.

7. Form 496. From stone wall, diameter 10 in.

8. Form 501A. MARTINVS F (IV or VI), white ware.

9. Form 497. Diameter 14 in.

10. Form 497. Diameter 13½ in.

Description of Fig. 68

1. Form 496. Very large, diameter c. 18 in.; good buff ware. H/B stamp 35 from body of kiln 31.

2. Form 496. Diam. c. 15 in.; good buff, large mixed grit.

3. Form 496. Good buff ware. H/B stamp 35.

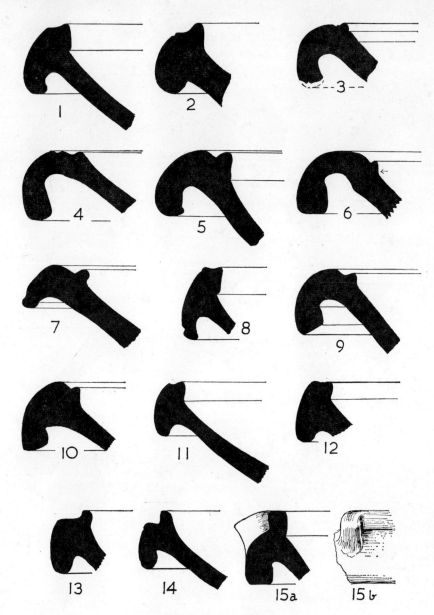

FIG. 67. Mortarium-rims. (½)

11. Form 498. Diameter c. 12 in., from kiln 19.

12. Form 498. Diameter 11½ in., from kiln 19.

13. Form 504 var. Diameter c. 12 in., from general debris.

14. Form 504 var. Diameter 9 in. with slight groove near lower edge of flange, from kiln 19.

15. Form 504. Part of spout, diameter 11 in., from kiln 19.

4. Form 496. Moulded under rim; diam. 10¾ in., underfired white-buff. Mixed grit. From 8.

5. Form 497. Buff. H/B stamp 39.

6. Form 497. Buff, spoilt in firing, white and grey grit. Stamped SC...Pl, fig. 61, 22A.

7. Form 497. Buff, H/B stamp 37.

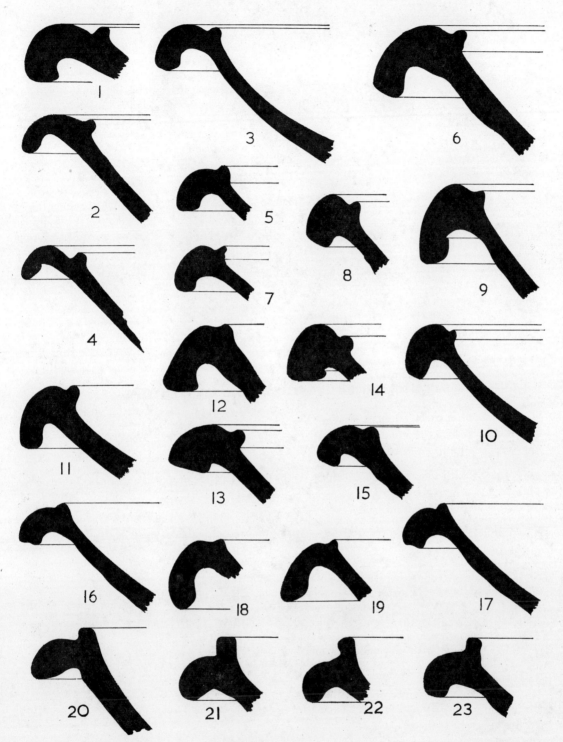

Fig. 68. Mortarium-rims. ($\frac{1}{2}$)

8. Form 497. White-buff, sandy, diameter *c.* 9¼ in. H/B stamp 37.

9. Form 497. White. H/B stamp 33.

10. Form 497. Yellow-buff, sandy. H/B stamp 37.

11. Form 497. Good buff. H/B stamp 39.

12. Form 497. Rim cut off flat beneath. Fine buff. H/B stamp 39.

13. Form 497. Rim cut off flat. beneath Very good buff. H/B stamp 32. Diameter *c.* 14 in. (2 exx.).

14. Form 497. Rim cut off flat. Buff. H/B stamp 30 (?).

15. Form 497. Buff. Diameter *c.* 14¼ in. H/B stamp 45.

16. Form 497. Buff. H/B stamp 38.

17. Yellow buff. Diameter 10⅝ in. H/B stamp 38.

18–23. Additions from the 1959 excavations. Nos. 18, 19 are stamped by BARO (see p. 110).

FLAGONS

In 1959 another plastically moulded neck was found, not so elaborate as that from kiln 13 (fig. 7, A–B, p. 11), but striking nevertheless. Its form (fig. 70, 1, pl. XIX *b,c*) follows no rule; it is bulbous at the top of a conical neck, which is not offset from the shoulder, and finishes with a simple, slightly everted lip. Upon this has been moulded a female face, with pellets for eyes, nose, and ears, the latter set much too high. The mouth is merely indicated by a slight hollow. No hair is shown, it is all concealed by an upright bandeau, which is flat on top and which is decorated all over with small circular impressions. These were probably made with the end of a quill and are exactly similar to those on fig. 7, A–B, and fig. 50, 4.[1] The ware is normal good buff; at the back of the head is the broken end of a three-ribbed handle.

Form 156. Flagon with cupped mouth, ridged or grooved outside.

These were one of the main products of the site; the fragments cannot be counted—not even the necks. A large quantity found by the stoke-hole of kiln 22 seemed undisturbed and provided (in 1933) the only two vessels which could be restored, fig. 56, 24–25. Other good examples were found in 1959 in pit 14 and are shown on fig. 70, 7–9. These are typical representatives of the form, which is, as May has observed, a local one, characterized by the regularly cupped mouth. The outside of the rim is sometimes carefully formed and stepped back, sometimes merely grooved in a continuous spiral. Other treatment is rare: a series of the unusual variations is given (fig. 56, 28–36).

There is nearly always an offset where the rim joins the neck, often very bold, the lower edge of the rim projecting strongly, rarely overhanging or undercut. Whether such variations have any chronological significance has yet to be learned.

The neck is short and curved, nearly always offset from the shoulder. The body is ovoid, with the greatest diameter in the lower half, or oval (which appears to be a later feature), or globular or oblate. The foot at its best has a footring with a bold and careful groove inside it. In some the footring is little more than formed by the groove, but still the work is careful. But there are very many of careless finish, though beaded and with some suggestion of the footring. Later the foot degenerates steadily, until in the fourth century it can be quite plain and flat.

The small pit F in site C4 (figs. 9 and 77) contained several barrow loads of fragments of these vessels. They had probably fractured in firing. Attempts to piece them together proved fruitless.

The four necks on fig. 56, 26–29 show the range of variation in form. The next five, 30–34 are not truly of this form and are as yet unclassified. Although well made hardly any two are alike.

No. 26 is not from the kilns. It was found in the filling of the adjacent well and may be Hadrianic. It is illustrated as the only example (other than no. 23) ever found with decoration. It has a double band of fine rouletting and is of fine white ware.

Form 362 (see p. 99 above). A single fragment of a neck in buff ware may possibly be misfired: it bears no trace of mica-coating. It has a bold thumb-grip on the handle, which is 1¼ in. wide and quite flat (fig. 56, 15).

More evidence for this form was found in 1959; on fig. 70 we show three more outlines:

Fig. 70, 4. Distorted mouth (waster), fine white ware; handle seems to have been of oval section.

Fig. 70, 5. Neck and shoulder, fine white-buff ware; the stout handle has a wide central fluting flanked by two ribs.

Fig. 70, 6. Complete neck and handle in fine white ware. Handle three-ribbed.

A very large rim of this form has two grooves outside the lip and a very stout two-ribbed handle; another large mouth is about 5 in. in diameter; yet another fragment has a large thumb-stop on the handle, upright and round, with a deep round impression for the thumb.

Form 363 (see p. 101 above). Fig. 56, 19–22 are examples of this form in white to red-buff ware. All show multiple mouldings on the neck, which expands above and has a groove at the lip. There was only one small rim-fragment in 1959.

Form 366 (see p. 101 above). The two necks, fig. 56, 17–18, are of a sandy, red-brown ware which suggests that they may be wasters from the mica-coated group. On the other hand, the outline in each case is different. Both are grooved on top, and the form of the neck varies. More important is the fact that the sides of the mouth are pinched together and lapped over—a clear-cut distinction in form. Fig. 70, 2, 3, shows two more

---

[1] Cf. Ludowici, *Rheinzabern* iv, p. 244, K.25.

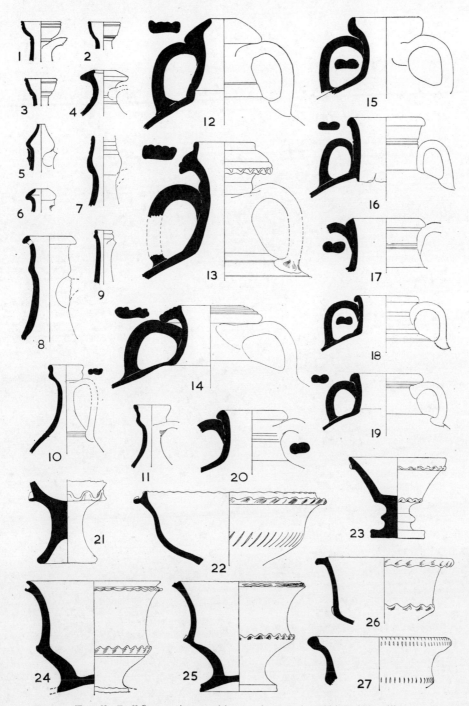

Fɪɢ. 69. Buff flagons, jugs, and incense-burners (pp. 124–8, 133). (¼)

necks which are exactly similar; some fragments found in 1959, like fig. 56, 18, are too small for description.

Form 376. Cup-mouthed flagon with long neck.

The three cupped necks, fig. 69, 1–3, are quite different in style from f. 156. They are of good buff to white ware, and are very carefully made, with neat grooves at top and bottom outside. It is unfortunate that the remains furnish no more information on the shape, and there is no more complete example in the Museum. They are from the general filling of the enclosure. Another exactly like no. 1 was found in 1959.

Form 149(?). Flagons with flat rim and short neck.

Fig. 69, 4 represents four rims, one from kiln 20, one from kiln 19, all hard buff ware. The outline is quite like the first-century type, but the two grooves on the neck are distinctive. In 1959 we gained more evidence for this form. We had five more necks in which the top is truly conical and straight. All were white or buff.

But a further seven complete necks are evidence for a second form in which the conical top is rounded convexly in outline; of these we illustrate four:

Fig. 70, 10. Fine yellow-buff ware, rather soft. Handle two-ribbed.
Fig. 70, 11. One of two examples; white ware, handle two-ribbed.
Fig. 70, 12. Fine yellow-buff ware, rather soft. Handle two-ribbed.
Fig. 69, 6. A small example found in 1933.

Form 367. Flagon with cupped mouth with constriction in rim.

Two rims only, fig. 69, 10–11, both from kiln 19. No. 10 is of hard buff ware with tall, curved neck and two grooves on the shoulder. Another similar fragment may belong to the same vessel, but if so it had two handles, which is hardly likely. There is a small hole against the handle. No. 11 is similar but larger. Both handles are three-ribbed. No more found in 1959.

Odd necks (figs. 69 and 70)

Fig. 69, 7 is of hard buff ware and has a bulbous top tapering and cordoned upwards, the rim missing. The spring of the handle is indicated. There is no parallel so far. From kiln 19.

Fig. 69, 8 is a large neck of soft buff ware. The same remarks apply.

Fig. 69, 9 is a tall cylindrical neck with handle attachment high up at the rim. The latter is doubly beaded and slightly hollowed inside. Soft creamy ware. Waste heap.

Fig. 70, 25. Part of a grooved neck with remains of handle. Buff ware (59). 1959.

JUGS

Two-handled jugs (fig. 69)

The three most remarkable of these are singletons and have not been classified. No. 12 is of fine hard buff ware and has a certain resemblance to no. 4 and the first-century flagons. These it surpasses in size, and the handles are broad and four-ribbed. The only parallel is a neck in the Museum large enough to be called an amphora (May, *Colchester*, pl. LXIX, 342).

No. 13 is a most distinctive neck of fine hard buff ware. It is an elaboration of the preceding with the addition of an upright lip and a groove and frill on the rim. There is a cordon on the neck above the handles, which are thick, broad, and five-ribbed. There are strong indentations on each side of the handles at the base, and two grooves on the shoulder. Form 370 (see p. 187).

No. 14 is another unusual neck, but not without parallel for there are three similar in the Museum, and a fourth in fine red ware, but with only one handle. All are reeded on the sloping rim, and the handles seem regularly four-ribbed. Hard buff ware. In 1959 we had the good fortune to find most of the upper part of one of these, so that we now have more than half of the outline:

Fig. 70, 13. Very fine and thin white ware, very soft and underfired. There are three pairs of low cordons, carefully made, on the body. The vessel was somewhat distorted. The handles have the section shown and are easily recognized; there were several fragments of similar mouths and of similarly cordoned bodies. We have no clue to the type of foot used.
Fig. 70, 14. Buff ware; probably simply a variant of the preceding; the handles are quite typical.
Fig. 69, 15. A large cupped mouth, quite smooth on the outside, with two-ribbed handles. Found in the enclosure south of kiln 21.
Fig. 70, 15. Another found in 1959, quite similar but more tapered and the handles not ribbed. Buff with white surface.

There are fragments of handles similar to those of no. 15, and two rim-fragments of this outline but twice the diameter. Some of the handles are equally large. A number of fragments of large handles have a large, round thumb-impression, or a row of such impressions, at the base of the handle. Such handles may be smooth or two-ribbed, or four-ribbed. We do not know to what form of neck they belonged.

Fig. 70, 16. A very large neck in fine buff ware, found in pit 14.
Fig. 70, 17. In fine soft yellow-buff ware: part of an outsize pedestal-foot or trumpet-shaped mouth.
Fig. 70, 18–22. Five large rims which we cannot attribute to forms, all in white or buff ware, mostly underfired; there are fragments of others. No. 19 is later than kiln 31A, being built into kiln 31.

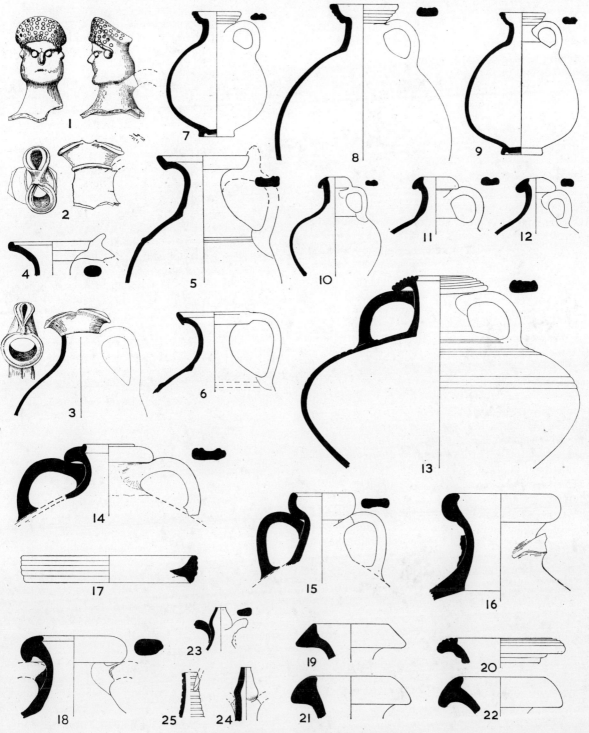

Fig. 70. Buff flagons and jugs (pp. 124–8). (¼)

Form unclassified. Small two-handled jugs with nipple-shaped mouth and very small orifice.

The evidence is small, only the few necks we have from our site; I cannot recall seeing one in the Museum. There is no doubt about the double handles, but we know nothing of the rest of the vessel.

> Fig. 69, 5. Small neck, white ware; handles gone.
> Fig. 70, 23. White ware, underfired.
> Fig. 70, 24. White ware. Half only preserved.

Form 167C. Two-handled jug with more or less cylindrical neck.

This is the second-century form of the vessel which can be traced through from the Augustan form at Haltern (Loeschcke, types 50–52), see *Cam.* p. 249. The neck has become very short and nearly cylindrical, generally with two grooves. The lip is thick and beaded. The handles are short, roundly curved with two ribs. One in the Museum has a very oblate body with a thick flat foot. Fragments show that ours were similar. We illustrate (fig. 69, 16–20) five out of quite a number of fragments. No. 16 is of creamy buff ware, over-fired. The handles are unusually low and the joint with the neck clumsy; another similar, but with higher handles is from kiln 17. No. 17 is normal, from the same kiln, and there is another like it from the enclosure. No. 18 is of soft, dark buff ware. There are fragments of two more, but with no offset at the shoulder (f. 167D), from kiln 20. No. 19 is fine hard buff, nearly white, low and wide, possibly later than the rest, from under the stone wall. No. 20 is a good normal example in fine buff ware. A complete example is illustrated in May, *Colchester*, pl. XLVII, 199.

The form was again well represented in 1959. A complete neck like fig. 69, 17, underfired buff with white surface, has a double groove at the level of the handles, as has another like no. 16. There are four like no. 17, underfired, and three well fired (one from kiln 31) and examples like nos. 18 and 19. Fragments of the side with the very marked curve were not uncommon; the bases seem not to be identifiable. Two fragments of form as no. 19 bear traces of a thin and poor red coating.

PEDESTALLED VASES

Form 207. Tall pedestalled vases. These were present in large numbers and in two groups which differ little except in size and thickness of wall. The vessels are distinguished by their fine texture, but the very quantity of the fragments has prevented attempts to restore them.

They are remarkable in that they so closely follow the outline of the well-known pre-Roman f. 204, which

died out in the middle of the first century. The larger group are very large and heavy, especially in the pedestal. The lighter necks have not survived so well. The general outline must have been nearly symmetrical, with the base and top almost of the same pattern, and the body more or less oval. Such bases have been found from time to time in Colchester, but it was not until 1932 that we were able to publish a complete outline (*Col. Mus. Rep.* 1932, p. 24, pl. VII, 6, here reproduced, fig. 71, 1). It is of fine buff ware, with polished surface decorated with red-brown paint, and was found at the Essex County Hospital. Painting was not much in fashion with our potters and neither neck nor base is accurately paralleled by ours, so that this vessel is probably later.[1]

The second group is similar to this vessel in being much lighter in build. On fig. 71, nos. 2–6 are from tops; no. 4 seems of the smaller category, the rest of the larger. No. 2 reeded, of hard buff ware, has a cordon and groove on the neck. There is a suggestion, which, however, is not borne out by the other fragments, that it might have had a handle. Found with the mass of flagon necks on site C4.

Nos. 3–5 are good buff ware from the enclosure, the east end of the stone wall, and kiln 17A respectively. No. 6 we take to be from a neck; fine hard yellow-buff ware, decorated with two bands of rouletted 'chessboard' pattern. From filling over kiln 19. No. 7, with the same decoration, may be the rim of the same neck, but might equally well belong to a foot. Soft white ware, from east end of stone wall.

No. 9 is part of a pedestal of quite unusual pattern, following the shape of the foot of f. 202, and decorated with a frill. Two fragments, both from the enclosure, in hard buff ware.

No. 10 is a base of the lighter group and matches the top, no. 2, above; fine buff ware. Others are shown on fig. 72, 4, 7, 21, 22.

Fig. 71, nos. 11–16, are bases of the heavy group, selected from a large number. They are of various qualities and shades of buff ware. Some are decorated with frills, others with grooves, and a few with notching, but most are quite plain. While most have the high floor of no. 1, no. 15 has a low floor. Most from the enclosure, but no. 13 from the stone wall.

Additional finds in 1959 included the pieces shown on fig. 72, 1–7. No. 1 is good buff ware with double grooves on body. Nos. 2 and 3 are in fine white ware, polished, and in yellow-buff respectively. Both had a band of barbotined rings in red paint. Some other large vessels, of form unknown, had been uniformly red-coated, and we must decide that red paint was not so rarely used by our potters as we had supposed.

These pedestal vases would appear to be a local

---

[1] But more evidence of painting has come up in 1959, cf. fig. 72, 2, 3, and p. 96.

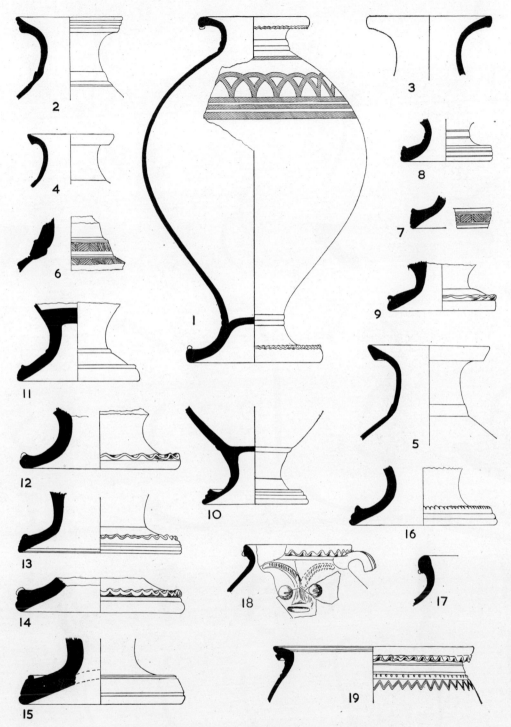

FIG. 71. Pedestalled urns and honey-pots (pp. 128, 133). (¼)

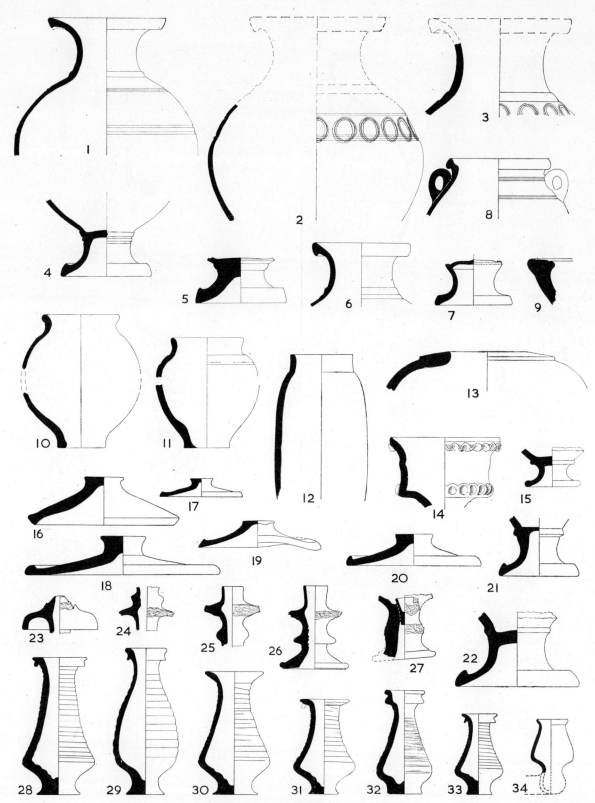

FIG. 72. Various buff vessels (pp. 110, 128, 133–4). ($\frac{1}{4}$)

peculiarity, for they do not seem to have been reported from elsewhere, even on other sites where native pre-Roman pedestalled forms existed.

BOWLS

The chief forms of bowls in buff, white, or red ware are shown on fig. 73. They are not very numerous, and it is worthy of note that they seldom, if ever, occur in deposits in the Roman town. In fact they are so restricted and local in distribution that it has not been considered desirable to give all of them form-numbers.

Fig. 73, no. 1. Several fragments of one heavy basin of thick, hard white-buff ware. The rim, flattened on top and projecting inwards, is decorated with a continuous row of deeply impressed ovals (1a), and provided with at least two wide and narrow lugs or handles. All eight fragments were found littered around inside the enclosure.

No. 2. Part of a bowl with reeded rim; sandy, pale yellowish clay. Kiln 19.

No. 3. Part of a similar bowl, but the side sharply carinated. Clay sandy, red-buff, gritty. The angular form was perhaps the more common, and the following rims belong to bowls of this type. Kiln 19.

No. 4. Clay soft buff, diameter enormous. Kiln 17.

No. 5. Clay pale buff, from under the stone wall. Diameter very large.

No. 6. Clay soft drab-buff. Diameter very large. Kiln 17.

No. 7. Clay hard brown-buff. Kiln 19, another similar from under stone wall, sandy pale buff. Both of very large diameter.

No. 8. Similar to last. Sandy buff ware. Kiln 19. Huge.

No. 9. Two rims, hollowed as for a lid, one in flower-pot red ware from over the enclosure, the other in soft bright red. Kiln 19. Diameter very large.

No. 10. Two fragments (fitting) of another hollowed rim, even larger, in dark buff ware. Again the diameter is enormous.

No. 11. Rim in hard red ware reminiscent of f. 246. From site C4 at 18 in.

No. 12. Unusual rim of rough brown-buff ware, from the enclosure. Diameter very large.

No. 13. Large rim belonging to the series of 2–8 above, but tilted upwards; soft, coarse red ware with grey core, very large. From the enclosure.

No. 14. Represents a large number of fragments of vessels which may have been bowls or lids, or intended to serve as either. The ware is thin but the finish is not fine; if anything the outside is the finer, suggesting a primary purpose as a lid. The ware is a sandy brown-buff, and the vessels vary much in diameter and curve of wall, but not in design. They are associated almost entirely with the enclosure, though odd pieces occur all over the site. None found in 1959.

No. 15. Part of a small bowl of soft buff ware. The form is 318 (Hofheim 129). The ledge of the rim is imperfect. This is the only fragment of this form found on the site, and it could well be a stray from the earlier period. Kiln 17.

Nos. 16 and 17. Two unusual rims, the first with a groove, soft buff ware, the second soft white ware. Both had decoration of three rounded projections on the rim, in the first case with three shallow, round impressions as well. Both are from over the enclosure.[1]

No. 18. Part of a bowl in buff ware from kiln 19.

No. 19. Bowl found in several fragments from the filling of the enclosure. Hard white ware, surface rough owing to a small, dark, gritty content.

No. 20. Form 306. Two fragments of a bowl in soft buff ware, from the enclosure, and the stone wall. Four similar rims came from the enclosure, all hard, white-buff ware, and a complete example (fig. 74, 1) was found in 1956. (See p. 165.)

No. 21 shows a huge rim in soft buff ware, from the enclosure, and no. 22 another small rim in white-buff ware, also from the enclosure.

Nos. 23–27 are of rims of various vessels of uncertain form.

No. 23. Soft sandy buff ware, with some mica. Kiln 17, unstratified.

No. 24. Three fragments, sandy red with grey core. Site C4. Unstratified.

No. 25. Soft sandy buff ware. Diameter very large. There are several small holes pierced through the side under the rim $\frac{5}{8}$ to $\frac{7}{8}$ in. apart, but one fragment shows that there was a space of $3\frac{1}{2}$ in. at least with no holes. The three fragments were found in the enclosure.

No. 26. Soft sandy buff ware. Diameter c. 10 in. (?). Enclosure.

No. 27. Two examples, unstratified. Diameter c. $10\frac{3}{4}$ in.

Nos. 28 and 29. See colour-coated ware, pp. 101, 107.

No. 30. Sandy buff ware with fine mixed grit. Apparently never polished. Two fragments from kiln 17 (a similar rim from the enclosure is black, micaceous).

The vessels on fig. 73 have been illustrated rather fully because they are remarkably isolated so far as parallels are concerned, and they are, moreover, of very rare occurrence among the vast quantities of Roman wares found in Roman levels in and about Colchester. They can hardly have been in production long or in large quantities. There is no doubt that vessels like no. 14 were being produced in some numbers, for our collection of fragments is large, but they are seldom found off the site.

The large bowls, nos. 2–13, so strongly resemble the large examples of f. 243 of the first century in many respects that one cannot but think of them as derivatives. On the other hand, f. 243 does not seem to have continued in existence except in the derivative ff. 244–6, with which our rims (except no. 11) have only a formal connexion. Possibly we have here a case of atavism, where the form has developed to a stage approximating to the original form.

No. 14 is represented by over fifty fragments, mostly large and cleanly broken, yet few will join up, and our figure is the only complete section obtained. Most bases are not so thick, and in some the offset at the greatest diameter is very pronounced or even a raised line. The clay is always brown-buff, carelessly smoothed on the outside. Largest diameter about $6\frac{3}{4}$ in. Most were found on the west side of the enclosure (kilns 19 and 22) and may be associated with kiln 22. One fragment is from the stone wall.

[1] Compare fig. 86, 8, 9 from kiln 24.

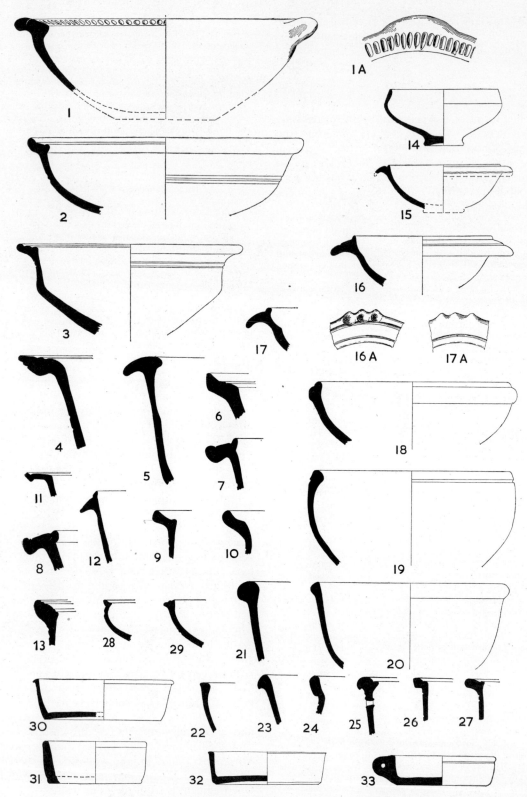

FIG. 73. Bowls and lamp-holders (pp. 101, 107, 110, 131). (¼)

BOTTOMLESS JARS

Fig. 72, nos. 10, 11 shows two rims drawn out with two bases beneath them so as to give a good impression of the appearance of these vessels. No less than 12 rims, 9 base-fragments, and 28 body-fragments were found among pottery connected with the final base floor of kiln 30. They explain the few examples found elsewhere in the excavations.

They are of rough-and-ready make, of buff clay like that of the kiln-tubes, and like them also the ware is brittle from repeated exposure to great heat. Some have traces of red clay burnt on to them and may have been buried in kiln walls. All were made with the base open in the middle, the opening being usually left quite rough and unfinished. Of the over fifty sherds hardly any two join, and the number of vessels represented must be large.

I do not know of any parallel, nor have I any idea what the purpose of these vessels may have been. It seems quite clear they were made on the spot for the potters' own use in their work.

Tall jar. Fig. 72, 12 is from a large fragment of hard, rough, buff ware, scarcely smoothed. The surface is splashed with red paint, fallen while the vessel lay horizontal. From the black ash in pit 13.

FORM 288. FACE-URNS, ETC. (FIG. 71)

There were many fragments of large buff urns or vases, most of which seem to have carried some form of decoration. So far none has been restored, but two examples can be illustrated.

Fig. 71, no. 17, a brown-buff frilled rim, diameter 7¾ in. Site C4.

No. 18, several fragments of a soft buff face-urn which had three handles. The face applied in high relief and the rim frilled. Many similar vessels are in the Museum, some in graves and always in association with 'Antonine' pottery, therefore of second- or third-century date. May, pl. LI, A, illustrates seven such. Nearly all are in our buff ware and many of them were doubtless made in these or neighbouring kilns. Under stone wall.

No. 19 is part of a large reeded rim of soft sandy buff ware with frill, two grooves on shoulder, with a row of impressions between, and a narrow combed wavy line below. It is probably from a 'honey-pot'. Unstratified.

Among the fragments is a rim similar to no. 18 but much larger. Brown-buff ware, frilled, diameter 7¾ in., from site C4. Two more fragments of frilled rims, diameter *c.* 12 in., coarse buff ware, were found.

In 1933 the fine example of f. 177 was found in grave 302 (fig. 79, 5 and p. 144), and in 1959 several more rims of ff. 170, 175, and 177, with fragments of handles and especially of the unmistakable flat bases with beaded offset.

FORM 198. INCENSE CUPS (FIG. 69)

Frilled, pedestalled bowls. These have been fully discussed by Wheeler (*Brecon Gaer*, 225, with numerous references). The various shapes are too many to number separately.

The fragments found in the kilns were not numerous, though varied enough. All useful fragments are shown on fig. 69, nos. 21–27. They are crude and heavy in design, and most are of a coarse, sandy clay which fires buff or red.

No. 21 is soft red ware, probably misfired. Found near kiln 15. So tall a pedestal is unusual. It could perhaps have suited a bowl similar to the next.

No. 22, several fragments in coarse red-brown ware, one from kiln 17B, the rest from the filling of the enclosure, all from a wide shallow bowl with rounded carination, which is decorated with oblique incisions. Pedestal missing.

No. 23, soft yellowish-white ware, almost intact. The solid pedestal and conical body with flat interior base are most unusual. From filling of enclosure over kiln 19.

Nos. 24 and 25. These alone bear a general resemblance. They are of very coarse buff ware and come from the upper filling of the enclosure. The rim of the base of no. 24 is missing and the upper rim and frill of no. 25. The form of the base is quite unusual.

No. 26, soft red ware, possibly once white coated, from under the stone wall. It appears distorted in firing, so the diameter is approximate. The rim is flat with weak frilling.

No. 27, soft red ware, from a smaller bowl somewhat similar to no. 22, with buff surface. Rim and carination notched, foot lost.

There are a few more fragments including two rims like no. 26 from site C4, and a piece of a pedestal found with the wasters in pit C17. A few fragments were found in 1959.

The few fragments found in 1959 are all red-buff ware; three pedestalled bases all have a cordon, one other fragment gives a body-outline, the rest are small fragments, but seem to show that a frill at the carination was usual. Fig. 72, 14 is red-buff, coarse, unsmoothed; 15 is similar.

According to Wheeler, loc. cit., notching began to replace frilling about the middle of the second century, later becoming general. Discoveries at Colchester are completely in agreement.

UNGUENT POTS (FIG. 72)

Remains of these were plentiful, not only in these excavations, but also among remains found from time to time in previous years in this locality. No less than five could be restored and others nearly so. Although these better-preserved vessels occurred here and there in the general filling of the enclosure, together with fragments, a deposit of rings which had become detached from the lower lip in firing was found in the stoke-hole of kiln 22, and one may presume that a batch of these vessels had been made shortly before the kilns were abandoned. Nearly all seem to have been wasters. The commonest faults are the bursting of the base (owing to the excessive amount of material there) and the splitting off of the lower rim, seen in our fig. 72, 30, 31. In that figure nos. 28–33 are all in rough buff ware and all much alike. The lower lip of the rim is usually much the smaller: only occasionally is it the larger, as in no. 32. None of our vessels has the narrow foot of form 389B.

The production of these pots is evidence that there was at least one local firm of unguent manufacturers of sufficient standing to place considerable orders for them, and possibly quite a large proportion of these vessels found in Britain may have come from Colchester.

Several different forms are found locally, but we have only three from these kilns:

Form 389. Tall, carinated body on a small, solid base, which is carelessly finished. The body tapers upwards, with incurved sides, to a small mouth with double, pulley-like rim. The mouth is trumpet-shaped inside. The whole body is spirally grooved down to the carination. We illustrate four, fig. 72, nos. 28, 30, 31, 33, all in the same buff ware.

Form 389A. Very similar to the preceding, but the mouth cupped within, and the base shorter and broader, and more carefully made. The spiral grooving careless. Same ware. Fig. 72, 32.

Form 389C. Also similar to the preceding, but the body bulbously curved outwards and the grooving lighter. The clay is whiter. Fig. 72, 29.

TRIPLE VASES

There is one cup from a triple vase, fig. 72, 34. The clay is fine soft buff, with remains of a dark chocolate coating, and the cup sat on a ring of comparatively large diameter, with a large opening connecting the two. Found near kiln 19.

Another fragment from a hollow ring was found in the rubbish around the enclosure. It is of soft yellowish ware and preserves the base of a cup which has a small perforation through to the ring, but the opening is plugged by a pellet of clay which the potter has neglected to remove. Compare *Cumb. and Westm. Trans.* xxx (1930), no. 100a, period I, second century. A third fragment was found in 1959.

CHEESE PRESSES

Part of a typical base, with concentric ridges and perforations, was found in 1959, in red-buff ware. Another base with several perforations of $\frac{1}{4}$ in. diameter was probably from a colander.

HORS-D'ŒUVRE DISH

A few fragments of soft red ware very underfired yielded, after much study, the restoration shown on fig. 74, nos. 3, 3a. It is nearly 12 in. in diameter, with a circular compartment in the centre and the remaining space divided into four by vertical walls. The rim has a ledge for a lid. We know of no parallel.

LARGE BOWL

The large bowl, fig. 74, 4, is of very soft ware, buff, underfired; it is simply made, of conical form, with heavy, rounded rim and flat base. The body is pierced by four round holes all about $\frac{3}{4}$ in. above the base. Found by Mr. Calver. Compare a similar bowl found with remains of T.S. manufactory, Chenet, p. 53, pl. III.

AMPHORA. FORM 188 (FIG. 74, 2)

This amphora is constantly turning up in Roman Colchester. The characteristics of the type are the very flat shoulder and absurdly small foot with footring. The short, broad handles are easily recognized, but the mouth resembles that of the globular f. 187, except that, as a rule, there is no offset inside the lip. One neck in the Museum bears a stamp, but this is the only stamp on this form of which we have heard.

The complete upper half of one vessel was found sunk in the ground, upside down, in the west bank of the stoke-yard of kiln 30. Its mouth was plugged with lead. It had no doubt been placed there as some convenience to the potters in their work, but there was no clue in the contents to what this purpose was. There was only earth and potsherds of the kiln period.

The drawing of this vessel, fig. 74, 2, is at one-sixth scale. Other fragments were found, from one of which the base in the drawing is taken.

COARSE WARE LIDS (FIG. 72)

This is a dull and perhaps unprofitable subject, but the lids which occurred must be recorded. They are nearly all buff, so we place them here. They all have a central knob which is flat on top and is usually unfinished, still showing the mark of the wire with which they were cut off the wheel.

There are five forms of rim, classified according to the outline of the lip. If this is carefully moulded we have:

1. A bevelled lip, rounded beneath and projecting more or less sharply upwards (fig. 72, 17, 19, 20). There were seventeen of these.

2. A rounded lip with a rather flattened beading (fig. 72, 18). Five of these.

If the rim is not carefully moulded it may take one of the following three forms:

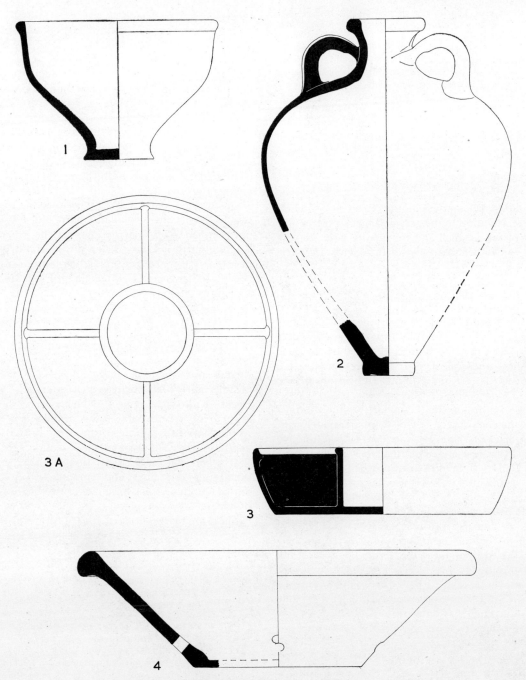

FIG. 74. Large buff vessels (pp. 131, 134). (All ¼ except no. 2, ⅙)

3. An oblique lip, cut off with blunt edges top and bottom. The top edge may rise a little. Five of these (fig. 72, 16).

4. The lip is simply tapered off to a more or less sharp edge (not figured). One only.

5. The lip is turned inwards for more than half a circle, so that it turns up inside. One is shown fig. 98, 15. They are mostly red and sandy, but some are grey. It is doubtful whether this form was made in these particular kilns.

I am not aware of any chronological value in these coarse-ware lids. I have often thought that lids are most common in Trajanic levels, but have no proof of the validity of the observation.

GREY WARES

It would appear that our potters devoted comparatively little attention to the grey and black pottery; the quantity of this is small and the quality poor, though we must remember that most of the sherds are likely to have been wasters.

PLATTERS AND BOWLS

Form 37. Wide bowl or porringer with slightly curved wall; the lip as a rule heavily beaded and of triangular section. The side is rounded or bevelled into the base and almost invariably decorated with a scored lattice pattern and polished all over, inside and out.

Of some 150 fragments the majority came from the filling of the enclosure; a few of them are made of the universal black cooking-pot ware charged with minute white grit, the rest are of normal fine grey to black ware, which is a muddy brown when badly fired. Several fragments are discoloured through being in an oxidizing flame. Quite a number of fragments are decorated with a wavy line on the side instead of latticing, an unusual feature.

Fragments of this form were found here and there all over the area of the Camulodunum excavations from 1930 onwards, but always high up so that they could not ever be said to have been definitely in use before A.D. 60. They must, however, have begun to appear soon after that date.

Quite a number (about 20) were found under the stone wall.

Form 38. Wide bowl or porringer with straight side, bearing a heavy, beaded rim of three-quarter round to triangular section, and joining the base by a distinct bevel. Polished all over and not decorated. (For illustrations see figs. 6, nos. 13, 14; 93, 1–3.) These were much more common than f. 37. Of over 260 rims some thirty were found under the stone wall, the rest chiefly from the enclosure. Only a small proportion are of the cooking-pot ware; the bulk are of various colours and qualities of the local clay.

Form 39. Shallow dish with curving, upright wall, the same general shape as f. 17, but not so splayed. The ware is the universal black cooking-pot ware and therefore not local, and the outside is scored with the usual intersecting arcs and looped scrabble under the base. There were only three fragments; one under the stone wall and two near kiln 19. A complete example in grave 320 is on fig. 78, 7.

Form 40. Wide bowl or porringer with straight side and simple lip bevelled at junction with base. Fine grey ware, polished all over, occasionally decorated with a wavy line on the side. Over forty fragments, eight under the stone wall. Seven belong to f. 40B, having a groove below the lip.

Unclassified bowl. Fig. 75, 3 shows the outline of two fragments of a bowl of fine, hard, bluish-grey ware, not polished except on top of rim. The general form is reminiscent of *Cam.* f. 246, but the rim droops like that of a f. 37. Decoration, a fine lattice pattern between pairs of grooves. Found in pit F, site C4, among a quantity of wasters.

JARS AND COOKING-POTS

Form 268A. Oval or ovoid jar smoothed but never polished in any part, the side usually curving in to the slightly spreading base. Base unfinished, always showing the mark of the wire which severed it from the wheel. Rim offset at neck, which is very short, and sharply everted. In A the rim is of thick and rounded section, in B it is thin in section, with almost straight, parallel sides. The ware of the A section can be very coarse and coarsely gritted; that of the B section is usually darker, finer and smooth, never coarsely gritted. Both sections have one or two grooves on the shoulder.

There are many varieties, for the form was the commonest in use over a long period in Colchester. The following are illustrated:

Fig. 76, 1. A waster of thin brown ware, with some black colouration of the surface, found with wasters in pit C17. Form 268B.

Fig. 76, 2. A waster found near kiln 15, brown clay with rough, brown and black surface. Form 268A.

Fig. 76, 3. Thin brown-black ware. Unstratified.

Fig. 76, 4. Hard brown to grey-black ware; from pit G in site C4. Form 268B.

Fig. 75, 6. Intact example found upright in the filling of the enclosure as if intentionally buried there. It is of the B class, with the rim hollowed for a lid, as is not infrequent (p. 19).

Fig. 75, 9. Another example of group B found isolated in area L.

There were over 100 rims of group A compared with some dozen of group B, so that, although one of the latter was found in the stoke-hole of kiln 20, the evidence is that group A was being made in our kilns and that the rims of group B are generally of later date and of adventitious occurrence, the majority of the dozen or so being odd vessels apparently buried at the time of the later burials, or fragments thrown in with the filling after our kilns had fallen into disuse. On the other hand, the presence of fig. 76, 1 in pit C17 shows that group B was already in production before our kilns closed down.

this also is underfired and is triply latticed like the first.

Four fragments came from kiln 17, the rest from the enclosure.

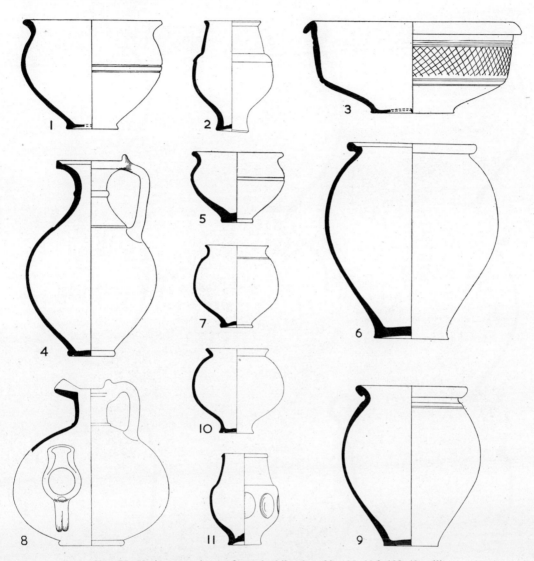

FIG. 75. Various vessels, not from the kilns (pp. 99, 105, 136, 138–40). (¼)

the other hand, the presence of fig. 76, 1 in pit C17 shows that group B was already in production before our kilns closed down.

Form 278. Ovoid jar with broad, curved, sharply everted rim. Polished top and bottom, the intervening space decorated with scored lines.

About eighty vessels were represented in all. Two from near kiln 15 are shown on fig. 76, 5 and 6; the former is a waster. The ware is soft and brownish, misfired. Another was found in fragments in kiln 16;

Form 279. Tall cooking-pot of the same general shape as f. 278, but usually rather differently outlined at the offset of the neck, and nearly always of black cooking-pot ware charged with minute white grit. The whole was dipped in an intense black coating, top and bottom were polished and the space between latticed.

There are three main subdivisions of this form:

A. Body barrel-shaped, rim short and upright, slightly curved, often bearing a wavy line on the neck. Latticing tall and close. The type is Hadrianic-Antonine.

B. Body taller, tending to be wider at the top, rim much broader and curved, usually slightly thickened at extreme lip. Lattice not so tall. Our example, fig. 76, 9, was found on site C4. Only five other fragments were found.

sionally two) grooves on the shoulder. Base neatly finished and often grooved beneath. Newstead type. The typical clay is nearly white, with pale, pearly grey polished surface which is usually slightly micaceous. Other wares occur.

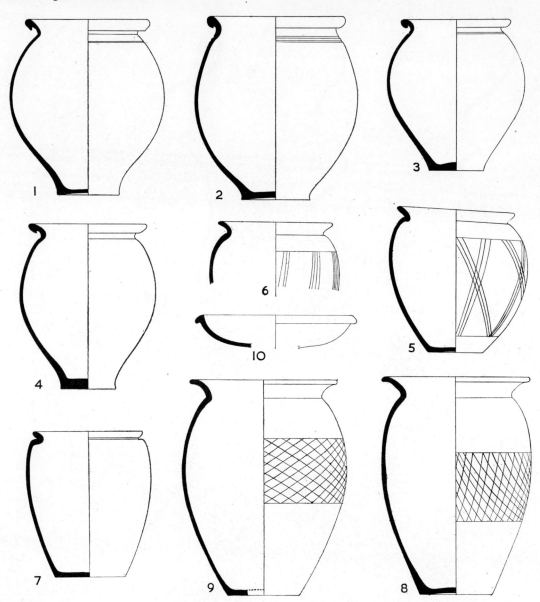

FIG. 76. Jars and cooking-pots (pp. 136–8, 141, 146). (¼)

C. Body tall, definitely wider at the top; rim very wide, usually exceeding the greatest diameter of the body. Latticed band now very narrow and the lattice very oblique and widely spaced. Our fig. 76, 8 is intermediate between B and C. The ware is an unusual fine brown-grey, perhaps a local copy.

Form 299. Wide bowl of S-section, without offsets, the lip either simple or beaded, with one (very occa-

Fig. 75, 1 is a typical example from pit F, site C4.
Fig. 75, 5 is another, the base beaded. Unstratified.

There were also about twenty-four fragments from the enclosure, from under the stone wall, and from site C4.

SITE C4, THE STONE WALL AND GRAVES (FIGS. 9 AND 77)

A scene of activity, such as is suggested by the eleven kilns found in a small area in 1933 and 1959, might be expected to have remains of some variety lying around the site. And so, indeed, it proved, though the first hopes that a maze of dark marks in the yellow sand only 6 in. under the turf might yield the plans of the dwellings or workshops of the potters were not fulfilled.[1] An area over 100 ft. long and 25 ft. wide was stripped and was known as 'Site C4'. The markings

inhumation, grave 554, distinguishable as a rect·angular mark in the filling. There had been a coffin 7 ft. 2 in. long by 2 ft. 6 in. wide, with iron nails at the corners and at intervals along the sides. Of the skeleton no trace remained.

At the west end of the coffin a much darker and almost rectangular mark showed the position of a box, which contained a jar f. 279c (cf. fig. 78, 8) lying on its side. The sides of the box had been 9–11 in. long, but they had been distorted by collapse. Three iron nails belonging to the bottom of the box remained in position on one side and two on the other. The jar

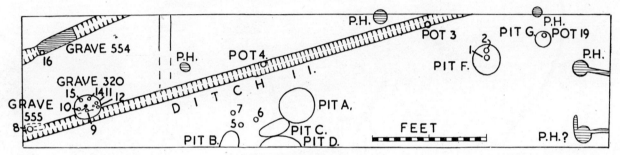

FIG. 77. Plan of Site C4.

which drew our attention to it proved to be without plan or co-ordination, and had to be dismissed as left by tree-roots or rabbit-burrows (the field was formerly known as 'The Warren').

Nevertheless, much was found in stripping this area, and no doubt a somewhat similar harvest would be reaped by stripping further. The subsoil is a very soft yellow sand and is crossed diagonally by the traces of the Palisade and ditch II. These, which are attributed to Boudicca, have been fully discussed and described in *Camulodunum*.[2] The very soft sand had not preserved their outline; the bottom appeared shallow and rounded. A curious feature was a trench or ditch crossing the berm at an angle just east of graves 554 and 320. It was similar in form to the Palisade trench but contained pottery of the kiln period. It was probably dug for an inhumation and contained the colour-coated beakers fig. 75, 10 (unclassified) and 11 (f. 408–9, fluted), which would go well with such circumstances. The topsoil, only 6 in. deep on the north side where first opened, rapidly deepened downhill to 18 in. or 2 ft. at the south side, and we found that the upper (north) part of the site had been denuded since ancient times leaving ditch II little more than 2 ft. wide and 18 in. deep. Its filling of uniform dark sandy material was interrupted here and there by later burials and pits, as was that of the Palisade trench.

The west part of the Palisade trench contained an

was crushed by earth pressure, and its contents, as it lay on its side, had left an intensely black and soot-like deposit $1\frac{1}{4}$ in. thick on the inside. The surrounding earth was also very dark.

Two post-holes of about 2 ft. diameter and 18 in. deep stood on the north lip of ditch II. Their sides were vertical; the western hole was a little farther from the centre line of the ditch than the eastern. Another similar, but 2 ft. 9 in. in diameter and 10 in. deep, was found near the south lip of the ditch, near pit G, and a fourth half-way down the east side of the area (marked P.H.). There was a mark like that of a sleeper-beam running SE. from it, and there were two lighter marks running from pit H, which was of the same dimensions exactly and presumably to be considered as another post-hole; the pottery from it. was of the time of Claudius–Nero. The pottery in the filling of the other holes was all of the kiln-period. They could, accordingly, have belonged to some part of the potters' establishment, but only stripping to a much greater extent than we were able to do could establish their nature.

Pit F, a shallow depression in the sand, about 5 ft. in diameter, produced about two barrow-loads of broken flagons of the cup-mouthed f. 156, including the one with barbotine decoration (fig. 56, 23) and other pottery. The vessels had apparently all cracked in firing; none except that figured could be restored. Two vessels, fig. 75, 1 and another not now identifiable,

---

[1] See note on Mittelbronn, p. 34.

[2] *Cam.*, p. 40.

were found upright among these fragments and are regarded as a possible burial (grave 557).

Pit G was very small and contained sherds of the kiln-period, and the jar f. 268B (fig. 76, 4), of thin, hard, brown to grey-black ware.

Near the centre of the south side a cluster of small pits with rounded bottoms was found, shown by the letters A, B, C, D on the plan. They were empty

paint. The handle was already broken off when it was buried, and the mouth is distorted, either in firing or in modelling the head.

Only a few feet east of grave 555 a group of seven vessels stood spaced out in an oval, as if around an inhumation. A few small pieces of unburnt human bones were actually found in the centre. This is grave 320, which comprised (fig. 78):

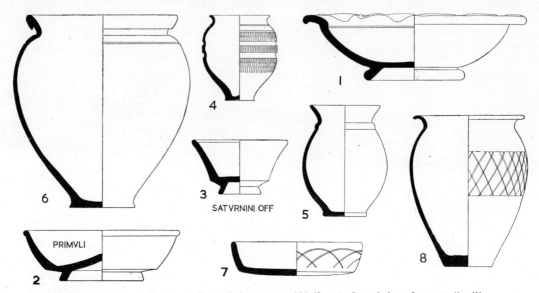

FIG. 78. Nos. 1–7, group of vessels from grave 320 (for no. 8 see below, footnote 1). (¼)

except for a beaker f. 402 (fig. 55, 4), which was in pit A. It is of yellowish ware with dark purple coating. The bell-mouth and pill-box foot indicate a fourth-century date. Near the other pits and shown on the plan by three circles were three other vessels:

Fig. 75, 2, beaker f. 395, creamy ware, red to chocolate coated, presumably from the Nene potteries.
Fig. 78, 8, cooking pot of fine pale grey ware, f. 278.
Fig. 75, 5, bowl f. 299, light grey ware, polished.

The first was lying on its side; they were not closely associated but they, or some of them, may have accompanied an inhumation; if so, nothing else of it remained. Close by lay a coin of Cunobelin, at the same level, and a piece of mould for coin-flans—relics of the early occupation.

In the SW. corner lay the scanty remains of a skeleton with a fine mask-mouthed flagon at its feet (grave 555). It was laid in ditch II, head to the east. The vessel, fig. 82, 1, is of buff ware decorated in red

No. 1. T.S. bowl f. 36, fine ware.
No. 2. T.S. bowl f. 18/31, stamped PRIMVLI.
No. 3. T.S. cup f. 33, stamped SATVRNINI OFF (C.M. 285–92.39).
No. 4. Small beaker, f. 397, rough dark grey ware, two deep girth grooves and three rouletted bands. Found inside the T.S. cup.
No. 5. 'Poppy-head' beaker, fine polished grey ware, f. 123.
No. 6. Cooking pot of f. 268, pale grey ware.[1]
No. 7. Platter of black ware, f. 39, scored intersecting arcs.

Two other vessels, marked 4 and 3 on plan, were found almost intact in the filling of ditch II. Pot 4, fig. 55, 3, is a very tall beaker f. 392 of rough light red ware, perhaps red coated (cf. one from Caistor-by-Norwich, Atkinson, T. 17, attributed to c. A.D. 200–50). The other is of f. 108, of grey ware; it contained burnt matter, possibly charcoal, but no bones. The first may have belonged to a grave, but the second should be of first-century date.

The topsoil was full of pottery fragments of the kiln

---

[1] The field-records of 1933 were lost in a flood, but most of the essential information was duplicated in one way or another. This is one of the obscure points. Evidence differs on the identity of nos. 5 and 6 in this group. They are either fig. 78, 5 and 6, or no. 8 on that figure and a fluted beaker of grey ware, f. 406, like

fig. 86, 7. We can rule out fig. 78, 8 at once, but the beaker, f. 406 could belong to the group. Fig. 78, 8 is of fine *pale grey* ware and remains without exact provenance; it was probably one of those numbered 5, 6, 7 on the plan, fig. 77.

period, with some of the mid-first century (e.g. stamps of PATER . . ., GABRVS, MINVSO F, OF FIRM, LICINVS). The latter were more frequent in the ditch and in the SE. corner. There was a single fragment of red-brown, gritted ware of Iron Age A.

Pit C17 was an oval pit of no great size, dug to receive a very large quantity of fused wasters of colour-coated beakers (f. 391). A large block from this mass is illustrated pl. XVIII c. There was little else in this pit save a waster of f. 268 (fig. 76, 1).

Pit C19 was large and only found in a small trench cut after the season ended. It was full of fragments of the kiln period and with raw brown clay. From it came the object illustrated in Fig. 50, 3, made of soft buff ware.

Apart from the retaining wall of the enclosure there were only two attempts at masonry.[1] Just west of site C4 there was a lightly built rectangular foundation, consisting of small irregular uncoursed pieces of hard, pale, blue-grey Kentish ragstone. The top was 14 in. below the surface, and the height was 1 ft. 8 in. The mortar was soft and white, and the whole was set directly on the soft sand filling of ditch II. It could not have supported any great weight. It measured 4 ft. 6 in. to 5 ft. square.

The other case was very different. Not far east of the enclosure lay a long line of masonry, apparently the foundation of a wall. A shallow trench had been cut in the soft sand and filled with broken pottery of all kinds from the kiln waste-heap, mixed with mortar. Upon this footing, above the sand-level, was laid a foundation of small irregular pieces of the same bluish Kentish rag stone only 19 in. wide. There was no regular facing present, nor any regular coursing. Both ends were broken and the foundation could not be traced farther, though it might have continued to the east, where there was an area of confused broken pottery as if the foundation had been disturbed and scattered. But this more resembled the base of a waste heap, so large and extensive was it. There was no indication that the wall had ever extended north or south to enclose a space.

Materials for masonry are so scarce here that these two features must have had a serious purpose. The wall is paralleled by one at Heiligenberg[2] which pointed directly to the entrance and centre of an enclosure comprising four kilns. It was explained as a roadway, though it was only 75 ft. long and 3 ft. 6 in. wide. Ours points to no structure, so far as we know, and is of lighter build, being only 18 in. wide and 20 ft. long. It would serve as the foundation for the wall of a building. Possibly one may find some similarity between it

and the long platforms which are laid out in brick-yards, upon which the moist bricks are stacked to dry under low roofs. Something similar may well have been used to provide for the drying of the pottery vessels.[3]

The rectangular foundation is paralleled by one of sandstone adjoining the Linwood East Kiln.[4] It measured about 5 ft. by 3 ft. Another such was found at Rough-piece[5] and these are comparable to clay floors found near other New Forest kilns.[6] They were clearly used in preparing the clay or the vessels for firing.

Examination of the pottery in the foundation of the 'wall' showed that it contained every sort of pottery made on the site except Samian moulds and decorated ware from them. The only contribution this makes to the history of the site is to suggest that decorated Samian was the last branch of the work to be undertaken, which is perhaps what one would expect.

COINS

Very few coins were found in the excavation of the kilns, and a large part of them is illegible.

1. As, Domitian (probably); corroded, but not much worn. Found in the rubbish layer at east end of the stone wall.
2. As, Domitian (?); much worn. Found in the rubbish layer immediately north of kiln 21.
3. As, Hadrian, M. & S. 577 (Britannia type), condition fine, slightly worn. Found in the rubbish layer.
4. Sestertius, M. Aurelius; very worn, possibly M. & S. 960 or 969, certainly after A.D. 164. Found in the rubbish layer.
5. As, M Aurelius (?); very worn, clipped and marked as if clipping had been done with a circular punch. Illegible. Found in the rubbish layer.
6. Small bronze, Constantine II or Constantius II, rev. *Gloria Exercitus*. Two standards. Mint illegible. Condition fair. Found in south part of site C4 at depth of 18 in.
7. Small and thin bronze of only 10 mm. diameter, preserving part of the die only (but the edges are broken). Small diademed head and reverse like *Salus Reipublicae* type, but barbarous. Theodosian or later. Found over kiln 19.

The following are quite illegible:

8. Fragments of a plated coin, denarius or antoninianus of around A.D. 220. Found over the clay floor by well 5 (about 100 yds. SE. of kiln-enclosure).
10. Hopelessly corroded, similar flan and size. Unstratified.
11. Similar second brass, heavily encrusted, and with a heavy deposit of pitch ($\frac{1}{8}$ in. thick) on one side. Found in top soil on north part of site C4.

The two rubbish layers (one north of kiln 21, the other at the east end of the stone wall) were undoubtedly contemporary, and the first five coins, found in them, constitute the coin-evidence for the date of the kilns. We have to accommodate two very

---

[1] But see the 1959 excavations, pp. 41 ff.
[2] Forrer, p. 24, fig. 5.
[3] But see note on Mittelbronn, p. 34.

[4] *Antiq. Journ.* xviii, 121.
[5] Ibid.
[6] Ibid., p. 122.

worn coins of M. Aurelius, so our date must be late in the second century; but these two coins may belong to any part of a more or less lengthy life of the firm. The absence of later coins suggests that they belong to its later days.

The two fourth-century coins are contemporary with the late pottery and burials found on site C4 and in the filling of the enclosure. We had no other evidence of the nature of the fourth-century use of the site.

SUMMARY OF THE KILNS FOUND IN 1933 AND 1959

All the kilns (nos. 15–22) found in 1933 were up-draught kilns of Grimes's type I. The Sigillata kiln (no. 21) was very similar to his type VI, though smaller.

Though stone is sometimes used in building kilns (e.g. Heiligenberg) tile was more generally used, if not extensively, at least to build the furnace-arch and walls. In these particular kilns at Colchester, as at many other places, clay was used almost exclusively in the smaller kilns, strengthened by pieces of tile and pottery. Tiles were properly built into the entrances of kilns 15, 19, and 22, and in the body of kiln 30 (phase IV); otherwise they only occur irregularly placed here and there (see also kilns 25 and 26). Spoilt pots are used in the entrance of kiln 20.

In many cases where clay was used the central support for the oven floor was not of continuous clay, like the walls, but built of rectangular blocks, made to suit the job in hand, the sizes varying accordingly. These were noted in kilns 19, 20, and 22 (see also kiln 24, where the vaulting was done with similar voussoir blocks).

The date of the activity of these kilns depends on the following evidence. That of the stratification was negligible, for the remains were mixed directly with those of the earlier occupation which ended about A.D. 65 (*Camulodunum*, pp. 26, 43). The only inter-mediate remains consisted of some evidence of Hadrianic occupation around well 5, whence also comes a fused mass of flagons f. 154–5 (pl. XX *a*), which is late first-century, and a few sherds found loose over the site which appear to be Flavian (p. 76).

The soil also contains coins and pottery (the latter chiefly connected with burials) later than the kilns, but not associated with any regular occupation level.

The coins associated with the kilns are few, as usual on pottery sites, and the latest, of M. Aurelius, was found in the rubbish dump and must therefore be contemporary with our kilns. It is a very worn sesterce bearing the titles Armeniacus and Parthicus and there-fore not earlier than A.D. 165, but must have seen twenty years' wear or more before it was dropped. A date about A.D. 190 is the earliest reasonable for it.

The internal evidence of the pottery may be sum-marized as follows. The imported decorated sigillata comprises 80 pieces, of which two are Flavian. Of the rest 46 (some of which fit together) have been illus-trated. Of the total (excluding the Flavian) 46 have a good dark glaze and are mostly Lezoux ware, while 32 are of a paler and poorer ware, undoubtedly East Gaulish. Unfortunately they preserve few types, and one can only say the general appearance fits in with that of the Sigillata from Niederbieber, which dates from A.D. 190. If one assumes that this is contemporary with our kilns, then we have 41 per cent. of the whole contemporary, and nearly 60 per cent. from the pre-ceding, Antonine, period. The position is similar to that shown in the chart in *Camulodunum* (p. 175) where in the first three periods, up to Nero, the contemporary ware outnumbered the older ware in use by two to one. In our case the figures are reversed, becoming two to three. They are not so reliable as the others, both be-cause the number of sherds is smaller, and because the distinction in style is not so clear cut. Some of the Lezoux pieces may be later than Antonine, while some of the East Gaulish pieces are almost certainly Antonine. But our figures may be taken as a maxi-mum for the proportion of contemporary ware, and yield a clear verdict that the proportion of new ware imported had declined steeply.

The ware made on the site is in general style com-parable to that of the East Gaulish potteries, the most valuable dated group of which is that from Nieder-bieber (A.D. 190–260). The plain band above the ovolo is frequently very wide, a late feature, paralleled by our figs. 26–27, but only found once among the Lezoux sherds.

The late tendency of the decorated ware is con-firmed by the very strong representation of f. 79 among the plain ware, for the form is mainly post-Antonine.[1]

By contrast the potter's names all fall too early to fit into this picture. The explanation is that they have been dated only on very broad principles, for the Antonine wall is the latest source for historically dated stamps, and the wreck on the Pan Rock the latest archaeologically dated. Four of our continental names are of Pan Rock date (*c.* A.D. 190), and our series of names must be brought down to this date, subject to allowance for survival on the scale of our chart in *Camulodunum*, already quoted.

The huge quantity of colour-coated wares is useful for the negative evidence of the absence of forms such as 395, 407, and 408, and of painted decoration, all of

---

[1] I rely on the fact that I do not know of its occurrence on the Antonine Wall; but it will not be surprising if it turns up there.

which were certainly in fashion by the middle of the third century and probably, to some extent, before. The presence of flagons of f. 363 is important as giving us the beginning of the series of ledged flagons better known in f. 365, which was so plentiful at Niederbieder (A.D. 190–260).

The buff ware consists more of vessels which call for dating rather than those which can aid it. The great variety of mortarium-rims on the whole continues the Antonine Wall series, but gives us a date for the prevalence of f. 501 and a date for the beginning of f. 504.

We assume, therefore, a date about A.D. 190–200 for the activity of our kilns, which was followed very closely by that of kiln 24, where a slightly later mortarium form appears, with f. 504 now in quantity, while the colour-coated ware continues almost unchanged.

It is not, of course, impossible that some of our kilns may have been in production from a date earlier than 190. Evidence for any change in fashion between the products of one kiln and another was sought in vain, but it is possible that fashions in the coarser wares were not changing much. Indeed, we know it was so in the case of cooking-pots and flagons of ff. 268 and 156. We do not suggest a date earlier than about 175 for the earliest activity.

Generally speaking the evidence for the incidence of Sigillata in this country after about A.D. 180 is that the previously great flow of imported ware diminished in a remarkable way. Later sites as a rule are poor in it, and in a large collection, such as Colchester, it is clear from the very small proportion of late products such as those from Trier that very little ware was being imported. The reason for this is unknown, but the poor quality of the ware may have been partly to blame. The lack of imports probably provided our potters with an incentive to try their hand. It may well have had similar results elsewhere, but, if so, the products are not so far self-evident in our collections. We may be fairly sure, however, that there are at least one or two more such sites as ours yet to be found. Oswald's list contains many names with numerous British records and yet as little known as ours. There is part of a mould at York, another was found at Pulborough, and there is a third in Hull Museum from near Peterborough. The more conclusive evidence of rings and tubes, so far not forthcoming, may well have been missed (or dismissed) as commonplace coarse ware fragments. Their publication in their true light here may lead to their identification in future and thus to the discovery of further sites. There was one small piece of mould of our potter A in Colchester Museum (May, pl. XXXII, E) for years before further evidence turned up and the site was found, and, though the

bulk of the remains was so large, it was not spread over a wide radius and did not show on the surface.

The collection of decorated Sigillata in Colchester Museum is probably the largest in the country, for every piece has been carefully collected. It is easy to be wise after the event, but a close scrutiny of the collection would have revealed evidence of a fabric agreeing with no known continental source, and therefore probably of local manufacture. The same may be true of other localities.

The discovery of this Sigillata kiln has not contributed much to our knowledge of the methods of the potters. Apart from the moulds little or none of their tools or utensils has survived. The ruins of the kiln add little to Forrer's analysis of the evidence at Heiligenberg, and correspond closely to the round kilns found there. The only other sites which have furnished useful information are Eschweiler Hof and Aquincum. On most sites kilns of varied shapes occur, especially large rectangular ones, some of which are associated with Sigillata waste-heaps, and there was no circular kiln of our type at Aquincum, nor any remains of rings or kiln tubes. At these sites the rectangular kilns should have retained at least some trace of the use of these, but did not do so. It would appear that Sigillata could be produced without them, but how is not so clear, for saggers were also not in evidence. We can shed no light on this.

Our kilns are sufficiently varied in form and size to cover any minor requirements ancillary to the manufacture of Sigillata (as suggested by Forrer, pp. 45, 47).

The method of manufacture has been described (p. 32). Two punches for impressing patterns were found, but none for names. The numerous fragments of moulds show that there were two distinct potters making them, whom we have designated A and B (pp. 44 ff.), and who largely used punches in common. The decorated fragments indicate the existence of a third potter C (p. 74), who has a more conventional style and is connected with Trier, the other two betraying only a very slight connexion with Blickweiler. Potter C may have started the business and then moved on, taking his moulds with him. None of our moulds is signed.

The Sigillata side of the business may have developed later than the coarser wares, and did not fare at all well. The ware at its best is a bright tile red, with a good, pale, almost orange-red glaze. But the result was, it seems, rarely attained, the local clay proving unsuitable. Difficulties found in the firing were probably due to this, for otherwise the potters seem to have known their technique well enough. In the end they abandoned their project, whether to try again elsewhere we do not know.

The mortarium trade fared better, and we now find

that something like one-third of the mortaria found in Scotland came from our firm.[1] If our potters held one army contract they probably held others.

The potters would appear to have owned the ground and lived near their work, for some at least of the burials were contemporary with their activities (see pp. 144–7 ff. below). Domestic occupation and scattered tesserae from a pavement were found near the entrance

The lead had lined a stout wooden coffin which measured 6 ft. 3 in. by 17 in., and 11 in. high. Remains of iron nails were found at the corners and one side. The lid was decorated on the inside by repeated impressions of a short moulded batten (pressed in the sand mould, in which the lead was cast). The remains of the skeleton were too fragile to move, and the coffin has not been emptied.

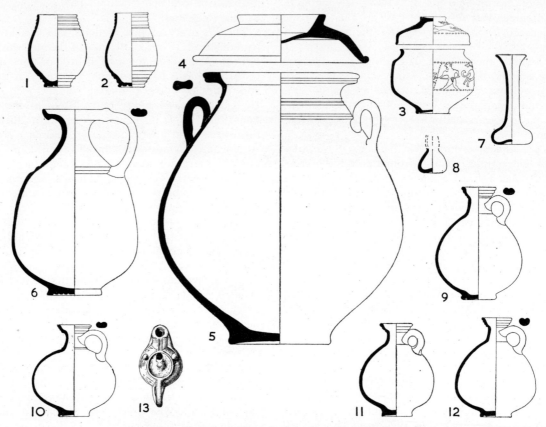

FIG. 79. Vessels from amphora-burial, grave 302 (pp. 144–6). ($\frac{1}{4}$)

through ditch I in region 3, and also on top of the hill south of the Waterworks enclosure, with second- or third-century pottery, but there is no definite connexion between these remains and the potteries.

There remain to mention several other entries on fig. 9 which do not belong to the first-century occupation, but to the kiln-period or later. They are as follows:

Grave 296. Lead coffin, containing a skeleton. Found at a depth of 5 ft. in the filling of ditch IB in 1932. It was much flattened by earth-pressure, which had pressed out the outline of the skeleton on the lid, even forcing some of the larger joints through the metal.

The excavation for this grave had been a wide, bowl-shaped one, measuring 12 ft. by 9 ft. with rounded corners.

About a foot from the head, which lay to the NE., lay the remains of a wooden casket bound with thin bronze at the corners, the key still in the iron lock. It had contained two small glass phials, one of which could be repaired. C.M. 293–6.[1]

Grave 302 (figs. 79–81). A large group contained, with one exception, in an amphora, f. 187, the top of which had been chiselled off to allow the insertion of the objects. It was found only a little distance east of the lead coffin and so near the surface that the plough

[1] Information kindly supplied by Mrs. K. Hartley.

[1] *C.M. Report*, 1933, p. 10.

had removed the rim of the amphora. The latter was fractured and could not be removed intact. The interior was very carefully excavated, from the bottom upwards. The objects lay in sandy soil which had completely filled the amphora. All the small objects lay near the bottom; they had probably been in a wooden box which had decayed away, though no iron nails were found. These objects were:

Four small bronze studs, two bronze tacks (exactly like modern tin-tacks) and the umbonate head of a bronze nail. Fig. 81, 4. These may have belonged to a mirror-case, as may a small bronze clamp or pivot. Fig. 80, 9.

Twenty small glass beads, some cylindrical, some spherical, of green or dark blue glass. These were found by putting the earth twice through a sieve. Fig. 80, 11.

Above these the vessels (fig. 79) had been set in the amphora with the urn in the central position.

A 'Honey-pot' with single band of impressed chequered

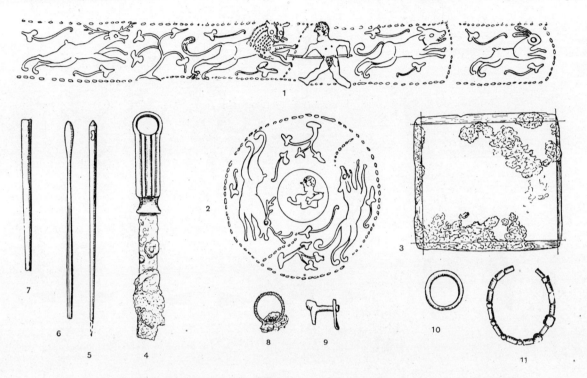

FIG. 80. Barbotine decoration and small objects from amphora-burial, grave 302 (beads $\frac{1}{1}$, rest $\frac{1}{2}$).

A bronze brooch in the form of a duck, length $1\frac{5}{8}$ in. Fig. 81, 1. I know of no parallel.

A bronze brooch of original design. The curved bow is of V-section, with a broader, flat portion above and below. The conical terminals are finely turned out of bone. Length $1\frac{1}{4}$ in. Fig. 81, 2. Again there is no parallel.

A rectangular mirror of speculum metal, rough and unfinished at back. A darker marking round the edges indicates that it was mounted in a case of wood or leather. Size $3\frac{1}{8}$ by $2\frac{7}{8}$ in. Fig. 80, 3.

An iron knife with fluted bone handle ending in a ring for suspension. Fig. 80, 4.

A bone needle, and part of a bone pin, also two small moulded terminals of turned bone and three bone disks with central opening. The diameters are 21, 26, and 23 mm. respectively. Figs. 80, 5, 7 and 81, 5, 6a–c.

A bone finger-ring of plain, circular pattern. Fig. 80, 10.

A handle of a bronze spatula; the missing end could not be found. Fig. 80, 6.

A small bronze ring, minutely cross-ribbed, with a shapeless piece of corroded iron (?) adhering. Fig. 80, 8.

pattern, fine hard buff ware (fig. 79, 5). This was covered by a T.S. dish, f. 18/31 (fig. 79, 4), stamped TOCCA FX, a potter ascribed by Oswald (p. 318) to Lavoye, Avocourt, and Blickweiler and dated Trajan–Antonine. Our stamp appears to be the same as Blickweiler no. 28D.[1] The vessel was chipped when buried, but it formed a perfect cover, and the bones in the urn were clean and dry as when buried. Stamp on fig. 81, 3.

A beautiful little bowl, small variety of f. 308, colour-coated ware decorated in barbotine with lid to match (figs. 79, 3; 80, 1, 2). There is no doubt it was made on the site. The clay is thin, hard, reddish, with a purplish metallic colour-coating. The decoration includes human figures and shows considerable originality.

Four small flagons of fine buff ware, f. 156, probably made on the site (fig. 79, 9–12). They had been stoppered with wax (?) plugs, which are now nodules of hard earth. The interiors were thus sealed, and from them samples of floccose vegetable deposits were obtained which await analysis.

The flagons are partly covered on the outside with a white deposit like lime, though no lime was found in the amphora.

Two small beakers of colour-coated ware, of the unusual f. 404. Local reddish clay with purplish-chocolate slip. Fig. 79,

[1] And see Ludowici, *Rheinzabern*, v, 13, TOCCA F (a) on f. Lud. Sb, and ibid. v, 231, six different matrices of TOCCA F.

1, 2. Cf. *Rheinzabern*, ii, 154, fig. 17, also our own fig. 47, 11–16 and p. 82.

A small lamp of reddish-buff ware, slightly micaceous, of the form known as '*firma*'. There is no name beneath, but a double footring. Fig. 79, 13.

A glass unguentarium nearly complete, but broken, and the bulb only of a second one. Fig. 79, 7 and 8.

Grave 549. Only 6 ft. west of no. 302 remains of another amphora of f. 187 were found upright in the ground, much disturbed. With them was found a bone ring exactly like fig. 81, 6*a* and *b*, but intermediate in size, and a bone cylinder 3·7 cm. long and 2 cm. in

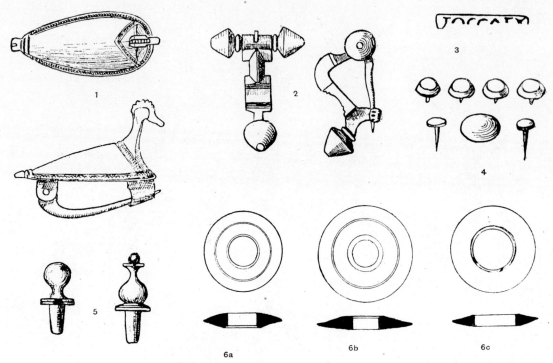

FIG. 81. Small objects from amphora-burial, grave 302 (p. 145). 1, 2, 4, bronze, 3 pottery, 5–6 bone. ($\frac{1}{1}$)

Finally, set outside the amphora, but clearly belonging to it, a fine flagon of thin reddish ware, f. 383, which had been mica-coated. The shoulder has a false cordon, and there are three grooves inside the footring. Fig. 79, 6.[1]

Some of the vessels were probably made on the site. The date should be about A.D. 190, despite the TOCCA stamp.

Grave 319. Six vessels, fig. 82, 3–7, found together, somewhat damaged, but presumably a burial group. The position was not far from the last, and was actually over the top of the pit Y40. The depth was about 2 ft. 6 in. The vessels were:

Not illustrated. T.S. dish f. 31. Stamped GABRVS F. Colchester ware.
Fig. 82, 3. Colour-coated beaker of the globular f. 396, red ware, chocolate coated.
4. Another beaker, similar ware, but of the usual f. 391, rough cast.
5–7. Three flagons f. 156, the mouth of one missing, bodies globular, footrings poor, handles two-ribbed. C.M. 280–4.39.
Date probably similar to last.

diameter. Fragments of a jar f. 268 (fig. 76, 2) were found close by.

Grave 550. A single large urn, f. 280 (fig. 82, 2), of brown-grey ware, with horizontal lines on the upper part of the body was found dug into the filling of the stoke-hole of kiln 16. It contained burnt bones.

An almost exactly similar vessel was found in the lowest level of the 'Mithraeum', with a coin of Constans. *Roman Colchester*, fig. 65, 62.

Grave 551. An urn of f. 268 of fine hard, pale grey ware was found upright in the ground in the filling above kiln 20. It contained only earth, and there was no trace of a skeleton. It may not represent a grave.

Grave 553. Remains of a skeleton and coffin found in 1933 about 44 ft. NW. of the kiln enclosure. Part only of the skull remained and a few fragments of the rest of the skeleton, including two *tibiae*. Although so much was missing, including all the vertebrae, the presence of three large jet beads in position on the breast showed that the interment had not been disturbed. It

[1] *C.M. Report*, 1935, 18–26, figs. 4–7; *Ill. London News*, 23 Sept. 1933, 473.

lay 2 ft. 6 in. from the surface with head to the east; the irregular mark of the coffin, with nails around it, showed it to have been a short and broad chest in which the body could not have lain straight.

The three beads were found lying end to end, so can hardly be regarded as pendants. They must have been

Taf. 26, no. D13, and she figures spirally fluted rods, ibid., p. 121, D2, Taf. 33–34, G5, 1; G9, 1; G10.

KILN 23

This kiln, found on the east side of region 4 in the excavations of 1938, was rectangular in plan and

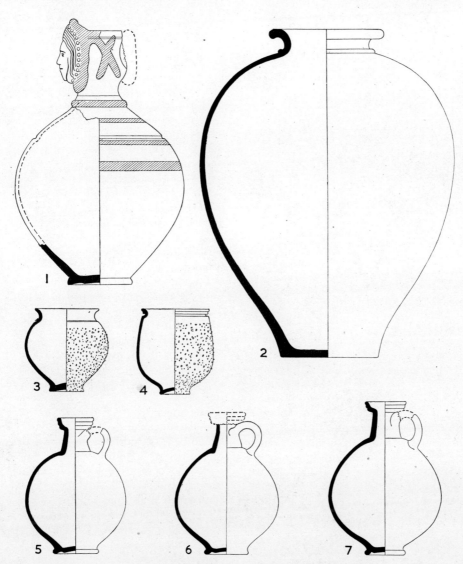

FIG. 82. Vessels from graves (pp. 140, 146). (¼)

used in combination with others of perishable material. This is confirmed by the parallel of a grave at Coninzheim (Prov. Limbourg) in which was a single bead similar to our end pair, with two small jet pendants. Here again there must have been other beads. The bead is like our two, but with plain mouldings and no incised crosses. A spirally fluted bead like our middle one is figured by Fraülein Hagen in *B.J.*, 142 (1937),

poorly preserved, being nowhere more than 9 in. high. The walls were of clay, 8 in. thick, where preserved, for much of them had been destroyed. The flue-space measured 5 ft. 8 in. by 4 ft. 2 in. with a central support projecting from the back wall, 4 ft. 6 in. long by 14 in. wide. The stoke-hole, which was imperfect, was only 15 in. wide at the mouth, splaying to 2 ft. wide inwards. The burnt clay floor was mostly missing.

The interior was packed with remains of flagons and jugs embedded in fragments of burnt clay and ashes. We reproduce on figs. 83 and 84 the plan and pottery from the Camulodunum Report. The full account will be found there, pp. 107–8 and 282, and a photograph, pl. XII. The plan on the right of the kiln in fig. 83 is that of Pit L19, which was clearly cut for the making of a kiln. Since it is not a kiln we have not said more

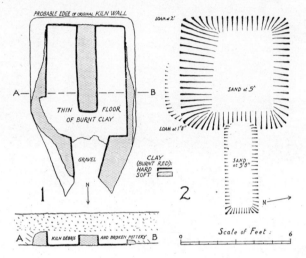

FIG. 83. Plan of kiln 23.

than this. Its contents (*Camulodunum*, 281 and pl. XII, 2) were of a date about A.D. 60 or 61.

The activity of this kiln was almost certainly ended by the Boudiccan revolt in A.D. 61. The ware made in it seems to have been all buff, comprising ff. 17 (in its latest and poorest form), 62, 94B, 149 or 150, 154, 171, 244. Among the 154's was the neck and handle of a 'puzzle jug' (this was later stolen from the site) which is shown on fig. 84, 1*a*. A long tube depending from the neck made it impossible to empty more than half the vessel by pouring in the normal way. The remaining liquid could only be poured out through the hole through the handle.

KILN 24 (Pl. XXI *a*)

On 23 May 1946 it was observed that the foundations for the new N.A.A.F.I. Club, which was being erected on the Abbey Field, had cut through the remains of a Roman potter's kiln.[1]

The new building has two square projections on its west side, and the kiln lies under the first stanchion south of the NW. angle of the northern of these two projections. The centre line of the kiln has a magnetic

bearing of 02 degrees, and the stoke-hole was directed to the north. The stanchion-hole had cut away a large segment of the kiln, and before permission to excavate could be obtained, a further trench, for the wall, cut away part of the central support and of the west side of the stoke-hole. It also, of course, caused the wanton removal of all the contents of the kiln along this line. The initial damage was done at the best-preserved part of the kiln, where the burnt clay wall was still standing to 3 ft. 8 in. above the floor, with its top only 14 in. below the surface. We found that elsewhere the walls had been reduced to less than 2 ft. 6 in., but that the central support still stood to nearly 3 ft. in part. Only in the northern part of the east wall of the stoke-hole was the wall seriously reduced—to about 4 in. The west wall had, it seemed, been good, but had been removed by the workmen, so that we had to draw all our evidence for the entrance to the flue from what was left of the east side (fig. 85).

The kiln was long and pear-shaped in plan. The floor, part of which remained just within the entrance and again towards the far end of the flues, was of hard-burnt natural sand. Upon it lay a dark layer, of variable thickness, averaging about 2–3 in., consisting of greyish or black ash, with some charcoal, and full of fragments of vitrified clay which had fallen from the walls or roof. There seemed to be evidence that this deposit consisted of two layers, and this appearance was most marked at the entrance. The lower layer was of clean grey ash, shading to black on top, and only a half to one inch thick; it lay directly upon the floor, and was only seen where the floor was preserved. At the entrance this layer ran under the yellow plugging (see below).

The upper layer was thicker, and mostly black, and was largely made up of vitrified fragments. These would be detached from the walls when the wood fuel was thrust in. Both layers contained fragments of pottery. Those in the lower were from colour-coated beakers and buff flagons: those in the upper were similar, but larger, and included fragments of mortaria. Those in the lower layer were all very small.

The entrance, which was probably about 18 in. wide, had a rounded-oblong block of clay set across it, at a distance of 17 in. This had been damaged by the workmen, but its dimensions could be worked out as about 17 by 10 in. It was certainly intact to about 1 ft. of its height. The upper part was of clay burnt bright red, but not so hard as the lower. Embedded in this was a number of fragments of pottery, chiefly large fragments of mortaria, and one of them was very firmly fixed in the top of the firmer lower part. This block stood directly on the burnt floor, which must have been

---

[1] We are indebted to the alertness of the boys of Mr. Chisnell's school, who, inspired by him, noticed and reported this discovery.

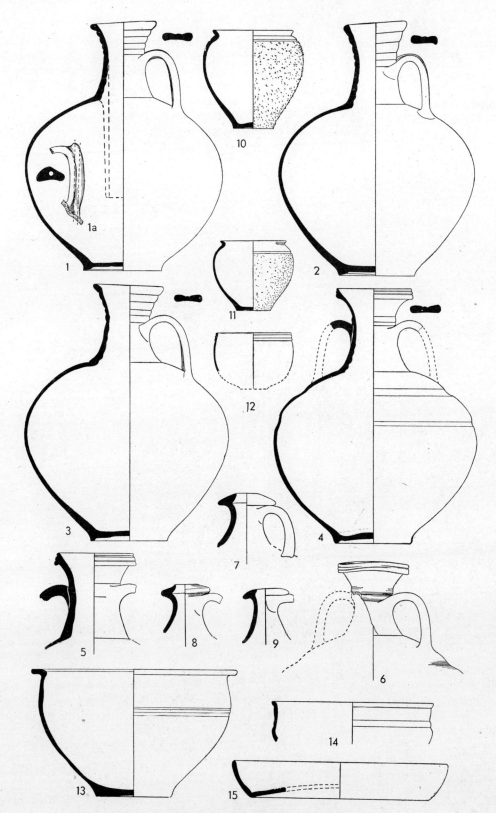

FIG. 84. Pottery from kiln 23 (p. 148). (¼)

built-out to receive it. After the deposit of the lowest layer of ash its inner face seemed to have been patched, for there was a second burnt face, about 2 in. thick, standing against the first, but on top of the ash.

In subsequent use the left opening between the block and the flue had been plugged by a mass of very sandy yellow clay, which was very firm and compact, and had intermixed with fragments of hard-burnt clay from the structure of the kiln, a few of them quite large, some from flat slabs nearly 3 in. thick, some of which showed they had been mixed with hay or straw. One fragment appeared to be from a plano-convex disk about 9 in. diameter, with rounded edge about 1 in. thick, increasing to about 2 in. inwards. The centre was not

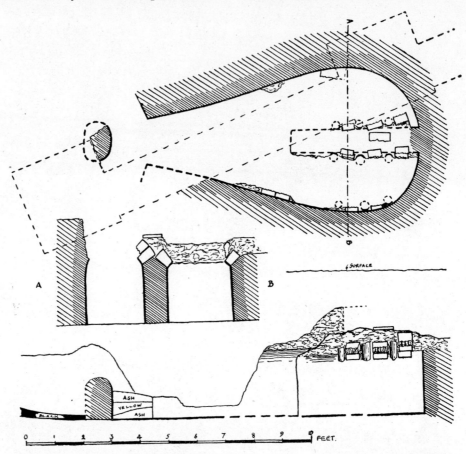

FIG. 85. Roman potter's kiln (no. 24), found under the N.A.A.F.I. Canteen on the Abbey Field.

been laid to continue the line of the kiln wall up to the block, no doubt to exclude an unwanted draught from the NE. This layer contained no pottery and was laid directly upon the lower ash.

The ash over this, naturally, joined up with the ash along the flue, and may have been so left after working it, or it may have been thrown there when the stoker's emplacement was filled in. This latter hollow, from which the fuelling was done, could not be explored. It was probably at least 8 ft. wide N.–S., its bottom sloping up from 5 ft. deep at the kiln to 4 ft. 3 in. where last seen, well marked by a black layer of ash, charcoal and pottery. Above this the filling consisted of lumps of clay burnt red, but still soft,

preserved. This may well have been part of a potter's wheel.

The kiln itself had been built in the usual manner. A hole made of appropriate shape in the ground had been lined with 15 in. of clay, the inner face of which was modelled to the shape required. The subsequent firing baked the clay of the wall a bright red to a depth of about 6 in. This wall was vertical for some 20 in. at which level it begins to curve inwards for the vaulting. Matching it a central support was built against the south end-wall, 4 ft. 6 in. long and 10½ in. thick. It was preserved nearly a foot higher than the outer walls, and retaining more of the vaulting than they. It was most probably built up of rectangular blocks of clay, as in kilns 19, 20, and 22 of 1933, but we did not break it down to find out.

The filling of the body of the kiln consisted entirely of the remains of the structure. Directly upon the ashes lay a loose mass of whole or fragmentary voussoirs from the vaulting and broken pieces of very hard-burnt and brittle material, probably from the floor. There were also a number of fragments of tiles, both tegulae and imbrices, and probably, building tiles. This material practically filled the space up to the tops of the walls and upon it lay a further mass of fragments of a softer nature and paler, yellow-red colour. These probably came from the dome, but it was observed that the clay filling the space between the voussoirs on the central support was of this colour, so that the floor too may have been of this nature. Fragments of pottery were found in this filling, but most were lower down.

The lower, hard-burnt filling was full of cavities. It was carefully examined for snail-shells and the like, but was perfectly clean and barren. It is clear, therefore, that we are dealing with a rapid and intentional destruction, which was at once so sealed down that snails never had access.

The vaulting was done with separate arches of clay blocks shaped as voussoirs, measuring 6 in. back to front, the smaller end 3 in. wide, the larger just over 4 in. There are slight variations in these measurements, but these occur more in the length, which is normally 7 in. There are definite remains of three such arches (see the top of the central support in fig. 85), which were rather irregularly spaced, and, to judge from the visible remains, set out by eye with little regard for symmetry. They can only be said to be generally at right angles to the axis; they were probably not very even in height, or in construction, for the noses of some projected more into the kiln than of others, as can be seen from their vitrification.

The spaces between vary from $4\frac{1}{2}$ to 6 in. At each end they were luted with clay to form a round opening continuing the line of the wall through the floor above. The remaining space was then filled with luting (of the yellowish clay noted above), through which further holes were made, probably simply one about the centre. The lateral holes vary from 4 to 5 in. in diameter, but the scanty remains of the others seem to indicate a diameter of only 2 in. One fragment of the floor shows this very clearly.

The floor was undoubtedly laid on a levelling make-up of the yellowish clay. A fragment of tile apparently in position, on top of the central support, and 35 in. above the floor, is probably only part of the make-up. It is not at all burnt on top. The fragment of floor already mentioned shows glassy grey vitrification on the upper side, and is about 2 in. thick, of very good

clay, quite like a building-tile, but specially made for the purpose. Heavy fragments of softer clay, about 3 in. thick and mixed with grass, are difficult to explain. But it seems almost certain that this kiln had a long use. Everywhere the walls were ready to peel, revealing another vitrified surface, showing that they had been patched again and again. Repairs had also been made to the main structure. A block of yellowish clay had been inserted into the highest remaining part of the east wall, as a springing for the arch, which must have required replacement. Our fragments of the structure, therefore, may include portions of successive alterations of varying character.

Exploration around the kiln was unfortunately impossible. In the small space cleared immediately west nothing was found at the old surface-level, except a few sherds of pottery and a large irregular block of Kentish rag, 2 ft. long by 18 in. wide and thick. One face only was flat, but not smoothed. There was nothing beneath it.

The bulk of the pottery recovered was found by the workmen when cutting the staunchion-hole into the emplacement outside the stoke-hole. It is described below. There is no difference in nature between the pottery from the different levels. Nothing else was found at the kiln, except a beaker, fig. 86, 1, quite intact, which a workman told me he found low down, near the north end of the central support. It is difficult to see how it could come there at all, especially without being broken.

The extensive trenching over the site, for foundations, revealed little of interest. Here and there a few small sherds were found at about 2 ft. to 2 ft. 6 in. deep, indicating the old ground-level. But in the SE. corner of the excavation for the cellar there seemed to have been a shallow pit running somewhat deeper, in which lay food-bones and broken pottery of late second- or third-century date.

A workman also showed me a silver denarius of Marcus Aurelius, in good condition, Concord type, TR.P.XVI (M. & S. no. 37, Cohen 36), dated A.D. 161-2, which he said he found on the site.

In the filling of the kiln were found two fragments of a curious tile, measuring only 5 in. wide by something over $6\frac{1}{2}$ in. long (broken off) and a little over $\frac{1}{2}$ in. thick. One side was curiously mottled with white, which may have been mortar or pipeclay. Some fragments of ordinary tile showed the same markings. These were found in the filling of the west flue about a foot above the floor.

THE POTTERY OF KILN 24
(FIGS. 86 AND 87)

Considering the small space excavated the pottery found was in very large quantity. The largest bulk of it consisted of fragments of mortaria, all of a hard and good, almost white clay. But the most numerous vessels were colour-coated beakers. If these two groups were removed little would be left, comprising mostly remains of flagons and jars.

off straight as in no. 3. There were also a number of vessels of f. 406 of which no. 7 is the only section which could be obtained. These are always fluted, usually plain, with or without rouletting at the top, and rarely rough-cast. The only unusual pieces were a rim, no. 6,

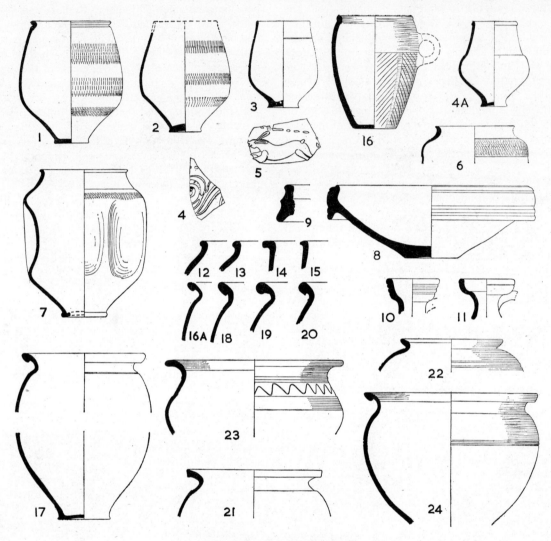

FIG. 86. Pottery from kiln 24. ($\frac{1}{4}$)

Colour-coated ware. The fragments are of buff to red-brown ware, thin, hard (as a rule) and finely coated, much cleaner and harder than those from the 1933 kilns. The vast majority are of ff. 391 and 392, fig. 86, 1–3, the latter found intact in the flue.[1] Nearly every vessel was rouletted with multiple bands. The figures are typical. More angular carinations did not occur, and most bases are moulded beneath, not cut

and a tall, slender handle of a flagon like fig. 56, 14, but quite plain.

Buff ware. Only three distinct types of mortaria occurred. A large and heavy series of f. 497 (fig. 87, 1) is characterized by absence of groove between lip and the flat top of the flange. One of these (no. 2) could be restored. Unfortunately it is not stamped. Among the others, which are closely similar (nos. 1, 3, and 4)

[1] Nos. 4 and 5 are the only pieces of barbotine.

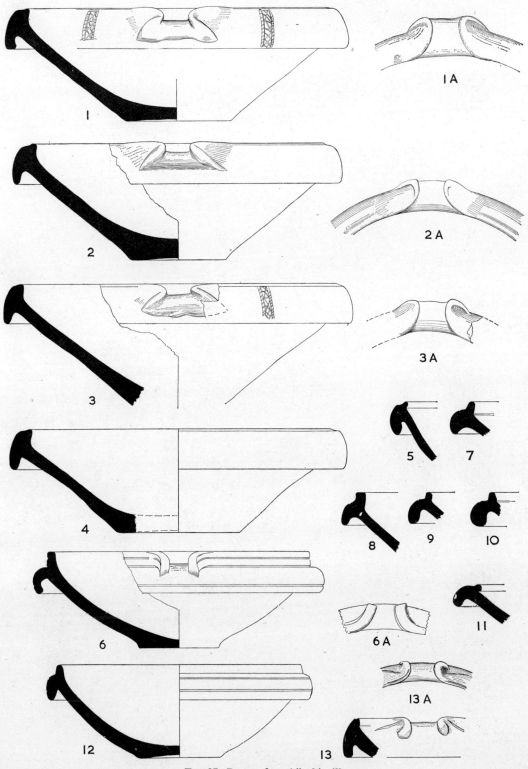

FIG. 87. Pottery from kiln 24. (¼)

there were four or five stamps, all from the same matrix. They are meaningless, but not of 'herring-bone' type (fig. 60, 26A). A slight variant is no. 5.

The second group was twice as numerous as the first, consisting of f. 504 well represented by fig. 87, no. 6. Others often omit the groove on the flange. The range

of them ringed (f. 156) as fig. 86, no. 10, and only one with a groove, no. 11.

Four buff rims remain; fig. 86, nos. 12–13 are from jars or bowls of uncertain form. Nos. 14–15 are from vertical-sided bowls of uncertain form.

Grey ware. The remaining fragments were almost

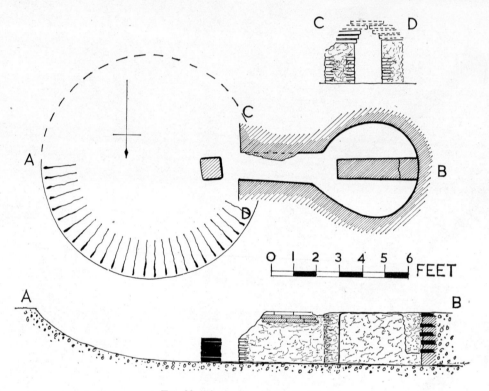

FIG. 88. Plan and section, kiln 25.

of variants is illustrated by nos. 7–10, of which only 7 and 8 are repetitive. This form (504), which scarcely appeared in the 1933 kilns, here is more numerous than f. 497, and it seems we are privileged to see the birth of a type. No. 12 is quite unusual and No. 11 was a singleton. None of these vessels was stamped.

The third type, f. 498, was represented by the one rim (with spout), fig. 87, nos. 13 and 13*a*, only. The ware is darker, almost buff, and it was not produced in this kiln. It may be a stray. It is certainly a later type than the preceding.

The only buff bowls were two small ones, f. 300, shaped like mortaria, but without grit, and probably without spouts. They are fig. 86, nos. 8 and 9, the latter a small fragment only. The clay is fine, nearly white.

Though there were fragments of many flagons there were remains of only four mouths, all cupped. Three

certainly intended to be grey, but most of them are burnt to some shade of red.

Fig. 86, 16. The fragments of a handled beaker of f. 124 in black cooking-pot ware, the polished surface scored with a chevron-pattern. This was stratified with the rest, but was certainly not made in this kiln. The only other such foreign fragments were one or two of black platters of f. 40.

There was a quantity of remains of grey jars f. 268, most of which were misfired red. They are illustrated by nos. 16A–20.

No. 17 is made up of a top and a base which may or may not belong to one pot.

No. 21, also burnt red, is unusual, looking like late f. 267. It is in the coarse-ware class.

No. 22. Burnt red, is in the fine class, being polished. It is very like f. 108.

No. 23. Partly red and partly grey, is from a polished bowl decorated with a wavy line. As yet unclassified, it is perhaps a late phase of f. 218.

No. 24. Also found in red and grey fragments, a bowl after

the style of f. 221, but also related to 299. This had been, at least in part, built into the body of the kiln.[1]

Remains of platters were scarce; they are represented by three rims of f. 38. One pale grey, the rest yellowed; a chip of f. 39, and one of f. 40 with practically no bevel and poorly polished.

KILN 25 (PL. XXIb AND FIG. 88)

In September 1952 a kiln was found in altering ground levels on the playing field of Endsleigh School,[2] immediately west of Kingswode Hoe. The site is only 120 yds. SSE. of kiln 7. The new kiln was excavated by Mr. J. Williams, Headmaster, and Mr. J. B. Baird. It was of the usual long pear-shape, with a central support united to the back wall. The overall length, inside, was 7 ft. 9 in., but there was a solid block of tiles laid in clay opposite the entrance (as in several of our kilns), measuring 1 ft. square. Adding this to the length we get 9 ft. 6 in. The inside width was just under 4 ft. and the central support was 3 ft. 6 in. long by 11 in. thick, built of rectangular clay blocks as we have seen in many cases. At the back a gap had been broken in it, and in pulling it away the clay had been pulled out from between the courses of tile which made up the wall (see section, fig. 88).

The walls still stood 2 ft. 2 in. high and were built of tiles laid in courses with very wide joints of clay, which had fired red. They were about 8 in. thick, but this was variable, and they became thicker at the entrance. The stoke-hole was 13 in. wide, also built of tiles laid in clay, and had been closed at the top by laying the tiles in oversailing courses.

Nothing remained of the oven floor and dome except fragments, among which, on the floor of the flues, lay the vitrified remains of long, hollow flue-tiles. One of these was complete, though fractured, and it is possible the same might be said of the others. It seems possible that they may have been used to support the vault of the flues and floor of the oven in some way.

A quantity of fragments of plates of clay, mixed with grass or straw, were found. These were presumably used in covering the vessels after they were assembled for firing.

There were also several fragments of a mould or moulds for some large object such as a bust or a mask. Three of these are shown on pl. XV, B, with casts from them beneath.

The uppermost pieces of tile on the square block fitted together to make up nearly half of a flat tile which had probably been about 20 in. square. It was only $\frac{1}{2}$ in. thick and was decorated with combed wavy lines as is usual on flue-tiles. A few other small pieces

of similar tiles were found among the pottery. Similar tiles have not been recorded in Colchester before. They all have a nail-hole near each corner. The back is left quite rough and unfinished (pl. XXIIa).

There was not a great quantity of pottery, and it only came from the flues and stoke-hole, for there was no litter found around the kiln nor any waste heap. All the pottery worthy of illustration has been figured (fig. 89).

1. Several fragments of a large bowl of polished red ware copying f. Drag. 37, decorated with repeated impressions of a stamp resembling a portcullis, used in two rows, the lower one made with the upper tip of the stamp only. Compare the fine red bowl with impressed pattern of swastikas, &c., from the pit in Dr. Wirth's garden. *Roman Colchester*, fig. 111, 4.

2. A few small fragments from a similar bowl, underfired, the red surface dull brown and soapy. Decoration in rows made with an ovolo stamp, and lines of rouletting.

3. Representative of several examples of f. 395, restored in drawing from a split and distorted waster.

4. Representative of several examples of f. 409, restored in drawing from a distorted waster.

5. One of several fragments of f. 407, some of which are wasters.

All these are in chocolate-coloured ware and vitrified.

6. Rim of f. 316 in polished red ware as found at Kent Blaxill's, cf. *Trans. Essex Arch. Soc.* xxv, 52, fig. 4, 8.

7. The only fragment decorated with a scroll of white paint. The colour-coating is red.

8. Fragment of a coarse vessel of plain red ware, not polished. It appears to be without parallel.

9, 10, 12–14. Examples of mortarium rims of ff. 498 and 499, all in the usual pale buff ware. Diameter of 9 *c.* 16 in., of 12 *c.* 18 in., of 13 *c.* 12$\frac{1}{2}$ in.

11. Part of a light mortarium with simple thumbed spout, buff ware, f. 505 (variant).

15. Rim of f. 504 (variant). Diameter *c.* 12$\frac{1}{2}$ in.

16–20. Rims of an unclassified form of mortarium[3] in which we, surprisingly, discover a new form which almost returns us to the first-century f. 192. The flange, however, is not so massive and more lobed beneath, and the beading is substantially heavier. This must be a late type. Diameters: 17 *c.* 12$\frac{1}{2}$ in., 18 *c.* 26 in., 20 17$\frac{3}{4}$ in., rest uncertain.

21. One of several rims of f. 305, which were in polished grey ware, none was black. That illustrated is misfired soft red.

22. Top of a flask of polished grey ware, f. 119. Compare the similar vessels from the fourth-century deposit, *Roman Colchester*, fig. 63, 49–54.

23. Top of a vase of f. 280, grey ware, burnt red. Partly polished and with a rouletted band. There were at least two others variously decorated.

24–25. Rims of grey jars f. 268A and B. 24: grey, diameter 6$\frac{1}{2}$ in.; 25: red, no groove, diameter 5$\frac{3}{4}$ in.

26. Red. Diameter 13 in., seems to have been polished and if so is not f. 268.

27. Fragment of a grey face urn.

27 *bis*. Rim f. 307, polished grey ware.

28. Rim f. 279, in black cooking-pot ware.

---

[1] Some months later, when laying a drain some 6 ft. north of the kiln, a single example of f. 409 was found (fig. 86, 4a). It must have been whole or nearly so. The ware is bright tile-red. The fact that burials of all periods have turned up in this area

must make it doubtful whether this can truly be assigned to the kiln or not.

[2] Now in the Sussex Road housing estate, see kiln 32 (p. 168).

[3] Now form 508.

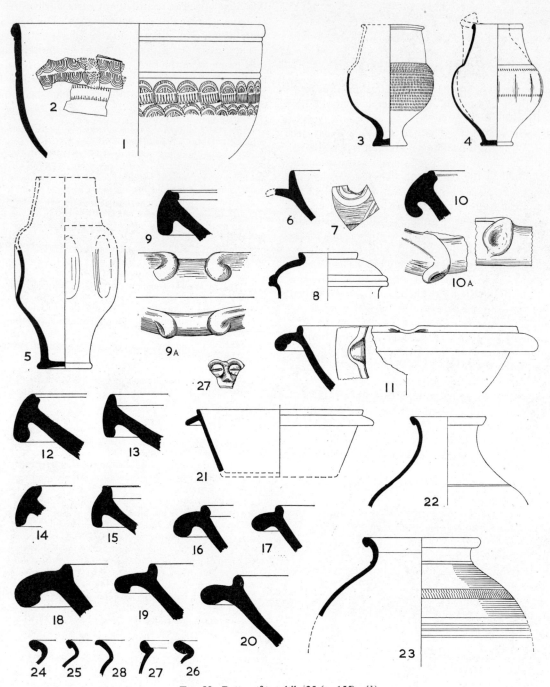

FIG. 89. Pottery from kiln 25 (p. 155). ($\frac{1}{4}$).

KILNS 26–28 FOUND IN 1955

In the summer of 1955 construction was begun on a certain section of the proposed ring road which crosses the Lexden Road by traversing field 1214 on the north side and then following the boundary between fields 1211 and 1216 on the south side. The first operation but we had already ascertained that there were other kilns, and through the kindness of Mr. Williams we were able to resume the work at a later date. One disadvantage of this was that the *exact* relationship of kiln 27 to the other two could not be measured. Our plan shows it approximately (fig. 90).

Though kiln 27 was the first to be found, the next,

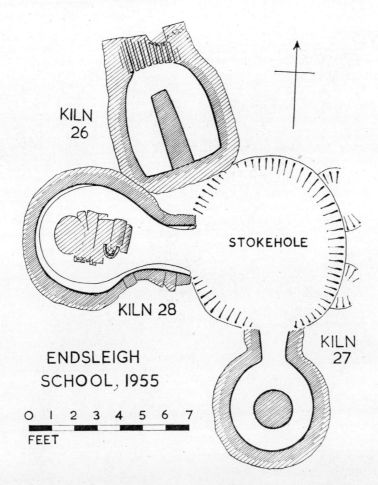

FIG. 90. Plan of kilns 26–28.

was the laying of the 'Southern Outfall Sewer', which was built over the whole course of the proposed road.

Field 1214 was used by Endsleigh School as a playing field, and in cutting across it kiln 27 was discovered. Mr. J. Williams, headmaster of the school, kindly gave the Museum permission to excavate it. In this we were greatly assisted by Mr. J. B. Baird and others of the school, and also by the cordial cooperation of the contractors and their men employed on the sewer.

After kiln 27 was cleared it became necessary to fill in so that the contractors could complete their work,

kiln 26, was so much earlier in date that we have reversed their order.

The two late kilns, 27 and 28, shared a common stoke-hole, which had cut two earlier pits. One of these was of the first century, the other was barren.

KILN 26

The natural development of the excavation moved from kiln 27 to the mouth of kiln 28, the existence of which had been deduced in advance. It was, however, quite unexpected to find yet another kiln standing almost on top of kiln 28. It was even more surprising that this kiln should turn out to be about 200 years older than the one below it.

Kiln 26 was squarish in plan, and in this respect reminds us that our other first-century kiln (kiln 23, p. 148) was also of this shape. It was built of broken tiles laid in clay, and the walls were about 11 in. thick. The battered and possibly weatherworn arch of the fire-hole still stood; it faced north. The south wall of this kiln came so close to the wall of kiln 28 that it almost oversailed it. The base of the walls of kiln 26 were at about the same level as the top of the walls of kiln 28 (at this point), i.e. about 2 ft. 6 in. from the surface.

The walls stood from 16 to 24 in. high and the central support was of the same construction, tile laid in clay, 3 ft. 4 in. long and 9 in. to 1 ft. wide. The flues occupied a space measuring 3 ft. 10 in. wide at the south, where it was rather square, by 4 ft. 6 in. long; the north end was much narrower than the south, but rounded, so that we do not give its width. The fire-hole was only 21 in. long, 21 in. wide, and 18 in. high.

The floor of the flues had perished and all we found was gravel burnt purplish red. Upon it lay about 15 in. of filling and then a layer of broken tile and clay from the destruction of the kiln.

Most of the extensive array of flagon necks were found just inside or outside the mouth of the kiln. Joints were found between pottery from this kiln and from the early pit cut by the stoke-hole of kilns 27 and 28.

KILN 27

This kiln was circular, with a very short fire-hole. The walls were of clay, with a little tile, and about 8 in. thick; they stood at most points to a height of 20 in. All above this had been destroyed. The central support was circular and 1 ft. 10 in. in diameter, made of clay. The circular flue was about 3 ft. 6 in. in diameter, but this was variable, for the walls sloped in places. The fire-hole was about 18 in. wide, and little over 1 ft. long.

The floor of the flues, vitrified like the walls, remained, and the flues were full of pottery—they had been filled up from the waste-heap.

Most of this pottery consisted of coarse grey cooking-pots (f. 268A). Next in numbers, but fewer, were the platters of f. 38 and f. 40. In much smaller quantity were fragments of mica-coated wares, polished black and grey ware, latticed jars, and vessels with chess-board rouletting.

KILN 28

This kiln was pear-shaped, with a wide fire-hole facing east and opening into the same shallow stoke-hole as

that of kiln 27. The flue-space was 4 ft. wide by nearly 7 ft. long at floor level, but the walls sloped outwards somewhat. The central support was confused; it did not connect with the back wall; at the back it consisted of a round column of clay, but this was extended forwards by a rough construction of fragments of tiles, tegulae and imbrices with nothing to hold it together. The whole was suspect, for it bore very little trace of burning, while the walls of the flue were vitrified. The fire-hole at its narrowest part was 14 in., widening outwards to 21 in. The wall on its south side stood 26 in. high, that on the north 14 in. The floor had lain at about 3 ft. 9 in. from the modern surface, but little of it remained.

THE POTTERY OF KILNS 26–28
(Figs. 91–94)

The pottery divides into the first-century products of kiln 26 and the third-century wares of kilns 27 and 28. The latter two used one stoke-hole and can hardly be separated; in any case their products were of types which changed but little, so that no difference is to be expected. In each case, however, it will be necessary to devote some attention to the sherds which were not made on the site, but which make some contribution towards dating.

KILN 26

Though the types made in this kiln are datable to the mid-first century in themselves, the date is confirmed by the following sherds, some of which are from the kiln-debris, some from the pit and some unstratified among the later debris. There was no first-century occupation level discernible. The scraps of *Cam.* ff. 5, 12, 17, 21, 56 and copy, 59, 62, 71, 112, 113, and 204, suggest that the potters were native Belgae, and the quantity of domestic ware of ff. 241 and 266 bears this out.

The Samian ware is equally conclusive; see p. 160.

The pottery made in the kiln is as follows, but we have included some pieces which were merely associated and probably not made on the site.

White and Buff Wares (Fig. 91)

Flagons and jugs. The quantity of fragments and the number of complete or nearly complete necks, show that the last loading of this kiln consisted of white and buff flagons; of these the best preserved are figured:

Form 140. Nos. 1–8 are red-buff necks of the general shape of 140, but much smaller, and with the neck tending to expand more downwards; the handles are only three-ribbed. They did not occur at Camulodunum, or at least, not exactly as here.

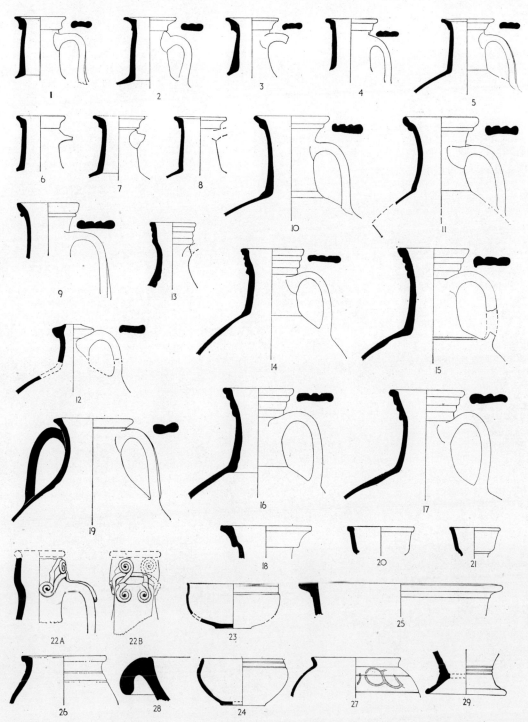

FIG. 91. Pottery from kiln 26. (¼)

No. 18 is a white rim, a variant of f. 140 which also occurred at Camulodunum.

There are also 11 more red-buff fragments and 7 white, plus 30 bases and 14 handles, also in white or red-buff. Eleven fragments of large four-ribbed handles could belong to the typical f. 140 or to f. 143 (see below), and there were remains of 12–13 bases with the square footring of f. 140. The red-buff ware here described has large whitish flecks in it, as if boulder clay had been used.

Form 143. Nos. 9–11 are of large size, with four-ribbed handles, and all of white clay. In addition to these, three handles may belong to this type. This curved neck, with a large upper lobe, occurred in large and small sizes at Camulodunum.

Form 149. No. 12 is a single neck in buff ware, with broad, flat handle.

Form 154. Nos. 13–17 show necks of this type; the first five are red-buff, the last is nearly white. The handles are three-ribbed and much curved. No. 13 is unusual in having the lower ring so much off-set and is reminiscent of f. 153.

There were also a white rim and handle, and 15 red-buff rims. Possibly the handles were sometimes two-ribbed, for there are 8 such, of large size, and one with no ribs. There are 18 bases with rounded footring and broad groove inside, two of them so large that they most probably belonged to this form.

Form 170. Nos. 20–21 show two small rim-fragments; they are of thin, hard, creamy ware charged with dark sand. Compare *Camulodunum*, fig. 52, 10.

Form unclassified. No. 19. Several fragments of a two-handled jug-neck in white ware. The neck is curved, with a simple rim which is flat on top. The handles are two-ribbed.

There are other unclassified fragments, but of no significance except the curious handle, no. 22A and B, of buff ware, broad and flat, and decorated with applied spirals. Though found on the site of kiln 26 it rather bears the smack of the later period, but this must remain uncertain.

HONEY POTS

Form 175. Fragments of honey-pots were few. No. 26 (distorted) shows a white-buff waster of this form; there was another rim, buff. There were also five fragments of two simply outcurved rims in creamy ware charged with dark sand. Five flat bases in similar ware, with no beading or other offset, go well with these.

MORTARIUM

Form 195. Fig. 91, no. 28 is a typical rim in creamy white ware with quartz grit running over the rim. Since it stands alone it may not have been made here.

BOWLS

Form 246 (?). Fig. 91, no. 25, a single rim in creamy white ware, flat on top, with two grooves, is perhaps a variety of this type, otherwise it is quite unclassified. Fig. 92, nos. 33, 34 are very large bowls in dark grey native ware.

BEAKER

Form 100. No. 27 shows the rim and shoulder of a beaker approximately of this form, bearing remains of a pattern of overlapping circles on the shoulder. The ware is creamy white and the circles are applied in a pale pink, chalky slip.

There were also one fragment of a tettine, a base like a samian f. 33, two pieces of buff lids and the base of a red cup f. 62, which is mentioned again below.

GREY AND BLACK WARES

These fragments were not at all numerous, and after all those which pretty certainly belonged to the late period had been sorted out there was little left. It is doubtful whether any of it was actually in this kiln.

Form 62. Fig. 91, nos. 23, 24 are copies (?) of this form, the first in thin hard rather rough red ware, the second fine, thick, polished grey ware.

Form 204. Fig. 91, 29 is a single base in native brown ware.

Small coarse pots and jars were the most plentiful, and all were of native ware, being ill levigated, brown to black, 'knobbly' surfaced, and soft. There were at least two examples of the rare f. 242 (fig. 92, nos. 30, 31) and rims of f. 266, besides a number of fragments. Several of these vessels had several pieces fitting together.

Large coarse storage jars. These also were of the native brown ware; the only recognizable rims were of f. 270; but there was a number of fragments of a blue-grey waster of f. 272, which is Roman. This will restore as fig. 95, 1.

Form 230. The finer (polished) fragments included a number giving the section through a bowl of this form (fig. 92, 32) in thick, soapy, polished brown-black ware.

On f. 268 see under that paragraph under kilns 27 and 28 (p. 164).

OTHER EARLY WARES TO BE CONNECTED WITH KILN 26

Samian. There were six small pieces of Drag. f. 29 and two of early f. 30. The two which preserve some decoration are Claudius–Nero. Plain forms are represented by ff. 15/17 (3), 18 (2), and 27 (4).

Gallo-Belgic, &c. There was one rim each of ff. 5 and 12, and a chip probably f. 56 in T.N. Two chips of a beaker ff. 74 or 79 and part of a pedestal base of T.R. 3 were found, also one fragment of f. 112, four of 113. A possible piece of lid f. 17; a grey copy of f. 56, several fragments of f. 59; fragments of two cups

ber of iron nails. The latter may indicate that wood from demolished structures was burnt in the kiln.

DATE OF KILN 26

The consensus of this evidence is that this kiln was

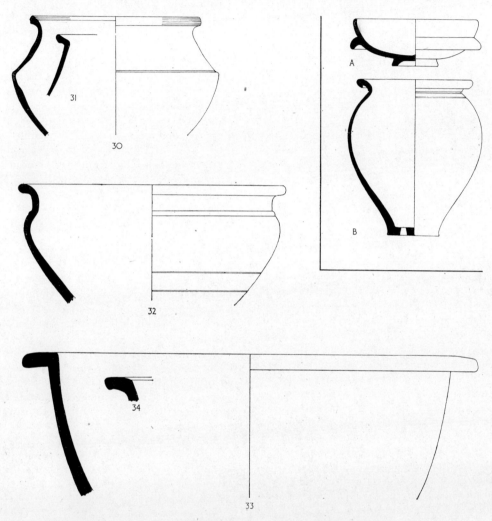

FIG. 92. Nos. 30–34, from kiln 26 (p. 160). A and B from stone building (p. 43). (¼)

f. 62 (fig. 91, nos. 23, 24). The first of these is red, the second polished grey ware. Ten or more fragments of f. 108, mostly Roman but some native, and a few fragments of ff. 115 and 119.

The hard white jug f. 161 is represented by two pieces, and there are fragments of native finer ware including a platter rim f. 21 and ff. 218 and 231, also a pedestal-base of f. 204 (fig. 91, no. 29).

Also to be mentioned as found here are several fragments of one or more human skulls, and quite a num-

active when the above wares were in use, which could be in periods IV, V, or VI of Camulodunum (see that Report, pp. 27–44). Period V is that of the short-lived triumph of Boudicca in A.D. 61. The pieces of skull would be simply explained if we assumed our kiln ended with the destruction of that year. There is nothing in the pottery more indicative of date than this, and nothing to disagree with it. This being so, the pots in figs. 84 and 91 should be contemporary and should correspond (as they do to a considerable extent).

THE POTTERY FROM KILNS 27 AND 28
(FIGS. 93–94)

The products of these kilns were, with few exceptions, dull and uninteresting. The number of fragments was very great (see the table, pp. 177–8, where in the case of the commonest vessels only rim fragments have been counted) and the majority of them were very small, though there were many complete bases, and in a few cases some large fragments would fit together. An exhaustive trial was made, as the available staff and time allowed, to see what would fit together, but it became apparent that no useful result could be obtained without a totally unjustifiable expenditure of time and labour. The following is the best that could be made of the remains. The forms are taken in the order used in the Museum work, and partly published in *Camulodunum* and *Roman Colchester*.

PLATTERS AND BOWLS

Form 37. The absence of this form is so significant that it must be mentioned.

Form 38. The straight-sided bowl with heavy beaded rim, polished all over and with no decoration. It may be large or small in diameter, and tall or short in height. The bevel at junction of wall and foot is a regular feature except that in the fourth century examples begin to appear without it. There are none such here. The ware is a good dark grey (disregarding variations in firing, especially among wasters). Fig. 93, nos. 1–3, illustrate these vessels, which were very numerous and especially connected with kiln 27, where two half-vessels were found in one piece, an exceptional circumstance on the site. They are not deep (no. 1); the very deep form was hardly represented; the average form is shown by nos. 2 and 3.

Form 39. Platter with low, curved wall and simple lip. (The standard type is of black cooking-pot ware, and is scored outside with intersecting arcs; it does not occur here.) A few rims of grey ware may be classed as of this form, but may be merely rims of f. 40 with more curve than usual. No. 4 is an example. Two have a sharply incised groove below the lip, which is quite foreign to f. 39.

Form 40. Straight-sided bowl with bevelled foot and simple rim. A, with a groove under the rim; B, without groove. This groove is smooth, not sharply incised. The vessels are polished all over, or were intended to be. They were very numerous; the wavy line sometimes used on the outside scarcely appears here. Fig. 93, 5–7, show three normal examples with groove. No. 8, without groove, illustrates the shallower form which is as common as the deeper no. 9. This is a variant of f. 40A, the groove very wide and almost double, the ware

dark grey-black, polished outside but not inside; it does not appear to be of the same ware as the rest. No. 10 is an unusual rim, also in a strange black ware polished all over.

CUP OR BEAKER

Form 69B. Cylindrical bowl decorated with wavy lines between grooves. The form was originally described from fragments found at Camulodunum supported by others from Twitty Fee Camp at Danbury. These were of a red to buff, soapy, native ware, undoubtedly Belgic.

We have fragments of three or more examples in a pearly grey ware, far removed from Belgic, but the form and decoration are almost unchanged. The form of the rim, and the ware itself, correspond exactly with the products of kilns 27 and 28, especially fig. 94, 41. All the fragments come from the common stoke-hole, so on all counts we have classed them as of the third century.

Fig. 93, 11 shows a body made up from several fragments with a rim added from another vessel.

FACE URNS

Form 288. Fig. 93, 12. The Museum has a series of very globular light buff face-urns found in graves with second-century pottery, and these graves may extend into the third century. In these the rim, in passing from lip to shoulder, describes a semicircle.

From these kilns we have a quantity of small and worn fragments of similar vessels, apparently from an old firing of one of the kilns. They differ only in two respects; the rim is more upright, and the clay is a dull, dirty, greyish white and sandy; it is difficult to imagine that they would take a polish. The body seems to have been less globular, but the small size of the fragments, and the likelihood of their being wasters, precludes a definite judgement on this. The form of handles, frilled rim, and the flat base with beaded off-set are enough to satisfy us that we have here the third-century continuation of f. 288.

BOWL

Form 316 (fig. 93, 13). Fragments making nearly half of this bowl were found in the mouth of kiln 26. The ware is good, nearly white, with a chocolate red coating on the outside, possibly also on the inside, but it is not there now. The vessel is mis-shapen, but no other similar fragments were found, and it hardly seems possible that such bowls were made in our kilns. It is uncertain whether it was associated with kiln 26 or with the later ones. However, since it is a copy of the samian f. Drag. 38, which we are accustomed to

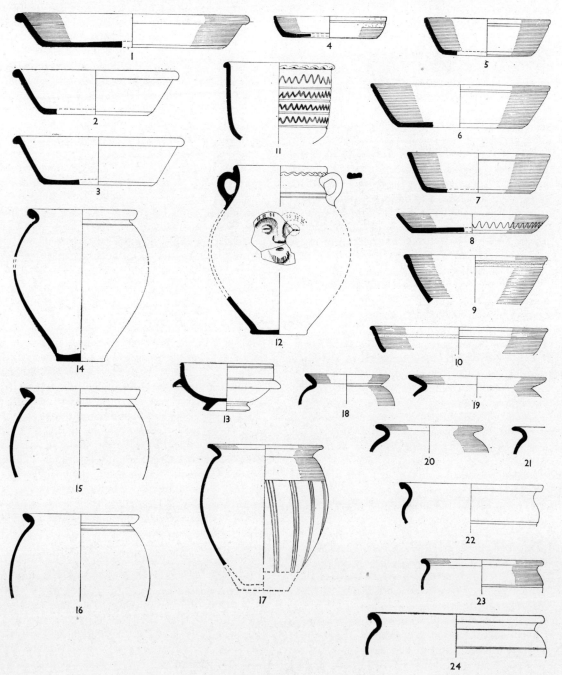

FIG. 93. Pottery from kilns 27 and 28. ($\frac{1}{4}$)

meet in the fourth century, and occasionally earlier, and since it is certain that f. Drag. 38 was not available to copy at the period of kiln 26, we have associated it with the later kilns.

COOKING-POTS

Form 268. This is the commonest cooking-pot in Colchester and neighbourhood. The rim is sharply but roundly outcurved so that it usually has a 'bunched-up' appearance. The lip is very thick and rounded or triangular in section, the hollow at the neck being usually very deep and short, but very variable. Immediately below the offset of the neck there is a groove, sometimes two. The whole vessel is merely smoothed, never polished in any part, and the base always retains the curious marks of the wire with which it was cut off the potter's wheel. The ware is, or was, intended to be a thin, hard, brown-grey to black, but the colour varies greatly according to the mixing and firing.

Fig. 93, 14 is dull red, with brown to grey-black exterior; it is from the common stoke-hole. No. 15 is grey to red ware, from kiln 27. The edge of the rim is very square. Several others similar were found from kilns 27 and 28. No. 16 is mottled red and black, very thin, with a few sparse grains of white quartz, from kiln 27.

The great quantity of these vessels indicated in the table (p. 178) is from a count of the rim-fragments only; side fragments and bases were equally numerous: many of the bases extended to the lower third of the body. A number of rims is shown as from kiln 26, and it was noticeable that they all seemed to have a browner colour than the rest. This may be due to the difference caused by the quantity of red and buff ware present there: at any rate we do not feel that we can accept this form as possibly made at the time of kiln 26. In the first century the common cooking-pot was f. 266, which certainly prevailed up to about 100 and perhaps even to 120 and later. By Flavian times, however, it had changed, inasmuch as the base becomes polished, and as time goes on the polished area mounts higher. At the same time f. 268 appears in great numbers and takes over the role of the unpolished vessels.

Form 279. The universal Romano-British cooking pot, of black ware, charged with minute white quartz grit, polished top and bottom and latticed, is always scarce in Colchester, apparently having little chance in competition with f. 268. It is represented by *one* rim only, no. 21. The lip projects so far that it must be of late third- or fourth-century date.

HOUSEHOLD JARS

Form 278. A universal form, parallel to f. 279, but the ware is usually grey. It is so similar to 279 that it is sometimes doubtful to which form to assign a piece.

On the whole f. 278 should have a quite sharp angle between base of rim and shoulder, a distinction which is clear in our two nos. 17 and 21. Though many fragments were found they were very varied; there was here no standard size, ware, or decoration. Instead of the usual lattice we have groups of several lines, or the same crossed to make a multiple lattice. I had previously connected this fashion with the Antonine period, but we must now allow it to be later. The ware is mostly a red-brown to grey-black, and some of the vessels are small enough to be called beakers.

A new feature is a series of jar-rims of a variant form, in which the rim is straight, and turned out sharply, with more or less of an acute angle at the shoulder. Fig. 93, nos. 18–20 are representative of eleven such rims. We know nothing of the body or foot. No. 18 is pale grey polished; no. 19 is grey-black to brown, possibly polished, diameter $7\frac{3}{4}$ in.; no. 20 is pale grey, probably once polished, all three from the common stoke-hole.

FINE-WARE BOWLS

Form 299. This standard type, which was first published in the Newstead Report (Curle's type 46) and which was accordingly for some time regarded as Antonine, has now been shown to last through, at Colchester, into the fourth century, generally preserving the same pale clay and darker, slightly micaceous surface, the product, apparently, of one pottery only.

However, other potteries did make it on occasion, as here. The neck runs into the shoulder without offset (we call them 'S-bowls'), and there is a groove near the maximum diameter. The finish of the foot, very good at first, varies later, and can be crude in the fourth century. These vessels were made in our kilns in their usual brown-grey ware, and the rims have either a simple lip or are beaded or overhung. Fig. 93, nos. 22, 23 illustrate the type.

But this form (299) is attended by a shadow; every now and then a vessel appears which one would class as 299, but the rim is offset from the shoulder (the ware is never that described as standard for f. 299 above), and I have often hesitated whether to make f. 299 embrace these or not. Our potters certainly made both varieties, and no. 24 illustrates the offset rim. It is grey-brown: from the common stoke-hole.

These vessels belong to the finer ware group, and much of their surface is polished. Remains were numerous but small, so that we have no body-outline or base. The numbers were probably much higher than we have shown, for there were many polished rims which could not be allocated to forms, and most may have belonged to the present group.

Narrow-necked Vessels

Form 280. Large jars with comparatively narrow mouth were represented by a few fragments from all places, but they were, with one exception, very scrappy and of poor finish; nothing can be said of the body proportions.

Fig. 94, 25 shows the largest fragment; grey ware, not (now) polished, from the common stoke-hole.

Form 281. Flasks with narrow mouth (diameter about 3 in.); there are a few unimportant fragments, but the following are worthy of note:

No. 26, an unusual neck of pale grey ware with a pressed-out cordon. No handle joined the rim, but there could have been one lower down. The form is unclassified, but see the neck with frilled rim, *Roman Colchester*, fig. 64, 57 and 58, which would go well with some of our rouletted wares here. Kiln 27.

No. 27. A similar neck, but lacking cordon; the ware is again light grey. From its general appearance the vessel could have been a flagon, but we cannot say whether it had a handle or not. Common stoke-hole.

No. 28. A more normal neck, very near to f. 281. Hard, fine, dark grey ware, polished. Kiln 26.

No. 29. This has an exceptionally narrow throat; fine dark grey ware, polished. Common stoke-hole.

Bowls

Form 305. The well-known straight-sided bowl with ledged rim, which is characteristic of the fourth century, is represented here by one rim only, in polished grey ware. We do not know when this form began. One found at Gellygaer must belong to some occupation of a later date than the original occupation of the fort (c. A.D. 103–21), and so far as I know no example of this form has been found in circumstances which compel us to date it earlier than the fourth century.

So, unless our rim is purely a stray (and we have no other strays) it brings our date up to the fourth century or very close to it. The only argument to the contrary is the sherds of Antonine Samian ware, and these will have to be regarded as survivals.

Form 306. Nos. 30–32 illustrate this form, which has only been recorded previously from Colchester. When I first saw it I connected it with similar bowls found at Kastel Alzei, which is fourth-century, and its occurrence in the 'Mithraeum' confirmed me (*Roman Colchester*, fig. 67, 87). But since then it has turned up not only in these kilns, but in the early second-century kilns at Ardleigh. It therefore begins then; not, I think, earlier, and must continue until at least 300, and it may or may not be a survival in the 'Mithraeum'.

The form is a very simple funnel shape, with a broad thickened rim like a collar, made generally by simply turning down the last inch or so of the lip. The whole is smoothed but never polished, the base, not smoothed

beneath, preserving the mark of the wire. In these respects the type is in the same 'service' as f. 268, and it is beginning to show signs of having had the same long life. (See p. 131 (no. 20) and fig. 74, 1.)

Fig. 94, 30. Large fragment, red-brown, with black surface. Common stoke-hole.

No. 31. Fine light grey. Stoke-hole of kiln 26.

No. 32. Sandy red-brown with blackish surface. Ibid.

Form 307. Nos. 33–35 illustrate this type, which is a wide-mouthed bowl made in much the same ware and style as f. 278. The rim is a large, projecting beading with a hollow inside for a lid. The top and bottom are polished, and the side usually bears a decoration of groups of scored lines, or a multiple lattice. This, I have thought, connects them with the decoration on the late fourth-century handled jars from the Signal Stations (e.g. Scarborough, *Arch. Journ.* lxxxix, 228, pl. I, 1–2), but here again, later evidence shows it was certainly current earlier. I first met it in the many lots of unstratified pottery from various sites in Colchester; then it turned up in the 'Mithraeum' (*Roman Colchester*, fig. 65, 65), and now we have it here. It looks like proving a concomitant of f. 278, just as f. 306 links up with f. 268.

Fig. 94, 33. Light grey; rim polished, body scored with groups of three lines. Common stoke-hole.

No. 34. Grey. Diameter c. 6¾ in. Ibid.

No. 35. Grey. Same diameter. Ibid.

Flask and Flagons (Fig. 94)

Form 283 (?) No. 36. Grey ware, white coated; the grey was probably intended to be red. The form is exactly 283, and the ware could agree, but if so this rim is the largest yet recorded for the form. It should date about 330, but we do not know how early it began. From the common stoke-hole.

Form 360. No. 37. A flanged neck of soft red ware, red-coated; careless work. Kiln 26, to which it could not possibly belong.

No. 38 is part of a flagon neck, very distorted, bright red ware; the handle is darker, but fits to the rim, probably intended to be mica-coated, but not so. Common stoke-hole.

No. 39. Flagon-neck and handle, brown-red clay, mica-coated. Common stoke-hole.

These two necks are of forms as yet unclassified. The first is very reminiscent of the bronze flagon at Colchester which contained a silver hoard dating to about A.D. 230. The second is equally close to another Colchester flagon of mica-coated ware. Both of these have tubular spouts, whereas ours have slightly pinched spouts. The fact that the handle is attached to the rim cuts them off from the classified forms with pinched spouts. For the present we regard them as a variant of f. 361, and we place them in the third century.

Form 389. Only four fragments of unguent pots were found; they call for no comment.

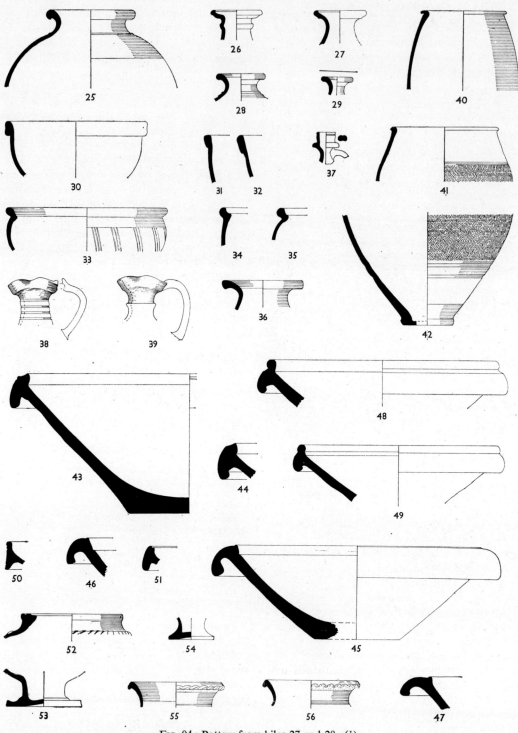

FIG. 94. Pottery from kilns 27 and 28. (⅓)

BEAKERS AND ROULETTED DECORATION

The true f. 391 is in colour-coated ware, which these kilns did not make, but they did make grey copies of the form, rather larger than the originals. I had not noticed such vessels before in Colchester.

Fig. 94, 40. Several fragments making a large piece, fine dark grey ware, polished outside. Kiln 27 and common stoke-hole. There were several other rims similar in form and ware.

It is of f. 108, but would not be easily confused with the first and early second-century examples, not only because of the decoration, but because the foot has no groove beneath and is not quite of the usual shape. The ware is a pale red-brown with a darker brown-grey surface.

MORTARIA

The fragments of mortaria were not numerous in

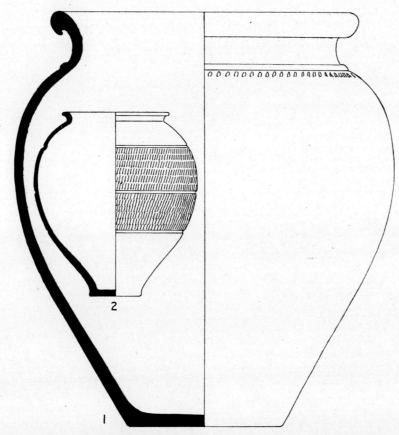

FIG. 95. Vessels from kilns 26 (no. 1, p. 161) and 28 (no. 2, p. 167). (¼)

No. 41. Another copy of f. 391 in good pale grey ware, polished, and with a coarse 'chessboard' rouletting. Kiln 28.

No. 42. Base of a crudely finished vessel in brown-grey ware with darker surface, partly ill-polished, and decorated with horizontal grooves and crude 'chessboard' decoration. Kiln 28.

There were many fragments of grey or brown-grey ware bearing rouletted decoration. Most of it was 'chessboard', but some was of the usual type. The vessels concerned were of several forms, but the pieces were all very small, often worn, and scarcely a joint could be found. There was reason to suspect that ff. 280 and/or 281 were present, also f. 406.

Fig. 95, no. 2. One vessel only could be restored.

comparison with the other wares, and the pieces were larger, in many cases fitting together. The various types represented are illustrated by fig. 94, nos. 43–51.

43. Many fragments making the most part of a vessel f. 497, but lacking the spout. Greyish buff ware with small, mixed grit. Kiln 28.

44. Similar rim, with grooves on flange, white-buff ware, with mixed grit. Part of the spout shows that it had a short side-rib only extending across the flat top of the rim. Kiln 28.

Another similar, sandy yellow, has one groove; a third is white with no grooves. From Kilns 28 and 27 respectively.

Similar rim, buff with white grit. Diameter large. Kiln 28 with two more similar.

Another rim, similar but heavier; creamy buff ware with

mixed grit. Ten fragments, diameter *c.* 14 in. One other similar. Kiln 28.

45. Rim f. 497, buff with red and white grit. Kiln 28. There is also half the spout of another similar rim.

46. Similar rim, buff, mixed grit, the white grit large. Kiln 28.

47. Another, soft buff, the mixed grit running over the rim. Kiln 28.

48. Rim of f. 504. Dull buff with small mixed grit which ends an inch below the interior offset. The remaining space is covered with slight horizontal grooving. Kiln 28. Three more rims have this outline, but the grit rises higher and there is no grooving.

49. Another rim f. 504, white-buff ware. Grit small, white, ends ⅜ in. below offset, with grooving as on no. 48. Kiln 28.

50. Rim f. 501. Buff ware, much underfired, with very small mixed grit. Diameter 8¼ in. Kiln 27.

51. Rim f. 498, yellow-buff ware. Diameter 10½ in. Common stoke-hole.

VARIOUS

After going through a mass of pottery there is always a residue of oddments, most of which have not sufficient character to merit separate mention. The following may be mentioned in this case (fig. 94):

52. Three fragments of a curious rim in very hard, grey-black to brown ware (like some medieval ware), fluted on top and very sharply stabbed on the shoulder. Common stoke-hole.

53. Another pedestal-base, perhaps of an incense burner, grey-buff, waster, smoothed, not polished. Common stoke-hole.

54. Pedestal-base, very small, pale grey. Common stoke-hole.

55. Frilled rim of red ware, formerly polished. Common stoke-hole.

56. Another frilled rim, fine hard grey ware, polished. Common stoke-hole.

KILNS 29–31

These were found in 1959 on the site of the 1933 kilns and are described with them, pp. 34–43.

KILN 32

In 1959 the fields south and west of Kingswode Hoe were developed as a building-estate and a new street

¹ Since the above was written Mr. H. C. Calver has come forward with the following account of this incident. The pit excavated by Mr. Campen and Mr. Jarmin was the stoke-hole. After they left it Mr. Calver continued and excavated the kiln itself, which lay immediately to the west and was connected to the stoke-hole by a short furnace-flue.

The kiln was circular, with clay wall about 12 in. thick. The overall diameter was 5 ft. 9 in., giving an internal diameter of about 3 ft. 9 in. The floor of the oven had collapsed into the flues, but the central support remained in position. The flues were full of soot.

At the back of the kiln, lying on the collapsed floor, were two rows of vessels, mostly fluted beakers, partly nested together and lying on their sides. These vessels he subsequently gave to Mr. Campen, and it is some of these which we have illustrated. Mr. Calver says they were 31 in number.

His sketch-plan shows the stoke-hole as D-shaped, the rounded side towards the kiln. He states that its sides were lined with flat tiles (one is illustrated on pl. XXII *b*) laid edgeways.

was made westwards from Sussex Road, with another running northwards from it up towards the hedge which passes the south side of kiln 7. In making the first street nothing was found save the trace of ditch IA (explored in 1932, see *Cam.*, plan, pl. cxii). In stripping the topsoil from the northwards road a number of dark marks in the subsoil indicated the presence of scattered pits, many of which were accompanied by pottery. The pottery was mixed, consisting of remains of the Belgic and Claudius–Nero period, and of potter's waste of late third-century or fourth-century date. One pit in particular was very clearly defined, though the description of it, as given by the several amateurs who dug it, varies from that of a simple pit to a complete kiln. The former view is perhaps the most likely to have been correct.

Colchester Museum has but one archaeological assistant, and at the time this activity was going on it was quite impossible to find opportunity to watch this estate as it should have been. It was not possible to dig the pits which lay under the new street, and not practicable to dig at random looking for others. The Museum collected some pottery, and Mr. M. J. Campen secured the bulk of the pottery from the prominent pit we have mentioned.¹

Disregarding the first-century material the pottery is all late and is all potter's waste, a large proportion of it being underfired. There were also fragments of vitrified kiln-wall. Mr. Campen gave the bulk of his pottery to the Museum: the pick of it he retains at his house, and we are greatly indebted to him for permission to draw and publish it.

The pottery from the several different spots on this N.–S. road, west of Kingswode Hoe, is all homogeneous and can be described straightforwardly as a single deposit.

The best ware made was colour-coated and it is of great interest, for it is comparatively well preserved, the style is new, as are some of the ideas in the decora-

On the north side of the entrance to the kiln Mr. Calver found a platform made of these same tiles (cf. the ovens between kilns 20 and 21, and adjacent to kiln 30). Lying on this were the remains of two remarkable vessels and a fragment, possibly from a mask (fig. 99).

The two vessels are of a coarse, sandy buff ware, the first much darker than the second.

No. 1 has a domed top and is completely closed save for the small round spout. Near the base, on the opposite side, is a large, solid knob. We know of no parallel for this.

No. 2 is a tall bottle-shaped flask with spreading mouth and flat base. The general shape, though not the rim, is reminiscent of our fig. 72, no. 12. Both vessels are irregularly formed and carelessly made, as if for the potter's own use only.

No. 3 is a fragment of very soft, underfired, whitish-buff clay, thin on the decorated face, but about ¼ in. thick on the side running back from it. The inner edge is broken all along. Our drawing is purely conjectural, but compare pl. XVIII *a*.

tion. This applies to the barbotine; rouletting was employed freely, but rough-casting or sanding was hardly used at all, many vessels were quite smooth, and the number of folded vessels was very great.

BARBOTINED WARE (FIGS. 96, 97)

The more decorative vessels are either of ff. 391 or 392; no human figures appear, but we have animals and floral scrolls, with lavish use of imbricated scales. The style of the animals is very different from that of the earlier kilns. There is a double groove above the decoration, and a new feature is the introduction of a rouletted band above it.

The beakers are taller and larger than those we have encountered hitherto; the rising base, offset by a beading, rarely has a groove beneath. There is also a new modification of the rim of f. 392 (fig. 97, 4).

The fabric of the decorated pieces is very uniform; they could nearly all have come from one firing. The paste is buff, creamy or yellowish, with very rarely a red tinge. The coating is a fine, even, matt chocolate, only varying in depth of colour.

Mr. Campen has many more fragments besides those illustrated, but they are mostly small and add nothing to our inquiry. The best examples are illustrated on figs. 96 and 97.

Fig. 96

1. Fragment in 'hunt-cup' style; two rouletted bands above the double groove.
2. Most part of a fine beaker decorated with vertical bands of overlapping scales; a broad, thin scale used singly and smaller, thicker scales used double, the bands alternating with vertical bead-rows. Rouletted band at top as before. There are fragments of other beakers with the same design.
3. Large fragment of a similar beaker, the decoration entirely of imbricated scales, arranged in triangular blocks alternately upright and pendant. A space left between them is traversed by a single oblique line of scales. There are fragments of others with this same pattern.
4. Single fragment of somewhat similar design, having an upright triangle of scales, the space to the right of which has had some loose kind of design which is not intelligible.
5. Two large joining fragments; this bowl carried two seamonsters only; they are displayed on fig. 97, 1 and are of a new type and style.
Fig. 97, 2 shows another fragment bearing part of the same beast; this fragment is underfired. The animal is presumably a capricorn.
6. This beaker may have been of f. 391 or 392; the decoration is parallel lines of barbotine applied very fluid, making a broad band with a raised rib. There were a few other fragments.
7 and 8 are examples of f. 392 decorated with broad bands of rouletting. There were many similar fragments, some in fabric quite like those already described: others have the same paste but are much darker in the coating.
9 and 10 are examples of the smaller f. 392, which are quite smooth and have the simple, cut-off foot. These, too, are often very dark in colour. Compare fig. 55, 3.

11 is a rare and fine example of f. 397; the ware is fine, hard red, with a dark-chocolate to black coating.
12–15 are examples of the commonest vessel on the site, the folded beaker f. 407A. Nos. 12 and 14 are hard red and orange-red ware, the others are buff, all have chocolate coating. The decoration is usually simply rouletting above and below the folds; but some examples are smooth all over; imbricated scales on the ridges (no. 15) are rare.

It will be seen that the forms carry on directly from those which were so popular in the kilns of 1933 and 1959, but they tend to be larger and taller. Another great difference between the two sites is the quantity of f. 407.

In fig. 97 we have attempted to demonstrate the difference in the style of the barbotine work. Nos. 1 and 2 have already been noticed.

3. A stag seized by what should be a lion, but hardly resembles one!
4. A stag with a new type of antler; new, too, is the idea of carrying the antlers beyond the double groove.
5. This piece is worthy of note; the ware is a pale yellow-buff, underfired, so that the glittering black glaze is falling off. The fine rouletted bands and neat scroll-work, together with the black finish would label this piece as finest Rhenish ware, were it not for the fact that the vessel is underfired.
6. Several fragments of a very distinctive beaker, f. 392; thin hard buff ware, with a glossy red to chocolate-black coating. The scroll-work is sharp and fine and the leaf is *applied*. At 6a the main fragment is displayed, and shows the mark where another applied leaf has fallen off. The fragment b shows there was another fine bead-row below the decoration; c and d are shown with the turning-marks horizontal, but they may be upside down.
7. The only fragment found from a grey face-urn.

Nos. 5 and 6 are a surprising discovery; they undoubtedly suggest that our potters may have been making this very fine ware. We shall, however, have to have a great many more wasters before we can feel really confident on the matter. The present few sherds are not adequate for so important a conclusion.

MORTARIA (FIG. 98, NOS. 1–6)

In an assemblage such as that with which we are dealing Samian ware is hardly to be expected, and in fact there is only one possible fragment. It is the rim of a mortarium f. Drag. 45, finely potted and quite thin (fig. 98, 1). The ware is of very fine grain, but is overfired nearly black, so that it is not certain whether it was meant to be Samian or colour-coated. However, the fine grit and the shape identify it with Samian, whereas nothing connects it with the colour-coated technique.

The upright rim is slightly convex outwards, and there is no internal offset. These facts associate it with the latest examples of the form, such as Oswald and Pryce, pl. LXXIV, 2, 4, and 5, from Rheinzabern, Niederbieber, and Trier, the latter two judged to run into the third century.

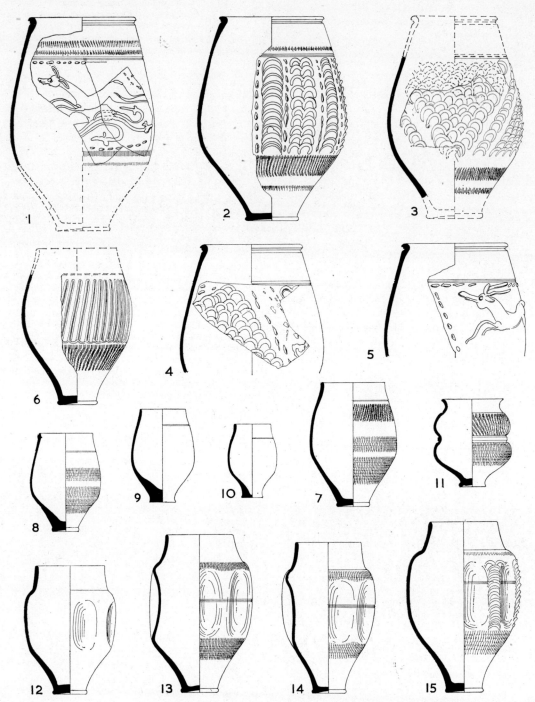

FIG. 96. Colour-coated beakers from kiln 32 (p. 169). (¼)

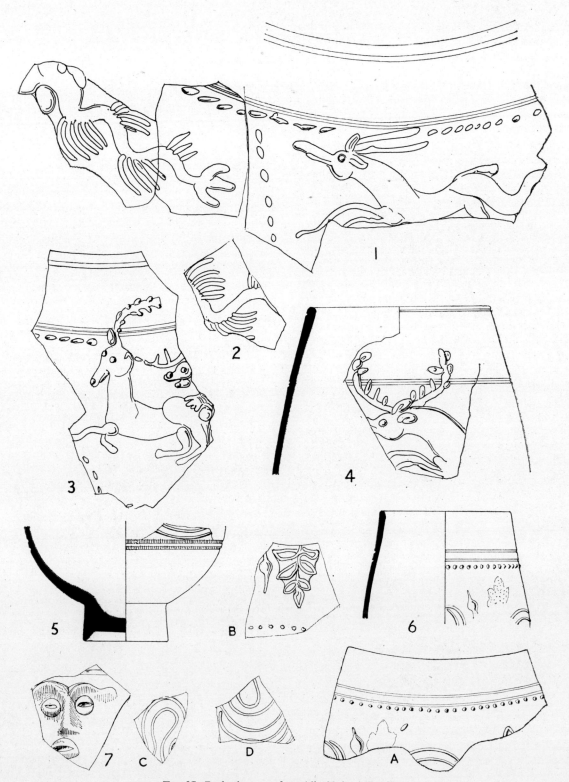

Fig. 97. Barbotine ware from kiln 32 (p. 169). (½)

The coarse-ware mortaria come next to the folded beakers in numbers and bulk. The many rim-fragments are broken small and have produced few joints, indicating a large number of vessels. There are four different types or forms.

Form 501B. There are only two rims and a fragment, in white and buff ware, one underfired. They are typical of those already published.

Form 504. There are sixteen rims in white and buff ware, mostly underfired; most have a groove on top and two grooves on the outside of the lip. None has a groove at the lower edge of the flange. The grit is small and mixed. We illustrate two:

> Fig. 98, 5. Good buff ware. Diameter *c.* 10½ in. The commonest outline.
> Fig. 98, 6. Creamy white ware, underfired. Diameter *c.* 13 in.

Form 508. Fig. 98, 4 is a huge rim in dark brown-buff ware. Diameter 20 in. or more, in six small fragments. The type is clearly in the same series as rims like fig. 64, 10, and is paralleled by nos. 16–20 on fig. 89. We now give this type a form-number.

Forms 498 and 499. These are not, perhaps, so easily separable as we once thought. We have before us a great bulk of fragments, mostly quite small and underfired, clearly one of the largest products of the site. The rim is nearly upright, convex outwards, and approaching the 'hammer-head' in section. The inner lip may be offset within or not, and generally has a groove on top. Sometimes there is a groove outside as well, approaching that of f. 499. Very occasionally there is no groove on top.

The grit is small and mixed. There are two types of spout:

> Fig. 98, 2. Rim more sloping than in the next figure; groove on top of lip and outside; spout projecting a little, the lips ending in round bosses each with a circular depression. This type of spout seems to go with the more sloping rim. Buff ware.
> Fig. 98, 3. Rim nearly upright, grooved on top. The spout scarcely projects at all and the lips end in very slight oval blobs.

There are over 160 rims of this type, mostly in underfired buff ware; very few are whitish. There were also many side and base fragments which cannot be allotted to forms.

GREY WARES (FIG. 98, NOS. 7–17)

The bulk of these is very moderate and the recognizable forms are few, for much of it is fragments of heavy bases, both fine and coarse.

Among the platters f. 37 has dropped out, though some of the f. 38's are very near it in form.

Form 38. There are twenty-one rims, two close to f. 37, the rest typical, except two which we illustrate:

> Fig. 98, 7. Grey-black ware, polished. Diameter uncertain, but very large.
> Fig. 98, 8. Red (probably intended to be grey), polished outside. Diameter *c.* 11 in.

Form 39. A single rim in fine hard pale grey ware.

Form 40. Only six rims. A number of base-fragments cannot be assigned to forms; one of them lacks the bevel.

COOKING-POTS AND JARS

These are not numerous and all are f. 268. One might have expected to find f. 268B but we seem to have only f. 268A. Much more work will have to be done on this form before we can say whether there is any chronological value in the rim-forms. We illustrate:

> Fig. 98, 9. A neck of almost standard form.
> Fig. 98, 10. A more upright and open neck, lacking the groove.

Of twenty-one rims, only one might be called f. 268B. As often happens, many are fired red, presumably by accident.

Form 278 is represented by six rims and a base. They call for no comment.

Form 299. There is one certain example and three possibles; also two rims of this style, but with offset neck:

> Fig. 98, 11. Grey ware, polished outside.
> Fig. 98, 12. Fine light grey ware, partly polished.

Form 307. Nine rims are of this type: most are underfired and some are red (in error). The standard type has a hollow for a lid:

> Fig. 98, 16. Very fine grey-black ware, polished. Typical.
> Fig. 98, 17. Drab grey ware, perished; was probably polished. Has no hollow for lid. There are seven more similar rims.

Form 280. There are two rims of this form or something similar.

Form 407A. There are some twenty fragments of folded beakers in grey ware; they seem to have been quite like these in colour-coated ware. A few fragments of grey jars show rouletting on the shoulder (cf. fig. 96, 12–14):

> Fig. 98, 13. A black rim of unknown form.
> Fig. 98, 14 is a black rim, hard ware, not polished but very smooth and slightly micaceous. This could be f. 306.
> Fig. 98, 15. There are a number of fragments of these lids with incurved lip. They are always in sandy ware and usually red, as ours.[1]

FACE-URNS

It remains to mention that there is a quantity of fragments of red ware which has been coated with a white or cream wash. We have noted this before and have regarded it as a fourth-century fashion (e.g. *Roman*

---

[1] There is a fragment in the Museum (38.38) apparently of this form stamped AV·CF.

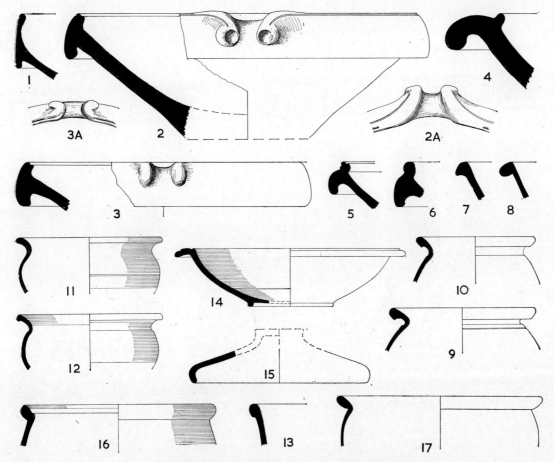

FIG. 98. Coarse wares from kiln 32 (pp. 169–72). (¼)

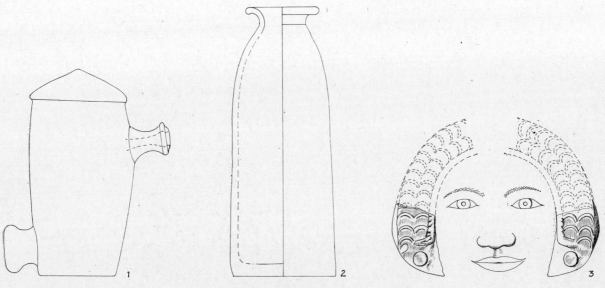

FIG. 99. Vessels and fragment from kiln 32. (¼)
(See footnote, p. 168.)

Colchester, fig. 60, 4 and fig. 63, 48). The only recognizable pieces belonged to the handled face-urns, f. 288. Two frilled rims and a handle certainly are of this type. The examples in the Museum, however, are not, so far as we can ascertain, red ware white coated, but white or buff right through.

The date of this kiln must fall later than that of the 1933–59 site, and must come before the general use of all-black grit in mortaria, and, indeed, before the introduction of many familiar fourth-century types of

Fig. 100

1. Rim of a mortarium, a distorted waster, the ware now grey with a paler grey coating and small, mixed grit. The very upright rim carries three broad grooves. One cannot be certain, but one can strongly suspect that the ware was intended to be white or buff, white coated, and that the present colour is due to over-firing. No fragment preserves a spout.

2 and 3 are similar rims, one with the grooves in two pairs, resembling f. 501, the other grooved like no. 1. Diameters uncertain. There were many fragments of these vessels.[1]

4 is a mortar-rim of different pattern; the ware is the same; the grit is very fine and white. Diameter uncertain.

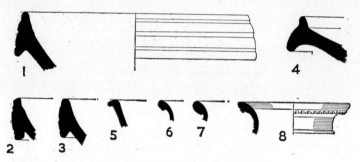

FIG. 100. Pottery from kiln 33. ($\frac{1}{4}$)

vessel. This does not, however, preclude the early part of the fourth century. Having regard for the continuity evident from the earlier kilns, and the lack of definitely fourth-century types, it seems best to us to date the activity of this kiln between 250 and 300. Certain things are notably absent, e.g. the mortarium ff. 500 and 503, small beakers like f. 408, and cooking-pots f. 279.

KILN 33

In the winter of 1959–60 the Museum learnt that a kiln had been discovered a few years earlier on the nursery gardens known as Strowlger's Ground. Inquiries were made and a small quantity of pottery which had been gathered up at the time of the discovery was acquired for the Museum. The site was about where C is marked on the plan (fig. 1). The remains are quite certain evidence of a kiln, and nearly all the sherds are potter's waste. They are unfortunately limited in quantity, and we show what we can on fig. 100.

Most of the remains are of mortaria, and of a type which we have not seen before, making the nearest approach, perhaps, that we yet have in Colchester to the 'hammer-head' type.

5 is the rim of a bowl, dark grey ware, polished both sides. Diameter uncertain.

6 and 7 are rims of f. 268. Both are red, but were probably intended to be grey.

8 is the frilled neck of a flask in fine light grey ware. This frilling of necks, especially high up under the rim, seems to have been fashionable in the fourth century, which is not to say that it never occurs earlier. Cf. *Roman Colchester*, fig. 64, 57, 58 (f. 297); also f. 290.

There is practically nothing here paralleled in any of our other kiln-deposits, and I have the feeling that this is perhaps the latest kiln of our series so far. One has, however, no cogent reason for putting it very late. I will provisionally suggest an early fourth-century date.

This discovery confirms the contention of the late Mr. P. G. Laver that he had evidence for a potter's kiln in this vicinity. There is also the record that a large amount of burnt earth and brick rubble was found in the NW. part of Mr. R. W. Wallace's garden (this I take to mean about 500 yds. NW. of C on the plan). The deposit was 50 yds. long by 20 ft. wide and 3 ft. thick. The depth from the surface was 2 ft. 'It was composed mostly of burnt clay, rather like insufficiently burnt ballast, intermixed with pieces of thin bricks, flue tiles and Roman roof tiles. None of these showed signs of use. All appearances were as seen where bricks are burnt in clamps at the present

---

[1] The form occurs at Canterbury, *Arch. Cant.* lxv, fig. 5, 31, fourth-century. In the same figure nos. 25 and 30 are very like our fig. 100, 4. They were late third to early fourth-century. See also Chenet, p. 73, fig. 23, fourth-century.

day. The clay would originate from the necessity of plastering up some vacancies to force the fire in other directions. Appearances of a similar character to this were seen by H. Laver previously.'[1]

We give this for what it is worth, with a very uncomfortable feeling about the 'pieces of thin bricks'.

There is in the Museum a quantity of pottery marked as found in April 1934 in Serpentine Walk at the corner of Margaret Road (just a little east of C on the plan, fig. 1). Its nature is rather surprising:

The date of the deposit is not easily fixed. The bowls (fig. 101, 1, 2) of f. 246 would appear to follow upon the standard Sheepen type (*Cam.*, pl. LXXX), which was, however, represented. Of the two illustrated, the first has three very fine grooves on the flange, two scored lines on the wall, and a deep groove. The side is well sloped outwards.[2]

No. 2 approximates more to an Antonine type. The flange is polished, without grooves; there are two scored lines on the wall and a minute groove at the

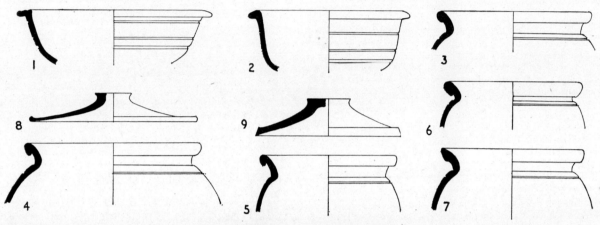

FIG. 101. Pottery from Queen's Road. ($\frac{1}{4}$)

Buff. Many fragments of an amphora f. 188; four mortar-rims of f. 497 of the style favoured by Martinus, and two are actually stamped by him. The buff rim of a hemispherical bowl, rouletted, resembling one found in the 1933 kilns.

Grey. One rim f. 38.

Colour-coated. Two bases f. 391 or 392, apparently *overfired*.

Either the Martinus firm had a branch here, or the Museum label is in error.

OTHER POSSIBLE SITES

QUEEN'S ROAD

The evidence in this case is slight. In 1933, during the extension of Queen's Road, a large quantity of pottery was recovered. The general impression it gave was that it came from one deposit, as it appeared homogeneous. The fragments were unusually even in size, but none were large. The ware varied in colour, consisting almost entirely of ff. 246 and 268, of a dirty almost sooty, grey ware. In this respect they closely resembled the grey ware from kilns 7–11. The impression created was that the bulk was refuse from a site where these vessels were being made. Form 268 made up about two-thirds of the bulk.

[1] *T.E.A.S.* x, 325.

angle. From just above this groove the lower part is polished. Thus we see here some departure from the typical form of 246.

3–7 are rims of jars, all with a small groove on the shoulder. Their position in the typological series of f. 268 has yet to be determined. Some are undercut, others not, but all have at least a slight flattening of the curve inside the lip.

8–9 are two lids which were in larger fragments than the rest. They are remarkable in that both were made with a hole through the top.

Analysis of the Pottery

Sigillata. Three chips ff. Drag. 18 (late), 33 (good), 31 (poorish, with part stamp apparently reading **ALL**...).

Colour-coated. Four small fragments, local ware, approximately Antonine.

Buff (few). One chip of a late f. 167 and five fragments of body of a similar jug. Several small and worn fragments of a red flagon, white-coated outside and bearing horizontal bands of red paint. There is a small two-ribbed handle which may have belonged to this. Twenty-one indeterminate fragments.

Grey. Nine fragments of native coarse ware of *c.* A.D. 10–50; five of f. 246; thirty-eight rims and over a hundred body fragments of f. 268, few fitting together. The ware is variable in colour, thickish to thin, sandy brown-black, hard but brittle. There was not much incurve of the side to the base.

[2] But this has perhaps very little significance.

Platters were merely represented, ff. 37 (four, and a variant), 38, 40. There were ten fragments of lids, some indeterminate rims, fragments of food bones, and two pieces of daub (C.M. 177.43).

CROUCH STREET

When the large shop, no. 105 Crouch Street (B on fig. 1), was erected in 1934 a great quantity of pottery was found, mostly towards the rear of the premises, which gives a strong impression that there lay close by yet another site where the potters of kilns 15–17 were working. The pottery is as follows:

Sigillata. Forms 18/31 or 31, stamped GL....; 31 or Sb (13); 33, base stamped REGALIS. F; 36, 38, 79; of decorated ware one useless fragment of f. 30; and an indeterminate plain base with illegible stamp.

Colour-coated (all local). Forms 391–2 (24, some barbotined and a few fluted) and a lid for f. 308; there were some further fragments which might not be local, and a late Rhenish base.

Mortaria. Forms 497(6) and 498, two with herring-bone stamps; 501*b*; and one uncertain.

Amphorae, &c. Form 187 (17); three fragments of flagons; honey-pot rim; fragment of bowl of unknown form with impressed concentric circles round bulge (West Stowe ware?); f. 156 (23) (necks and many fragments); f. 194 var.; f. 167c; ff. 362, 363; the top of an ointment pot and a frilled rim.

Grey and Black. Platters. Forms 17D, 37 (2), 38 (6), 40A; bowl f. 246; jars ff. 268, 278 (2), and fragments, one with graffito XIII.

Glass. Three large lumps of fused black glass; another piece of some sort of fused glass.

Tile. Fragment of red tegula and white imbrex.

Possibly all this fictile debris (save the early forms of the grey) may have been connected with kilns 3 and 4, which lay only about 100 yds. to the west.

Jars ff. 266 (4 or 5), 270 (native), 271 (Romanizing), 272 and other large fragments.

POSSIBLE TILE-KILNS

When the by-pass road was laid out the ground-level was reduced for it from a point about 200 yds. west of Sheepen Farmhouse, the excavation becoming a cutting across the north part of field 495, the east hedge of which stands on a sharp scarp. All the flat ground up to this scarp was littered with fragments of Roman tile at a depth of 2–3 ft., lying in a dark muddy mass, which also produced several Roman horseshoes. The cutting showed that the scarp itself was the almost vertical face of the London clay, standing as it was left by the Roman brickmakers. West of this, in field 495, the plough grates over tiled masonry at two or three different points, and there is broken tile scattered about. There is good reason to hope that here some of the Roman tile-kilns may exist in fairly good preservation. The site lies north-west of no. 26 on fig. 1.

CHRONOLOGICAL CHART

Of the thirty-three kilns which we have recorded,

only ten have provided us with pottery which can be described and discussed. The most important point, calling for as precise an answer as possible, is the date at which each of them was active.

Our only coin-evidence is the latest coin found near our 1933 kilns, a worn one of M. Aurelius. Without such evidence, and without any seal by later and datable strata, we are thrown back on internal evidence. This has, up to now, consisted of the pottery itself; but recently a new technique has been introduced, which attempts, by measuring the residual magnetism left in the clay at the last firing of the kiln, to tell us approximately the date of that firing.

In our case, by co-operation with Mr. J. Belshé and the Science Laboratory at Cambridge, samples of the structure of kilns 29 and 30 were examined. The samples from kiln 29 gave a clear result of *c.* A.D. 210,[1] those from kiln 30 were at variance among themselves, a fact which may be due to their being taken from different parts of the kiln, and, at the time they were taken, it was not understood that they were of different dates.

The internal evidence of the pottery is worked out as follows:

Kiln 25, having ff. 305, 316, and 395, must be of the fourth century, and is the latest of our series, its only rival being kilns 27 and 28 which have ff. 283, 305, 316, which are also of the fourth century, but perhaps a little earlier. There is not much in it.

Kilns 23 and 26 present no difficulty; the former is dated to A.D. 61, and the latter is somewhat later, but certainly of the first century.

The most critical and difficult point is the date of the kilns found in 1933 and 1959. Reporting on the 1933 kilns soon after their excavation, I gave them a date of *c.* A.D. 190. This was based on a worn coin of M. Aurelius and the great numbers of Samian platters f. Walters 79. These I was hardly able to find anywhere other than at the Pudding Pan Rock, the accepted date for which was, at that time, A.D. 190. The decorated Samian seemed to agree pretty well with that at Niederbieber (A.D. 190–260) and I finally proposed a date about A.D. 190–200. There was the further consideration that we were dealing with a period during which the practice of stamping mortaria with names had lapsed and that of stamping with herring-bone or chevron stamps was introduced; a period, moreover, preceding the time beyond which mortaria ceased to be stamped at all. The suggested date agreed with all of this.

There was another consideration; years ago in trying to order and classify the pottery from the Roman cemeteries of Colchester I was forced to the conclusion that the term 'Antonine' in dating pottery had

---

[1] But such dates are of course only approximate at present.

long been used wrongly. It originated, I suppose, in its application to the latest pottery found on the Antonine Wall. This in its turn was dated by coins and Samian ware. Any pottery like it was automatically labelled 'Antonine' and supposed to date to the reigns of Antoninus Pius, M. Aurelius, and Commodus.

Examination of the Colchester grave-groups using this yardstick showed that if there were x grave-groups of the first century and x grave-groups of the fourth century, there were 2x grave-groups of the second century and none of the third. It became quite clear that the prevailing conception was wrong, and that 'Antonine' pottery must have extended over most of the third century besides the second half of the second.

Being unable to find f. 79 on sites definitely dated before 180 or 190, and finding it very common here, I thought it necessary to suppose that it had a *floruit* sometime after that date. Indeed, I was now ready to extend the date well into the third century if necessary, but not to place it earlier. I might have derived further confidence from Miss Kenyon's very late dating[1] of the colour-coated beakers (ff. 391, 392), but I was unable to use that because I feel very strongly that it is several decades too late (see p. 102).

But now comes a problem; it turns out that something like one-third of the mortaria found in Roman Scotland came from these very kilns. They show the herring-bone stamps rather than the named stamps. I would expect them, therefore, to belong to the later activities of our firm. On my dating these would have to be attributed to the Severan campaign, but I understand that it is heresy to suggest that that campaign left any trace. On the other hand, I feel it is improbable that the *major part* of the activity of our 1933 and 1959 kilns took place before the end of the Antonine occupation of Scotland. One thing, however, seems ineluctable: Dr. K. A. Steer has found one of our products at the end of the Antonine I occupation. That being so, we have to suppose that our firm was active over a long period. There was little or nothing to suggest this in the finds of 1933; those of 1959, however, show things up very differently, and it is quite clear that the two kilns were rebuilt so often that quite a long period of activity is indicated.

One inconvenient result is seen in the pottery chart. I had supposed that the platter f. 37 had gone out of fashion about 140, or at least by 150, but it carries on nearly to the end of the century. My previous views on it are now proved wrong.

Having thus placed these kilns at about A.D. 175–210 we can look at the remainder. The quantity of remains from some of them is hardly adequate, and in other cases we do not know well enough how safely the finds are contemporary. A fourth-century piece from kilns 7–11 may be little more significant than the several such found in 1933 and 1959, which had nothing whatever to do with the kilns. With this in mind we assign kilns 7–11 to the late third or early fourth century rather than definitely to the fourth century Kiln 13a and b seems practically contemporary with the 1933–59 series.

Kiln 32 yielded a great quantity of pottery, from the shapes of which we can definitely say it was later than the 1933–59 series and earlier than the fourth century. It must fit into the period A.D. 210–300, and a reasonable conclusion would be c. 240–60. Then kiln 24 fits in between A.D. 210 and 240.

We are left with kiln 33, from which the remains are pitifully few. The mortarium shapes, however, agree with some from Canterbury which are dated to the late third or early fourth century, and this is the best we can suggest at present.

The series is not complete; the first half of the second century is not represented, nor is the last half of the fourth century.

Chronological Chart

The symbols in the chart below are as follows:

x = occurs		c.c. = colour coated	
n = small numbers		... = guide lines	
N = large numbers		--- = continuity of form	
E = early		NN = very large numbers	
L = late			

Kiln no.	23	26	15–31	13	1	24	32	7–11	27–28	25
Date	c60	c60	175–210	c190	c190	c220	c250	c300	c300	c350
f. 37			N------	5						
17	3+									
62	x---	-2								
69B	....								.3+	
94B	n									
100		x								
108		10								
140		70+								
143		6?								
154	N	-22+								
170		2								
171	n									
175		7--	----x?							
195		1								
221									...x?	
230		x								
242		2								
244	n									
246		1								
270		4+								
272		3								
149E	x--	--x								
149var.				9						
149L				x						
496				n						
156			NN---			4+				
157			x						.2+	
167C			n							
177			x							
188			n							
198			n							
204		1								
207			N							
247/8			n							
268A			150+	35+		n	21	NN	NN	2
268B			14				1			x
277			x	1	2?	1				

[1] K. M. Kenyon, *Excavations at the Jewry Wall Site, Leicester* (1948), 119–20.

Chronological Chart (*cont.*)

Kiln no.	23	26	15–31	13	1	24	32	7–11	27–28	25
Date	c60	c60	175–210	c190	c190	c220	c250	c300	c300	c350
f. 278			84	-3			-7	-x	-65	
279									1-	-1
280						.2	- n -	-34-	-3	
281								n	-18	
286							.x			
288			x				-n		-68+	
38			260+	-1		-3	-21	-x	-255	
39			3			-1	-1		-2?	
39C.C.			n							
40			40+	-2		-x	-6	-x	-141	
108L						.1			-1	
119L							.x			-x
124					.1					
283									1	
299			24+				-4?	-3+	-47	
300					.x					
305								1-	-n	
306			4	-1				-27-	-x	
307							-9	-x	-46-	-1
308			n				.x			
308(lid)			n							
316								1-	-1	
318			x							
360									1	
361B			4+							
362A			5+							
363			6							
364			2							
366			4							
367			2+							
375						x(?)				
376			n							
383										
389			N	-2					-8	
391			NN	-2		-N	-N	-x	-11	
392			N			-N	-N		-x	
395							x?	-n		
396			N							
397			n				-1			
404			x							
406			N			-n		-6	-163	
407							NN	-n		-n
409										-n
494			2							
497			NNN	-n		-n		-x	-12	
498					.1		160	-n	-1-	-n
499							+			-x
501			N	-x		-3	-x		-1	
504/5		n		3+	n-		-16			-x
508							.1			-n

There is little upon which to decide the terminal point of our chronology, that is, the date of kiln 25. It would appear that our whole series has to end before such time as small black grit became almost universal in mortaria; and before f. 305 became so remarkably popular as it certainly did in the second half of the fourth century. But is this necessary? The absence of some things such as the cooking-pots of f. 279 is due to the fact that they were not made locally; if our potters did not make mortaria with small black grit and not f. 305, then the absence of these forms is not conclusive. However, we do know that f. 305 was made in quantity not far away at Sible Hedingham, and there is one further body of evidence.

The graves found in site C4 and others found scattered about in the area are partly contemporary with the kilns, but a number of them are definitely later, and in these we find forms which our potters did not make, such as the mask-mouth flagon, fig. 82, 1,

and the cooking-pots f. 279, figs. 76, 8 and 78, 8, also the large f. 280, fig. 82, 2. The two vessels found inserted in the rubble of the building east of kiln 31 (fig. 92, A, B) are also later than our latest kiln, at least, in my opinion.

TABLE OF FORMS OF POTTERY VESSELS

This table was first published in *Roman Colchester*, pp. 280–92 in 1958. The material from the kiln-excavations of 1933 was available for its composition and was used. There is, neverthe-less, the additional information obtained from other sources, the most useful of which is the prolific pottery-site at Ardleigh which appears to be chiefly Trajanic. There are also one or two corrections to be made to the original table, and one or two second thoughts.

Nos. 1–275 were mostly published in *Camulodunum*: forms inserted later are shown on figs. 102, 103 below.

  1. Terra nigra platter. Scarce. Tiberian.
  2. Terra nigra platter. Highly polished. Common A.D. 25–50.
  3. Terra rubra and terra nigra platters. Common A.D. 25–50.
  4. Variants of last, terra nigra. Rare. A.D. 25–50.
  5. Terra rubra and terra nigra platters. Common. A.D. 25–50.
  6. Terra rubra platters. Scarce. Tiberian.
  7. Terra rubra and terra nigra platters. Common. A.D. 25–50.
  8. Terra rubra and terra nigra platters. Common. A.D. 25–50.
  9. Fine terra nigra platters. Rare. Claudian.
  10. Fine terra nigra platters. Rare. Claudian.
  11. Terra rubra platters. Rare. A.D. 25–50.
  12. Terra nigra platters. Very common. A.D. 25–50.
  13. Terra nigra platters. Not so common. Claudian.
  14. Poor terra nigra, or (mostly) grey. Common. Claudian and later.
  15. Fine terra nigra. Fairly frequent. Claudian.
  16. Terra nigra and fine grey. Common. Claudian–Flavian.
  17. Pompeian red, becoming very debased, finally Roman grey. Claudian–Flavian.
But this type occurs in various wares and forms throughout the Roman period.

21–33 are 'sub-belgic', that is native imitations of Gallo-Belgic platters, in soapy brown-black ware. Claudius–Nero.
  37. Fine black or grey, highly polished and latticed. Rim triangular in section. Very common from about A.D. 70. We had said 'to about 150', but it now appears that, even if we have to put the activity of our kilns back from 190 to as far as 150, we must give this type longer, and make it last at least up to 170.
  38. Black or grey, polished, with half-round rim. Not latticed. Omission of bevel at foot is fourth century, *c.* A.D. 120–400.
  39. Black cooking-pot ware, or fine grey. The former with scored pattern. Really continues f. 17. Fine grey runs through-out; the black not earlier than Hadrian–Antonine. *c.* A.D. 120–300.
  40. Fine grey or black, with or without groove and scoring. Very common; since it does not occur at Ardleigh we had better perhaps assume that its period begins after A.D. 120, perhaps after 130.

41. Porringer, native and Roman grey. Claudius–Nero.

42. Porringer, light, rough grey. Rare. Claudian.

43A. Flanged bowl. Rare. Neronian.

43B. The same, very large. Brown to grey. Rare. Claudian.

44A. Unusual bowl. Native and various. Rare. Claudian.

44B. Similar to 43 and 44, very large. Rare. Claudian. (But see 243 and 247–8.)

45A. Similar bowl on three feet. Native. Rare. Claudian.

45B. Tripod-bowl in fine pale grey. Rare. Claudius–Nero.

46. Roman bowl, resembling mortarium. Scarce. Claudius–Nero.

47A and B. Carinated bowls, native. Rare. Claudian.

48. Bowl, beaded rim, ware various. Rare. Claudian.

49. Deep bowl, high kick and footring. Terra nigra, grey copies. Rare. Claudian (?).

50. Later copy of the same. Terra nigra abroad, buff here. Claudius–Nero.

51. Bobbin-shaped bowl with high kick. Gallo-Belgic, various wares. Tibero-Claudian.

52A. Carinated bowl with everted rim. Grey. Solo. Claudian.

52B. Porringer with footring. Fine pale grey. Rare. Claudian (?).

52C. Hemispherical with moulded rim. Grey. Rare. Claudian.

53. Copy of Arretine cup. Various Gallo-Belgic wares. Rare. Tiberio-Claudian.

54. Similar, bell-shaped. Terra rubra. Rare. Tiberio-Claudian.

55. Imitation of Arretine cup. Red. Solo. Claudian.

56. Copy of Arretine cup. Terra rubra and terra nigra. Both common. Tiberio-Claudian.

57. Copies of same, native or Roman. Rare. Claudian.

58. Copies of Drag. 24/25. Terra rubra and terra nigra. Common. Claudian.

59. Native and Roman copies of 56–58 or their prototypes. Claudius–Nero.

60. Carinated cup (or lid?). Fine native. Rare. Claudian.

61A. Hemispherical cup, deep. Various wares. Rare. Augustus–Tiberius.

61B. Similar. Red wares. Rare. Tiberio-Claudian.

62. Similar. Standard type. Soft buff, colour-coated. Common. Claudius–Nero.

62B. Copies of last. Reddish wares. Rare. Claudius–Nero.

63. Similar bowls on three feet. Buff, colour-coated. Rare. Claudius–Nero.

64. Similar bowls in black egg-shell ware. Fairly common. Claudius–Nero.

65. Bowl in white egg-shell ware. Solo. Claudian.

66. Fragment, polished grey. Solo. Nero.

67. Native cup. Soapy black. Solo. Nero (?).

68. Copy of Drag. 29. Fine grey. Rare. Claudian-Flavian.

69A. (Hofheim 28B.) Terra rubra. Solo. Claudian (?).

69B. Copy of Drag. 30. Fine red-brown. Rare. Claudian-Flavian.

70. Handled bowl. Dark grey, white coated. Solo. Claudius–Nero?

71. (Not Colchester.) Copy of Arretine crater. Terra rubra. Augustus–Tiberius.

72. Pedestalled copies of Drag. 29. Terra rubra (not yet found at Colchester). Tiberio-Claudian.

73. Bell-shaped beakers. Terra rubra. Rare. Claudius.

74. Similar carinated. Terra rubra. Scarce. Tiberio-Claudian.

75. Various similar, with cupped mouth. Terra rubra. Rare. Claudian (?).

76. Ditto. Terra rubra. The commonest rim. Tiberio-Claudian.

77. Similar, almost cylindrical. Terra rubra. Rare. Claudian (??).

78. Similar, conical and carinated. Terra rubra. Occurs (?). Claudian (?).

79A. Similar. Terra rubra. Scarce. Tiberio-Claudian.

79B. Native copy, polished black. Solo. Nero.

81. Barrel-like beaker, cordoned. Terra rubra. Occurs (?). Claudian (??).

82. Carinated girth-beaker. Terra rubra. Rare. Tiberio-Claudian.

83. Copy of same. Native brown. Solo. Claudian.

84. Similar, not carinated. Terra rubra. Common. Tiberio-Claudian.

85. Copies of same, native and Roman copies. Rare. Claudian.

86. Funnel-shaped girth-beaker. Terra rubra. Occurs (?). Claudian (??).

87. Copies of same. Native and Roman. May occur. Claudian (?).

88. Roman girth-beaker? Thin fine grey. Solo. Nero.

91A and B. Globular beaker on pedestal-foot. Terra rubra. Fairly common. Tiberio-Claudian.

91C. Native copy, red-brown ware. Rare. Claudian (?).

91D. As 91A but rim everted. Terra rubra. Rare. Claudian (?).

92. Native copy of 91A, black-polished. Fairly common. Claudius–Nero.

93. Small beaker, very thin, horn-coloured. Rare. Tiberio-Claudian.

94. Ovoid to globular, colour-coated and rough-cast. A. Full-bodied, fine ware. Continental. Common. Claudius–Nero. B. Taller, poor ware and coating. Local. Common. Claudius–Nero.

95. Bossed beakers, mica gilt. Rare. Claudius–Nero.

96. Beaker with pointed studs. Roman grey. Rare. Claudius–Nero.

97. Beaker with blunt studs. Thin hard black. Rare. Claudian.

98–99. Rusticated beakers. Grey ware. Both rare. Claudius–Nero.

100. As 94A, but decorated in barbotine (Hofheim 118). Here only in grey. Rare. Claudius–Nero.

101. Folded beakers. Thin hard black (as 97). Rare. Claudius–Nero.

102. Ovoid beaker, upright rim grooved. Mica gilt. Fairly common. Tiberio-Claudian.

103. Unusual cordoned beaker. Grey, black-polished. Solo. Claudian.

104. Ovoid beakers with short rim. Black, almost egg-shell ware. Sometimes stamped. Rare. Nero-Domitian.

105. Small globular beakers on pedestal, buff, red-coated; another, not coated. Rare. Uncertain.

106–7. Vacant.

108. Ovoid beakers, taking the place of the rusticated type, the surface roughened instead by lines prodded with a comb. Very common. Claudius–Hadrian.

108B. Similar vessels, but much larger, and usually with two bands of prodding. Despite strong resemblance, this series seems distinctly later. All the evidence agrees in dating it from about 160 to 250.

109–12. Absent from Colonia.

113. Butt-beaker in white pipeclay, and copies. Scarce. Not after Nero.

114. White beakers with gilt rim. Scarce, in graves of Claudius–Nero.

115–18. Absent from Colonia.

119. Butt-beakers with distinct neck. These run through, almost without change (except in decoration) from the earliest

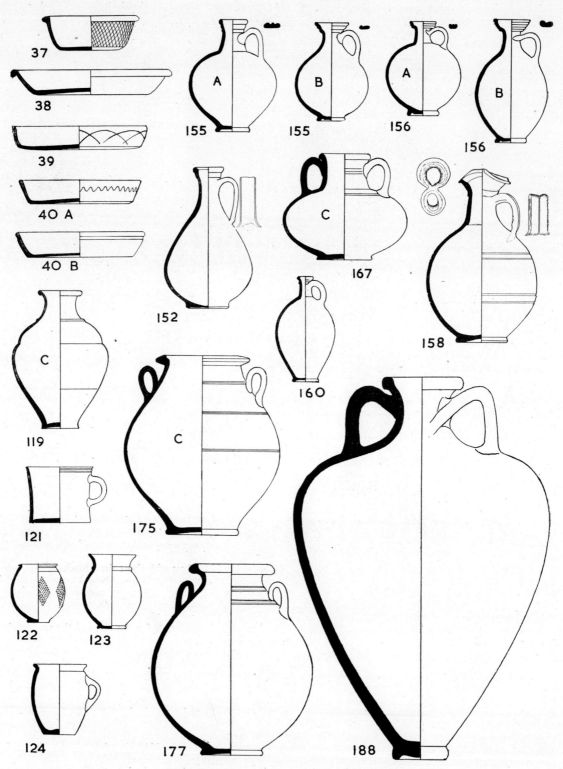

FIG. 102. The type-forms of pottery vessels. ($\frac{1}{6}$)

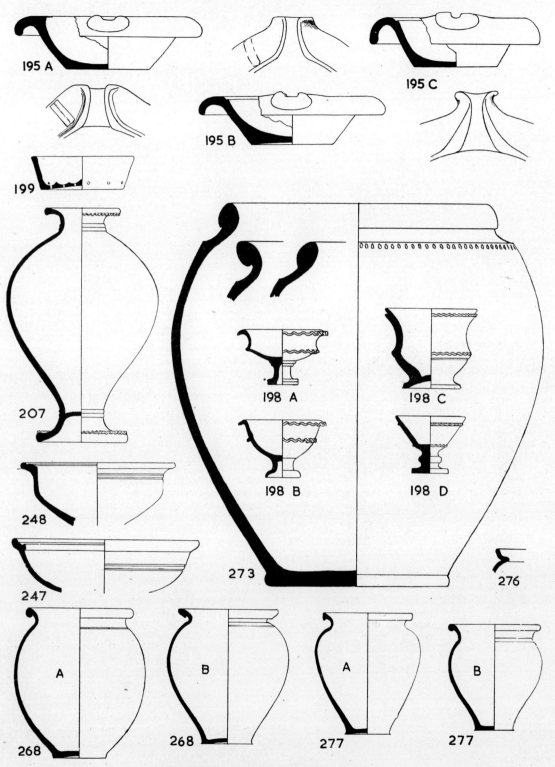

195 A

195 C

195 B

199

207

248

247

198 A

198 B

198 C

198 D

273

276

A
268

B
268

A
277

B
277

Fig. 103. The type-forms of pottery vessels. ($\frac{1}{6}$)

times to the fourth century, when they are exceptionally numerous in the 'Mithraeum' (with coin of Constans). Polished grey and black.

120. Sharply carinated beakers. The finest black (Gallo-Belgic) ones are absent. Inferior copies (some quite good) occur in graves up to Hadrian (i.e. *c.* 120). Claudius–Hadrian.

121. Handled mug with curved and outsplayed wall. Mid-first century (May, *Colchester*, grave 9).

122. Beaker, fine polished ware, decorated with panels of raised dots. The evidence is poor, but these seem to run from *c.* 150 to 350.

123. Taller beaker of 'poppy-head' shape, similar ware and decoration. Seems to occur in graves from about 100 to 200, but is still with us in the 'Mithraeum'. But the two fragments of ff. 122 and 123 found there may be rubbish-survivals.

124. Tall ovoid beaker, with or without handle. Rim very small. Not rare. Of over a dozen in the Museum few are datable. One at Brecon Gaer was dated early second century; our series seems to run evenly and continuously from *c.* 100 onwards. The evidence is from graves, and ends with two in a grave of about 350[1] and one with an inhumation.

125–30. Vacant.

139, 140. These possibly occur in the Colonia. Buff. Mid-first century.

141. Occurs in the west cemetery. Brown-buff. Scarce. Mid-to late first century?

142. Vacant.

143 and 144. Rare in Colonia. Buff. Mid-first century.

145. Vacant.

146. Buff flagon. A neck from pit I (*Roman Colchester*, fig. 53, 2) extends the life of this form to about 100.

147. Black flagon. Absent from Colonia. Mid-first century.

148. Flat- or conical-mouthed flagon. One in a grave of Flavian date. Not common; does not occur in the late second-century kilns.

149. Similar with short neck. Not uncommon. Claudius–Nero; not common in the late second century, but is certainly a standard type in kilns of that date, in a form slightly different from those of the first century.

150. Similar with tall, straight neck. This form certainly occurs in graves of Trajanic date. Period Claudius–Trajan. There is a doubtful reappearance of the type in the mid-fourth century.

152. Tall, pear-shaped flagon with long neck. Buff. This is an early type on the Continent. Here it appears in graves of about A.D. 80 and 120.

153. Ring-mouthed flagon. Early form. Tiberian.

154. Ring-mouthed flagon, Claudian form. The rings are many and are never boldly stepped outwards; the ringed portion, too, is usually but little outbent. There is a distinct footring. The typical form is common, but during the Flavian period modifications began to creep in. Nevertheless, f. 154 is still frequent *c.* 100, and the form continues popular in graves of Trajan–Hadrian date.

155. This is an omnibus number for the variants which fall between 154 and 156. It includes vessels like 154, but with markedly trumpet-shaped mouths, or without offset between neck and shoulder. It also includes vessels in which the rings are few and thick, as shown in the *Camulodunum* plates. The chief incidence of this type is from about 70 to 130, judging by the graves. One example of apparently about 175 is probably a stray.

156. This is another ring-mouthed flagon, like the last, but the mouth is markedly cupped inside. The footring is marked off by a deep groove from the centre of the base. The form is one of the most typical and local to Colchester. It is very common in the Trajan–Hadrian period, and hardly less so in the Antonine. It was still being made in quantities in our kilns about 190, and continues to be found in graves, and elsewhere, at least up to 350 ('Mithraeum', *Roman Colchester*, fig. 60, 3, 4, 5). In the latter part of its life a tall form appears alongside the familiar globular form, and the footring tends to disappear.

157–9. Three forms of spouted flagons. Incidence in colonia not yet known.

160. Tall flagon with narrow cylindrical neck. White ware. These are scarce. One in a grave seems to date to about 140.

161–6 do not occur in the colonia, though the commoner varieties occur in graves up to about A.D. 60.

167A. Augustan (as at Haltern); B, Claudian (as at Camulodunum); C, is the late form, in which the outline is blurred and softened. The way in which this is done can be seen in *Roman Colchester*, figs. 53, 3, and 61, 26, 27. The former is *c.* 100, the latter *c.* 350. The type is very common, but not in graves. A complete example is shown ibid., fig. 58, 7.

168–74. Absent from colonia.

175. The typical early form has been described in *Camulodunum*. With modifications it lasted on to about 140 (pit I, *Roman Colchester*, fig. 53, 4, 5, and graves).

176 and 177. It is now quite clear that 177 was made in our kilns in the second half of the second century. It is not quite certain that odd examples of f. 175 are not strays from the Claudian occupation. A detailed study of the considerable variety of 'honey-pots' in the Museum is desirable.

178–81. Vacant.

182–4. Spindle-shaped amphorae, common in the Colonia in the pre-Boudiccan level.

185. Sausage-shaped amphora; probably occurs as last, but not easily recognizable.

186. Radish-shaped amphora. A, with slender neck; B, similar, neck wider; C, neck very wide, rim now very short. All occur in Claudius–Nero level, but C is latest to appear and possibly lasts into Flavian times. Common.

187. Globular amphora, the commonest of the Roman period. Fragments are everywhere in the early and middle Empire. One has the impression that in the fourth century the vessels passed out of use, but there is no direct evidence. They are often used to contain burials and these are not later than about 200 (in Colchester).

188. Amphora with high shoulder and small footstand. This occurs not infrequently, but never in graves. It is post-Boudiccan. We can now say that this was in use in the last decades of the second century. It does not appear at the later kilns, but this is not conclusive.

189. Small, carrot-shaped amphora, horizontally fluted. Typically Claudius–Nero. Occurs in the Colonia, doubtfully as late as Vespasian, certainly not later.

190. Vacant.

191. Wall-sided mortarium. Early (Augustan) type. Very common on the Camulodunum site under Claudius and Nero. Less so in the Colonia. Not post-Boudiccan.

192. Heavily flanged mortarium. Neronian. Hard to identify among fragments from the Colonia. Same date as last.

193. Small mortaria with stubby rims. Pre-Boudiccan.

194. Mortarium with 'bunched-up' rim. Pre-Boudiccan.

195. Mortarium with broad, flat flange (favourite form of Q. VAL. VERANIVS). Frequent in Colonia, and apparently Vespasianic.

195B. Flange short, thick, curved, with grit over it. Frequent. Flavian.

---

[1] Grave 394, presumably an incineration, containing 8 vessels; unpublished.

195c. Flange broad, very much curved, arched above rim. Frequent. Flavian-Trajanic.

196 and 197. Unguentaria of thin fine red ware. Rare. Date uncertain, but perhaps all first century.

198. Incense cups. These have not been closely examined and there are many different forms.

199. Cheese press. The base has concentric furrows and ridges inside, with perforations in furrows and in wall. Not uncommon. Period uncertain. One is Neronian, others first century. We can now add that they occur throughout the second century at Ardleigh and Colchester.

200. Vacant.

201–5. Pedestalled vases.

206. Various Roman pedestal-bases. Little can be said of these for many of them probably belong to incense cups.

207. Large, buff, pedestalled vases. These were very common in the kilns of about 190. The only example which can be drawn complete is rather lighter in build than these, and is painted. We now find that red paint was used to some extent in our late second-century kilns, on this form as well as others.

208. Vacant.

209. Squat, carinated bowl with generous mouldings. Native, and rare, but lasted on through the Flavian period to c. 100.

210–17. Native bowls.

218A. The native form, or the Roman copy of it, remained in use up to about 100. It is frequent in the Colonia.

218B. The copies soon began to be latticed on the neck. The hard grey ware shows these to be developed Roman copies, and they appear in graves which may be dated up to 140. This latticing first appears (locally) about 70. The form is very common in the Ardleigh kilns, but is quite out of use in the late second century.

219 and 220. Absent from Colonia.

221 and 222. Wide bowls with small cordon (or not) at base of neck. No dating can be given for this very simple and characterless type, which occurs everywhere at all times.

223–6. The first three are native; the last is purely Roman, but cannot be dated at present.

227. Bowl with incurved neck. The Roman series are true copies of the native original and are frequent in graves of the Flavian-Trajan period. It occurred in small numbers at Ardleigh.

228. Somewhat similar bowl, also derived from a native prototype. Possibly same dating.

229, 230. Absent from Colonia.

231. Absent from Colonia.

232. Large, tall vase with narrow mouth. Bulge at base of neck, between cordons, scored oblique strokes or latticed. Runs continuously from Claudius up to c. 100, and thereafter appears in graves up to about 180.

233–5. Absent from Colonia.

236. Small flask with oblate body and strong cordon or bulge at neck. Rare type; occurs in a grave about 100.

237–40. Vacant.

241. Cancelled, now vacant.

242 (includes former 241). Biconical bowls with everted, flat rim. Numbers of these appear in pit I (*Roman Colchester*, fig. 54, 10–14) in Roman ware, thus continuing the popularity of this common Claudian type. But how long it remained in use after 100 we do not know.

243–5. Early versions of the following form.

246. Grey bowl with flat, reeded rim. Common in the earlier levels, latest appearance in pit I (ibid., fig. 54, 9). Very rare in graves, and the evidence as to its use after about 100 is inadequate. One would not be surprised if it was current until about 120.

247 and 248. Vacant.

249–63 do not occur in the Colonia.

264. Native cooking-pot. One of these occurs in a grave (141) which is probably Flavian.

265 and 266. The most common cooking-pot of the mid-first century, with offset neck and beaded lip, often undercut. Begins in native ware and romanizes to hard grey. Peculiarity is that the base is polished. The greater the polished area the later the date. Very common in graves from Claudius to Trajan. Not so common in pit I (*Roman Colchester*, fig. 56, 47–53 and 58–60) as might be expected. Late and tall examples (B) seem to be early second century, but so far positive evidence is lacking for the demise of the type.

267A is absent from the Colonia; B, with flat rim, occasionally occurs in graves of the first century, up to about 90. The type is never common in Colchester.

268. Ovoid cooking-pot, smoothed, but never polished anywhere. Underside of foot always bears mark of the wire which cut it from the wheel. Rim nearly always undercut; neck short, with groove on shoulder.

268A. Rim fat, and roundly curved outwards. Material often rather coarse and gritty. Body usually squat. One of the most common Roman vessels. Most numerous in graves which we judge to be Hadrianic, but probably begins about 100. This form was made in fair quantity at Ardleigh, but was outnumbered by f. 266. An example in grave 126, which is not later than Flavian, is abnormal and may be intrusive; at any rate we hesitate to begin the type so early. It continues to appear in graves up to 250, and is still present in the 'Mithraeum' with a coin of Constans.

268B. Rim thinner, flat on the inside, the ware usually thinner and finer, the body often markedly incurved to the foot. Doubtfully represented in graves round about 100; well attested thus and in general use from about 120 to 200; not proved, but no doubt present from 200 to 250, when it again appears in a grave, and in the 'Mithraeum' about 350, and with inhumation burials.

These are beyond question the commonest vessels in Roman Colchester.

269. Jars or cooking-pots with hooked rim-section. This type is not yet substantiated.

270–1. Large storage-jars of native ware. Absent except in the Claudius–Nero levels.

272. Large storage-jars of f. 266 but with polished rim and band of finger-tipping on shoulder. They begin full and round (*Camulodunum*, pl. LXXXIV) and gradually become taller. The type is one of the most common and was much favoured for burials up to about 140. Thereafter its continuity is in doubt. There is a possible burial about 220, and in the 'Mithraeum' (c. 350) the type is only represented by two miniature vessels (*Roman Colchester*, fig. 69, 121–2), which can hardly be accounted of the same class.

273. Very large storage-jars about 2 ft. high and nearly as much in diameter. Roman development of the native 270–2. Rim fat, oval section, may be upright or sloped inwards or outwards. Begins round about 60 and runs on. A complete example in the Museum contains a burial of about 150 or soon after. Its later history is quite unknown.

274. Vacant.

275. Large storage-vessels with broad, flat, inturned rim. The few examples in the Colonia are all probably Claudius–Nero.

276. Jar with tallish rim deeply hollowed inside. These are usually of a very coarse ware and seem to be of late date, but good evidence is lacking.

277. Jar or cooking-pot similar to 266 but rather tall, with rim cut off vertically. This type is now substantiated in our late second-century kilns, though not in large numbers.

278. The common grey (or black) latticed jar, ubiquitous on Roman sites. Always popular, its maximum frequency here is from c. 100 to 140, and is scarcely diminished up to 200. It still

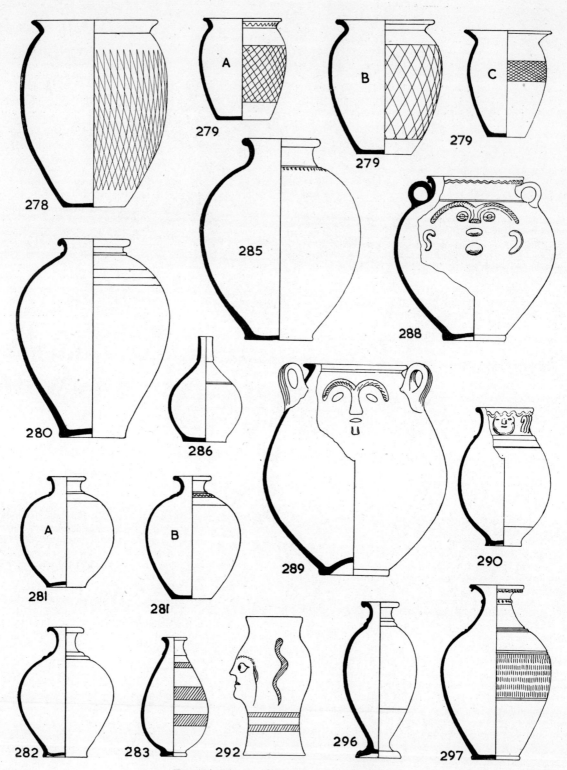

FIG. 104. The type-forms of pottery vessels. ($\frac{1}{6}$)

FIG. 105. The type-forms of pottery vessels. ($\frac{1}{6}$)

appears in graves throughout the third century and remains with us in the 'Mithraeum' *c*. 350. How soon it started is uncertain—probably in Flavian times, for it does not appear before about 70. The form changes scarcely at all. Taller examples may be third century.

279. The common black cooking-pot with latticed side.

279A. Fairly broad, with tall lattice and short almost upright rim, often with a wavy line scored round the outside. Hadrianic on Hadrian's Wall, the type is so scarce in Colchester that we have no dating evidence for it.

279B. Still as broad, but the rim now almost as wide as the greatest diameter. The latticing tends to become wider-spaced and not so upright. Sometimes it is reduced in height. The form is universal, but in Colchester local products held the market, and it is not common in graves. One can be dated to about 200. Another was found in the 'Mithraeum' with coin of Constans, and another with an inhumation burial. The dating is therefore about 200 to 350.

279C. The latest form is smallish, and tall, with the rim now very wide and often exceeding the width of the body. The lattice occupies a narrow band, and its angle is 45° or less. The evidence is 'Mithraeum', a grave of about same date, and an inhumation. Date, fourth century, *c*. 325 to 400.

280. Large narrow-necked storage-jars. These resemble the handled jars of the Yorkshire Signal Stations, but have a long life. They possibly begin under Hadrian, appear in graves of *c*. 150, are most numerous in graves of 200–50, but run on to 400. Early examples are full and round, later ones are taller and ovoid. Very common.

281. Flasks with narrow necks. There are many of these, and it is not easy to decide how many types to make (cf. f. 282). The present form is nearly globular at first, nearly always with a small cordon at neck. Two in grave 8 are very doubtfully Neronian; then they appear now and then in graves from about 100 right through, being especially numerous in the 'Mithraeum' (*c*. 350) and occurring in inhumations.

282. Flask with narrow neck, shoulder sloping up to neck. Commonly white coated, with painted bands. In graves from *c*. 250 to 350.

283. Tall flask, buff, with painted bands. First appears, apparently, about 200, but more usual about 300–30, and occurs with inhumations. Chiefly fourth century.

284. Vacant.

285. Large, tall, narrow-necked jars. Usually with finger-tipping round neck. Frequent; but the evidence for date is small. Latter half of first century (*Roman Colchester*, pit I, fig. 53, 8).

286. Ovoid flask with tall cylindrical neck. Copied from a glass form, rare. Three occurrences in graves seem to date to 160, 260, and 380 (approximately). Further evidence is needed, but the form seems late.

287. Large grey face-urn, no frill or handles. Undated. Rare. We can now quote small fragments from Ardleigh dated *c*. 100–120.

288. Frilled face-urn with (usually) three handles. Buff ware. Many whole vessels in Museum, fragments are not rare. Datable graves seem Hadrianic, but one is about 200. Date *c*. 120–200.

289. Large buff face-urn. One only, not dated.

290. Face urns of polished red ware. These are small and quite distinctive. There is no evidence for dating save the activity of the potteries which made them. Possibly fourth century.

291. Vacant.

292. Face-urn of white ware. Features painted. Rare, no dating.

293–5. Vacant.

296. Tall ovoid flask on pedestal-foot, very finely made of polished red ware. Late fourth century. A standard type.

297. Vase of f. 119, but with frilled rim and prodded cordon on neck. Rare. Two in 'Mithraeum' *c*. 350; one in grave 320 may be of about 290.

298. Carinated bowl with broadly outcurved top. The base often pierced as a strainer. Date uncertain, but occurs in 'Mithraeum' *c*. 350.

299. Bowl of S-shaped outline. Usually of fine, pearly grey ware and slightly micaceous. Groove on shoulder. The form is Newstead 46. In Colchester it was certainly common by 150, and in use through the third century, and is still frequent in the 'Mithraeum', *c*. 350. We now find this was made at Ardleigh in the early second century.

300. Buff bowl, with wall-side, like late mortaria, small. Rare. Was made in a Colchester kiln of *c*. 200.

301. Bowl resembling 298, but rim more upright. Rare. Seems Flavian in grave 45 and Antonine in grave 90.

302. Bowl shaped like a small cauldron, bulged below and straight above, with or without handles containing rings which may be loose or fixed. Not common, but several examples. Only date so far grave 408, *c*. 275.

303. Platter of polished black cooking-pot ware with flat rim. A well-known type which begins under Hadrian or Pius and is typically Antonine or later. One fragment in the 'Mithraeum' may be an intrusion.

304. Similar bowl, deeper, same ware. On the flat rim is a groove. Side scored as on f. 39 and f. 305A. Common, but dating uncertain. Not in graves. Probably Antonine onwards, certainly in 'Mithraeum' (15 exx.) about 350.

305. Bowls with ledged rim. Straight side, no bevel.

305A. Black polished cooking-pot ware. Exterior scored as ff. 39 and 304. A very common late Roman type, probably in use from about 250 to 400. Earlier evidence still lacking.[1]

305B. Polished grey ware. A wavy line on the inside wall does not occur in Colchester. One of the commonest of late Roman vessels. Occurs in grave with coin of Postumus, and in another which may be fourth-century. Rarely used in graves.

306. Bell-shaped bowls of coarse grey ware. Dating uncertain; one in a grave seems late Antonine. Fragments occur in the 'Mithraeum'. The dating seems approximately 175–350 or later.

307. Wide bowls, with broad base, grey ware, with barrel-markings. The rim often hollowed for lid. These begin about 200, occur in graves in the first half of the third century, and are still with us in the 'Mithraeum', *c*. 350. Fairly common.

308. Colour-coated bowl, with lid. Sometimes angularly built (Corbridge, *Arch. Ael.* 3rd ser., viii, pl. XII (63)): here they are always rounded. The ware may be Castor or local. The ugly base of *Antiq. Journ.* XX, 506, occurs here in Castor ware in flagons and in polished red ware, e.g. *Roman Colchester*, figs. 61, 28 and 62, 45. Large examples are not uncommon, but are fragile and fragmentary. An unusually small one is in a grave of *c*. 190; none in 'Mithraeum'. Date *c*. 180–200, perhaps to 300.

309. Bowl with incurved lip like f. 251. Rare. Late Antonine.

310. Wide bowls with beaded rim, copies of T.S. f. Lud. Sb. These occur from time to time in various wares. A fine grey one is in a Hadrianic grave. Fine polished grey one in 'Mithraeum' and one in Castor ware in grave 394, of about same date (*c*. 350).

311. Small bowl beaded and flanged (copy of T.S. f. Ritt. 12), the bead evanescent. Flange often rouletted. Fine hard polished grey. Type seems early. Neronian. Not common. There was at least one example at Ardleigh, Trajanic.

312. Bowl with wide vertical collar. Not dated. Rare.

313. Bowl with curved rim. A good example in pit I, *c*. 100 (*Roman Colchester*, fig. 55, 33). Not dated at present.

---

[1] We regard *Gellygaer*, pl. XII, 11, as a stray.

314. Carinated bowl with necked and beaded rim. Nearly always in red-coated ware, generally ascribed to the New Forest. Often decorated in white paint. Occurs in inhumation graves only. Fourth century, and perhaps second half only.

315. Shallow, rounded bowl with ledged rim, and footring. There are possibly subdivisions, for one is in a grave of Trajanic-Hadrianic date and another was in the 'Mithraeum' (c. 350). Little known as yet.

316. Bowl copying T.S. f. 38. The form varies somewhat. The New Forest examples are very true to the original. A series which occurs fairly regularly in very late deposits in Colchester is wider and shallower, with a heavy, squarish footring. The ware is a red-buff, partly polished. All seem to be second half of fourth century.

317. Bowl with flatly curved rim. Copied from Sigillata forms, especially by New Forest potteries. Usually red ware, red-coated, sometimes decorated with white paint. Fourth century.

318. Hemispherical bowl with curved flange and bead-rim. Little known as yet. There are two examples in a Neronian grave.

319. Vacant.

320. Conical beaker on footring, copy of T.S. f. 30. These are made in red or black polished ware, variously decorated with impressed patterns. Some were made in kilns at West Stowe, near Bury St. Edmunds. See P. Corder, in *Antiq. Journ.* xxi, 296. Date uncertain, perhaps late first and second century.

321. Hemispherical bowl with simple lip. One in pit I (*Roman Colchester*, fig. 55, 31), c. 100. Others, quite small, are in New Forest ware (red-coated) and are fourth century.

322. Wide bowl with strainer-spout in form of a boar's head. Fine thin buff, mica-coated. Occurs in pit I (ibid., fig. 54, 46), c. 100. Not common.

323. Similar bowls, carinated, the spout usually quite simple, but sometimes showing eyes and tusks of the boar. Polished grey ware. Fairly frequent. Occurs in Belgic level at Ardleigh.

324. Vacant.

325. Vacant.

326. Wide, carinated bowls with two handles. Buff ware. Fairly frequent. No dating as yet.

327. Vacant.

328. Grey jars resembling f. 278, except that the rim is small beading. Dating perhaps much the same. One in a grave of Trajanic date.

329. Wide bowls, copies of T.S. f. 29. Fine polished brown, grey, or black ware. Decorated with groups of incised lines, often in festoons. Made at West Stowe (see f. 320). Not rare. Also made at Ardleigh, Trajanic.

330. Hemispherical bowls, copies of T.S. f. 37, in same ware and decoration as last (see f. 320). Not rare. Ardleigh, Trajanic.

331. Carinated bowls with tall, cupped rim and two handles. Usually white ware, poorly finished, sometimes with scored groups of lines on wall. Not rare. Dating uncertain save one in pit I (*Roman Colchester*, fig. 55, 34), c. 100.

332. Wide bowl with vertical, reeded rim. White ware. Rare. No date.

333. Copies of T.S. f. 27. These are in grey or buff ware, sometimes mica-coated. They vary much and are infrequent. One in pit I (ibid., fig. 54, 19) is c. 100.

334. Tall cylindrical beaker on pedestal foot. Rare. Red, red-coated New Forest ware, decorated with white paint. Presumed late fourth century.

335. Vacant.

336. Cup or bowl with curved, drooping rim. Rare. No date.

337. Small vessel with thick, beaded rim. Coarse whitish ware. These were sometimes used as crucibles. Newstead, type 20.

338. Small bowl, polished grey ware with rounded impressions and bosses. Late fourth century.

339. Small flask with large bulge round shoulder. Fine polished light red, decorated with bosses. With inhumation burial. Fourth century.

340. Similar vessel, without bulge. Fine polished grey ware, decorated with bosses and hollows. Rare. Presumably fourth century.

342. Oblate, rounded beaker, with tall curved rim and simple lip. Rare. No date.

343. The same, later form, taller, and the neck now little curved. Typical are the small, fine, black-glazed Rhenish beakers, which first appear about 210(?). Others are still with us in the fourth century, e.g. *Roman Colchester*, figs. 71, 141 and 41, 10 (St. Martin's House), the former red, the latter black. The very tall neck appears alongside the short.

344. Hemispherical bowl, copy of T.S. f. 37, in red ware, with some slight incurve at top. Flavian. Rare in Colchester, more common on military sites. Newstead, type 44.

345-54. Vacant.

355. Large two-handled jug, white ware. It seems certain that these were made in our late second-century kilns.

356. Tall flagon with incurved lip, offset shoulder and cordons on neck. Castor ware. Late fourth century.

357. Two-handled jug. Castor ware. Late fourth century.

358. Flagon in buff ware. Not dated.

359. Two-handled jug with cupped mouth. Little known. No date.

360. Flagons with ledged rim. In various wares, with various modifications of form. In Castor ware with coins of Tetricus. Common at Niederbieber (190–260). Wheeler dates them c. 220–350. Common in Colchester, perhaps from c. 200 on.

361. Flagons with beaked spout. Usually red ware, mica-coated. Made here c. 190. Terminal dates unknown. Bronze original also made here, one containing a hoard of about A.D. 230. Not common.

362. Flagon imitating a well-known bronze form. Usually red ware, mica gilt. Made here about 190. Not uncommon.

363. Flagon, no dating, probably c. 190–210.

364. Flagon with very narrow neck, tall and curved, with simple lip. Mostly in fine polished red ware. Not dated, but probably third to fourth century.

365. Flagon with conical, reeded mouth. Usually in the same polished red ware. Occurs in graves from about 240, and in 'Mithraeum', c. 350.

366. Flagon with pinched spout, the sides lapped over. Handle below mouth. These were made in our kilns at the end of the second-century.

367. This form, which we did not illustrate in *Roman Colchester*, will be found on our fig. 69, 10, 11. We still lack the complete outline. The date is late second century.

368. Flagon with elaborately moulded mouth, neck very narrow. Fine polished red ware (see ff. 364–5). Probably fourth century.

369. Flagon with human mask on mouth. These are in many different wares, some white, with features coloured brown-red. Occur frequently with inhumations, presumably c. 350–400. Common.

370. In *Roman Colchester* we could only show a mouth and handles; we can now show the most part of the vessel, fig. 70, 13. The date is late second century.

371. Tall, colour-coated flagon. The ware seems Castor. Decorated with white paint. Rare. Should be fourth century, but this uncertain.

372. Tall flagon copying a bronze form, with or without

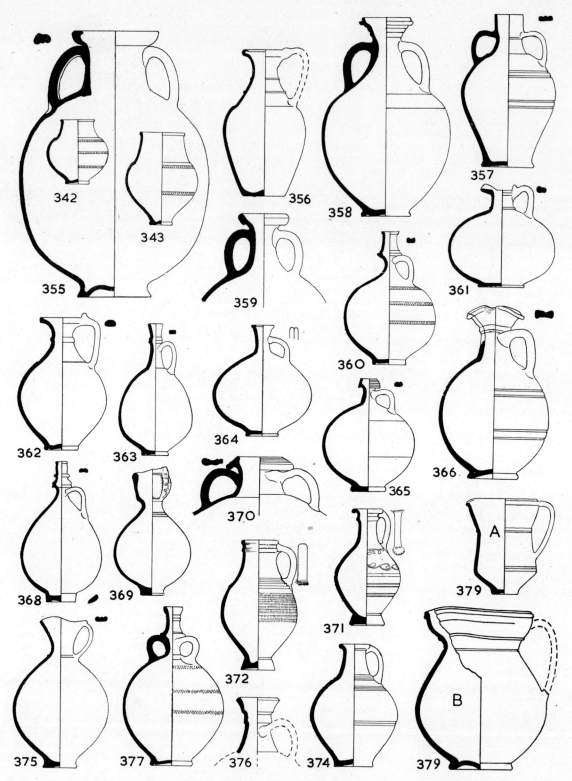

FIG. 106. The type-forms of pottery vessels. (⅙)

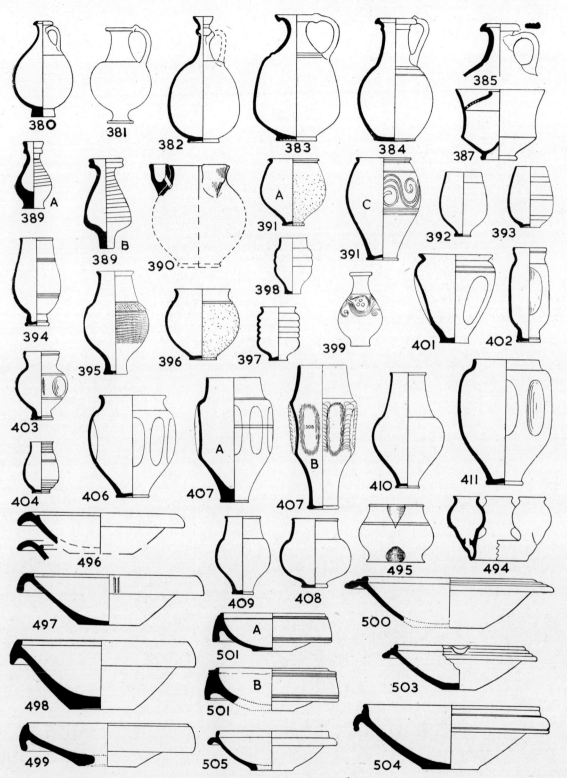

FIG. 107. The type-forms of pottery vessels. (⅙)

pinched spout. Castor ware here. At Silchester with coins to Arcadius, and seems equally late here.

373. Two-handled jug with cupped mouth. Buff. Rare. No date.

374. Flagon with conical neck and beaded rim. A late type, but no dating as yet.

375. Flagon with pinched spout, handle on rim. Castor ware. Not common. Possibly fourth century. Two fragments of one of these were found on the kilns-site in 1959. The value of their evidence is doubtful.

376. This form is our fig. 69, 1, 2, 3. We still know little of its general form, but it was in use at the end of the second century.

377. Two-handled flagon with narrow neck and ledge. Castor ware. One in 'Mithraeum', another with an inhumation. Rare.

378. Pear-shaped flagon with cylindrical neck and upright collar-rim. One with an inhumation. Rare.

379. Flagon with wide mouth, shaped to spout. Once in grave possibly c. 100.

380. Flagon with conical mouth and very narrow neck. Fine polished red ware. Occurs with an inhumation. Not rare.

381. Flagon on pedestal foot. Colour-coated ware, decorated in barbotine. Occurs with inhumation.

382. Tall, pear-shaped flagon, white ware, or buff, mica-coated. Occurs in a grave of c. 200.

383–5. Vacant.

386. Vacant.

387. We apologize for stating in *Roman Colchester* that this form has an 'upright, collared rim', which appears to be nonsense.

388. Vacant.

389A and B are forms of unguent-pots which seem to be numerous throughout the period, though commonest, perhaps, in the second century. They were made in kiln 22.

390. Large jars with several small cups on the shoulder, against the rim. No dating material as yet.

391. Cup or beaker with corniced rim. The greatest diameter low down (in contrast to f. 94). A short; B tall. Base beaded and grooved, or quite plain. Not before A.D. 120 (?) and then runs into the fourth century. Very common.

392. Vessels of the same outline except that the lip is quite simple. Appears later, perhaps not before 150. Both forms are typically colour-coated ware. There are grey copies of both. Very common. A short; B tall with almost a carination.

393. Similar beaker, tall, with rounded base and footring. Third to fourth century? Colour-coated ware.

394. Colour-coated beakers with cylindrical foot. Fourth century. Fairly frequent.

395. Colour-coated beaker with a rouletted bulge at base of tall neck; globular body with small foot. There are grey copies. Fourth century.

396. Globular beakers with upright, outcurved rim. Colour-coated ware; plain or folded. Late second and early third century. Not common.

397. Similar beakers, but the body variously constricted. Rare. Late second century.

398. Similar beakers, the body horizontally fluted, the top tapering to simple lip. Rare. Third century (?).

399. Small vase of colour-coated ware, very scarce. Fourth century.

400. Vacant.

401. Fluted beaker of conical outline. Grey ware. Fourth century.

402. Tall colour-coated beaker with cupped mouth and cylindrical foot. Sides with four foldings. Fourth century.

403. Similar beaker, but globular body, with four flutings. Fourth century.

404. Ovoid beaker, colour-coated, with several cordons at lip. Rare. Late second century.

405. Ovoid beaker with everted lip, fluted on body. Grey ware. Uncertain.

406. Similar beaker with marked shoulder, insloping neck, with sharply beaded rim. Grey ware, fluted. Late second and early third centuries.

407. Tall ovoid beaker with tall neck, conical or curved, the lip simple. Fluted. Colour-coated and grey ware. Third and fourth centuries.

408. Oblately ovoid to globular beakers or bowls with insloping neck and rim as 406. Beaded base. Various wares, copying the fine metallic Rhenish ff. 342, 343. Sometimes fluted. Third and fourth centuries.

409. Similar beakers with tall, almost straight neck, rim beaded. Foot usually very small. Colour-coated. Sometimes fluted. Fourth century.

410. Ovoid beaker reducing below to very small foot, sometimes pedestalled like 394. Fluted. Grey or black ware. Fourth century.

411. Upright beaker, the sides nearly parallel, marked shoulder with medium tall, straight, insloping neck with simple rim. Common in colour-coated ware and copies in various wares. Late second and third centuries.

Honey-pots. These vessels are most striking to the eye, but are difficult to classify, and we have little upon which to date them. Some early ones are already dealt with under 175–7. Possibly the following could be telescoped to fill the three numbers 178–80. They are too many and varied to be illustrated here.

412. Honey-pot. Fat rim, two small handles close up. Greatest diameter low down. Buff. Mid- to late second century.

413. Honey-pot. Fat rim, always hollowed inside. Very similar to last. White or buff. Frequent. c. A.D. 120–50.

414. Honey-pot. Tall and ovoid, greatest diameter very low down. Handles fairly low. Neronian-Flavian.

415. Honey-pot. Body very evenly rounded, greatest diameter in middle, handles high up. Foot heavily beaded. Buff. Rounded rim has a groove inside. Mid-second century (?).

416. Honey-pot. Similar to the last, but more full-bodied. Buff. Rare. Third century.

417. Honey-pot. Rim broad, grooved on edge, no neck; handles close up, three-ribbed. Solo. Unknown date.

418. Honey-pot. Fat rim with groove inside. Body ovoid on a tallish foot. Handles high up. Buff. Unknown date.

419. Honey-pot. Like 414 and 418, but taller, no groove on rim, and upper part nearly conical. Third or fourth century (?).

420–93. Vacant.

494. Triple vase, three cups, without offset shoulder, standing on a hollow ring. Buff, not polished. Rare. Made in our late second-century kilns.

495. Triple vase, the three cups almost globular, on small feet, with tall, offset necks. Usually red, white, or buff coated, once buff ware; one painted as *Roman Colchester*, fig. 63, 48. Rare. Fourth century.

496 (follows on *Cam.* f. 195). Mortarium with rolled rim rising above the beading. Uncommon in Colchester. It seems that we must bring this form down to much later than 'Trajan-Hadrian'.

497. Mortarium with rolled rim of approximately quandrant-section. The beading level with it, or rising above—great variety in outline. Very common. Buff. Late second century.

498. Mortarium, similar, but rim at a very steep angle. Common. Buff. Late second and third century.

499. Mortarium. Similar, but lacking beading. Buff. Frequent. Third century.

500. Mortarium. Large beading, ledge more or less horizontal and fluted. Buff, often biscuit-colour. Rare. Third century.

501A. Mortarium. 'Wall-sided' type, wall sloping outwards, buff or white. Common. Second half of second century.

501B. The same, but the wall nearly vertical. Late second century.

502. Mortarium with upright beading; the broad ledge smooth, but beaded beneath. White, buff, or biscuit. Common. Late second century onwards. Resembles 505.

503. Mortarium. Similar, but the ledge fluted. Not common. Buff to biscuit. Late third to fourth century (?).

504. Mortarium with prominent beading of squarish section, the ledge rolled down as a quadrant in section. White. Frequent, Late second to third century.

505. Mortarium, similar, but the beading is usually grooved on top, and the narrow ledge is always beaded beneath. Buff or red ware, white-coated, grit a coralline pink. Common. Fourth century.

506. Mortarium. 'Hammer-head' type. Very rare here. White or buff. Fourth century.

507. Mortarium. Rim bunched up. Rare. Uncertain date.

508. Mortarium. Heavy rolled rim with beading. Fourth century. See fig. 98, 4.

INDEX

Serpentine Walk, 175.
Shaw, J., 50.
Sheepen, 83.
  Farm, 11.
  Farm house, 176.
Sible Hedingham, 178.
site C4, 139–41.
skeleton, human, 19.
Smith, C. Roach, 1.
Smith, Dr. R. Sauvan, 2.
Southend Museum, 112.
Sprater, F., 26, 27, 28, 29, 31.
Stanfield, J. A., and Simpson, G., 85, 90.
Steer, Dr. K. A., 177.
Stevenson, R. B. K., 1.
stone building, 42.
  Kentish Rag, 8, 18, 19, 41, 42, 141, 151.
  septaria, 18.
  wall, the, 17–19, 41, 80, 82, 141.
Strowlger's Ground, 174.

Sussex Road, 90, 168.

Technical College, 48, 113.
Thornborough, Bucks., 107.
tile kilns, 3, 11, 176.
tiles, as kiln roof, 29.
  with nail holes, 155.
  stamped, 9.
Toppesfield, 107.
town wall, rampart of, 82.
Trier, 83, 90–91, 96, 108, 143.
tubes, *see* clay.

Unguent manufacturers, 134.

Vint Crescent, 1.
vintage ceremony, Romano-British, 93.

wall, stone, 17–19, 41, 80, 82, 141.
  clay, 43.

clay and tile, 38.
Wallace, R. W., 174.
Walters, H. B., 33, 46.
Warren, The, 139.
Warwickshire mortaria, 115.
Wax stoppers, 145.
Weisenau, 16.
well 5, 142.
West Lodge, 96.
Wheeler, Sir Mortimer, 102, 133.
Williams, J., 155, 157.
Wire, Wm., 2, 3, 9, 87.

Xanten, 96.

York, mould from, 43, 143.
Yorkshire signal stations, 8.

Zugmantel, 82.

PLATE I

a. Kiln 15, from west (p. 13)

b. Kiln 16, from south (p. 13)

c. Kilns 17 A and B, from south (p. 16)

PLATE II

a. Kiln 18, from south (p. 17)

b. Kiln 19, from east (p. 19)

c. The Kiln-enclosure, from south (pp. 17–20)

PLATE III

a. Mouth of Kiln 21 (p. 20)

b. Kiln 20, with Kiln 19 beyond (p. 19)

c. Part of the Enclosure, showing Kiln 21, Oven, and Kiln 20 (pp. 17–20)

PLATE IV

a. Kiln 22, from south (p. 20)

b. Oven (left) and Kiln 20 (p. 19)

PLATE V

a. Kiln-tubes and other structural details from Kiln 21 (pp. 23–25). (*c.* $\frac{1}{7}$)

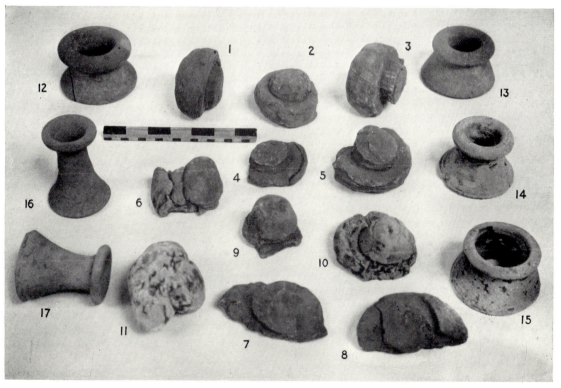

b. Clay plugs and kiln-props (pp. 25–26, 33–34). (*c.* $\frac{1}{4}$)

Structural remains from the Samian Kilns

PLATE VI

b. Clay rings and short tubes (pp. 22–24)

a. Clay rings (pp. 22–24). (c. ¼)

PLATE VII

a. Kiln 29, from south (p. 35)

b. Stone wall, from west. (p. 41)

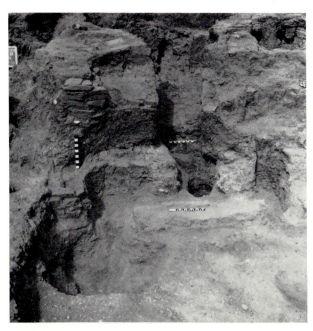

c. Mouth of Kiln 30 (Phase IV) with mouth of Phase III and its plug below, from south (pp. 35–37, 40)

d. Kiln 31, from south-east (p. 39)

PLATE VIII

a. Floor of Kiln 31, with mortarium-stamps (p. 39)

b. Kiln 30, Phase I, and Kiln 31A (pp. 35–37)

PLATE IX

a. Kiln 30 (left), late phase, and Kiln 31 (pp. 35–41)

b. Kilns 30, 31A, and 31 (pp. 35–41)

PLATE X

a. Kiln 30, from north. Phase IV (p. 40)

b. Kiln 31, interior, from south (p. 39)

c. Buried clay wall, from west (p. 43)

d. Stone building, from south-east (pp. 42–43)

PLATE XI

a. Mould of Potter A. Diameter 10¼ in. (p. 50)

b. Mould of Potter B. Diameter 7¼ in. (pp. 47, 49)

PLATE XII

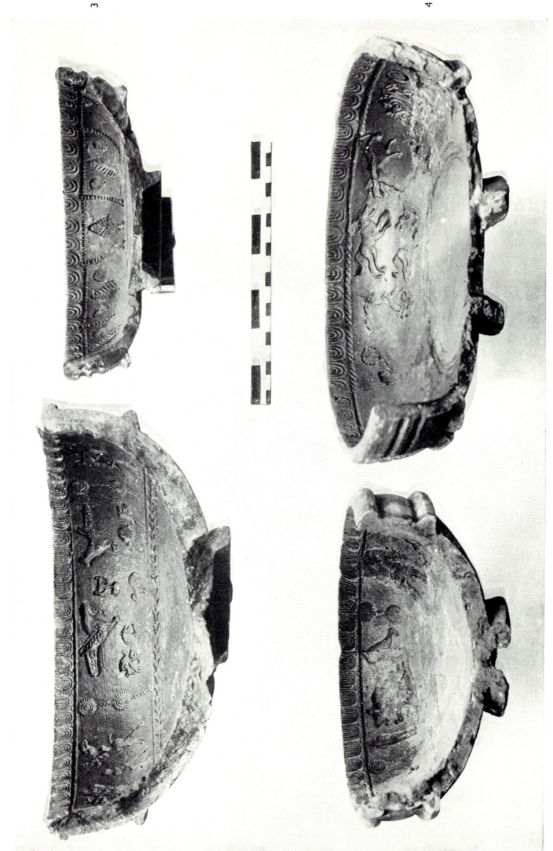

Moulds 1, 2, Potter A; 3, 4, Potter B (pp. 47–49)

PLATE XIII

a. Bowl, form Drag. 30, by Potter A. Diameter 5⅜ in. (pp. 33, 49)

By permission of Hull Museum

b. Mould (right) and cast from it, Hull Museum (p. 46)

PLATE XIV

Decorated ware by Potter A (p. 49)

PLATE XV

a. View of Kiln 30, from west (p. 40)

b. Three fragments of mould(s) from Kiln 25, with impressions from them
below (p. 155)

PLATE XVI

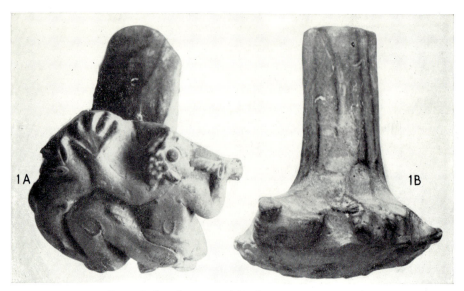

a. Potter's hand-stamp, side views (pp. 50, 69). ($\frac{1}{1}$)

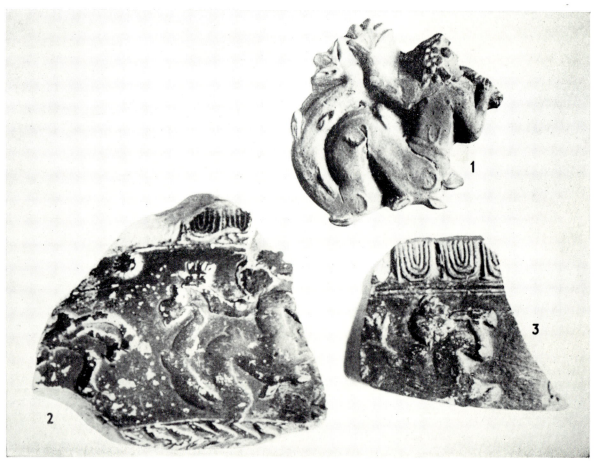

b. Flat view of same stamp, and ware with same motif. ($\frac{1}{1}$)

PLATE XVII

a. Fragments of moulds for lamps and impressions from them (p. 109). ($\frac{3}{8}$)

b. Fragment of aedicula (?) (p. 108). ($\frac{4}{5}$)

c. Mould for lamp (p. 109). ($\frac{4}{5}$)

PLATE XVIII

a. Mould for life-size mask or bust with impression from it (right), and fragment of bust or mask (above) (p. 108). (*c.* $\frac{1}{3}$)

b. Fused samian platters (pp. 32–33). ($\frac{3}{8}$)

c. Fused beakers (pp. 102, 141). ($\frac{1}{2}$)

PLATE XIX

a. Pottery palette (p. 109). ($\frac{1}{1}$)

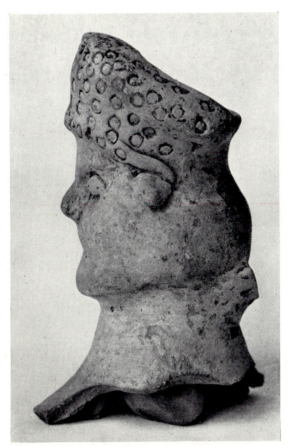

b. Flagon neck, side view. (Scale nearly $\frac{1}{1}$)

c. The same, front view (p. 124)

PLATE XX

a. Mass of fused flagons, form 154/5 (pp. 76, 142). (Scale nearly ½)

b. Barbotined hunt-cup, form 391 (p. 93, note). Maximum diameter 5¼ in.

PLATE XXI

a. Kiln 24, from north (p. 148)

b. Kiln 25, from east (p. 155)

PLATE XXII

a. Tile from Kiln 25 (p. 155). (*c*. $\frac{1}{4}$)

b. Tile from near Kiln 32 (p. 168, note). (*c*. $\frac{1}{4}$)